Ingo Wegener

Complexity Theory

Ingo Wegener

Complexity Theory

Exploring the Limits of Efficient Algorithms

Translated from the German by Randall Pruim

With 31 Figures

 Springer

Ingo Wegener
Universität Dortmund
Fachbereich Informatik
Lehrstuhl Informatik II
Baroper Str. 301
44221 Dortmund
Germany
wegener@1s2.cs.uni-dortmund.de

Translated from the German „Komplexitätstheorie – Grenzen der
Effizienz von Algorithmen" (Springer-Verlag 2003 , ISBN 3-540-00161-1)
by Randall Pruim.

ISBN-13 978-3-642-05914-8   e-ISBN-13 978-3-540-27477-3

Springer is a part of Springer Science+Business Media

springeronline.com

© Springer-Verlag Berlin Heidelberg 2010
Printed in Germany

Cover design: KünkelLopka, Heidelberg

Printed on acid-free paper 33/3142/YL - 5 4 3 2 1 0

Preface to the Original German Edition

At least since the development of the theory of NP-completeness, complexity theory has become a central area of instruction and research within computer science. The NP $\neq$ P-problem represents one of the great intellectual challenges of the present. In contrast to other areas within computer science, where it is often suggested that nearly all problems are solvable with the aid of computers, the goals of complexity theory include showing what computers cannot do. Delineating the boundary between problems that can be efficiently solved and those that can only be solved with an unreasonable amount of resources is a practically relevant question, but so is the structural question of what determines the complexity or "complicatedness" of problems.

The development of complexity theory is presented in this book as essentially a reaction to algorithmic development. For this reason, the investigation of practically important optimization problems plays a predominant role. From this algorithmic perspective, reduction concepts can be thought of as methods to solve problems with the help of algorithms for other problems. From this it follows conversely that we can derive the difficulty of a problem from the difficulty of other problems.

In this book we choose an unusual approach to the central concept of nondeterminism. The usual description, based on computers that guess a correct computation path or for which a suitable computation path exists, is often confusing to students encountering nondeterminism for the first time. Here this description is replaced with an introduction to randomized algorithms. Nondeterminism is then simply the special case of one-sided error with an error-rate that may be larger than is tolerable in applications. In this presentation, nondeterministic algorithms can be run on normal computers, but do not provide a satisfactory solution to problems. Based on experience, we are hopeful that this algorithmic approach will make it simpler for students to grasp the concept of nondeterminism.

Since this is not intended to be a research monograph, the content has been limited to results that are important and useful for students of computer science. In particular, this text is aimed at students who want an introduction to complexity theory but do not necessarily plan to specialize in this area. For this reason, an emphasis has been placed on informal descriptions of the proof ideas, which are, of course, followed by complete proofs. The emphasis is on modern themes like the PCP-theorem, approximation problems, randomization, and communication complexity at the expense of structural and abstract complexity theory.

The first nine chapters describe the foundation of complexity theory. Beyond that, instructors can choose various emphases:

- Chapters 10, 13, and 14 describe a more classically oriented introduction to complexity theory,
- Chapters 11 and 12 treat the complexity of approximation problems, and
- Chapters 14, 15, and 16 treat the complexity of Boolean functions.

Many ideas have come together in this text that arose in conversations. Since it is often no longer possible to recall where, when, and with whom these conversations were held, I would like to thank all those who have discussed with me science in general and complexity theory in particular. Many thanks to Beate Bollig, Stefan Droste, Oliver Giel, Thomas Hofmeister, Martin Sauerhoff, and Carsten Witt, who read the [original German] manuscript and contributed to improvements through their critical comments, and to Alice Czerniejewski, Danny Rozynski, Marion Scheel, Nicole Skaradzinski, and Dirk Sudholt for their careful typesetting.

Finally, I want to thank Christa for not setting any limits on the time I could spend on this book.

Dortmund/Bielefeld, January 2003   *Ingo Wegener*

Preface to the English Edition

This book is the second translation project I have undertaken for Springer. My goal each time has been to produce a text that will serve its new audience as well as the original book served its audience. Thus I have tried to mimic as far as possible the style and "flavor" of the original text while making the necessary adaptations. At the same time, a translation affords an opportunity to make some improvements, which I have done in consultation with the original author. And so, in some sense, the result is a translation of a second edition that was never written.

Most of the revisions to the book are quite minor. Some bibliography items have been added or updated; a number of German sources have been deleted. Occasionally I have added or rearranged a paragraph, or included some additional detail, but for the most part I have followed the original quite closely. Where I found errors in the original, I have tried to fix them; I hope I have corrected more than I have introduced.

It is always a good feeling to come to the end of a large project like this one, and in looking back on the project there are always a number of people to thank. Much of the work done to prepare the English edition of this book was done while visiting the University of Ulm in the first half of 2004. The last revisions and final touches were completed during my subsequent visit at the University of Michigan. I would like to thank all my colleagues at both institutions for their hospitality during these visits.

A writer is always the worst editor of his own writing, so for reading portions of the text, identifying errors, and providing various suggestions for improvement, I want to thank Beate Bollig, Stefan Droste, Jeremy Frens, Judy Goldsmith, André Gronemeier, Jens Jägersküpper, Thomas Jansen, Marcus Schaefer, Tobias Storch, and Dieter van Melkebeek, each of whom read one or more chapters. In addition, my wife, Pennylyn, read nearly the entire manuscript. Their volunteered efforts have helped to ensure a more accurate and stylistically consistent text. A list of those (I hope few) errors that have escaped detection until after the printing of the book will be available at `ls2-www.cs.uni-dortmund.de/monographs/ct`

Finally, a special thanks goes to Ingo Wegener, who not only wrote the original text but also responded to my comments and questions, and read the English translation with a careful eye for details; and to Hermann Engesser and Dorothea Glaunsinger at Springer for their encouragement, assistance, and patience, and for a fine *Kaffeestunde* on a sunny afternoon in Heidelberg.

Ann Arbor, January 2005   *Randall Pruim*

It is possible to write a research monograph in a non-native language. In fact, I have done this before. But a textbook with a pictorial language needs a native speaker as translator. Moreover, the translator should have a good feeling for the formulations and a background to understand and even to shape and direct the text. Such a person is hard to find, and it is Randall Pruim who made this project possible and, as I am convinced, in a perfect way. Indeed, he did more than a translation. He found some mistakes and corrected them, and he improved many arguments. Also thanks to Dorothea Glaunsinger and Hermann Engesser from Springer for their enthusiastic encouragement and for their suggestion to engage Randall Pruim as translator.

Bielefeld/Dortmund, January 2005   *Ingo Wegener*

Contents

1 Introduction 1
  1.1 What Is Complexity Theory? 1
  1.2 Didactic Background 5
  1.3 Overview 6
  1.4 Additional Literature 10

2 Algorithmic Problems & Their Complexity 11
  2.1 What Are Algorithmic Problems? 11
  2.2 Some Important Algorithmic Problems 13
  2.3 Measuring Computation Time 18
  2.4 The Complexity of Algorithmic Problems 22

3 Fundamental Complexity Classes 25
  3.1 The Special Role of Polynomial Computation Time 25
  3.2 Randomized Algorithms 27
  3.3 The Fundamental Complexity Classes for Algorithmic Problems 30
  3.4 The Fundamental Complexity Classes for Decision Problems .. 35
  3.5 Nondeterminism as a Special Case of Randomization 39

4 Reductions – Algorithmic Relationships Between Problems 43
  4.1 When Are Two Problems Algorithmically Similar? 43
  4.2 Reductions Between Various Variants of a Problem 46
  4.3 Reductions Between Related Problems 49
  4.4 Reductions Between Unrelated Problems 53
  4.5 The Special Role of Polynomial Reductions 60

5 The Theory of NP-Completeness 63
  5.1 Fundamental Considerations 63
  5.2 Problems in NP 67
  5.3 Alternative Characterizations of NP 69
  5.4 Cook's Theorem 70

6   NP-complete and NP-equivalent Problems 77
   6.1   Fundamental Considerations 77
   6.2   Traveling Salesperson Problems 77
   6.3   Knapsack Problems 78
   6.4   Partitioning and Scheduling Problems 80
   6.5   Clique Problems 81
   6.6   Team Building Problems 83
   6.7   Championship Problems 85

7   The Complexity Analysis of Problems 89
   7.1   The Dividing Line Between Easy and Hard 89
   7.2   Pseudo-polynomial Algorithms and Strong NP-completeness . . 93
   7.3   An Overview of the NP-completeness Proofs Considered 96

**8   The Complexity of Approximation Problems – Classical
     Results** 99
   8.1   Complexity Classes 99
   8.2   Approximation Algorithms 103
   8.3   The Gap Technique 106
   8.4   Approximation-Preserving Reductions 109
   8.5   Complete Approximation Problems 112

9   The Complexity of Black Box Problems 115
   9.1   Black Box Optimization 115
   9.2   Yao's Minimax Principle 118
   9.3   Lower Bounds for Black Box Complexity 120

10   Additional Complexity Classes 127
   10.1 Fundamental Considerations 127
   10.2 Complexity Classes Within NP and co-NP 128
   10.3 Oracle Classes 130
   10.4 The Polynomial Hierarchy 132
   10.5 BPP, NP, and the Polynomial Hierarchy 138

11   Interactive Proofs 145
   11.1 Fundamental Considerations 145
   11.2 Interactive Proof Systems 147
   11.3 Regarding the Complexity of Graph Isomorphism Problems . . . 148
   11.4 Zero-Knowledge Proofs 155

**12   The PCP Theorem and the Complexity of Approximation
     Problems** 161
   12.1 Randomized Verification of Proofs 161
   12.2 The PCP Theorem 164
   12.3 The PCP Theorem and Inapproximability Results 173
   12.4 The PCP Theorem and APX-Completeness 177

13 Further Topics From Classical Complexity Theory 185
    13.1 Overview 185
    13.2 Space-Bounded Complexity Classes 186
    13.3 PSPACE-complete Problems 188
    13.4 Nondeterminism and Determinism in the Context of Bounded
        Space 191
    13.5 Nondeterminism and Complementation with Precise Space
        Bounds 193
    13.6 Complexity Classes Within P 195
    13.7 The Complexity of Counting Problems 198

14 The Complexity of Non-uniform Problems 201
    14.1 Fundamental Considerations 201
    14.2 The Simulation of Turing Machines By Circuits 204
    14.3 The Simulation of Circuits by Non-uniform Turing Machines .. 206
    14.4 Branching Programs and Space Bounds 209
    14.5 Polynomial Circuits for Problems in BPP................. 211
    14.6 Complexity Classes for Computation with Help 212
    14.7 Are There Polynomial Circuits for all Problems in NP?....... 214

15 Communication Complexity 219
    15.1 The Communication Game 219
    15.2 Lower Bounds for Communication Complexity 223
    15.3 Nondeterministic Communication Protocols................ 233
    15.4 Randomized Communication Protocols 238
    15.5 Communication Complexity and VLSI Circuits 246
    15.6 Communication Complexity and Computation Time 247

16 The Complexity of Boolean Functions 251
    16.1 Fundamental Considerations 251
    16.2 Circuit Size 252
    16.3 Circuit Depth 254
    16.4 The Size of Depth-Bounded Circuits 259
    16.5 The Size of Depth-Bounded Threshold Circuits............. 264
    16.6 The Size of Branching Programs......................... 267
    16.7 Reduction Notions.................................... 271

Final Comments 277

A Appendix.. 279
    A.1 Orders of Magnitude and O-Notation 279
    A.2 Results from Probability Theory 283

References.. 295

Index 301

1

Introduction

1.1 What Is Complexity Theory?

Complexity theory – is it a discipline for theoreticians who have no concern for "the real world" or a central topic of modern computer science?

In this introductory text, complexity theory is presented as an active area of computer science with results that have implications for the development and use of algorithms. Our study will lead to insights into the structure of important optimization problems and will explore the borders of what is algorithmically "possible" with reasonable resources. Since this text is also especially directed toward those who do not wish to make complexity theory their specialty, results that do not (yet) have a connection to algorithmic applications will be omitted.

The areas of complexity theory on the one hand and of the design and analysis of efficient algorithms on the other look at algorithmic problems from two opposing perspectives. An efficient algorithm can be directly applied to solve a problem and is itself a proof of the efficient solvability of the problem. In contrast, in complexity theory the goal is to prove that difficult problems cannot be solved with modest resources. Bearers of bad news are seldom welcome, and so it is that the results of complexity theory are more difficult to communicate than a better algorithm for an important problem. Those who do complexity theory are often asked such questions as

- "Why are you pleased with a proof that a problem is algorithmically difficult? It would be better if it had an efficient algorithmic solution."
- "What good are these results? For my particular applied problem I need an algorithmic solution. Now what do I do?"

Naturally, it would be preferable if a problem proved to be efficiently algorithmically solvable. But whether or not this is the case is not up to us. Once we have agreed upon the rules of the game (roughly: computers, but more about that later), every problem has a well-defined algorithmic complexity. Complexity theory and algorithm theory are both striving to estimate this

algorithmic complexity and so to "discover the truth". In this sense, the joy
over a proof that a problem is not efficiently solvable is, just like the joy over
the design of an efficient algorithm, the joy of finding out more about the true
algorithmic complexity.

Of course, our reaction to the discovery of truths does depend on whether
hopes were fulfilled or fears confirmed. What are the consequences when we
find out that the problem we are investigating is not efficiently solvable? First,
there is the obvious and very practical consequence that we can with good
reason abandon the search for an efficient algorithm. We need no longer waste
our time with attempts to obtain an unreachable goal. We are familiar with
this from other sciences as well. Reasonable people no longer build "perpetual
motion machines", and they no longer try to construct from a circle, using
only straight edge and compass, a square with the same area (the proverbial
quadrature of the circle). In general, however, people have a hard time with
impossibility results. This can be seen in the large number of suggested designs
for perpetual motion machines and the large number of attempts to square a
circle that are still being made.

Once we have understood that we must accept negative results as well
as positive results, and that they save us unnecessary work, we are left with
the question of what to do. In the end, we are dealing with an algorithmic
problem the solution to which is important for some particular application.
Fortunately, problems in most applications are not unalterably determined.
It is often tempting to formulate a problem in a very general form and to
place very strict demands on the quality of the solution. If such a general
formulation has an efficient solution, great. But when this is not the case, we
can often specialize the problem (graphs that model street systems will have
low degree because there is a limit on the number of streets that can meet at
a single intersection), or perhaps a weaker form of solution will suffice (almost
optimal may be good enough). In this way we come up with new problems
which are perhaps efficiently algorithmically solvable. And so impossibility
proofs (negative results) help us find the problems that are (perhaps "just
barely") efficiently solvable.

So complexity theory and the design and analysis of efficient algorithms
are the two areas of computer science which together fathom the borders
between what can and cannot be done algorithmically with realistic resource
requirements. There is, of course, a good deal of "cross-pollination" between
the two areas. Often attempts to prove the impossibility of an efficient solution
to a problem have so illuminated the structure of the problem that efficient
algorithms have been the result. On the other hand, failed attempts to design
an efficient algorithm often reveal just where the difficulty of a particular
problem lies. This can lead to ideas for proving the difficulty of the problem.
It is very often the case that one begins with a false conjecture about the
degree of difficulty of a problem, so we can expect to encounter startling
results in our study of the complexity of problems.

As a result of this introductory discussion we maintain that

The goal of complexity theory is to prove for important problems that their solutions require certain minimum resources. The results of complexity theory have specific implications for the development of algorithms for practical applications.

We have up until now been emphasizing the relationship between the areas of complexity theory and algorithm design. Now, however, we want to take a look at the differences between these areas. When designing an algorithm we "only" need to develop and analyze *one* algorithm. This provides an *upper bound* for the minimal resource requirements with which the problem can be solved. Complexity theory must provide *lower bounds* for the minimally necessary resource requirements that *every* algorithm that solves the problem must use. For the proof of an upper bound, it is sufficient to design and analyze a *single* algorithm (and algorithms are often designed to support the subsequent analysis). Every lower bound, on the other hand, is a statement about *all* algorithms that solve a particular problem. The set of all algorithms for a problem is not a very structured set. Its only structural characteristic is that the problem be solved. How can we make use of this characteristic? An obvious way to start is to derive from the structure of the problem statements that restrict the set of algorithms we must consider. A specific example: It seems clear that the best algorithms for matrix multiplication do not begin by subtracting matrix elements from each other. But how does one prove this? Or is a proof unnecessary, since the claim is so obvious? Quite the opposite: The best algorithms known for matrix multiplication do in fact begin by subtracting matrix elements (see, for example, Schönhage, Grotefeld, and Vetter (1999)). This clearly shows the danger in drawing very "obvious" but false conclusions. Therefore,

In order to prove that the solution of a particular problem requires certain minimal resources, all algorithms for the problem must be considered. This is the source of the main difficulty that impedes achieving the goals of complexity theory.

We now know what kind of results we desire, and we have indicated that they are difficult to come by. It sounds as if we want to excuse in advance the absence of results. This is indeed the case:

None of the most important problems in complexity theory have been solved, but along the way to answering the central questions many notable results have been achieved.

How do we imagine this situation? The cover of the classic book by Hopcroft and Ullman (1979), which includes an introduction to complexity theory, shows a picture in which a curtain in front of the collection of truths of complexity theory is being lifted with the help of various results, thus allowing a clear view of the results. From our perspective of complexity theory, the curtain has so far only been pushed aside a bit at the edges, so that we can clearly see some "smaller truths". Otherwise, the opaque curtain has been replaced by a thinner curtain through which we can recognize a large portion of the truth, but only in outline and with no certainty that we are not falling prey to an optical illusion.

What does that mean concretely? Problems that are viewed as difficult have not actually been proved to be difficult, but it has been shown that thousands of problems are essentially equally difficult (in a sense that will be made precise later). An efficient solution to any one of these thousands of problems implies an efficient solution to all the others. Or stated another way: a proof that any one of these problems is not efficiently solvable implies that none of them is. Thousands of secrets have joined together to form one great mystery, the unmasking of which reveals all the secrets. In this sense, each of these secrets is just as central as every other and just as important as the great mystery, which we will later refer to as the $NP \neq P$-problem. In contrast to many other areas of computer science,

Complexity theory has in the $NP \neq P$-problem a central challenge.

The advantage of such an important and central problem is that along the way to its solution many important results, methods, and even new research areas are discovered. The disadvantage is that the solution of the central problem may be a long time in coming. We can learn something of this from the 350-year search for a proof of Fermat's Last Theorem (Singh (1998) is recommended for more about that topic). Along the way to the solution, deep mathematical theories were developed but also many false paths were followed. Only because of the notoriety of Fermat's Last Theorem was so much effort expended toward the solution to the problem. The $NP \neq P$-problem has taken on a similar role in computer science – but with an unfortunate difference: Fermat's Last Theorem (which says that there are no natural numbers x, y, z, and n with $n \geq 3$ such that $x^n + y^n = z^n$) can be understood by most people. It is fascinating that a conjecture that is so simple to formulate occupied the world of mathematics for centuries. For the role of computer science, it would be nice if it were equally simple to explain to a majority of people the complexity class P and especially NP, and the meaning of the $NP \neq P$-problem. Alas, this is not the case.

We will see that in the vicinity of the $NP \neq P$-problem important and beautiful results have been achieved. But we must also fear that much time may pass before the $NP \neq P$-problem is solved. For this reason, it is not necessarily the best strategy to aim directly for a solution to the problem. Yao (2001) compared our starting position to the situation of those who 200 years ago dreamed of reaching the moon. The strategy of climbing the nearest tree or mountain brings us closer to the moon, but it doesn't really bring us any closer to the goal of reaching the moon. The better strategy was to develop ever better means of transportation (bicycles, automobiles, airplanes, rockets). Each of these intermediate steps represented an earth moving discovery. So it is with complexity theory at the beginning of the third millennium: we must search for intermediate steps and follow suitable paths, even though we can never be certain that they will lead to our goal.

Just as those who worked on Fermat's Last Theorem were "sure" that the conjecture was true, so it is that today the experts believe that $NP \neq P$ and, therefore, that all of the essentially equally difficult problems mentioned above are not efficiently solvable. Why is this so? From the opposite assumption that $NP = P$ one can derive consequences that contradict all our convictions, even though they have not been proven false. Strassen (1996) has gone so far as to elevate the $NP \neq P$-conjecture above the status of a mathematical conjecture and compared it with a physical law (such as $E = mc^2$). This, by the way, opens up the possibility that the hypothesis that $NP \neq P$ is true but not provable with our proof techniques. But at this point we are far from being able to discuss this background seriously. Our main conclusion is that it is reasonable to build a theory under the hypothesis that $NP \neq P$.

Many results in complexity theory assume solidly based but unproven hypotheses, such as $NP \neq P$.

But what if $NP = P$? Well, then we must make fundamental modifications to many of our intuitions. Many of the results discussed here would in this case have other interpretations, but most would not become worthless. In general, complexity theory forms an intellectual challenge that differs from the demands of other areas of computer science. Complexity theory takes its place in the scientific landscape among those disciplines that

seek to probe the boundaries of what is possible with available resources.

Here the resources are such things as computation time and storage space. Anyone who is interested in the boundaries of what is (and is not) practically feasible with computers will find that complexity theory provides important answers. But those who come to complexity theory only wanting to know pragmatically if the problem they are interested in can be efficiently solved have also come to the right place.

1.2 Didactic Background

The main goal of this text is to provide as many as possible with a comfortable introduction to modern complexity theory. To this end a number of decisions were made with the result that this text differs from other books on the subject.

Since complexity theory is a polished theory with many branches, some selection of topics is unavoidable. In our selection, we have placed a premium on choosing topics that have a concrete relationship to algorithmic problems. After all, we want the importance of complexity theory for modern computer science to be clear. This comes at the cost of structural and abstract branches of complexity theory, which are largely omitted. In Section 1.3 we discuss in more detail just which topics are covered.

We have already discussed the difficulties of dealing with negative results and the relationship to the area of algorithm design. With a consistent perspective that is markedly algorithmic, we will – whenever it is possible and reasonable – present first positive results and only then derive consequences of negative results. For this reason, we will often quantify results which are typically presented only qualitatively.

In the end, it is the concept of nondeterminism that presents a large hurdle that one must clear in order to begin the study of complexity theory. The usual approach is to first describe nondeterministic computers which "guess" the correct computation path, and therefore can not actually be constructed. We have chosen instead to present randomization as the key concept. Randomized algorithms can be realized on normal computers and the modern development of algorithms has clearly shown the advantages of randomized algorithms (see Motwani and Raghavan (1995)). Nondeterminism then becomes a special case of randomization and therefore an algorithmically realizable concept, albeit one with an unacceptable probability of error (see Wegener (2002)). Using this approach it is easy to derive the usual characterizations of nondeterminism later.

We will, of course, give complete and formal proofs of our results, but often there are ugly details that make the proofs long and opaque. The essential ideas, however, are usually shorter to describe and much clearer. So we will include, in addition to the proofs, discussions of the ideas, methods, and concepts involved, in the hope that the interplay of all components will ease the introduction to complexity theory.

1.3 Overview

In Section 1.1 we simplified things by assuming that a problem is either algorithmically difficult or efficiently solvable. All concepts that are not formally defined must be uniquely specified. This begins already with the concept of an algorithmic problem. Doesn't the difficulty of a problem depend on just how one formulates the problem and on the manner in which the necessary data are made available? In Chapter 2 we will clarify essential notions such as algorithmic problem, computer, computation time, and algorithmic complexity. So that we can talk about some example problems, several important algorithmic problems and their variants will also be introduced and motivated. To avoid breaking up the flow of the text, a thorough introduction to O-notation has been relegated to the appendix.

In Chapter 3 we introduce randomization. We discuss why randomized algorithms are for many applications an extremely useful generalization of deterministic algorithms – provided the probability of undesirable results (such as computation times that are too long or an incorrect output) is vanishingly small. The necessary results from probability theory are introduced, proved, and clarified in an appendix. In the end we arrive at the classes of problems that we consider to be efficiently solvable.

The number of practically relevant algorithmic problems is in the thousands, and we would despair if we had to treat each one independently of the others. In addition to algorithmic techniques such as dynamic programming that can be applied to many problems, there are many tight connections between various problems. This is not surprising when we look at several variations on the same problem, but even problems that on the surface appear very different can be closely related in the following sense. Problem A can be solved with the help of an algorithmic solution to problem B in such a way that we need not make too many calls to the algorithm for B and the additional overhead is acceptable. This implies that if B is efficiently solvable, then A certainly is. Or said in another way: B cannot be efficiently solvable if A is algorithmically difficult. In this way we have used an algorithmic concept (which we will call reduction) to derive the algorithmic difficulty of one problem from the algorithmic difficulty of another. In Chapter 4, this approach will be formalized and practiced with various examples. Of special interest to us will be classes of problems for which every problem can play the role of A in the discussion above and also every problem can play the role of B. Then either all of these problems are efficiently solvable or none of them is. In Chapter 5 we introduce the theory of NP-completeness which leads to the class of problems already discussed in Section 1.1, and to which belong thousands of practically relevant problems that are either all efficiently solvable or all impossible to solve efficiently. The first possibility is equivalent to the property NP = P and the second to NP $\neq$ P. This makes it clear why the NP $\neq$ P-problem plays such a central role in complexity theory. Now the reductions introduced in Chapter 4 receive their true meaning, since they are used to show that the problems considered there belong to this class of problems. In Chapter 6 we treat the design of such reductions in a more systematic manner.

Chapters 7 and 8 are dedicated to the complexity analysis of difficult problems. We will investigate how one can determine the dividing line between efficiently solvable and difficult variations of a problem. The important special case of approximation problems is handled in Chapter 8. With optimization problems we can relax the demand that we compute an optimal solution if we can be satisfied with an "almost" optimal solution, in which case "almost" must be quantified. For a few problems, results from previous chapters lead relatively easily to results for such approximation problems. To obtain further results by means of reductions, it is necessary to introduce a generalized notion of approximation preserving reduction. Quite a number of approximation problems can be dealt with in this manner; nevertheless, there are also important (and presumably difficult) approximation problems that elude all these methods. Classical complexity theory at this point runs up against an insurmountable obstacle; newer developments are presented in Chapters 11 and 12.

Complexity theory must respond to all developments in the design of efficient algorithms, in particular to the increased use of randomized search heuristics that are not problem specific, such as simulated annealing and genetic algorithms. When algorithms do not function in a problem-specific way, our otherwise problem-specific scenario is no longer appropriate. A more appropriate "black box scenario" is introduced in Chapter 9. In this scenario we have the opportunity to determine the difficulty of problems directly, without any complexity theoretic hypotheses.

Not until the early 1990's when the enormous efforts of many researchers led to the so-called PCP Theorem (probabilistically checkable proofs) was it possible to overcome the previously discussed obstacle in dealing with approximation problems. But even now, over a decade after the discovery of this fundamental theorem, not all of its consequences have been worked out, and the result is still being sharpened. On the other hand, there is still no proof of even the basic variation of the PCP Theorem that can be presented in a textbook. (A treatment of this theorem in a special topics course required 12 two-hour sessions.) Here we will merely describe the path to the PCP Theorem and the central results along this path.

Not until Chapter 10 will we take a brief look at structural complexity theory. We will investigate the inner structure of the complexity class NP and develop a logic-oriented view of NP. From this perspective it is possible to derive generalizations of NP which form the polynomial hierarchy. This will provide a better taxonomy for the classes that depend on randomized algorithms. We also obtain new hypotheses which have a strong basis, although not as strong as that for the NP $\neq$ P-hypothesis. Later (in Chapters 11 and 14) we will base claims about practically important problems on these hypotheses.

Proofs have the property that they are much easier to verify than to construct. Thus it is possible to understand in a reasonable amount of time an entire textbook, even though the discovery of the results it contains required many researchers and many years. Generally, proofs are not presented in a formal and logically correct manner (supported only by axioms and a few inference rules); instead, authors attempt to convince their readers with less formal arguments. This would be easier to do using interactive communication (which can be better approximated in a lecture than in a textbook or via e-learning). Teachers since the time of Socrates have presented proofs to students in the form of such dialogues. Chapter 11 contains an introduction to interactive proof systems. What does this have to do with the complexity of problems? We measure the complexity in terms of how much communication (measured in bits and communication rounds, in which the roles of speaker and listener alternate) and how much randomization suffice so that someone with unlimited computational resources who knows a proof of some property (e.g., the shortest route in a traveling salesperson problem) can convince someone with realistically limited resources. This original, but seemingly useless game, turns out to have a tight connection to the complexity of the problems we have been discussing. There are even proof dialogues by which the second person can be convinced of a certain property without learning anything new about the proof (so-called zero-knowledge proofs). Such dialogues have an obvious application: The proof could be used as password. The password could then be efficiently checked, without any loss of security, since no information about the password itself need be exchanged. In other words, a user is able to convince the system that she knows her password, without actually providing the password.

After this preparation, the PCP Theorem is treated in Chapter 12 and the central ideas of the proof are discussed. The PCP Theorem will then be used to achieve better results about the complexity of central approximation problems.

Chapter 13 offers a brief look at further themes in classical complexity theory: space-bounded complexity classes, the complexity theoretic classification of context sensitive languages, the Theorems of Savitch and of Immerman and Szelepcsényi, PSPACE-completeness, P-completeness (that is, problems that are efficiently solvable but inherently sequential), and #P-completeness (in which we are concerned with the complexity of determining the number of solutions to a problem).

Chapter 14 treats the complexity theoretic difference between software and hardware. An algorithm (software) works on inputs of arbitrary length while a circuit (hardware) can only process inputs of a fixed length. While there is a circuit solution for every Boolean function in disjunctive normal form (DNF), there are algorithmic problems that are not solvable at all (e.g., the Halting Problem, software verification). The question here will be whether algorithmically difficult problems can have small circuits.

Chapter 15 contains an introduction to the area of communication complexity. Once computer science was defined as the science of processing information. Today the central role of communication is beyond dispute. By means of the theory of communication complexity it has been possible to reduce many very different problems to their common communication core. We will present the fundamental methods of this theory and some example applications.

Boolean (or more general) finite functions clearly play an important role in computer science. There are important models for their computation or representation (circuits, formulas, branching programs – also called binary decision diagrams or BDDs). Their advantage is that they are independent of any short term changes in technology and therefore provide clearly specified reference models. This makes concrete bounds on the complexity of specific problems interesting. Here, too, lower bounds are hard to come by. In Chapter 16, central proof methods are introduced and, together with methods from communication complexity, applied to specific functions.

1.4 Additional Literature

Since we have restricted ourselves in this text to an introduction to complexity theory, and in particular have only treated structural complexity very briefly, we should mention here a selection of additional texts. To begin with, two classic monographs must be cited, each of which has been very influential. The first of this is the general introduction to all areas of theoretical computer science by Hopcroft and Ullman (1979) with the famous cover picture. (An updated version of this text by Hopcroft, Motwani, and Ullman appeared in 2001.) The book by Garey and Johnson (1979) was for many years *the* NP-completeness book, and is still a very good reference due to the large number of problems that it treats. The *Handbook of Theoretical Computer Science* edited by van Leeuwen (1990) provides above all a good placement of complexity theory within theoretical computer science more generally. This book, as well as books by Papadimitriou (1994) and Sipser (1997), treat many aspects of computational complexity. Those looking for a text with an emphasis on structural complexity theory and its specialties are referred to books by Balcázar, Díaz, and Gabarró (1988), Hemaspaandra and Ogihara (2002), Homer (2001), and Wagner and Wechsung (1986). More information about the PCP Theorem can be found in the collection edited by Mayr, Prömel, and Steger (1998). The book by Ausiello, Crescenzi, Gambosi, Kann, Marchetti-Spaccamela, and Protasi (1999) specializes in approximation problems. Hromkovič (1997) treats aspects of parallel computation and multiprocessor systems especially thoroughly. The complexity of Boolean functions with respect to circuits and formulas is presented by Wegener (1987) and Clote and Kranakis (2002), and with respect to branching programs and BDDs by Wegener (2000). The standard works on communication complexity are Hromkovič (1997) and Kushilevitz and Nisan (1997).

2

Algorithmic Problems and Their Complexity

2.1 What Are Algorithmic Problems?

The notion of "problem" as it is commonly used is so general that it would be impossible to formalize. In order to restrict ourselves to something more manageable, we will consider only "algorithmic problems". By an algorithmic problem, we mean a problem that is suitable for processing by computers and for which the set of correct results is unambiguous. The problem of finding a just sentence for a defendant is not algorithmic since it depends on matters of judicial philosophy and is therefore not suitable for processing by computers. On the other hand, the problem of translating a German text into another language is suitable for processing by computers, but in this case it is not clear which results should be considered correct. So in the sense of complexity theory, the translation problem is not an algorithmic problem either. A good example of an algorithmic problem is the computation of a shortest path from s to t in a graph in which s and t are among the vertices, and each edge is associated with a positive cost (which we may interpret as distance or travel time).

An *algorithmic problem* is defined by

- a description of the set of allowable inputs, each of which can be represented as a finite sequence over a finite alphabet (the symbol set of our computer); and
- a description of a function that maps each allowable input to a non-empty set of correct outputs (answers, results), each of which is also a finite sequence over a finite alphabet.

Note that according to our definition, a problem does not consist of a single question to be answered but of a family of questions. For a given problem these questions are typically related and have a simple "fill-in-the-blank" structure. Each input (also called an instance) fills in the blanks differently, but otherwise the questions are identical. Often this is described as in the following example:

Instance: A positive integer n.
Question: Is n prime?

By restricting to finite sequences and finite alphabets we have matched the capabilities of digital computers. For any processing of arbitrary real numbers, it is necessary to approximate them in one way or another. Often algorithmic problems like the shortest path problem have short informal descriptions that do not specify the input format. Graphs can be represented as adjacency matrices or adjacency lists, for example, and the distance values can be represented in binary or in decimal. The design of a good algorithm for a problem can depend heavily upon the input format. This is especially the case if we want to measure the computation time very precisely. It can be shown, however, that often all "reasonable" input formats for "a" problem lead to algorithmically similar problems. (The adjacency matrix of a graph can be very efficiently computed from adjacency lists and vice versa, for example.) We will therefore only describe the input format as precisely as is necessary. In particular, we will specify the parameters that we consider the computation time to depend on (the number of vertices in a graph presented as an adjacency matrix, or the number of vertices and edges in a graph represented by adjacency lists). Artificial lengthenings of the inputs, such as the unary representation of numbers (in which n is represented by $n + 1$ 0's), will not be allowed unless we explicitly say the opposite. To be precise, we must also first check each input to make sure it is allowable (syntactically correct). Since this can be done efficiently for all the problems treated in this book, we will not discuss this aspect any further. Instead, we will try to concentrate on the core of the problem.

It is worth mentioning that we are only distinguishing between correct and incorrect solutions. Thus all correct outputs are "equally good". This reflects our goal of making the required resources, especially the required computation time, the focus of our observations. Of course, correct outputs (paths from s to t) can be of different quality (length). The obvious thing to do then is to redefine "correct" so that only those outputs of optimal quality (shortest paths) are considered to be correct outputs. In the case of difficult problems, we may declare all outputs that fall short of optimal quality by at most a certain percentage to be correct (approximation problems).

Although algorithmic problems can have several correct answers, we will always be satisfied with a single correct answer. If there are many correct answers, the listing of all correct answers may take too long. For example, cities like Manhattan can be represented as numeric grids $\{0, \ldots, n\} \times \{0, \ldots, m\}$ where each (i, j) is an intersection and the streets run horizontally and vertically between intersections. If $n \leq m$, then there are at least 2^n shortest paths from $(0, 0)$ to (n, m), and listing them all would be too much work even for modestly sized n. In most applications, a description of a single shortest path suffices. We can, however, change the problem so that we now only consider lists of all shortest paths to be correct solutions, or we could demand a list of

$\min\{a, b\}$ shortest paths, where a is the actual number of shortest paths and b is some specified bound. Since formally in each case we are looking for one of potentially many correct answers, we refer to such a problem as a *search problem*. If, as in the case of the search for a shortest path, we are looking for a solution that is in some way optimal, we will refer to the problem as an *optimization problem*. Often, it is sufficient to compute the value of an optimal solution (e.g., the length of a shortest path). These variants are called *evaluation problems*. Evaluation problems always have unique solutions. In the special case when the only possible answers are 0 (no) and 1 (yes), and we must decide which of these two possibilities is correct, we speak of a *decision problem*. Decision problems arise naturally in many situations: Does white have a winning strategy from a given configuration of a chess board? Is the given number a prime number? Is it possible to satisfy the prescribed conditions? The important special case of determining if a program is syntactically correct for a particular programming language (the word problem) has led to the alternative terminology for decision problems, namely (formal) languages. Optimization problems have obvious variants that are decision problems: Is the length of the shortest path from s to t bounded by l?

> *Algorithmic problems include all problems that can be handled by computers and for which we can unambiguously distinguish between correct and incorrect solutions. Among these are optimization problems and problems with unique solutions such as evaluation problems and decision problems. Different input formats for the same "problem" lead to different algorithmic problems, but typically these problems are algorithmically very similar.*

2.2 Some Important Algorithmic Problems

In order to have enough examples at our disposal, we now want to introduce ten important families of problems:

- traveling salesperson problems;
- knapsack problems (the best selection of objects);
- partitioning problems (bin packing problems, scheduling problems);
- surveillance (or covering) problems;
- clique problems;
- team building problems;
- optimization of flows in networks;
- championship problems in sports leagues;
- verification problems; and
- number theoretic problems (primality testing, factoring).

This list contains the most well-known algorithmic problems. They have simple and clear descriptions and, for the most part, great practical importance. Some problems rarely arise in their "pure" forms but are frequently at the core of other problems that arise in applications.

The *traveling salesperson problem* (TSP) is the problem of finding a shortest round trip circuit that visits n given cities and returns to its starting point. The cities are denoted by $1, \ldots, n$ and the distances between the cities by $d_{i,j}$, $1 \leq i, j \leq n$. The distances are chosen from $\mathbb{N} \cup \{\infty\}$, and the value ∞ represents that there is no direct connection between two particular cities. A circuit is a permutation π of $\{1, \ldots, n\}$ so that the cities are visited in the order $\pi(1), \pi(2), \ldots, \pi(n), \pi(1)$. The cost of a circuit π is given by

$$d_{\pi(1),\pi(2)} + d_{\pi(2),\pi(3)} + \cdots + d_{\pi(n-1),\pi(n)} + d_{\pi(n),\pi(1)}$$

and a circuit with minimal cost is to be computed. There are many possible variations on this problem. TSP (or TSP_{OPT}) denotes the general optimization problem; TSP_{EVAL} and TSP_{DEC} denote the related evaluation and decision problems. For the latter, the input includes a bound D, and it must be determined whether there is a circuit that has cost not exceeding D. We will also consider the following restricted variants:

- TSP^{SYM}: the distances are symmetric ($d_{i,j} = d_{j,i}$);
- $\text{TSP}^{\triangle}$: the distances satisfy the triangle inequality, that is, $d_{i,j} \leq d_{i,k} + d_{k,j}$;
- $\text{TSP}^{d\text{-Euclid}}$: the cities are points in d-dimensional Euclidean space $\mathbb{R}^d$ and the distances correspond to Euclidean distance (L_2 norm);
- TSP^{N}: the distances come from $\{1, \ldots, N\}$;
- DHC (Directed Hamiltonian Circuit): the distances come from $\{1, \infty\}$, and the usual input format is then a directed graph containing only those edges that have a cost of 1;
- $\text{HC} = \text{DHC}^{\text{SYM}}$: the symmetric variant of DHC, for which the usual input format is an undirected graph containing only those edges that have a cost of 1.

Further variations are introduced in the monograph by Lawler, Lenstra, Rinnooy Kan, and Shmoys (1985) that deals exclusively with TSP. For all versions there is an optimization variant, an evaluation variant, and a decision variant, although for DHC and HC we only consider the decision variant (whether the graph contains a Hamiltonian circuit). The inputs consist of the number n and the $n(n-1)$ distances, but it is customary to express the computation time in terms of n. For DHC and HC, the number of edges m is also relevant. It is important to note that neither n nor m measure the length of the input over a finite alphabet, since this depends on the size of the distances $d_{i,j}$. Using the usual binary representation of natural numbers, $d_{i,j}$ has length $\lceil \log(d_{i,j} + 1) \rceil$.

For TSP we have listed as examples many variants (although far from all), and we have also discussed the relevant parameters more closely (n, or (n, m), or essentially the bit length of the input). For the remaining problems, we will introduce only the most important variants and mention the relevant parameters only when they do not arise in a manner that is similar to our discussion of TSP.

Travelers who want to stay within a limit of 20 kg per piece of luggage established by an airline are dealing with the *knapsack problem* (KNAPSACK). The weight limit $W \in \mathbb{N}$ must be observed and there are n objects that one would like to bring along. The ith object has weight $w_i \in \mathbb{N}$ and utility $u_i \in \mathbb{N}$. Travelers are not allowed to take objects with a total weight that exceeds W. Subject to this restriction, the goal is to maximize the total utility of the selected objects. Here, too, there are variants in which the size of the utility values and/or the weights are bounded. In the general case, the objects have different utility per unit weight. KNAPSACK* denotes the special case that $u_i = w_i$ for all objects. In this case, the goal is merely to approach the weight limit as closely as possible without going over. If in addition $W = (w_1 + w_2 + \cdots + w_n)/2$, and we consider the decision problem of whether we can achieve the maximum allowable weight, the resulting problem is equivalent to the question of whether the set of objects can be divided into two groups of the same total weight. For this reason, this special case is called the *partition problem* (PARTITION). A book has also been dedicated to the knapsack problem, see Martello and Toth (1990).

The partition problem is also a special case of the *bin packing problem* (BINPACKING), in which bins of size b are available, and we want to pack n objects of sizes $u_1, u_2, \ldots, u_n$ into as few bins as possible. But we can also view BINPACKING as a very special case of the *scheduling problem*. The class of scheduling problems is nearly impossible to gain an overview of (Lawler, Lenstra, Rinnooy Kan, and Shmoys (1993), Pinedo (1995)). In each case tasks must be divided up among people or machines subject to different side constraints. Not all people are suited for all tasks, different people may take different amounts of time to complete the same task, certain tasks may need to be completed in a specified order, there may be earliest start times or latest completion times (deadlines) specified, and there are different optimization criteria that can be used. As we go along, we will introduce several special cases.

A typical surveillance problem is the art gallery problem. The challenge is to monitor all walls of an art gallery with as few cameras as possible. We will restrict our attention to surveillance problems on undirected graphs, in which case they are often called covering problems. In the *vertex cover problem* (VERTEXCOVER), each vertex monitors all edges that are incident to it, and all edges are to be monitored with as few vertices as possible. In the *edge cover problem* (EDGECOVER), the roles are reversed: each edge monitors the two incident vertices, and the vertices are to be monitored with as few edges as possible.

The vertices of a graph can be used to represent people; the edges, to represent friendships between people. A *clique* is defined as a group in which each person likes each other person in the group. The following problems do not appear to have direct connections to applications, but they occur frequently as parts of larger problems. In the *clique cover problem* (CLIQUECOVER), the vertices of a graph must be partitioned into as few sets as possible, in such a way that each set forms a clique. In the *clique problem* (denoted CLIQUE), a largest possible clique is to be computed. An *anti-clique* ("no one likes anyone", between any two vertices there is not an edge) is called an *independent set*, and the problem of computing a largest independent set is INDEPENDENTSET.

Team building can mean dividing people with different capabilities into cooperative teams in which the members of the team must get along. For k-DM (k-dimensional matching, i.e., the building of teams of size k), we are given k groups of people (each group representing one of the k capabilities), and a list of potential k-member teams, each of which includes one person from each of the capability groups. The goal is to form as many teams as possible with the restriction that each person may only be assigned to one team. 2-DM is also known as the *marriage problem*: the two "capabilities" are interpreted as the two genders, a potential team as a "potential happy marriage", and the goal is to maximize the number of happy heterosexual marriages. This description of the problem does not, of course, reflect the way the problem arises in actual applications.

In the *network flow problem* (NETWORKFLOW) one seeks to maximize flows in networks – another large class of problems, see Ahuja, Magnanti, and Orlin (1993). We are only interested in the basic problem in which we seek to maximize the flow from s to t in a directed graph. The flow $f(e)$ along an edge e must be a non-negative integer bounded above by the capacity $c(e)$ of the edge. The total flow that reaches a vertex $v \notin \{s,t\}$, i.e., the sum of all $f(e)$ with $e = (\cdot, v)$, must equal the total flow that leaves v, i.e., the sum of all $f(e)$ with $e = (v, \cdot)$ (Kirchhoff rule). The source vertex s cannot be reached via any edge, and the terminal vertex (sink) t cannot be left via any edge. Under these conditions, the flow from s to t, i.e., the sum of all $f(e)$ with $e = (s, \cdot)$ is to be maximized. One can easily argue that this model is not suited for maximizing traffic flow, but we will see that flow problems arise in many different contexts.

The problems we have considered to this point have the property that their optimization variants seem to be the most natural version, while the evaluation and decision variants are restricted problems, the solutions to which only cover some aspects of the problem. The *championship problem* (CHAMPIONSHIP) is fundamentally a decision problem. A fan wonders at a particular point in the season whether it is (at least theoretically) possible for his favorite team to be the league champion. Given are the current standings for each team and a list of the games that remain to be played. The chosen team can become the champion if there are potential outcomes to the remaining games so that in the end no other team has more points (if necessary, the team may need to also have the best goal differential). In addition, one of the following rules must specify how points are awarded for each game:

- The a-point rule: After each game a points are awarded ($a \in \mathbb{N}$), and every partition of a into b points for Team 1 and $a - b$ points for Team 2 with $0 \leq b \leq a$ and $b \in \mathbb{N}$ is possible.
- The $(0, a, b)$-point rule: The only possibilities are $b : 0$ (home victory), $a : a$ (tie), and $0 : b$.

In fact, in various sports, various point rules are used: the 1-point rule is used in sports that do not permit ties (basketball, volleyball, baseball, ...). The 2-point rule (equivalent to the $(0, 1, 2)$-point rule) is the classic rule in sports with ties (team handball, German soccer until the end of the 1994–95 season). The 3-point rule is used in the German Ice Hockey League (DEL) which awards 3:0 for a regulation win, 2:1 for a win in overtime or after penalty shots. The $(0, 1, 3)$-point rule is currently used in soccer. Further variations arise if the remaining games are divided into rounds, and especially if the games are scheduled as in the German soccer Bundesliga (see Bernholt, Gülich, Hofmeister, Schmitt, and Wegener (2002)). This problem, of practical interest to many sports fans, will also lead to surprising insights.

With the class of verification problems (see Wegener (2000)) we move into the domain of hardware. The basic question is whether the specification S and the realization R of a chip describe the same Boolean function. That is, we have descriptions S and R of Boolean functions f and g and wonder if $f(a) = g(a)$ for all inputs a. Since we carry out the verification bitwise, we can assume that $f, g : \{0, 1\}^n \rightarrow \{0, 1\}$. The property $f \neq g$ is equivalent to the existence of an a with $(f \oplus g)(a) = 1$ ($\oplus = \text{EXOR} = \text{parity}$). So we are asking whether $h = f \oplus g$ is satisfiable, i.e., whether h can output a value of 1. This decision problem is called the *satisfiability problem*. Here the input format for h is relevant:

- SAT_{CIR} assumes the input is represented as a circuit.
- $\text{SAT} = \text{CNF-SAT} = \text{SAT}_{\text{CNF}}$ assumes the input is represented as a conjunction of clauses (which are disjunctions of literals), i.e., in conjunctive (normal) form.
- $\text{DNF-SAT} = \text{SAT}_{\text{DNF}}$ assumes the input is represented as a disjunction of monomials (which are conjunctions of literals), i.e., in disjunctive (normal) form.

Other representation forms will be introduced later. We will use k-SAT to denote the special case that all clauses have exactly k literals. For SAT and k-SAT there are also the optimization versions MAX-SAT and MAX-k-SAT, in which the goal is to find an assignment for the variables that satisfies as many of the clauses as possible, i.e., one that produces as many clauses as possible in which at least one of the literals is assigned the value 1. These optimization problems can no longer be motivated by verification problems, but they will play a central role in the treatment of the complexity of approximation problems. In general, we shall see that, historically, new subareas of complexity theory have always begun with the investigation of new satisfiability problems.

So satisfiability problems are motivated by an important application problem but also take center stage as "problems for their own sake".

Modern cryptography (see Stinson (1995)) has a tight connection to number theoretic problems in which very large numbers are used. Here we must take note that the binary representation of an input n has a length of only $\lceil \log(n + 1) \rceil$. Already in gradeschool, most of us learned an algorithm for adding fractions that required us to compute common denominators, and for this we factored the denominators into prime factors. This is the problem of *factoring* (FACT). Often it suffices to check whether a number is prime (*primality testing*). PRIMES, the problem of deciding whether or not a positive integer n is prime, was our first example of an algorithmic problem on page 12.

With this colorful bouquet of central and practical algorithmic problems we can discuss most complexity theoretical questions.

2.3 How Is the Computation Time of an Algorithm Measured?

A first attempt at a definition of the complexity of an algorithmic problem might look like the following:

> The complexity of an algorithmic problem is the amount of computation time required by an optimal algorithm.

But after a bit of reflection, this definition proves to be deficient:

- Is there always an optimal algorithm?
- What is in fact the computation time required by an algorithm?
- Is it even clear what an algorithm is?

We need to pursue these questions before we can develop a complexity theory of algorithmic problems. Sufficient for our purposes will be a largely intuitive notion of algorithm as an unambiguous set of instructions which (in dependence on the input for the algorithmic problem under consideration) specifies the steps that are to be carried out to produce a particular output. The algorithm is called *deterministic* if at every moment the next step in the computation is unambiguously specified. In Chapter 3 we will expand the notion of algorithm to include randomized algorithms, which can have the next step in the computation depend on random bits. The description of "algorithm" that we have chosen allows us the same freedom that those who design and publish algorithms allow themselves.

The computation time t of an algorithm A for an algorithmic problem still depends on at least the following parameters:

- the input x,
- the chosen computer C,
- the chosen programming language L,
- the implementation I of the algorithm.

The dependence of the computation time on the particular input x is unavoidable and sensible. It is absolutely obvious that "larger" instances (say, 10^6 cities for TSP) require significantly more computation time than "smaller" instances (say, only 10 cities). But if computation time is also essentially dependent upon C, L, and I, and perhaps other parameters, then algorithms can no longer be sensibly compared. In that case, the most we could do would be to make statements about the computation time of an algorithm with respect to a particular computer, a particular programming language, and a particular implementation. But that sort of statement is rather uninteresting. In a very short time whatever computer we consider will become outdated. Even programming languages often have only a short season of interest, and those in use are constantly being changed. Certainly the computation time depends on these parameters, but we will see that this dependence is limited and controllable. Complexity theory and the theory of algorithms have chosen the following way out of this dilemma:

The notion of computation time will be simplified to that point that it only depends on the algorithm and the input.

Concretely, this means that we can give the computation time for an algorithm independent of whether we use a 50 year old computer or a modern one. Furthermore, our observations should remain true for the computers that will be in use 50 years from now. The goal of this section is to demonstrate that there is an abstract notion of computation time that has the desired properties.

Because of past and expected future advances in the area of hardware, we will not measure computation "time" in units of time, but in terms of the number of computation steps. We agree on a set of allowable elementary operations, among them the arithmetic operations, assignment, memory access, and the recognition of the next command to be performed. This model of computation can be formally defined using register machines, also called random access machines (see Hopcroft, Motwani, and Ullman (2001)). We will be satisfied with the knowledge that every program in every known programming language for every known computer can be translated into a program for a register machine and that the resulting loss in efficiency is "modest". Such a translation is structurally simple, but very tedious in practice.

The "modest" loss of efficiency can even be quantified. For each known programming language and computer there is always a constant c so that the translation of such programs into register machine programs increases the number of computation steps required by no more than a factor of c. And what about future computers? It is impossible to say for sure, but the evidence suggests that the possible effects will be limited. This conviction is summarized as the *Extended Church-Turing Thesis*. The classical Church-Turing Thesis says that all models of computation can simulate one another, so that the set of algorithmically solvable problems is independent of the model of computation (which includes both the computer and the programming language). The Extended Church-Turing Thesis goes one step further:

> *For any two models of computation R_1 and R_2 there is a polynomial p such that t computation steps of R_1 on an input of length n can be simulated by $p(t, n)$ computation steps of R_2.*

The dependence of $p(t, n)$ on n is only necessary in the case that an algorithm (like binary search, for example) runs for sublinear time.

Of course, it is not fair to consider all arithmetic operations to be equally costly computation steps. We consider division (to a fixed number of decimal places) to be more time consuming than addition. Furthermore, the time actually required depends on the lengths of the numbers involved. If we descend to the level of bits, then every arithmetic operation on numbers of bit length l requires at least $\Omega(l)$ bit operations. For addition and subtraction, $O(l)$ bit operations are also sufficient, whereas the best known algorithms for multiplication and division require $\Theta(l \log l \log \log l)$ bit operations. (The notation O, Ω, and Θ is defined in Appendix A.1.) For this reason it is fair, if not quite exact, to assign a cost of l to arithmetic operations on numbers of length l. This way of doing things leads us to the *logarithmic cost model*, which gets its name from the fact that the natural number n has a bit length of $\lceil \log(n + 1) \rceil$. This fair, but cumbersome cost model is only worth the effort if we actually need to work with very large integers. If on an input of length l we only use integers of length at most $s(l)$, these logarithmic costs only increase the number of computation steps by at most a factor of $O(\log(s(l)))$. Even for exponentially large integers, this is only a linear factor. Since we will never consider any algorithms which carry out arithmetic operations on larger integers than this, it will suffice to simply count the computation steps. This is referred to as the *uniform cost model*.

As a result of this discussion and abstraction, we can now speak of *the* computation time $t_A(x)$ of the algorithm A on the input x. We acknowledge that we are implicitly using a model of computation when we do this. Nevertheless, computation times like $O(n \log n)$ for sorting algorithms and $O((n + m) \log n)$ for Dijkstra's Algorithm hold for all known computers and programming languages.

The Extended Church-Turing Thesis must be checked in light of new types of computers. There is no doubt that it is correct in the context of digital computers. Even so-called DNA-computers "only" result in smaller chips or a higher degree of parallelism. This can represent an enormous advance in practice, but it has no effect on the number of elementary operations. Only the so-called quantum computers, which are designed to take advantage of quantum effects (there are many feasibility studies underway, but as yet no usable quantum computer has been built), allow for a new kind of algorithm, which can be shown to be incomparable with usual algorithms. In the case of quantum computation, the complexity theory is far ahead of the construction of computers. This branch of complexity theory must, however, be left for more specialized monographs (see Nielsen and Chuang (2000)).

In the area of digital computers then, upper or lower bounds for register machines imply similar bounds for all actual computers. Later we will need yet another model of computation. Register machines have free access (referred to as random access) to their memory: on input i it is possible to read the contents of the ith storage cell (formerly called a register). This global access to storage will cause us problems. Therefore, a very restricted model of computation will be introduced as an intermediate model. In this model, computation steps have only local effects, and this is precisely what simplifies our work.

The Turing machine model goes back to the English logician Alan Turing. Not only did his work provide the basis for the building of computers, but during World War II he also led a group that cracked the German secret code "Enigma". As in all models of computation, we assume unbounded space for the storage of data. For a Turing machine, this storage space is divided into cells which are linearly arranged, and each assigned an integer $i \in \mathbb{Z}$ consecutively. This linearly arranged storage space is referred to as a *tape*. At each step, the Turing machine has access to one of these tape cells. In addition, a Turing machine has a separate finite storage space (its "memory") which it can access at any time. In a single step, the Turing machine can modify its memory and the contents of the tape cell it is reading and then move to the left or right neighboring tape cell. Formally, a Turing machine consists of the following components:

- a finite state space Q, whereby each $q \in Q$ represents a state of the memory, and so a memory that can hold k bits can be described by $Q = \{0,1\}^k$;
- an initial state $q_0 \in Q$;
- a finite *input alphabet* Σ;
- a finite *tape alphabet* Γ which contains at least the symbols in Σ and an additional *blank symbol* $b \notin \Sigma$;
- a program $\delta : Q \times \Gamma \to Q \times \Gamma \times \{-1,0,1\}$; and
- a set of *halting states* $Q' \subseteq Q$, where $\delta(q,a) = (q,a,0)$ for all $(q,a) \in Q' \times \Gamma$, but $\delta(q,a) \neq (q,a,0)$ for all $(q,a) \in (Q - Q') \times \Gamma$.

The Turing machine works as follows: Initially, the input $x = (x_1, \ldots, x_n) \in \Sigma^n$ is in the tape cells $0, 1, \ldots, n-1$, and all other cells contain the blank symbol; the memory is in state q_0; and the machine is reading tape cell 0. At every step, if the machine is in state q, reading symbol a in tape cell i, and $\delta(q,a) = (q',a',j)$, then symbol a is replaced by symbol a', state q is replaced by state q', and cell $i+j$ is read in the next step. Although formally a Turing machine continues to process when it is in a halting state, the computation time is defined as the first point in time that the machine reaches a halting state. For search problems, the output is located in cells $1, \ldots, m$, where m is the least positive integer such that tape cell $m+1$ contains the blank symbol. For decision problems we can integrate the output into the state by partitioning the halting states into two disjoint sets: $Q' = Q^+ \cup Q^-$. We say that the input is *accepted* if the machine halts in a state $q \in Q^+$ and is *rejected* if the machine halts in a state $q \in Q^-$.

Turing machines have the property that in one step of the computation, only the memory, the tape head position, and the contents of the cell at that position play a role, and in the next step, only one of the neighboring cells can be accessed. For a practical application as a computer this is a huge disadvantage, but for the analysis of the effects of a computation step it is a decided advantage.

The (standard) Turing machine we have introduced has a single two-way infinite tape. A generalization to k tapes, such that at any point in time one tape cell is read on each of the k tapes, and the motion of the tape heads on different tapes may be in different directions, can be described by a program $\delta : Q \times \Gamma^k \to Q \times \Gamma^k \times \{-1, 0, 1\}^k$. Remarkably, register machines can be simulated with only modest loss in efficiency by Turing machines with a small number of tapes (see Schönhage, Grotefeld, and Vetter (1994)). These Turing machines can then be simulated easily with a quadratic loss of efficiency by a Turing machine with only one tape (see, for example, Hopcroft, Motwani, and Ullman (2001)).

From this we see that

> For every existing type of computer there is a polynomial p such that, on an input of length n, t computation steps with respect to the logarithmic cost model can be simulated by a Turing machine in $p(t, n)$ steps.

If we accept the Extended Church-Turing Thesis, then this is also true for all future digital computers.

2.4 The Complexity of Algorithmic Problems

We let $t_A(x)$ denote the computation time of algorithm A on input x in the unit cost model for a chosen model of computation (for example, register machines). We can now try to compare two algorithms A and A' for the same problem in the following manner: A is at least as fast as A' if $t_A(x) \leq t_{A'}(x)$ for all x.

This obvious definition is problematic for several reasons:

- The exact value of $t_A(x)$ and therefore the comparison of A and A' depends on the model of computation.
- Only for very simple algorithms can we hope to compute $t_A(x)$ for all x and to test the relation $t_A(x) \leq t_{A'}(x)$ for all x.
- Often, when we compare a simple algorithm A with an algorithm A' that is more complicated but well-tailored to the problem at hand, we find that $t_A(x) < t_{A'}(x)$ for "small" inputs x but $t_A(x) > t_{A'}(x)$ for "large" inputs x.

The first and third problems we meet with the simplification that we compare computation times with respect to order of magnitude or asymptotic rates of growth. We deal with the second problem by measuring the computation time, not for each input x, but for each input "size" (bit length, number of vertices in a graph, number of cities for TSP, etc.). Although different inputs for TSP that have the same number of cities can have very different length (measured in bits), once we have chosen the meaning of size, we will use this when we refer to the "length" of an input, which we will denote by $|x|$. The most commonly used measurement for computation time is *worst-case runtime*:

$$t_A(n) := \sup\{t_A(x) : |x| \le n\} .$$

Frequently $t_A^*(n) := \sup\{t_A(x) : |x| = n\}$ is used, and $t_A^* = t_A$ when t_A^* is monotonically increasing. This is the case for most algorithms. The use of $t_A(n)$, ensures that the worst case runtime is always a monotonically increasing function, and this will be useful later.

Now we can describe how we compare two algorithms A and A' for the same problem.

The algorithm A is asymptotically at least as fast as A' if $t_A(n) = O(t_{A'}(n))$.

This simplification has proved itself (for the most part) to be quite suitable. But in extreme cases, it is an over-simplification. In applications, for example, we would consider $n \log n$ "for all practical purposes" smaller than $10^6 \cdot n$. And the worst case runtime treats algorithms like QuickSort (which processes "most" inputs more quickly than it does the "worst" inputs) very harshly. One workaround for this is to consider *average-case runtime*. For a family of probability distributions q_n on the inputs of length n, we define

$$t_A^q(n) := \sum_{x:|x|=n} q_n(x) \cdot t_A(x) .$$

For another possibility see the discussion of QuickSort in Section 3.2.

But the notion of average computation time does not work well for two reasons. The main reason is that for most problems we do not know which probability distributions q_n on the inputs are a good model of "reality". Rather than achieve unusable results on the basis of a poor estimate of q_n, it is more reasonable (even if more pessimistic) to use the maximal runtime as a measure. Furthermore, from a pragmatic view, we see that the determination of worst case runtime is possible for many more algorithms than is the case for average-case runtime.

Finally we can say that the *algorithmic complexity* of a problem is $f(n)$ if the problem can be solved by means of an algorithm A with a worst case runtime of $O(f(n))$, and every algorithm for this problem has a worst case runtime of $\Omega(f(n))$. In this case the algorithm A has the asymptotically minimal runtime. We do not define the algorithmic complexity of a problem, however, because problems do not necessarily have an asymptotically minimal runtime. There could be two algorithms A and A' such that neither $t_A(n) = O(t_{A'}(n))$ nor $t_{A'}(n) = O(t_A(n))$ hold. (See Appendix A.1 for examples of such runtimes.) Even when the runtimes of algorithms are asymptotically comparable, there may not be a best asymptotic runtime. Consider, for example, algorithms A_ε with runtimes $3^{1/\varepsilon}n^{2+\varepsilon} + O(n^2)$. Then the runtime of algorithm A_ε is $\Theta(n^{2+\varepsilon})$, so A_ε is asymptotically better than $A_{\varepsilon'}$ whenever $\varepsilon < \varepsilon'$. But it does not follow from this that there is an algorithm that is asymptotically at least as good as all of the A_ε's. Indeed, in this example it is not possible to obtain a better algorithm by combining algorithms from the family A_ε. In the general case, we must be satisfied with giving lower or upper bounds. In our example, the algorithmic complexity is bounded above by $O(n^{2+\varepsilon})$ for every $\varepsilon > 0$, and bounded below by $\Omega(n^2 \log^k n)$ for every $k \in \mathbb{N}$.

> *The algorithmic complexity of a problem is bounded above by the asymptotic worst case runtime of each algorithm that solves the problem. If every algorithm that solves a problem requires a certain asymptotic worst case runtime, this results in a lower bound for the asymptotic complexity of the problem. In the case that the upper and lower bounds are asymptotically the same, we obtain the algorithmic complexity of the problem.*

Fundamental Complexity Classes

3.1 The Special Role of Polynomial Computation Time

In the last chapter we discussed the difficulties that arise when defining the algorithmic complexity of problems. In general, there are only upper and lower bounds for the minimal asymptotic worst case runtime. But in this case the upper and lower bounds are so close together, that their difference plays no role in deciding whether or not a problem is efficiently solvable. Therefore, in the future we will speak of the complexity of algorithmic problems. If the complexity, as discussed above, is not defined, then we will use upper bounds for positive statements about the solvability of a problem and lower bounds for negative statements.

A problem with algorithmic complexity $\Theta(n^2)$ is more efficiently solvable than a problem with algorithmic complexity $\Theta(n^3)$ — but only with respect to the chosen model of computation. If we choose the random access machine, or the closely related modern digital computer, as our model of computation, then the statement above is at least correct for large values of n. But if we switch to Turing machines, it is possible that the first problem now requires $\Theta(n^4)$ steps while the first problem may still be solvable in $\Theta(n^3)$ steps. From the perspective of particular applications this is irrelevant since we are not forced to use inefficient computers like Turing machines. It is different in the case of "better" models of computation. Perhaps better computers could lead to different amounts of improvement for the two problems. If we take the Extended Church-Turing Thesis as a basis, we can't rule out the possibility of computers on which the first problem would require time $\Theta(n^2)$ but the second could be solved in time $\Theta(n \log n)$. At present (and presumably in the future as well), the difference in computing time between $\Theta(n^3)$ and $\Theta(n^2)$ is substantial, if we are speaking in terms of the random access machine model. But this argument applies only to the area of design and analysis of algorithms and has nothing to do with the algorithmic complexity of the problem. From the point of view of complexity theory, the Extended Church-Turing Thesis is assumed, so for a polynomial $p(n)$, computation times $t(n)$ and $p(t(n))$

are indistinguishable. Since reading and processing at least a large portion of the input is unavoidable (except in the case of very simple problems like searching in a sorted array), the algorithmic complexity for cases of interest will always be at least linear. So polynomial computation times are first of all indistinguishable from each other and secondly the best achievable results. As a result of the previous discussion, we maintain that

> *For the practical application of algorithms, the minimization of the worst-case runtime stands in the foreground, and improvements of polynomial, or logarithmic, or even constant factors can be significant. In complexity theory, polynomially related runtimes are indistinguishable, and problems that can be solved in polynomial time are the most efficiently solvable problems.*

Definition 3.1.1. *An algorithmic problem belongs to the complexity class* P *of polynomially solvable problems if it can be solved by an algorithm with polynomial worst-case runtime.*

Problems in P will be considered efficiently solvable, although runtimes like n^{100} do not belong to algorithms that are usable in practice. But we have said that the Extended Church-Turing Thesis does not allow for any smaller class of efficiently solvable problems. More interesting for us, however, is the converse: problems that are not in P (with respect to worst-case runtime) are not efficiently solvable. This seems reasonable, since any such algorithm has a runtime of $\Omega(n^k)$ for each constant k.

There is another property that distinguishes polynomial computation times. When new computers are faster than old computers, the runtime for every computation decreases by a factor of c. We can also ask how much we can increase the length of the input, if the available computation time t remains constant. If the computation time of an algorithm is n^k and $t = N^k$, then the new computer can perform $cN^k = (c^{1/k}N)^k$ computation steps, and can therefore process an input of length $\lfloor c^{1/k}N \rfloor$, in time t. So the length of inputs that can be processed has been increased by a constant factor of $c^{1/k} > 1$, which decreases as the degree of the polynomial increases, and for increasing k approaches a value of 1. For computation times like $n^2 \log n$ or sums like $2n^3 + 8n^2 + 4$ these considerations become more complicated, but for polynomial computation times there is always a constant $d > 1$, dependent upon c and the computation time, so that the length of inputs that can be processed increases by a factor of at least d. This is not true for any superpolynomial computation time, and for exponential computation times like $2^{\varepsilon n}$, the length of inputs that can be processed increases only by an additive constant term $a = \varepsilon^{-1} \cdot \log c$, since $2^{\varepsilon(n+a)} = c \cdot 2^{\varepsilon n}$. These observations underscore the qualitative difference between polynomially and superpolynomially growing computation times.

3.2 Randomized Algorithms

We are familiar with situations from everyday life where decisions are made by chance (i.e., by means of randomization) when there are opposing interests. This is the case in sports, for example, when tournaments are drawn (although the randomness may be restricted by seeding of the participating players or teams), when choosing which goal is defended by which team, or which lanes are assigned to which runners. Even in the case of mayoral elections it may be that a tie is broken by casting lots. What we routinely accept as an everyday decision-making aid, we should not reject when solving algorithmic problems. If an algorithm is to process n objects one after the other, the chosen order has a large impact on the computation time, many of the $n!$ orderings are favorable, and we don't know how to efficiently select one of these favorable orderings, then it is useful to choose one at random. We will discuss what properties a randomized algorithm must have in order to be considered efficient.

We provide our computer with a source of random bits that generates one random bit in each computation step. For every t, the first t random bits are fully independent random variables $X_1, \ldots, X_t$ with $\mathrm{Prob}(X_i = 0) = \mathrm{Prob}(X_i = 1) = 1/2$. (For basic concepts of probability theory see Appendix A.2.) This can be realized by independent coin tosses, but this is not efficient. Modern computers provide pseudo-random bits which do not completely satisfy the required conditions. We will not pursue this topic further (for this see Goldreich (1998)) but will assume an ideal source of randomness. At the ith step, a *randomized algorithm* can read the ith random bit, and its action may depend on this random bit. Formally, we will describe a *randomized Turing machine*. The deterministic program δ will be replaced by a pair of programs (δ_0, δ_1). At the ith computation step program δ_{X_i} is used. The course of the computation is therefore directed by the input and the random bits.

If random algorithms with modest worst-case computation times always yield the correct result, then we can simply simulate them by deterministic algorithms that ignore the random bits. From a formal perspective, the deterministic algorithm can simulate the randomized algorithm for the case that $X_i = 0$ for all i. So we only gain something if we give up either the demand for a modest worst-case computation time or the demand that the result always be correct.

For every input x the computation time $t_A(x)$ of a randomized algorithm A is a random variable, and we can be satisfied if the *worst-case* (over all inputs up to a certain length) *expected* (averaged over the random bits) *runtime*

$$\sup\{E(t_A(x)) : |x| \leq n\}$$

is small. Consider our earlier example, in which there were a few bad orderings and many good orderings in which the objects could be considered. A specific example of this type could be a variant of QuickSort in which the pivot element is chosen at random. Our critique in Section 2.4 regarding the use of average-case computation time does not apply here. There the expected value was taken with respect to a probability distribution on the inputs of length n, which is unknown in practice. Here the expected value is taken with respect to the random bits, the quality of which we can control.

Purists could complain that in our example of QuickSort, random bits only allow for the random choice from among n objects when n is a power of two ($n = 2^k$). But this is not a problem. We can work in phases during which we read $\lceil \log n \rceil$ random bits. These $\lceil \log n \rceil$ random bits can be interpreted as a random number $z \in \{0, \ldots, 2^{\lceil \log n \rceil} - 1\}$. If $0 \leq z \leq n - 1$, then we select object $z + 1$, otherwise we continue to the next phase. Since each phase is successful with probability greater than $1/2$, Theorem A.2.12 implies that on average we will need fewer than two phases, and so the average computation time increases by at most a factor of 2 compared to the case where we could actually select a random $z \in \{1, \ldots, n\}$.

Definition 3.2.1. *We will let* EP *(expected polynomial time) denote the class of algorithmic problems for which there is an algorithm with polynomial worst-case expected runtime.*

Such algorithms are called *Las Vegas algorithms.*

We can generalize the QuickSort example in order to clarify the options of Las Vegas algorithms. If the maximal computation time is bounded for all inputs of length n and all random choices, we obtain finitely many deterministic algorithms by considering all possible ways of replacing the random bits with constants. How can the Las Vegas algorithms be better than each of these deterministic algorithms? Each deterministic algorithm could be efficient for many inputs, but inefficient for a few inputs, and in such a way that for each input significantly more algorithms are efficient than inefficient. This would lead to a good expected runtime for *each input*, but to an unacceptably high worst case runtime for each input because we do not know how to decide efficiently which randomly directed choice will help us out of our dilemma.

Now we consider two models where the correct result is not always computed, but where the worst-case runtime (taken over all inputs up to a certain length and all realizations of the random bits) is polynomially bounded. In the first model, algorithms are not allowed to produce incorrect results, but they are allowed to fail and end the computation with the output "I don't know" (or more briefly "?").

Definition 3.2.2. *We denote with* ZPP($\varepsilon(n)$) *(zero-error probabilistic polynomial) the class of algorithmic problems for which there is a randomized algorithm with polynomially bounded worst-case runtime that, for every input of length n, has a* failure-probability *bounded by* $\varepsilon(n) < 1$. *Such an algorithm either provides a correct result or fails by producing the output "?".*

In the second model, the algorithm may even provide incorrect results. Such an algorithm is called a *Monte Carlo algorithm.*

Definition 3.2.3. *We let* $\mathsf{BPP}(\varepsilon(n))$ *denote the class of algorithmic problems for which there is a randomized algorithm with polynomially bounded worst-case runtime that for every input of length n has an* error-probability *of at most* $\varepsilon(n) < 1/2$. *In the case of error, the algorithm may output any result whatsoever.*

The side condition that $\varepsilon(n) < 1/2$ is there to rule out senseless algorithms. Every decision problem, for example, has an algorithm with error-probability $1/2$: the algorithm merely accepts with probability $1/2$ and rejects with probability $1/2$ without even reading its input. (For those readers already familiar with the classes ZPP and BPP, we point out that we will shortly identify these familiar complexity classes with special cases of $\mathsf{ZPP}(\varepsilon(n))$ and $\mathsf{BPP}(\varepsilon(n))$, respectively.)

In the important special case of decision problems, there are two types of error. Inputs can be incorrectly accepted or incorrectly rejected. For some problems, like verification problems, the two types of error are not equally serious. Accepting a bad processor as correct has very different consequences from classifying a good processor as faulty. If we take the word 'verification' seriously, then the first type of error must not be allowed.

Definition 3.2.4. *We will denote by* $\mathsf{RP}(\varepsilon(n))$ *(random polynomial time) the class of decision problems for which there is an algorithm with polynomially bounded worst-case computation time and the following acceptance behavior: Every input that should be rejected, is rejected; and for every input of length n that should be accepted, the probability of erroneously rejecting the input is bounded by* $\varepsilon(n) < 1$.

This type of error is known as *one-sided error*, in contrast to the *two-sided error* that is allowed in $\mathsf{BPP}(\varepsilon(n))$ algorithms. Of course, in the case of one-sided error we could reverse the roles of inputs that are to be accepted with those that are to be rejected. From the point of view of languages, which correspond to decision problems (see Section 2.1), we are moving from the language L to its *complement*, denoted by $\overline{L}$ or co-L. So we denote by co-$\mathsf{RP}(\varepsilon(n))$ the class of languages L for which $\overline{L} \in \mathsf{RP}(\varepsilon(n))$. In more detail, this is the class of decision problems that have randomized algorithms with polynomially bounded worst-case runtime that accept every input that should be accepted, and for inputs of length n that should be rejected, have an error-probability bounded by $\varepsilon(n) < 1$.

Of course, we can only use algorithms that fail or make errors when the failure- or error-probability is small enough. For time critical applications, we may also require that the worst-case runtime is small.

> *Randomized algorithms represent an alternative when it is sufficient to bound the average computation time, or when certain failure- or error-rates are tolerable.*

This means that for most applications, randomized algorithms represent a sensible alternative. Failure- or error-probabilities of, for example, 2^{-100}

lie well below the rate of computer breakdown or error. Exponentially small error-probabilities like $\varepsilon(n) = 2^{-n}$ are, for large n, even better. If any failure or error is acceptable at all, then we should certainly consider a failure- or error-probability of $\min\{2^{-100}, 2^{-n}\}$ to be tolerable.

Although randomized algorithms present no formal difficulties, there are frequently problems with the interpretation of results of randomized algorithms. We will discuss this in the context of the primality test of Solovay and Strassen (1977), which is a co-RP(2^{-100}) algorithm. It is very efficient and has the following behavior: If the input n is a prime, it is accepted. If the input n is not a prime number, it is still accepted with a probability of at most 2^{-100}, otherwise it is rejected. So if the algorithm rejects an input n, then n is not a prime, since all primes are accepted. If, on the other hand, the algorithm accepts n, then the conclusion is ambiguous. The number n might be a prime or it might not. In the second case, however, this would have been detected with a probability bordering on 100 %, more precisely with probability at least $1 - 2^{-100}$. Since we need random prime numbers with many bits for cryptography, random numbers with the desired number of bits are checked with the primality test. Numbers that pass this test are "probably" prime. This language at first led to a rejection of the work of Solovay and Strassen. The referee correctly noted that every number either is or isn't a prime and never is prime "with a certain probability". But this objection does not go to the heart of the primality test. The term "probably" is not to be interpreted as the probability that n is a prime number. Rather, we have performed a test which prime numbers always pass but which composites fail with a probability of at least $1 - 2^{-100}$. So when we apply the primality test, on average at most every 2^{100}th test of a number that is not prime leads to acceptance of the number as a prime.

3.3 The Fundamental Complexity Classes for Algorithmic Problems

We now want to bring some order to the complexity classes P, EP, ZPP$(\varepsilon(n))$, BPP$(\varepsilon(n))$, RP$(\varepsilon(n))$, and co-RP$(\varepsilon(n))$, which we introduced in Sections 3.1 and 3.2. In particular, we are facing the difficulty that, due to the free choice of $\varepsilon(n)$, we have a multitude of different complexity classes to deal with. If one person is satisfied with an error-rate of $1/100$ but another insists on a bound of $1/1000$, then we want to know if they obtain two different classes of efficiently solvable problems. We will show that all error-probabilities that are not absurdly large give rise to the same complexity classes. But first we will show that it doesn't matter if we demand correct results with polynomially bounded worst-case expected runtime or polynomially bounded worst-case runtime with small probability of failure.

Theorem 3.3.1. $\mathsf{EP} = \mathsf{ZPP}(1/2)$.

Proof. $\mathsf{EP} \subseteq \mathsf{ZPP}(1/2)$: If a problem belongs to EP, then there is a randomized algorithm that correctly solves this problem and for every input of length n has an expected runtime that is bounded by a polynomial $p(n)$. The Markov Inequality (Theorem A.2.9) says that the probability of a runtime bounded by $2 \cdot p(n)$ is at least $1/2$. So we will stop the algorithm if it has not halted on its own after $2 \cdot p(n)$ steps. If the algorithm stops on its own (which it does with probability at least $1/2$), then it computes a correct result. If we stop the algorithm because it takes too long, we will interpret this as a failure and output "?". By definition, this modified algorithm is a $\mathsf{ZPP}(1/2)$ algorithm.

$\mathsf{ZPP}(1/2) \subseteq \mathsf{EP}$: If a problem belongs to $\mathsf{ZPP}(1/2)$, then there is a randomized algorithm with worst-case runtime bounded by a polynomial $p(n)$ that never gives false results and provides the correct result with probability at least $1/2$. We can repeat this algorithm independently as often as necessary until it produces a result, which will then necessarily be correct. By Theorem A.2.12 the expected number of repetitions is bounded by 2. In this way we obtain a modified algorithm that always provides correct results and has a worst-case expected runtime bounded by $2 \cdot p(n)$. This is an EP algorithm. □

On the basis of this theorem we will only consider worst-case runtime and various types of error-probabilities. The notation EP is unusual, and we have only used it temporarily. In the future we will consider only the ZPP-classes instead.

A $\mathsf{ZPP}(1/2)$ algorithm is like a coin toss in which we lose with probability at most $1/2$. If we repeat the coin toss several times, we will hardly ever lose every toss. For ZPP algorithms, one successful run without failure is sufficient to know the correct result (with certainty). This observation can be generalized to drastically reduce the failure-rate. This is referred to as *probability amplification*.

Theorem 3.3.2. *Let $p(n)$ and $q(n)$ be polynomials, then*

$$\mathsf{ZPP}(1 - 1/p(n)) = \mathsf{ZPP}(2^{-q(n)}).$$

Proof. We will repeat an algorithm with failure-rate of $1 - 1/p(n)$ a total of $t(n)$ times, whereby the individual runs are fully independent, i.e., each new run uses new random bits. If all of the runs fail, then our new algorithm fails. Otherwise, every run that does not fail outputs a correct result, which we can recognize because it differs from "?". The new algorithm can output any one of these correct results. The failure-rate of the new algorithm is

$$(1 - 1/p(n))^{t(n)}.$$

We let $t(n) := \lceil (\ln 2) \cdot p(n) \cdot q(n) \rceil$. Then $t(n)$ is a polynomial, so the runtime of the new algorithm is polynomially bounded. Furthermore, since $(1 - \frac{1}{m})^m \leq$

e^{-1}, we have

$$(1 - 1/p(n))^{(\ln 2) \cdot p(n) \cdot q(n)} \leq e^{-(\ln 2) \cdot q(n)} = 2^{-q(n)} . \qquad \square$$

To reduce the failure-probability from $1 - 1/n$ to 2^{-n}, fewer than n^2 repetitions of the algorithm are required. Smaller failure-probabilities than $2^{-q(n)}$ are impossible with polynomially bounded runtimes. If the computation time is bounded by a polynomial $t(n)$, then there are at most $t(n)$ random bits, and so at most $2^{t(n)}$ different random sequences. Thus, if the algorithm fails at all, it must fail with probability at least $2^{-t(n)}$. Because they only allow polynomially bounded computation time, the ZPP$(\varepsilon(n))$-classes for all $\varepsilon(n)$ that do not approach 1 sufficiently quickly and are not equivalent to $\varepsilon(n) = 0$ collapse to the same class. Thus we obtain the following complexity classes.

Definition 3.3.3. *An algorithmic problem belongs to the complexity class ZPP if it belongs to ZPP$(1/2)$, that is, if there is an algorithm with polynomially bounded worst-case runtime that never produces incorrect results and for every input has a failure-probability bounded by $1/2$. An algorithmic problem belongs to ZPP* if it belongs to ZPP$(\varepsilon(n))$ for some function $\varepsilon(n) < 1$.*

ZPP algorithms are of practical significance, since the failure-probability can be made exponentially small. On the other hand, ZPP* algorithms that are not ZPP algorithms have no direct practical significance. Nevertheless, we will encounter the complexity class ZPP* again later and give it another name.

Our considerations in the proof of Theorem 3.3.2 can be extended to RP algorithms. If we repeat an RP$(\varepsilon(n))$ algorithm $t(n)$ times, every input that should be rejected will be rejected in each repetition. On the other hand, for inputs that should be accepted, the probability of being rejected in every repetition is bounded by $\varepsilon(n)^{t(n)}$. So we will make our decision as follows: If at least one repetition of the RP algorithm accepts, then we will accept; if all repetitions reject, then we will reject. Then the proof of Theorem 3.3.2 leads to the following result.

Theorem 3.3.4. *Let $p(n)$ and $q(n)$ be polynomials, then*

$$\mathsf{RP}(1 - 1/p(n)) = \mathsf{RP}(2^{-q(n)}). \qquad \square$$

The number of repetitions required is exactly the same as it was for the ZPP algorithms.

Definition 3.3.5. *A decision problem belongs to the complexity class RP if it belongs to the class RP$(1/2)$, that is, if there is a randomized algorithm with polynomially bounded worst-case runtime that rejects every input that should be rejected with probability 1 and has an error-probability bounded by $1/2$ for inputs that should be accepted. A decision problem belongs to RP* if it belongs to RP$(\varepsilon(n))$ for some function $\varepsilon(n) < 1$.*

Once again, RP algorithms and co-RP algorithms – like the primality test we discussed previously – are of practical significance, and the complexity class RP* will prove to be central for complexity theory and will later receive a different name.

The idea of reducing the error-probability by means of independent repetitions is not so easily extended to $\text{BPP}(\varepsilon(n))$ algorithms, since we can never be sure that a result is correct. If we consider an input x of length n then we get a correct result with probability of $s := s(x) \geq 1 - \varepsilon(n) > 1/2$. For $t(n)$ independent runs, we expect a correct result in $s \cdot t(n) > t(n)/2$ of the tries. In general, for a search problem we could obtain $t(n)$ different results and have no idea which result we should choose. For problems that have a single correct result the situation is better. We can take a *majority vote*, that is, we can choose the result that appears most often among the $t(n)$ repetitions of the algorithm. This majority decision is only wrong if fewer than $t(n)/2$ of the repetitions deliver the correct result. We can analyze this situation using the Chernoff Inequality (Theorem A.2.11). Let $X_i = 1$ if the ith repetition delivers the correct result, otherwise let $X_i = 0$. Then $\text{Prob}(X_i = 1) = s$, the random variables $X_1, \ldots, X_{t(n)}$ are fully independent, and $E(X) = s \cdot t(n)$ for $X = X_1 + \cdots + X_{t(n)}$.

So

$$\text{Prob}(X \leq t(n)/2) = \text{Prob}(X \leq (1 - (1 - 1/(2s))) \cdot E(X)) .$$

When applying the Chernoff Inequality, $\delta = 1 - 1/(2s)$ and

$$\text{Prob}(X \leq t(n)/2) \leq e^{-t(n) \cdot s \cdot \delta^2 / 2} .$$

Since $s \geq 1 - \varepsilon(n)$, this bound is largest when $s = 1 - \varepsilon(n)$.

For $t(n) := \lceil (2 \cdot \ln 2) \cdot q(n) \cdot p(n)^2 \rceil$, i.e., a polynomial, we obtain an error-probability that is bounded by $2^{-q(n)}$. For most optimization problems we can determine in (deterministic) polynomial time if two results have the same quality. Since the value of the optimal solution is unique, we can in this case reduce the error-probability in an analogous manner.

Theorem 3.3.6. *Let $p(n)$ and $q(n)$ be polynomials. If we restrict our attention to the class of problems with a unique solution or to optimization problems for which the value of a solution can be computed in polynomial time, then*

$$\text{BPP}(1/2 - 1/p(n)) = \text{BPP}(2^{-q(n)}) . \qquad \square$$

Theorem 3.3.6 covers the cases that are most interesting to us. Therefore, the following definitions are justified.

Definition 3.3.7. *An algorithmic problem belongs to the complexity class* BPP *if it belongs to* BPP(1/3), *that is, if there is a randomized algorithm with polynomially bounded worst-case runtime such that the error-probability for each input is bounded by 1/3. An algorithmic problem belongs to* PP *if it belongs to* $\text{BPP}(\varepsilon(n))$ *for some function $\varepsilon(n) < 1/2$.*

The designation "bounded-error" refers to the fact that the error-probability has at least some constant distance from $1/2$. The class $BPP(1/2)$ is just as senseless as the class $ZPP(1)$, since it contains *all* decision problems, even non-computable ones.

We repeat the definitions of our complexity classes P, ZPP, ZPP*, RP, RP*, co-RP, co-RP*, BPP, and PP informally. All of these classes assume a polynomially bounded worst-case runtime for their respective (randomized) algorithms. For the class P, the result of the algorithm must always be correct, so we have no need for random bits. For the classes ZPP and ZPP* errors are forbidden, but the algorithms may fail to give an answer. On the other hand, for the classes RP, RP*, co-RP, and co-RP* a one-sided error is allowed – for RP and RP* only if $x \in L$, and for co-RP and co-RP* only if $x \notin L$. Finally, for BPP and PP there may be an error on any input. ZPP, RP, co-RP, and BPP are complexity classes with bounded failure- or error-probabilities, while the classes ZPP*, RP*, co-RP*, and PP are complexity classes without reasonable bounds on the failure- or error-probabilities.

Algorithms with bounded failure- or error-probability lead to algorithms that are reasonably applicable in practice. Thus the complexity classes P, ZPP, RP, co-RP, *and* BPP *contain problems that, under different demands, can be considered efficiently solvable.*

We obtain the following "complexity landscape" for algorithmic problems, where the directed arrows represent subset relationships.

Theorem 3.3.8.

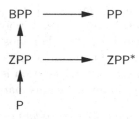

Proof. The relationships $P \subseteq ZPP$, $ZPP \subseteq ZPP^*$, and $BPP \subseteq PP$ follow directly from the definitions of these classes.

By Theorem 3.3.2,

$$ZPP = ZPP(1/2) = ZPP(1/3) \subseteq BPP(1/3) = BPP ,$$

since "?" in a BPP algorithm is an error.   □

One would like to show the corresponding relationship $\text{ZPP}^* \subseteq \text{PP}$, but this is presumably not true. A ZPP algorithm with failure-probability $1 - 2^{-2n}$, even if repeated independently 2^n times would still with high probability return "?" every time. We cannot return a correct result with an error-rate less than $1/2$.

When there are many possible results, "guessing the result" does not help. This suggests special consideration of complexity classes for decision problems. We have already seen (in Section 2.1) that optimization problems and evaluation problems have obvious variants that are decision problems. In Chapter 4 we will see that these decision problems are complexity theoretically very similar to their underlying optimization and evaluation problems. Therefore, we will focus on decision problems in the next section.

3.4 The Fundamental Complexity Classes for Decision Problems

The complexity classes P, ZPP, ZPP^*, BPP, and PP were defined for algorithmic problems. Since one-sided error only makes sense for decision problems, RP and RP^* were only defined for decision problems. If we focus on the class of decision problems DEC, then we have to consider the class $\text{P} \cap \text{DEC}$ instead of P, and analogously for ZPP, ZPP^*, BPP, and PP. Of course, $\text{P} \cap \text{DEC} \subseteq \text{RP}$, but $\text{P} \not\subseteq \text{RP}$, since the former contains problems that are not decision problems. But to the confusion of all who are introduced to complexity theory, P, ZPP, ZPP^*, BPP, and PP are used ambiguously to represent either the more general classes or the classes restricted to decision problems. The hope is that from context it will be clear if the class is restricted to decision problems. To avoid using unusual notation, we will also use the ambiguous notation and do our best to clarify any possible confusion. In this section in any case, we will always restrict our attention to decision problems.

Associated to every decision problem, i.e., to every language, is its complement, which we will denote as $\overline{L}$ or co-L. For complexity classes $\mathcal{C}$, we let co-$\mathcal{C}$ denote the class of all languages co-L such that $L \in \mathcal{C}$. Since only classes with one-sided error have asymmetric acceptance criteria, we have the following:

Remark 3.4.1. The complexity classes P, ZPP, ZPP^*, BPP, and PP are closed under complement. That is, P = co-P, ZPP = co-ZPP, $\text{ZPP}^* = \text{co-ZPP}^*$, BPP = co-BPP, and PP = co-PP.

For decision problems there is a more complete complexity landscape than for all algorithmic problems.

Theorem 3.4.2.

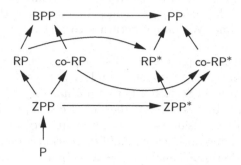

Proof. The inclusion P ⊆ ZPP and the "horizontal inclusions" between classes of practially efficiently solvable problems (bounded error) and the corresponding classes that do not give rise to practically useful algorithms, namely ZPP ⊆ ZPP*, RP ⊆ RP*, co-RP ⊆ co-RP*, and BPP ⊆ PP, follow directly from the definitions.

ZPP ⊆ RP, and ZPP* ⊆ RP*, since the answer "?" for a failure can be replaced by a rejection, possibly with error. Analogously, co-ZPP ⊆ co-RP, and since ZPP = co-ZPP, ZPP ⊆ co-RP as well. Similarly, ZPP* ⊆ co-RP*.

By Theorem 3.3.4,

$$RP = RP(1/2) = RP(1/3) \subseteq BPP(1/3) = BPP \ .$$

This is not surprising, since one-sided error is a stronger condition than two-sided error. Analogously, we have co-RP ⊆ co-BPP = BPP.

It remains to be shown that the inclusion RP* ⊆ PP holds, since co-RP* ⊆ co-PP = PP follows from this. For a decision problem $L \in$ RP* we investigate an RP* algorithm A and consider its worst-case runtime $p(n)$, a polynomial in the input length n. On an input of length n, the algorithm only has $p(n)$ random bits available. For each of the $2^{p(n)}$ assignments of the random bits the algorithm works deterministically. Thus we obtain a 0-1 vector $A(x)$ of length $2^{p(n)}$ that describes for each assignment of the random bits the decision of the algorithm (1 = accept; 0 = reject). For the RP algorithm A the following hold:

- For $x \in L$, $A(x)$ contains at least one 1.
- For $x \notin L$, $A(x)$ contains only 0's.

We are looking for a PP algorithm A' for L, that is, for an algorithm with the following properties:

- For $x \in L$, $A'(x)$ contains more 1's than 0's.
- For $x \notin L$, $A'(x)$ contains more 0's than 1's.

The idea is to accept each input with a suitable probability and otherwise to apply algorithm A. By doing this the acceptance probability is "shifted to the right" – from 0 or at least $2^{-p(n)}$ to something less than 1/2 or something greater than 1/2, respectively. This "shifting of acceptance probability" can be realized as follows: Algorithm A' uses $2p(n) + 1$ random bits. The first $p(n) + 1$ random bits are interpreted as a binary number z.

- If $0 \leq z \leq 2^{p(n)}$ (that is, in $2^{p(n)} + 1$ of the $2^{p(n)+1}$ cases), then we simulate A using the remaining $p(n)$ random bits.
- If $2^{p(n)} < z \leq 2^{p(n)+1} - 1$ (that is, in the other $2^{p(n)} - 1$ cases) the input is accepted without any further computation. Note that this happens for $(2^{p(n)} - 1) \cdot 2^{p(n)}$ of the $2^{2p(n)+1}$ total assignments of the $2p(n) + 1$ random bits.

The analysis of the algorithm A' is now simple.

- If $x \notin L$, then A never accepts. So $A'(x)$ contains only

$$(2^{p(n)} - 1) \cdot 2^{p(n)} = 2^{2p(n)} - 2^{p(n)} < 2^{2p(n)+1}/2$$

1's, and therefore more 0's than 1's.
- If $x \in L$, then $A'(x)$ contains at most

$$(2^{p(n)} + 1) \cdot (2^{p(n)} - 1) = 2^{2p(n)} - 1 < 2^{2p(n)+1}/2$$

0's, and therefore more 1's than 0's. $\qquad\qquad\square$

The proof of the inclusion $\mathsf{RP}^* \subseteq \mathsf{PP}$ only appears technical. We have an experiment that dependent on a property (namely, $x \notin L$ or $x \in L$) with probability $\varepsilon_0 < 1/2$ or $\varepsilon_1 > \varepsilon_0$, respectively, produces an outcome E (accepting input x). If we decide with probability $p < 1$, to produce the outcome E in any case, and with probability $1 - p$ to perform the experiment, then by the Law of Total Probability (Theorem A.2.2) we have new probabilities

$$\varepsilon_0' = p + (1-p)\varepsilon_0 = \varepsilon_0 + p(1 - \varepsilon_0)$$

and

$$\varepsilon_1' = p + (1-p)\varepsilon_1 = \varepsilon_1 + p(1 - \varepsilon_1) > \varepsilon_0 + p(1 - \varepsilon_0)$$

for the outcome E. Now it only remains to choose p so that

$$\varepsilon_0 + p(1 - \varepsilon_0) < 1/2 < \varepsilon_1 + p(1 - \varepsilon_1) \, .$$

Our work is only slightly more difficult because in addition we must see to it that p is of the form $t/2^{q(n)}$ for some polynomial $q(n)$ so that the new experiment can be realized in polynomial time.

To derive a relationship between ZPP, RP, and co-RP, we can imagine the associated algorithms as investment advisers. The ZPP adviser gives advice in at least half of the cases, and this advice is always correct, but the rest of the time he merely shrugs his shoulders. The RP adviser is very cautious. When the prospects for an investment are poor, she advises against the investment, and when the prospects are good, she only recommends the investment half of the time. If she advises against an investment, we can't be sure if she is doing this because she knows the prospects are poor or because she is cautious. With the ZPP adviser, on the other hand, we always know whether he has given good advice or is being cautious. With the co-RP adviser the situation is like that with the RP adviser, only the tendencies are reversed. His advice is risky. We won't miss any good investments, but we are only warned about poor investments at least half of the time. If we have both a conservative adviser and an aggressive adviser, that is, both an RP and a co-RP adviser, we should be able to avoid mistakes. This is formalized in the following theorem.

Theorem 3.4.3. ZPP = RP ∩ co-RP *and* ZPP* = RP* ∩ co-RP*.

Proof. We will only prove the first equality. The proof is, however, correct for all bounds $\varepsilon(n)$, and so the second equality follows as well. The inclusion ZPP $\subseteq$ RP ∩ co-RP follows from Theorem 3.4.2, so we only need to show that RP ∩ co-RP $\subseteq$ ZPP.

If $L \in$ RP ∩ co-RP, then there are polynomially bounded RP algorithms A and $\overline{A}$ for L and $\overline{L}$, respectively. We run both algorithms, one after the other, which clearly leads to a polynomially bounded randomized algorithm. Before we describe how we will make our decision about whether $x \in L$, we will investigate the behavior of the algorithm pair $(A, \overline{A})$.

- Suppose $x \in L$. Then since $x \notin \overline{L}$, $\overline{A}$ rejects the input, which we will denote by $\overline{A}(x) = 0$. Since $x \in L$, A accepts x with probability at least $1/2$, which we denote with $A(x) = 1|0$. So $(A, \overline{A})$ is $(1|0, 0)$.
- Suppose $x \notin L$. Analogously, $(A, \overline{A})$ is $(0, 1|0)$.

The combined algorithm $(A, \overline{A})$ has three possible results (since $(1, 1)$ is impossible). These results are evaluated as follows:

- $(1, 0)$: Since $A(x) = 1$, x must be in L. (If $x \notin L$, then $A(x) = 0$.) So we accept x.
- $(0, 1)$: Since $\overline{A}(x) = 1$, x must be in $\overline{L}$. (If $x \in L$, then $\overline{A}(x) = 0$.) So we reject x.
- $(0, 0)$: One of the algorithms has clearly made an error, but we don't know which one, so we output "?".

The new algorithm is error-free. If $x \in L$, then $\overline{A}(x) = 0$ with certainty, and $A(x) = 1$ with probability at least $1/2$, so the new algorithm accepts x with probability at least $1/2$. If $x \notin L$, then it follows in an analogous way that the new algorithm rejects with probability at least $1/2$. All together, this implies that the new algorithm is a ZPP algorithm for L.   □

3.5 Nondeterminism as a Special Case of Randomization

Now that we have introduced important complexity classes using randomization (which we consider as a key concept), we want to establish the connection to the classical use of nondeterminism. Once again in this section we will only consider decision problems.

With deterministic algorithms, the effects of the next computation step only depend on the information currently being read and the program instruction about to be executed. A randomized algorithm can at every step choose between two actions based on the random bit available for that step, whereby each action is performed with probability $1/2$. A nondeterministic algorithm can also choose at each step between two possible actions, but there are no rules about how the choice between the two actions is to be made. Formally, a nondeterministic Turing machine, just like a randomized Turing machine, has a pair of programs (δ_0, δ_1) available to it. This is more typically, but equivalently, described as a single function $\delta \colon Q \times \Gamma \to (Q \times \Gamma \times \{-1, 0, +1\})^2$, which contains both possible actions. An input is accepted if and only if there is a legal computation path, i.e., a sequence of actions that agree with the program, that leads to acceptance of the input.

Definition 3.5.1. *A decision problem L belongs to the complexity class* NP *(nondeterministic polynomial time) if there is a nondeterministic algorithm with polynomially bounded worst-case runtime that accepts every $x \in L$ along at least one legal computation path, and rejects every $x \notin L$ along every legal computation path.*

This is the complexity class that was discussed in Chapter 1 in the context of the NP $\neq$ P-hypothesis. It is admittedly difficult to imagine the way a nondeterministic machine works. The following explanations are frequently used:

- Algorithmically, all computation paths are tried out. If the maximal runtime is $p(n)$, this can be as many as $2^{p(n)}$ computation paths.
- The algorithm has the ability to "guess" the correct computation steps.

So we are dealing either with an exponentially long computation or with an unrealizable concept. Thus nondeterministic computers are considered to be a theoretically important but practically unrealizable concept. Randomization provides simpler access to the class NP.

Theorem 3.5.2. NP $=$ RP*.

Proof. The definitions of NP and RP* expect algorithms with polynomially bounded worst-case computation time $p(n)$ and two possible actions in each situation. For $x \notin L$, an NP algorithm must reject along every computation path, and for an RP* algorithm this must happen with probability 1. Since every computation path has a probability of at least $2^{-p(n)}$, the two requirements are equivalent. For $x \in L$, an NP algorithm must accept x along at least one computation path, and an RP* algorithm must reject with a probability less than 1. Once again, these two statements are equivalent.   □

An RP* algorithm, and therefore an NP algorithm, can be performed on a randomized computer with polynomially bounded computation time, and is therefore a realizable algorithmic concept. It just isn't practically useful due to the potentially large error-probability.

Nondeterminism is the same thing as randomization where one-sided errors and any error-probability less than 1 are allowed.

Now we can insert the results of Theorem 3.4.3 into Theorem 3.4.2 and reformulate Theorem 3.4.2 with the usual notation.

Theorem 3.5.3.

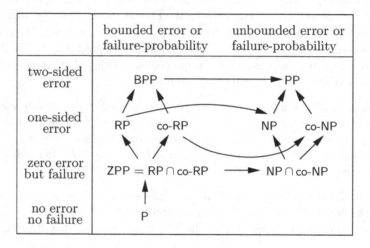

	bounded error or failure-probability	unbounded error or failure-probability
two-sided error	BPP	PP
one-sided error	RP co-RP	NP co-NP
zero error but failure	ZPP = RP ∩ co-RP	NP ∩ co-NP
no error no failure	P	

□

The rows and columns in the figure above reflect the characterization from the modern perspective with the focus on randomization. The terminology of the complexity classes arose historically, and are rather unfortunately chosen. For example, BPP (B = bounded) is not the only class for which the difference between the trivial error-probability and the tolerated error-probability is bounded by a constant; the same is true for RP algorithms and for the failure-probability of ZPP algorithms. In ZPP and BPP, the second P stands for probabilistic, and in RP, the R stands for random, although randomization is involved in all these classes. The classes PP and NP deal with randomized algorithms with unacceptable error-probabilities, but only PP indicates this in its name. Finally, the class NP ∩ co-NP, in contrast to ZPP = RP ∩ co-RP, has no real name of its own.

When the complexity class NP was "discovered" (in the 1960's), randomized algorithms were exotic outsiders, while formal languages had been highly developed as the basis for programming languages. A word belongs to the language generated by a grammar if there is a derivation of the word from the start symbol following the rules of the grammar. In this context, nondeterminism is more natural than randomization. Typically, we are not interested in the probability that a word is generated when randomly choosing an appropriate derivation rule for a left derivation from a context free grammar. With algorithms, on the other hand, the probability that a correct result is computed is important.

4

Reductions – Algorithmic Relationships Between Problems

4.1 When Are Two Problems Algorithmically Similar?

In complexity theory we want to classify problems with respect to their complexity. That is, we are satisfied to know which of the complexity classes introduced in Chapter 3 contain the problem we are considering and which do not. Later we will introduce additional complexity classes, and then we will extend our inquiry to include these classes as well. Two problems will be called *complexity theoretically similar* if they belong to exactly the same subset of the complexity classes being considered. We know many problems that are solvable in polynomial time, and therefore are complexity theoretically similar. Similarly, there are many problems that are not computable, that is that they cannot be solved with the help of computers. Still other problems are known to be computable but so difficult that they do not belong to any of the complexity classes we will consider. These problems are also similar in the sense just described. (Of course, it makes sense to distinguish between computable and noncomputable problems.) At the moment, we are not able to prove that a problem is in PP but not in P. This is because of our inability (mentioned already in Chapter 1) to show that problems cannot be solved in polynomial time, unless they are very difficult.

Fortunately, we are still able to show that many problems are complexity theoretically similar, i.e., that they belong to exactly the same complexity classes. The path to this at first surprising result consists of showing that the problems are actually *algorithmically similar*. If we can obtain from a polynomial time algorithm for one problem a polynomial time algorithm for another, and vice versa, then we know that either both problems belong to P or neither of them does.

We want to precisely define what it means for a problem A to be algorithmically no more difficult to solve than some problem B. Problems A and B are then algorithmically similar when A is algorithmically no more difficult than B and B is algorithmically no more difficult than A. The definition of "algorithmically no more difficult than" follows directly from our goals.

Definition 4.1.1. *Problem A is algorithmically no more difficult than problem B if there is an algorithm that solves problem A that may make use of an algorithm for B and has the following properties:*

- *The runtime of the algorithm for A, not counting the calls to the algorithm that solves B, is bounded by a polynomial $p(n)$.*
- *The number of calls to the algorithm that solves B is bounded by a polynomial $q(n)$.*
- *The length of each input to a call of the algorithm solving B is bounded by a polynomial $r(n)$.*

If there is an algorithm that solves B with runtime $t_B(n)$, then we obtain an algorithm for A with a runtime that can be estimated as follows:

$$t_A(n) \le p(n) + q(n) \cdot t_B\left(r(n)\right).$$

This estimate can be improved if we know that some of the calls to the algorithm for B are shorter. If $t_B(n)$ is polynomially bounded, then $t_A(n)$ is also polynomially bounded, and we can easily compute a polynomial bound for $t_A(n)$. Here we use the following three simple but central properties of polynomials p_1 of degree d_1 and p_2 of degree d_2:

- The sum $p_1 + p_2$ is a polynomial of degree at most $\max\{d_1, d_2\}$.
- The product $p_1 \cdot p_2$ is a polynomial of degree $d_1 + d_2$.
- The composition $p_1 \circ p_2$ (i.e., $p_1(p_2(n))$) is a polynomial of degree $d_1 \cdot d_2$.

What is interesting for us is the contrapositive of the statement above: If A does not belong to P, then B does not belong to P either. That is, from a lower bound $s_A(n)$ on the complexity of A, we are able to compute a lower bound $s_B(n)$ for the complexity of B. For the sake of simplicity, we will assume that the polynomials p, q, and r are monotonically increasing and let $r^{-1}(n) := \min\{m \mid r(m) \ge n\}$. Then

$$s_A(n) \le p(n) + q(n) \cdot s_B\left(r(n)\right),$$

$$s_A\left(r^{-1}(n)\right) \le p\left(r^{-1}(n)\right) + q\left(r^{-1}(n)\right) \cdot s_B(n)$$

and

$$s_B(n) \ge \frac{s_A\left(r^{-1}(n)\right) - p\left(r^{-1}(n)\right)}{q\left(r^{-1}(n)\right)}.$$

For the purposes of complexity theoretic classification it is sufficient if p, q, and r are polynomials. In fact, the bounds are better if the polynomials p, q, and r are "as small as possible". This concept can also be applied for randomized algorithms for B with bounded failure- or error-probability. Using independent repetitions the failure-rate of the algorithm for B can be reduced so that the total failure-rate when there are $q(n)$ calls is small enough.

In complexity theory the clearly understood term "algorithmically no more difficult than" is not actually used. Based on similar concepts from decidability theory and logic, we speak instead of reductions: We have reduced the problem of finding an efficient algorithm for A to the problem of finding an efficient algorithm for B. Since efficiency is in terms of polynomial time, and according to the Extended Church-Turing Thesis we may choose Turing machines as our model of computation, the statement "A is algorithmically no more difficult that B" is abbreviated $A \leq_T B$, and read "A is (polynomial time) Turing reducible to B". The notation $\leq_T$ indicates that the complexity of A is not greater than that of B. Now A and B are algorithmically similar if $A \leq_T B$ and $B \leq_T A$. We will write this as $A \equiv_T B$, and say that A and B are (polynomial time) *Turing equivalent.* [1]

Turing reductions are algorithmic concepts where, just like in top-down programming, we work with subprograms that have not yet been implemented. Of course in this case we do not always have the hope that we will be able to implement an efficient algorithm for B. Therefore, an algorithm for A that results from a Turing reduction to B is often called an algorithm *with oracle* B. We ask an oracle that – in contrast to the Oracle of Delphi – reliably provides answers for instances of problem B.

> *By means of Turing reductions we can establish algorithmic similarities between problems of unknown complexity.*

Before we get to specific Turing reductions, we want to establish a few extremely useful properties of this reducibility concept. Turing reducibility is trivially reflexive: $A \leq_T A$ for all problems A since we can solve instances of A by asking an oracle for A. Furthermore, $\leq_T$ is transitive:

$$A \leq_T B \text{ and } B \leq_T C \Rightarrow A \leq_T C.$$

The proof of this property is simple. We use the Turing reduction from A to B and substitute for each call to the oracle for B the given Turing reduction from B to C. Since every polynomial is bounded by a monotonically increasing polynomial, we will assume that the polynomials p_1, q_1, and r_1 in the definition of $A \leq_T B$ and the polynomials p_2, q_2, and r_2 in the definition of $B \leq_T C$ are monotonically increasing. The runtime of our C-oracle algorithm for A, excluding the calls to C, is bounded by $p_3(n) := p_1(n) + q_1(n) \cdot p_2(r_1(n))$; the oracle for C will be queried at most $q_3(n) := q_1(n) \cdot q_2(r_1(n))$ times for inputs of length at most $r_3(n) := r_2(r_1(n))$; and p_3, q_3, and r_3 are polynomials. Turing equivalence is an equivalence relation since $A \equiv_T A$ and

$$A \equiv_T B \Leftrightarrow B \equiv_T A,$$

and transitivity follows directly from the transitivity of $\leq_T$.

---

[1] When more general Turing reductions are considered, the notation $\leq_T^p$ is sometimes used for polynomially bounded Turing reductions to distinguish them from general Turing reductions. Since in this book all reductions will be polynomially bounded, we will omit the superscript.

Now we want to investigate the algorithmic similarity of problems in a few example cases. In Section 4.2 we will show that for the problems that are of interest to us, all variants of a problem are complexity theoretically equivalent. In Section 4.3 we will establish relationships between problems that appear to be very similar, or at least turn out to be very similar. The true power of Turing reducibility will be shown in Section 4.4 where we will be able to establish relationships between "very different" problems. In this section we will see that many of our Turing reductions are of a special type, and the special role of this type of Turing reduction will be discussed in Section 4.5. The techniques for designing Turing reductions go back to the influential work of Karp (1972).

4.2 Reductions Between Various Variants of a Problem

In Section 2.2 we introduced algorithmic problems including large groups of problems like TSP that have many special cases. That special problems like TSP^2 can be reduced to more general problems like TSP (i.e., that $TSP^2 \leq_T TSP$) is trivial (algorithms for more general problems automatically solve the more specialized problems), but not particularly enlightening. More interesting is the investigation of whether $TSP \leq_T TSP^2$, that is, whether a special case is already as hard as the general problem. Such results will be shown in Section 4.3 and in subsequent chapters. Surprisingly, it will be the case that $TSP \equiv_T TSP^2$.

Here we want to compare the complexity of evaluation and decision problems with their underlying optimization problems. Let A_{OPT}, A_{EVAL}, and A_{DEC} denote the optimization, evaluation, and decision variants of the problem A. We want to show that for many natural problems A,

$$A_{DEC} \equiv_T A_{EVAL} \equiv_T A_{OPT} .$$

We will not formalize a definition of degenerate problems (ones for which the three variants are not Turing equivalent), but we will give conditions under which the necessary Turing reductions are possible. We always have

$$A_{DEC} \leq_T A_{EVAL} ,$$

since we can compare the value of an optimal solution with the bound given in the decision problem. Solutions to optimization problems have a certain quality that is assigned a value. If this value can be computed in polynomial time for any solution, then

$$A_{EVAL} \leq_T A_{OPT} ,$$

since we can run the optimization algorithm to obtain an optimal solution and then compute the value of this optimal solution. All of the problems introduced in Section 2.2 satisfy this condition, as can be easily verified. The cost of a traveling salesperson tour, for example, can be computed in linear time.

To ensure that

$$A_{\text{EVAL}} \leq_T A_{\text{DEC}} \; ,$$

we use the following sufficient property: The value of each solution is a natural number, and we can efficiently find a bound B such that the value of an optimal solution lies between $-B$ and B, and the binary representation of B is polynomial in the bit length of the input. For the problems in Section 2.2, solutions are always non-negative, and are usually very easy to obtain. For example, we may choose B to be

- n for BinPacking, since it is always possible to use a separate bin for each item;
- n for VertexCover, CliqueCover, Clique, or IndependentSet, since the values of the solutions are the sizes of a subset of the vertices of the graph or the number of sets in a partition of the vertex set;
- m for the optimization variant of Sat, since the value of a solution is the number of satisfiable clauses;
- $a_1 + \cdots + a_n$ for Knapsack.

For TSP we also allow the distance ∞. Let d_{max} be the maximal finite distance. Then $n \cdot d_{max}$ is an upper bound for the cost of a tour that has finite cost. The cost of each tour is in $\{0, \ldots n \cdot d_{max}\} \cup \{\infty\}$.

In each case we have a list of possible solution values of the form $-B, \ldots, B$ or $-B, \ldots B, \infty$. We can use an algorithm for the decision problem to perform a binary search on these values, treating ∞ like $B + 1$. The number of calls to the decision problem algorithm is bounded by $\lceil \log(2B + 2) \rceil$, which is polynomially bounded. In many cases, roughly $\log(n)$ calls to the decision problem algorithm are sufficient. For problems that may have very large numbers as part of their input (like TSP and Knapsack), the number of calls may depend on the size of these numbers.

Finally, we want to investigate when we also have

$$A_{\text{OPT}} \leq_T A_{\text{EVAL}} \; .$$

We use the following method: First, we use the algorithm for A_{EVAL} to compute the value w_{opt} of an optimal solution. Then we try to establish portions of the solution. For this we try out possible decisions. If the solution value remains w_{opt}, we can stick with our decision; otherwise that decision was false and we must try out a new decision. By working this out for five specific problems, we will demonstrate that this approach can be routinely applied.

We will start with Max-Sat. Let w_{opt} be the maximal number of simultaneously satisfiable clauses. Let $x_1 = 1$. Clauses containing x_1 are then satisfied and can be replaced by clauses with the value 1, while $\overline{x}_1$ can be stricken from any clauses that contain it. (Any empty clause is unsatisfiable.) If the resulting set of clauses still has an optimal value of w_{opt}, then $x_1 = 1$ belongs to an optimal variable assignment, and we can look for suitable assignments for $x_2, \ldots, x_n$ in the resulting clause set. If the resulting set of clauses has an optimal value that is smaller than w_{opt} (larger is impossible), then we know that $x_1 = 1$ does not belong to an optimal variable assignment. Thus $x_1 = 0$ must belong to an optimal solution and we can search for suitable assignments for $x_2, \ldots, x_n$ in the clause set that results from setting $x_1 = 0$ in the original clause set. The number of calls to the algorithm for the evaluation problem is bounded by $n + 1$, all the calls are for instances that are no larger than the original, and the additional overhead is modest.

For the clique problem CLIQUE, we first determine the size w_{opt} of the largest clique. In order to decide if a vertex v *must* belong to a largest clique, we can remove the vertex and the edges incident to it from the graph, and check if the remaining graph still has a clique of size w_{opt}. If this is the case, then there is a clique of size w_{opt} that does not use vertex v. Otherwise the vertex v must belong to every maximal clique, so we remove v, the edges incident to v, and all vertices *not* adjacent to v from the graph and look for a clique of size $w_{opt} - 1$ in the remaining graph. By adding the vertex v to such a clique, we obtain the desired clique of size w_{opt}. Once again, $n + 1$ queries about graphs that are no larger than the original input suffice to find the optimal solution.

For TSP we can output any tour if $w_{opt} = \infty$. Otherwise, we can temporarily set finite distances $d_{i,j}$ to ∞ to see if the stretch from i to j must be in an optimal tour. If it is required for an optimal tour, then we return $d_{i,j}$ to its original value, otherwise we leave the value ∞. Once we have done this sequentially for all distances we obtain a distance matrix in which exactly the edges of an optimal tour have finite values. In this case the number of queries to the algorithm for the evaluation problem is $N + 1$, where N is the number of finite distance values.

The situation for the bin packing problem is somewhat more complicated. If we decide that certain objects go in certain bins, then the remaining capacity of those bins is no longer b, and we obtain a problem with bins of various sizes, which by the definition of BINPACKING is no longer a bin packing problem, so we can't get information about this situation by querying the evaluation problem. For a generalized version of BINPACKING with bins of potentially different sizes, this approach would work. But in our case we can employ a little trick. We can "glue together" two objects so that they become one new object with size equal to the sum of the sizes of the two original objects. If this doesn't increase the number of bins required, we can leave the two objects stuck together and work with a new instance that has one fewer object. If object i cannot be glued to object j, then this will subsequently be the case for all pairs of new superobjects one of which   contains object i and the other of which contains object j. So $\binom{n}{2}$ tests are sufficient. In the end we will have

w_{opt} superobjects, each consisting of a number of objects stuck together, and each fitting into a bin.

Finally we want to mention the network flow problem NETWORKFLOW. This problem is solvable in polynomial time (see, for example, Ahuja, Magnanti, and Orlin(1993)). So we can solve the optimization problem in polynomial time without even making any use of the evaluation variation.

> *The optimization, evaluation, and decision variants of the optimiza-*
> *tion problems that are of interest to us are all Turing equivalent. So*
> *from the point of view of complexity theory, we are justified in restrict-*
> *ing our attention to the decision variants.*

4.3 Reductions Between Related Problems

In this section and the following section we want to use examples to introduce and practice methods for designing Turing reductions. These examples have been chosen in such a way that the results will also be useful later. On the basis of the results in Section 4.2, we will always consider the decision variant of optimization problems. All of the problems treated here were defined in Section 2.2.

We begin with TSP and its variants. Since we will see later that DHC (the directed Hamiltonian circuit problem) is a difficult problem, the following theorem allows us to extend this claim to the problems HC, $TSP^\triangle$, TSP^2 (and also TSP^N for $N \geq 2$), and TSP.

Theorem 4.3.1. $DHC \equiv_T HC \leq_T TSP^{2,\triangle,\mathrm{sym}}$.

Proof. $HC \leq_T DHC$: This statement is easy to show. Undirected edges can be traveled in either direction. From the given undirected graph $G = (V, E)$, we generate a directed graph $G' = (V, E')$ with the same vertex set in which undirected edges $\{v, w\}$ in G are replaced by pairs of directed edges (v, w) and (w, v) from v to w and from w to v in G'. It is clear that G has an undirected Hamiltonian circuit if and only if G' has a directed Hamiltonian circuit. So we can make a call to the algorithm for DHC with input G' and use the answer (yes or no) as the answer for whether G is in HC. Directed graphs have more degrees of freedom, and so it is not surprising when a problem on undirected graphs can be Turing reduced to a problem on directed graphs.

$DHC \leq_T HC$: According to our last remark, this Turing reduction will be more difficult to construct. Our goal is use undirected edges but to force them to be traveled in only one direction. For this it suffices to replace vertices with tiny graphs. In polynomial time we will transform a directed graph $G = (V, E)$ into an undirected graph $G' = (V', E')$ that has a Hamiltonian circuit if and only if this is also the case for G. Then it will suffice to call the HC algorithm on graph G' and to copy the answer. Let $V = \{v_1, \ldots, v_n\}$. Then $V' := \{v_{i,j} \mid 1 \leq i \leq n, 1 \leq j \leq 3\}$. The vertices $v_{i,1}$, $v_{i,2}$, and $v_{i,3}$ are intended to "represent" the vertex $v_i \in V$. We always include the edges $\{v_{i,1}, v_{i,2}\}$ and $\{v_{i,2}, v_{i,3}\}$. An edge $(v_i, v_j) \in E$ is represented in G' by the edge $\{v_{i,3}, v_{j,1}\}$, and an edge $(v_k, v_i) \in E$ by the edge $\{v_{k,3}, v_{i,1}\}$. The direction of an edge in G that is adjacent to v_i is reflected in where the edge is attached to the vertex triple $(v_{i,1}, v_{i,2}, v_{i,3})$. At least the information about the direction of the edge is not lost. Figure 4.3.1 shows as an example the section of such a graph G that is adjacent to v_{10}.

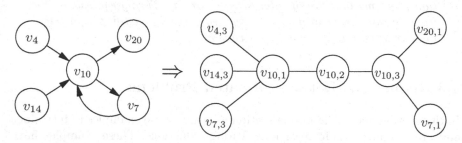

Fig. 4.3.1. Illustration of the Turing reduction DHC $\leq_T$ HC.

If G contains a Hamiltonian circuit, we can renumber the vertices so that this circuit is the vertex sequence $(v_1, v_2, \dots, v_n, v_1)$. Then G' contains the "corresponding" Hamiltonian circuit that results from replacing the edge (v_i, v_j) with the path $(v_{i,3}, v_{j,1}, v_{j,2}, v_{j,3})$. (This is only true for $n > 1$, but for $n = 1$ we don't need any oracle queries at all.)

Now let's assume that G' has a Hamiltonian circuit H'. In G', every vertex $v_{i,2}$ has degree 2. This means that the Hamiltonian circuit must contain the edges $\{v_{i,1}, v_{i,2}\}$ and $\{v_{i,2}, v_{i,3}\}$ for every $i \in \{1, \dots, n\}$. An undirected graph G' with Hamiltonian circuit H' always contains also the Hamiltonian circuit H'' formed by traversing H' in the reverse direction, so we can choose the subpath $(v_{1,1}, v_{1,2}, v_{1,3})$. Now H' must contain an edge from $v_{1,3}$ to a vertex $v_{j,1}$, for some $j \neq 1$. In order to reach $v_{j,2}$ along the circuit, the next portion of the path must be $(v_{j,1}, v_{j,2}, v_{j,3})$. This argument can be continued, until H' connects all the triples $(v_{i,1}, v_{i,2}, v_{i,3})$ in a suitable way. If the v_k-triple follows the v_i-triple, then we can choose the edge (v_i, v_k) in G.

HC $\leq_T$ TSP$^{2,\triangle,\mathrm{sym}}$: Let $G = (V, E)$ be an undirected graph for which we want to decide whether or not there is a Hamiltonian circuit. Then we can make the following query to a TSP-oracle. If $V = \{1, \dots, n\}$, then there are n cities. Let

$$d_{i,j} = \begin{cases} 1 & \text{if } \{i, j\} \in E \\ 2 & \text{otherwise.} \end{cases}$$

That is, we represent edges with short distances. A Hamiltonian circuit in G has cost n in the TSP problem. Every circuit that doesn't simulate a Hamiltonian circuit in G has cost at least $n + 1$. So by asking if there is a circuit with cost at most n we obtain an answer to the question of whether G has a Hamiltonian circuit. The TSP input has the distance values from the set $\{1, 2\}$ and is symmetric. Because the distances are from the set $\{1, 2\}$, the triangle inequality $d_{i,j} \leq d_{i,k} + d_{k,j}$ is always satisfied.

For all our reductions, we always want to give the required resources. For HC $\leq_T$ DHC the problems size is related to the number of vertices n and the number of edges m. Then $p(n, m) = O(n + m)$, $q(n, m) = 1$, and the new graph has n vertices and $2m$ edges. For DHC $\leq_T$ HC we have $p(n, m) = O(n + m)$, $q(n, m) = 1$, and the new graph has $3n$ vertices and $2n + m$ edges. For HC $\leq_T$ TSP$^{2, \triangle, \mathrm{sym}}$, we have $p(n, m) = O(n^2)$, $q(n, m) = 1$, and we obtain an instance of TSP with n cities. $\square$

We have already seen in this example that it is important that the properties of the instance to be solved be "coded into" an instance of the problem for which an algorithm is assumed. In particular, this is necessary when we want to reduce a problem like DHC to an "apparently more specialized" problem like HC. With closely related problems like those in the proof of Theorem 4.3.1 this can happen by means of *local replacement*. In local replacement, each simple component of an instance of one problem is represented by a little "gadget" in an instance of the other. 3-SAT is not only apparently but actually a special case of SAT. The following Turing reduction is a model example of local replacement.

Theorem 4.3.2. SAT $\equiv_T$ 3-SAT.

Proof. That 3-SAT $\leq_T$ SAT is clear. (But see the discussion following this proof.)

Now we must design a Turing reduction SAT $\leq_T$ 3-SAT. First, we note that clauses with fewer than three literals can be extended by repetition of variables to clauses that have exactly three literals. This is only a syntactic change, but it allows us to assume that all clauses have at least three literals.

Consider a clause $c = z_1 + \cdots + z_k$ (+ represents OR) with $k > 3$ and $z_i \in \{x_1, \overline{x}_1, \ldots, x_n, \overline{x}_n\}$. We want to construct clauses of length 3 with the "same satisfaction properties". We can't choose $z_1 + z_2 + z_3$, since we can satisfy $z_1 + \cdots + z_k$ without satisfying $z_1 + z_2 + z_3$. So we choose a new variable y_1 and form a new clause $z_1 + z_2 + y_1$. The new variable can satisfy the clause if c is satisfied by one of the literals $z_3, \ldots, z_k$. It doesn't make sense to now choose $z_3 + z_4 + y_2$ as the next clause, because then we could satisfy the new clauses without satisfying c. The trick consists of connecting the clauses in such a way that the new variables occur in two new clauses, once positively and once negatively, and thus connect these two clauses. All together the new clauses are connected like a chain. We will describe the new clauses for $k = 7$, from which the general construction is immediately clear:

$$z_1 + z_2 + y_1, \ \overline{y}_1 + z_3 + y_2, \ \overline{y}_2 + z_4 + y_3, \ \overline{y}_3 + z_5 + y_4, \ \overline{y}_4 + z_6 + z_7.$$

We do this for all clauses, using different new variables for each.

If the given set of clauses has a satisfying assignment, then we can assign values to the variables in such a way that the new set of clauses is also satisfiable. If c is satisfied, then $z_i = 1$ for some i. Thus one of the clauses of length 3 that came from clause c is already satisfied. All the clauses to the left of this clause can be satisfied by setting the positive y-literal to 1, and all the clauses to the right of this clause can be satisfied by setting the negative $\bar{y}$-literal to 1. In our example, if $z_3 = 1$, then we set $y_1 = 1$ and $y_2 = y_3 = y_4 = 0$.

On the other hand, if the new clause set is satisfied by an assignment, then it is not possible that all of the new clauses that come from c are satisfied by the y-literals alone. If i is the smallest index for which $y_i = 0$, then the ith clause ($z_1 + z_2 + y_1$ for $i = 1$, and $\bar{y}_{i-1} + z_{i+1} + y_i$ otherwise) is not satisfied by a y-literal. If all $y_i = 1$, then the last clause is not satisfied by the y-literals. Therefore, the assignment must satisfy at least one z_i, and hence satisfy c.

If we measure the input length in terms of the number of literals l in the clauses, then $p(l) = O(l)$, $q(l) = 1$, and $r(l) \leq 3l$.   □

It is always easier to reduce a problem to a more general problem. The reduction 3-SAT $\leq_T$ SAT, for example, is just as easy as the reduction $A \leq_T A$ for any problem A. The reductions HC $\leq_T$ DHC and HC $\leq_T$ TSP$^{2,\triangle,\text{sym}}$ were also Turing reductions from HC to more generalized problems. A Turing reduction $A \leq_T B$ of this kind is called a *restriction*, since problem A represents a restricted version of problem B. Another example is the following Turing reduction from PARTITION to BINPACKING.

Theorem 4.3.3. PARTITION $\leq_T$ BINPACKING.

Proof. PARTITION is a special case of BINPACKING in which there are only two bins and the objects are to completely fill the two bins. Formally, for PARTITION we are given the numbers $w_1, w_2, \ldots, w_n$, and the question is whether there is a set of indices $I \subseteq \{1, 2, \ldots, n\}$ such that the sum $\sum_{i \in I} w_i$ is equal to half the total sum $\sum_{i \in \{1, \ldots, n\}} w_i$. If we now apply a BINPACKING algorithm to the numbers $w_1, \ldots, w_n$ with two bins of size $b := \lfloor (w_1 + \cdots + w_n)/2 \rfloor$ we obtain the correct answer for PARTITION as well. In the case that $w_1 + \cdots + w_n$ is odd, then the instance is rejected in both cases. Otherwise the instances are equivalent since if the sum $\sum_{i \in I} w_i = b$, then $\sum_{i \notin I} w_i = b$, too. If we count the number of w-values as the size of the input, then $p(n) = O(n)$, $q(n) = 1$, and $r(n) = O(n)$.   □

Restrictions appear to be a simple, but not particularly interesting, tool, since we can already "see" that we are dealing with a generalization. Some problems, however, "hide" their commonalities so well that we don't immediately recognize the similarities. For example, CLIQUE, INDEPENDENTSET, and VERTEXCOVER are essentially the same problem. While this is immediately obvious for CLIQUE and INDEPENDENTSET, we have to look more closely to discover the similarity between these two problems and VERTEXCOVER.

Theorem 4.3.4. CLIQUE $\equiv_T$ INDEPENDENTSET $\equiv_T$ VERTEXCOVER.

Proof. CLIQUE $\equiv_T$ INDEPENDENTSET: With CLIQUE we are searching for cliques, and with INDEPENDENTSET we are searching for anti-cliques. If we construct the graph $G' = (V, E')$ from the graph $G = (V, E)$ such that G' includes exactly those edges that G does not include, then cliques are transformed into anti-cliques and vice versa. For this reduction $p(n) = O(n^2)$, since we consider all $\binom{n}{2}$ possible edges, $q(n) = 1$ and $r(n) = n$.

INDEPENDENTSET $\leq_T$ VERTEXCOVER: Let the graph $G = (V, E)$ and the bound k be an instance of INDEPENDENTSET. Then we let the VERTEXCOVER algorithm process the same graph, but with bound $n - k$. An independent set with k vertices implies that the remaining $n - k$ vertices cover all the edges. On the other hand, if $n - k$ vertices cover all the edges, then the k remaining vertices must form an independent set. So the VERTEXCOVER algorithm provides the right answer to the INDEPENDENTSET question. In this reduction $p(n, m) = O(n + m)$, since we must copy the graph G, $q(n, m) = 1$, and the new graph has the same size as the original.

VERTEXCOVER $\leq_T$ INDEPENDENTSET : This is shown using the same reduction as for INDEPENDENTSET $\leq_T$ VERTEXCOVER. $\qquad\square$

It is worth noting that our Turing reductions are very efficient.

4.4 Reductions Between Unrelated Problems

Now we want to find Turing reductions between problems that do not seem *a priori* to be very similar – not until we have demonstrated that there is a Turing reduction do we see that they are algorithmically similar. For example, we will show that the marriage problem 2-DM and the championship problem CHAMPIONSHIP with the a-point rule are special flow problems, i.e., that they are Turing reducible to NETWORKFLOW. Since NETWORKFLOW is solvable in polynomial time, 2-DM and CHAMPIONSHIP must also be in P. We get efficient algorithms for 2-DM and CHAMPIONSHIP directly from known efficient algorithms for NETWORKFLOW. In fact, when these reductions were designed, polynomial time algorithms for NETWORKFLOW were already known. But in principle, one could have designed the Turing reductions without knowing whether NETWORKFLOW is difficult or easy. Since these reductions serve to develop efficient algorithms, we will consider the optimization variants of 2-DM and NETWORKFLOW.

Theorem 4.4.1. 2-DM $\leq_T$ NETWORKFLOW.

Proof. The marriage problem 2-DM can be modeled as a graph problem. The vertex set consists of the set U, which represents the women, together with the set W that represents the men. An edge (u, w) with $u \in U$ and $w \in W$ represents a potential happily married couple. There are no edges between two vertices in U or between two vertices in W. The task is to find the largest possible set of edges in which no vertex appears more than once.

From this we construct the following input to a NETWORKFLOW algorithm. The edges are directed from U to W. We add to the graph two new vertices s and t, and edges from s to every vertex in U and from every vertex in W to t. All edges have capacity 1. An example is shown in Figure 4.4.1.

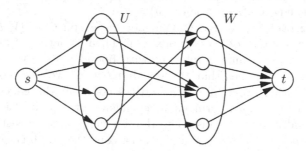

Fig. 4.4.1. Illustration of the Turing reduction 2-DM $\leq_T$ NETWORKFLOW.

The NETWORKFLOW algorithm produces a maximal flow. Since flows have integer values, each edge has a flow of either 0 (no flow) or 1 (some flow). We claim that the set of edges from U to W that carry some flow forms a maximum matching (when considered in undirected form).

This can be shown as follows: Suppose we are given a matching with k edges. After renumbering the vertices, we can assume this is $(u_1, w_1), \ldots,$ (u_k, w_k). Then there is a flow with value k that places flow on these edges and the edges $(s, u_1), \ldots, (s, u_k), (w_1, t), \ldots, (w_k, t)$. On the other hand, every flow with value k must use k edges that leave s and k edges that arrive at t. So k vertices in U receive flow, and k vertices in W must pass flow to t. Every vertex u_i, $1 \leq i \leq k$, must send its flow to a vertex w_j, $1 \leq j \leq k$. Since all the vertices $w_1, \ldots, w_k$ are reached, the k edges from U to V do not repeat any vertices and, therefore, form a matching.

For this reduction $p(n, m) = O(n + m)$, $q(n, m) = 1$, and the instance of NETWORKFLOW has $n + 2$ vertices and $n + m$ edges if the instance of the matching problem has n vertices and m edges. □

The work to solve 2-DM involves a linear amount of overhead plus the work required to solve an instance of the network flow problem for a graph with $n + 2$ vertices and $n + m$ edges. Furthermore, the instance of the network flow problem will have some special properties.

The championship problem CHAMPIONSHIP with the a-point rule (abbreviated a-CHAMPIONSHIP) can also be coded as a special network flow problem.

Theorem 4.4.2. *For the championship problem* a-CHAMPIONSHIP *with the* a-*point rule we have*

$$a\text{-CHAMPIONSHIP} \leq_T \text{NETWORKFLOW} .$$

Proof. First, we can assume that the selected team wins all its remaining games and by doing so attains a total of A points. For the other n teams and the other m games that remain to be played we need to decide if there are possible outcomes such that each team ends up with at most A points. Just as in the proof of Theorem 4.4.1, we will construct a network with four layers such that the edges only go from layer i to layer $i+1$. Layer 0 contains vertex s and layer 3 contains vertex t. Layer 1 contains m vertices that represent the m games to be played, and layer 2 contains n vertices that represent the n teams that still have games to play. There is no vertex for the selected team. There is an edge from s to each game vertex with capacity a, so the flow is bounded by $m \cdot a$. Our idea is to construct an instance of the network flow problem in such a way that a flow with value $m \cdot a$ simulates outcomes of the games that lead to a league championship for the selected team. Furthermore, it should not be possible for the chosen team to be league champion if the value of the maximum flow is less than $m \cdot a$.

Suppose a game vertex receives a flow of a from s which it must then pass along. The natural thing to do is to add an edge from each game vertex to each of the two teams playing in that game. The edges between layer 1 and layer 2 have capacity a to simulate the a-point rule. In this way the team vertices receive flow (or points) from the game vertices, perhaps so many points that they pass the selected team in the standings. If team j has a_j points so far, it may only win $A - a_j$ additional points in its remaining games. So the edge from team j to t has capacity $A - a_j$. (For an example, see Figure 4.4.2.)

If the selected team can become league champion, then the corresponding game outcomes lead to a flow with value $m \cdot a$. The vertex s sends flow a to each game vertex, which divides the flow among the two competing teams according to the outcome of the game. Since the jth team does not catch the selected team, it receives a flow of at most $A - a_j$, which it can pass along to vertex t.

On the other hand, every flow with value $m \cdot a$ "codes" outcomes of the games such that the selected team is league champion. Vertex s must send flow a to each game vertex in order for the total flow to be $m \cdot a$. Each integer partition at each game vertex symbolizes a legal outcome according to the a-point rule. In order to obtain a flow of $m \cdot a$, each team vertex must pass along all the flow entering it to vertex t. So team j receives a flow of at most $A - a_j$ (i.e., at most $A - a_j$ points).

The network has $n + m + 2$ vertices, $n + 3m$ edges, and can be constructed in time $O(n + m)$. □

Although the championship problem is really only a decision problem, the solution using the network flow problem not only provides a correct answer but also provides outcomes to the games that lead to league championship for the selected team. As an example, we consider an actual situation from the 1964–65 German soccer league (Bundesliga) when, with two games remaining for each team before the end of the regular season, the situation was not completely trivial. At that time the $(0, 1, 2)$-point rule (i.e., the 2-point rule) was being used. Of interest are only the following teams, their standings, and their remaining opponents.

Team	Points	Remaining Opponents
1. SV Werder Bremen (SVW)	37	BVB, FCN.
2. 1. FC Cologne (1. FC)	36	FCN, BVB.
3. Borussia Dortmund (BVB)	35	SVW, 1. FC.
4. 1860 Munich (1860)	33	MSV, HSV.
5. 1. FC Nurnberg (FCN)	31	1. FC, SVW.

If 1860 Munich wins its last two games, they will have 37 points, and could pass SVW based on a better goal differential. But then SVW would have to lose both of its games... If one completes this line of reasoning, one arrives at the conclusion that 1860 Munich cannot win the league championship.

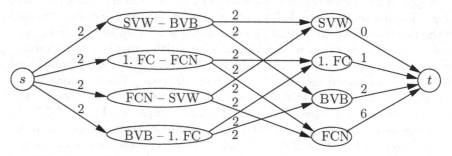

Fig. 4.4.2. Using Network Flow to decide the Championship Problem.

Now we come to reductions between problems that will later prove to be difficult. Since SAT will be the first problem that we will identify as difficult, and since we have already shown that SAT can be Turing reduced to 3-SAT, we will reduce 3-SAT to two further problems, the clique problem (CLIQUE) and the directed Hamiltonian circuit problem (DHC). As with many reductions, the Turing reduction from 3-SAT to CLIQUE is already in the monograph by Garey and Johnson. Sipser (1997) has presented simpler and clearer proofs for some reductions, including the reduction 3-SAT $\leq_T$ DHC.

For such different looking problems like 3-SAT and CLIQUE or DHC, the techniques of restriction and local replacement do not suffice for the design of a Turing reduction.

Theorem 4.4.3. 3-SAT $\leq_T$ CLIQUE.

Proof. An instance of 3-SAT is specified by the variables $x_1, \ldots, x_n$ and the clauses $c_1, \ldots, c_m$. For each clause we use a component that consists of a graph with three vertices and no edges. All together we have $3m$ vertices $v_{i,j}$ with $1 \leq i \leq m$ and $1 \leq j \leq 3$. The vertex $v_{i,j}$ represents the jth literal in the ith clause. The clause components now need to be connected via edges in a way that the edges reflect the satisfiability structure. So we connect two vertices $v_{i,j}$ and $v_{i',j'}$ from different components (i.e., $i \neq i'$) if and only if these two literals are simultaneously satisfiable, that is if they don't contradict each other. Two literals contradict each other precisely when one is the negation of the other. Since satisfiability of a 3-SAT formula means the simultaneous satisfiability of all m clauses, we are interested in cliques of size m. Our claim is that $c_1, \ldots, c_m$ are simultaneously satisfiable if and only if the graph $G = (V, E)$ that we have just described has a clique of size m. So we are able to use an algorithm for the clique problem to answer the satisfiability question for $c_1, \ldots, c_m$.

Let $a \in \{0, 1\}^n$ be a truth assignment for $x_1, \ldots, x_n$ that satisfies all the clauses. Then each clause contains at least one satisfied literal. For each clause we select one vertex that represents this satisfied literal. These vertices form a clique of size m in the graph G since they belong to different clause components and since the literals they represent are all satisfied by a, they cannot be contradictory.

On the other hand, let V' be a clique with m vertices from G. Since vertices in the same clause component are not connected by edges, and there are m clauses, there must be exactly one vertex from each clause component. Now we define a satisfying assignment $a = (a_1, \ldots, a_n)$. The vertices in V' represent literals. It is not possible for x_i and $\overline{x}_i$ to both be represented in V', since such vertices are not connected by edges in G. If the literal x_i is represented in V', then we let $a_i = 1$, otherwise we let $a_i = 0$. This assignment satisfies all the literals represented in V', and therefore all of the clauses.

The graph constructed in this reduction has $3m$ vertices and $O(m^2)$ edges. Furthermore, $p(n, m) = O(m^2)$ and $q(n, m) = 1$. $\qquad\square$

For later purposes it is interesting that the Turing reduction presented in the proof of Theorem 4.4.3 also constructs a connection between the optimization variants of these problems. The same arguments used in the proof of Theorem 4.4.3 lead to the conclusion that if k is the largest number of clauses that can be simultaneously satisfied, then the largest clique in G has k vertices, since from every assignment that satisfies l clauses, we can efficiently compute a clique of size l and vice versa.

This Turing reduction is illustrated on an example in Figure 4.4.3. For reasons of clarity rather than showing the edges of the graph, this figure uses dashed lines to show the edges *not* in the graph. The example formula has three clauses over four variables.

Theorem 4.4.4. 3-SAT $\leq_T$ DHC.

Proof. This Turing reduction uses variable components and clause components (see Figure 4.4.4). The clause component for each clause c_j consists of a single vertex that is also denoted c_j. The variable components are more complicated. If x_i and $\overline{x}_i$ occur a total of b_i times in the clauses, then the

$$x_1 + \overline{x}_2 + x_3$$

$$\overline{x}_1 + x_2 + \overline{x}_4 \qquad \Rightarrow$$

$$\overline{x}_1 + \overline{x}_2 + \overline{x}_3$$

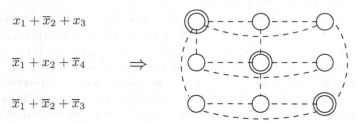

Fig. 4.4.3. An example of the Turing reduction 3-SAT $\leq_T$ CLIQUE. The dashed edges represent edges *not* present in the graph. A 3-clique representing the satisfying assignment $(1, 1, 0, 0)$ is indicated by double cirles.

component for x_i has exactly $3 + 2b_i$ vertices. The three vertices $v_{i,1}$, $v_{i,2}$, and $v_{i,3}$ form the border of the component. There are also edges $(v_{i,1}, v_{i,2})$, $(v_{i,1}, v_{i,3})$, $(v_{i,2}, v_{i+1,1})$, and $(v_{i,3}, v_{i+1,1})$, where we identify $n + 1$ with 1.

In Figure 4.4.4, $u \leftrightarrow w$ denotes the edges (u, w) and (w, u). The variable components are connected in a ring. If we ignore the clause components and always start Hamiltonian circuits at $v_{1,1}$, then we obtain exactly 2^n Hamiltonian circuits since at each vertex $v_{i,1}$ we can decide to go to $v_{i,2}$, then from left to right through the list to $v_{i,3}$, and finally on to $v_{i+1,1}$, or we can switch the roles of $v_{i,2}$ and $v_{i,3}$ and traverse the list from right to left. The idea of this construction is to identify these 2^n Hamiltonian circuits with the 2^n truth assignments for the n variables. The step from $v_{i,1}$ to $v_{i,2}$ is meant to symbolize the choice $a_i = 1$, and the step from $v_{i,1}$ to $v_{i,3}$, the choice $a_i = 0$.

Now the components need to be connected in such a way that satisfying assignments and Hamiltonian circuits on the whole graph correspond to each other. The linear list between $v_{i,2}$ and $v_{i,3}$ is divided into b_i groups of two adjacent vertices each. These groups correspond to the occurrence of x_i or $\overline{x}_i$ in the clauses. The variable x_i in c_j is represented by an edge "$\rightarrow j$" from the left vertex of the pair to c_j and an edge "$j \rightarrow$" from c_j to the right vertex of the pair. If our goal is achieved, we can apply a DHC algorithm to the constructed graph to answer the question of whether all the clauses are simultaneously satisfiable.

From a satisfying assignment a we obtain a Hamiltonian circuit as follows: We select in each clause one satisfied literal and the corresponding pair from one of the linear lists. From $v_{i,1}$ we select the edge to $v_{i,2}$ if $a_i = 1$, otherwise we choose the edge to $v_{i,3}$. Then we traverse the corresponding list. If we are coming from $v_{i,2}$ (i.e., going from left to right), then we encounter the left vertex of each pair first. One of these pairs will correspond to the clause c_j that contains the variable x_i. If this variable occurs positively in clause c_j, then at this point we can make a little detour, going from the left vertex to c_j and immediately returning to the right vertex of the pair. On the other hand, if x_i occurs negatively in c_j (i.e., the literal $\overline{x}_i$ occurs in clause c_j), then we can argue similarly that it is possible to traverse the list from right to left, again making our small detour along the way. In the end, each clause vertex c_j

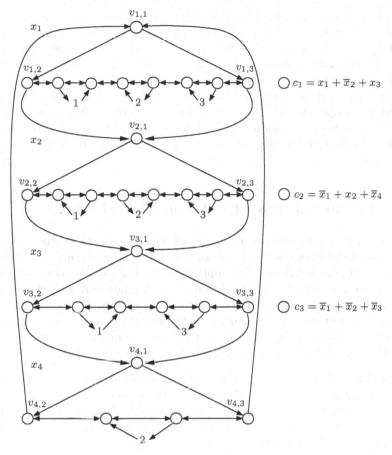

$\bigcirc c_1 = x_1 + \overline{x}_2 + x_3$

$\bigcirc c_2 = \overline{x}_1 + x_2 + \overline{x}_4$

$\bigcirc c_3 = \overline{x}_1 + \overline{x}_2 + \overline{x}_3$

Fig. 4.4.4. An example of the Turing reduction 3-SAT $\leq_T$ DHC. The notation "$\rightarrow i$" stands for an edge to vertex c_i, and the notation "$i \rightarrow$" stands for an edge from vertex c_i.

is integrated once in the Hamiltonian circuit corresponding to the assignment a, and so we obtain a Hamiltonian circuit on the entire graph.

Now suppose there is a Hamiltonian circuit on the entire graph. Every clause vertex must appear along this circuit. The vertex c_j is reached by an edge labeled "$\rightarrow j$" from a vertex u_j, and left by an edge labeled "$j \rightarrow$" to a vertex w_j. Our construction guarantees that the vertices u_j and w_j form a pair: The vertex w_j^* that forms a pair with u_j is only reached by two edges – one from u_j and one from c_j – so if w_j^* is not reached by the edge from u_j (because we leave u_j to go to c_j), then it must be reached by the edge from c_j, i.e., $w_j = w_j^*$. From this it follows that the Hamiltonian circuit on the entire graph arises by adding our little detours to an underlying Hamiltonian circuit on the variable components. This means we can consider the truth assignment that corresponds to this underlying circuit. If c_j is reached along the way through the x_i list, and if this list is traversed from left to right (i.e., starting at $v_{i,2}$), then $a_i = 1$ and x_i occurs positively in clause c_j since we were able to make a detour to c_j. A similar statement holds if we start at $v_{i,3}$ with $a_i = 0$ and x_i occurs negatively in c_j.

For each variable we have three vertices along the outline of the corresponding component, and for each clause we have a clause vertex and six vertices in three pairs among the variable components. So we have $3n + 7m$ vertices, each of degree at most three. Furthermore, $p(n,m) = O(n+m)$ and $q(n,m) = 1$. $\qquad\square$

4.5 The Special Role of Polynomial Reductions

Now that we have designed a number of Turing reductions and discovered surprising connections between very different looking problems, we notice that we have only made full use of the options of Turing reductions in Section 4.2. In Sections 4.3 and 4.4, each proof that $A \leq_T B$ made only a single call to the algorithm for B. For all reductions between decision problems, the answer to this single query to B could be used as the answer for our instance of problem A. With so many examples, this can't be merely coincidence, so we want to give these special reductions a name and a separate definition.

Definition 4.5.1. *The decision problem A is* polynomial time reducible *(or* polynomial-time many-one reducible*) to the decision problem B, denoted $A \leq_p B$, if there is a polynomial-time computable function f that maps instances of A to instances of B in such a way that for the corresponding languages L_A and L_B we have*

$$\forall x \; [x \in L_A \Leftrightarrow f(x) \in L_B] \; .$$

Since we only make one call to the algorithm for B and have no need to process the answer for B any further, we can capture all the work of this reduction in the computation of $f(x)$ from x. The condition "$x \in L_A \Leftrightarrow f(x) \in L_B$" guarantees that the decision as to whether $f(x) \in L_B$ agrees with the decision as to whether $x \in L_A$.

The terminology "many-one reducible" is meant to indicate that f is not required to be injective. Many-one reductions with injective transformations f play a special role that we do not investigate further. We will only mention that bijective transformations f represent an isomorphism between A and B.

We will call two decision problems A and B *polynomially equivalent*, denoted $A \equiv_p B$, if $A \leq_p B$ and $B \leq_p A$. Naturally, $\equiv_p$ is also an equivalence relation. Clearly $A \equiv_p A$, and the statements $A \equiv_p B$ and $B \equiv_p A$ are by definition equivalent. It only remains to show that $\leq_p$ is transitive, since the transitivity of $\equiv_p$ follows from this immediately. Let $A \leq_p B$ and $B \leq_p C$ as witnessed by the polynomial-time computable transformations f and g. The function $g \circ f$ then maps instances of A via instances of B over to instances of C and is computable in polynomial time. The last claim follows just as in the considerations of Turing reductions in Section 4.1. Finally, from

$$\forall x \ [x \in L_A \Leftrightarrow f(x) \in L_B] \quad \text{and} \quad \forall y \ [y \in L_B \Leftrightarrow g(y) \in L_C]$$

it follows that

$$\forall x \ [x \in L_A \Leftrightarrow g \circ f(x) \in L_C] \ .$$

More strongly restricted reduction notions like $\leq_p$ (as compared to $\leq_T$) allow for a finer differentiation between complexity classes. Polynomial reductions will prove to allow sufficiently many problems to be classified as complexity theoretically similar, while still being strong enough to potentially distinguish between the two kinds of one-sided error.

It is clear that for every language L, $L \leq_T \overline{L}$. In order to decide if $x \in L$ we use the algorithm for $\overline{L}$ to decide if $x \in \overline{L}$. By negating the answer we get the correct answer for $x \in L$. This negation of the answer is not allowed in polynomial reductions, so it is possible that for many languages L, $L \not\leq_p \overline{L}$ and that the two kinds of one-sided error are not complexity theoretically similar.

We have seen that Turing reductions we have constructed between decision problems – with the exception of $L \leq_T \overline{L}$ – have all been polynomial reductions. But polynomial reductions are limited to decision problems since, in general, a solution for an instance of an optimization problem B is not a solution for an instance of the optimization problem A.

Turing reductions serve to determine the algorithmic similarity of problems. For decision problems, polynomial reductions provide a finer classification and offer the possibility of distinguishing between the two variants of the concept of "one-sided error". Very differently formulated problems can prove to be algorithmically similar. Furthermore, the decision, evaluation, and optimization variants of many optimization problems are algorithmically similar.

We summarize the results of this chapter for decision problems, Turing reductions that are actually polynomial reductions, and drawing conclusions from the fact that NETWORKFLOW $\in$ P:

- 2-DM, a-CHAMPIONSHIP, NETWORKFLOW $\in$ P.

- PARTITION $\leq_p$ BINPACKING.

- SAT $\leq_p$ 3-SAT $\begin{array}{l} \leq_p \text{CLIQUE} \equiv_p \text{INDEPENDENTSET} \equiv_p \text{VERTEXCOVER} \\ \leq_p \text{DHC} \equiv_p \text{HC} \leq_p \text{TSP}^{2,\triangle,\text{sym}} \ . \end{array}$

5

The Theory of NP-Completeness

5.1 Fundamental Considerations

With the help of reduction concepts like $\leq_T$ and $\leq_p$, we have been able to establish the algorithmic similarity of a number of problems. To this point, however, we have been proceeding rather unsystematically, and have only been becoming familiar with these notions of reduction. Now we want to investigate what we accomplish with further reductions between important problems.

Turing equivalence ($\equiv_T$) is an equivalence relation on the set of all algorithmic problems, and so partitions this set into equivalence classes. On the set of equivalence classes, Turing reducibility ($\leq_T$) leads to a partial order if for any two equivalence classes $\mathcal{C}_1$ and $\mathcal{C}_2$ we define $\mathcal{C}_1 \leq_T \mathcal{C}_2$ if $A \leq_T B$ holds for all $A \in \mathcal{C}_1$ and all $B \in \mathcal{C}_2$. This is equivalent to $A \leq_T B$ for some $A \in \mathcal{C}_1$ and some $B \in \mathcal{C}_2$. Clearly P forms one of these equivalence classes. For $A, B \in$ P we have $A \leq_T B$, since we don't even need to use an algorithm for B in order to compute A in polynomial time. On the other hand, if $B \in$ P and $A \leq_T B$, then by definition $A \in$ P.

So if we get to know the partial order described by "$\leq_T$" on these classes, then we will have learned much about the complexity of all problems. We are, however, still far from such a complete picture. Based on the results of Chapter 4, we can hope to show that many problems belong to the same equivalence class with respect to $\equiv_T$. It follows that either all of these problems are efficiently solvable or none of them is. This is the formalization of the comment made in Chapter 1 that out of a thousand secrets, one great overarching secret is formed. The previous comment can be extended to the complexity class ZPP and to the class of problems contained in BPP that have unique solutions or are optimization problems for which the value of a solution can be computed in polynomial time. This follows from the results obtained in Chapter 3 that show that in these cases we can reduce the error- or failure-probability so that even polynomially many calls have a sufficiently small error- or failure-probability. If we use BPP to denote this restricted BPP-class as well, we obtain the following:

For any set of Turing equivalent problems and each of the complexity classes P, ZPP, *and* BPP, *it is the case that either all the problems belong to the complexity class or none of them do.*

If we restrict our attention to decision problems, then polynomial reducibility ($\leq_p$) is also available. Recall that for the relation $A \leq_p B$ to hold, on each instance of problem A the algorithm for B may only be called once, but must be called. Furthermore, the answer to this call must provide the correct answer for our instance of problem A. The first of these restrictions simplifies our considerations somewhat since it is no longer necessary to reduce the error- or failure-probability.

For any set of polynomially equivalent decision problems and each of the complexity classes P, ZPP, NP $\cap$ co-NP, RP, co-RP, NP, co-NP, BPP, *and* PP, *it is the case that either all the problems belong to the complexity class or none of them do.*

Because of the second condition on polynomial reductions, not all problems in P are polynomially equivalent. The class of decision problems that are solvable in polynomial time is subdivided into three categories:

- all problems for which no inputs are accepted,
- all problems for which every input is accepted,
- all other problems.

The first two equivalence classes offer no help as oracle, since they answer every query the same way, and for polynomial reductions this value cannot be changed. For all other problems A there is an input x that is accepted and an input y that is rejected. For a decision problem $B \in$ P we can show that $B \leq_p A$ as follows: On input z, we determine in polynomial time if $z \in B$. If $z \in B$, then we query the oracle A about x, otherwise we query about y.

Now we return to our main theme. We have a set of problems, among them some important problems, and we know that they are all Turing equivalent (or perhaps even polynomially equivalent), and we don't know a polynomial-time algorithm for any of them. Our previous observations lead to the following argument: We have so many different problems on which many computer scientists have worked hard for a long time. No one has found a polynomial-time algorithm for any of these problems. Based on the highly refined methods for the design and analysis of algorithms, we arrive at the suspicion that none of these problems is solvable in polynomial time. For each problem, this conjecture is supported by the failed attempts to solve all the other problems.

The theory of NP-completeness is the successful attempt to structurally support the conjectured algorithmic difficulty of classes of problems in view of the complexity classes considered in Chapter 3. In Chapter 4 we saw that it suffices to consider decision problems. The important optimization problems are Turing equivalent to their decision variants. So we are dealing with the complexity landscape described in Theorem 3.5.3. With the help of the following definition, we compare the complexity of a problem A with the most difficult problems in a complexity class C.

Definition 5.1.1. *Let A be a decision problem and C a class of decision problems.*

i) *A is C-hard with respect to polynomial reductions ($\leq_p$-hard for C), if $C \leq_p A$ for every $C \in C$.*

ii) *A is C-easy with respect to polynomial reductions ($\leq_p$-easy for C) if $A \leq_p C$ for some $C \in C$.*

iii) *A is C-equivalent with respect to polynomial reductions ($\leq_p$-equivalent for C) if A is both C-hard and C-easy with respect to polynomial reductions.*

iv) *A is C-complete with respect to polynomial reductions ($\leq_p$-complete for C), if A is $\leq_p$-hard for C and $A \in C$.*

The term "C-hard" signals that A is at least as hard as every problem in C. In particular, A does not belong to P if C contains any problems not in P. The counterpart of C-hard is C-easy. If A is C-easy and C contains only efficiently solvable problems, then A is also efficiently solvable. By considering all $C \in C$ in the definition of C-hard and only one $C \in C$ in the definition of C-easy, we are implicitly comparing A to a "hardest problem" in C. The complexity class C is thus represented (as far as its computational power is concerned) by its hardest problems. If A is C-equivalent, then $A \in$ P if and only if $C \subseteq$ P.

Since $\leq_p$ is only a partial order on the set of decision problems, a complexity class C can contain many "hardest problems" that are not comparable with respect to polynomial reductions. But if C contains a C-complete problem A, then the class of all C-complete problems forms an equivalence class with respect to $\equiv_p$ within the class C. This means that the C-complete problems are all equally difficult and are the hardest among the problems in C. If we suspect that C is not contained in P, then this is equivalent to the conjecture that none of the C-complete problems belongs to P. A proof of the C-hardness of a problem for a class C that is conjectured not to be contained in P is therefore a strong indication that this problem does not belong to P. Every C-complete problem is also C-equivalent, and by definition C-hard. Since $A \leq_p A$ and $A \in C$, A is also C-easy.

In order to include optimization problems, and in fact all algorithmic problems, in our considerations, we extend our definitions to these classes of problems. For this we must use Turing reductions in place of polynomial reductions.

Definition 5.1.2. *Let A be an algorithmic problem and let C be a class of algorithmic problems. Then the terms C-hard with respect to Turing reductions, C-easy with respect to Turing reductions, and C-equivalent with respect to Turing reductions are defined analogously to the terms in Definition 5.1.1 by replacing polynomial reductions ($\leq_p$) with Turing reductions ($\leq_T$).*

We follow the convention that C-hard, C-easy, and C-equivalent (without any mention of the type of reduction) will be understood to be with respect to Turing reductions. C-completeness, on the other hand, will be understood to be with respect to polynomial reductions. In fact, we did not even include completeness with respect to Turing reductions in Definition 5.1.2. A significant reason for this is the investigation of decision problems L and their complements $\overline{L}$. All the classes we are interested in are closed under polynomial reductions, but probably not all are closed under Turing reductions. In particular, it is possible that L be C-complete (with respect to polynomial reductions), but that $\overline{L} \notin C$. Many interesting classes are not known to be closed under complement, and if a class is not closed under complement, then Turing-completeness, while still sensible, has the funny property that the set of all problems Turing-equivalent to a Turing-complete problem is not entirely contained in that class. It is worth noting that if L is C-complete then $\overline{L}$ is at least C-equivalent.

Our goal is to prove that the decision variants of many of our problems are complete for some class C that is conjectured not to be contained in P. If the optimization variant of a problem is Turing equivalent to its decision variant, then it will immediately follow that the optimization problem is C-equivalent.

There are only a few decision problems that we know belong to ZPP, RP, co-RP, or BPP, that we don't know to be contained in P. This already makes the study of, for example, BPP-completeness less attractive. Furthermore, we are currently not at all sure that P $\neq$ BPP. The error-probability of BPP algorithms can be made exponentially small, and in many cases it has been possible to *derandomize* these algorithms, that is, to replace the randomized algorithm with a deterministic algorithm that has a runtime that is only polynomially greater than the original randomized algorithm. (See Miltersen (2001).) So BPP is generally considered to be "at most a little bit bigger than P". The situation looks very different for the classes NP ∩ co-NP, NP, co-NP, and PP. No one believes that such large error- or failure-probabilities can be derandomized. In Section 5.2 we will show that the decision variants of the important optimization problems are contained in NP. Since we don't believe them to be in NP ∩ co-NP, it makes sense to begin an investigation of the complexity class NP.

As we have already discussed, the complexity classes NP ∩ co-NP, NP, co-NP, and PP have no direct algorithmic relevance, but they form the basis for the complexity theoretical classification of problems. The decision variants of thousands of problems have been shown to be NP-complete, and their optimization variants to be NP-equivalent. So we are in the following situation:

Thousands of important problems are NP-complete or NP-equivalent. Either all of these problems can be solved in polynomial time and NP = P, or none of these problems can be solved in polynomial time and NP ≠ P.

The NP $\neq$ P-problem offers a central challenge for complexity theory and indeed for all of theoretical computer science. The Clay Mathematical Institute has included this problem in its list of the seven most important problems connected to mathematics and offered a reward of $1,000,000 for its solution.

We do not know if NP $= P$ or if NP $\neq$ P. Since all experts believe with good reason that NP $\neq$ P, a proof that a problem is NP-complete, NP-equivalent, or NP-hard is a strong indication that the problem is not solvable in polynomial time.

5.2 Problems in NP

We want to show that the decision variants of all the problems introduced in Section 2.2 belong to NP. To do this we must design NP algorithms, i.e., randomized algorithms with one-sided error where the error-probability must only be less than 1. Said differently: The probability that x is accepted is positive if and only if $x \in L$. These algorithms have no practical relevance, they only serve to show that the problems considered belong to the class NP.

Theorem 5.2.1. *The decision variants of all the problems introduced in Section 2.2 belong to the class NP.*

Proof. In this proof we will see that NP algorithms for many problems follow the same outline. For an input of length n, let $l(n)$ be the length of a potential solution. Then the following steps are carried out:

- The first $l(n)$ random bits are stored.
- These $l(n)$ bits are tested to see if they describe a potential solution. If not, the input is rejected.
- In the positive case, the solution is checked to see if it has the required quality, and if so the input is accepted.

Clearly every input that should not be accepted will be rejected with probability 1. If there is a solution with the required quality, then this solution will be randomly drawn with probability at least $2^{-l(n)} > 0$, so in this case the input is accepted. The computation time is polynomially bounded if $l(n)$ is polynomially bounded and testing whether a sequence of bits represents a solution and, if so, determining its quality can both be done in polynomial time. This is easy to show for the problems we are considering (and for many others as well).

Traveling Salesperson Problems (TSP): A tour is a sequence of n cities $i_1, \ldots, i_n \in \{1, \ldots, n\}$ and can be represented with $n\lceil \log(n+1) \rceil$ bits. It is possible to check in polynomial time whether $\{i_1, \ldots, i_n\} = \{1, \ldots, n\}$ (i.e., whether we have a tour at all), and if so it is possible in polynomial time to compute the value of the circuit.

Knapsack Problems: Each $a \in \{0,1\}^n$ represents a selection of objects. In linear time we can decide if this selection abides by the weight limit and, if so, the utility can also be computed in linear time.

Scheduling Problems (BINPACKING): We let $l(n) = n\lceil \log n \rceil$ and interpret the ith block of length $\lceil \log n \rceil$ as the number of the bin in which we place the ith object. We then check that no bin has been overfilled and finally determine the number of bins used.

Covering Problems (VERTEXCOVER, EDGECOVER): Each $a \in \{0,1\}^n$ or $\{0,1\}^m$ represents a subset of the vertices or edges, respectively. It is then easy to check if all edges or vertices are covered and to compute the number of vertices or edges selected.

Clique Problems (CLIQUE, INDEPENDENTSET, CLIQUECOVER): For CLIQUE and INDEPENDENTSET, the procedure is similar to that for VERTEXCOVER, this time testing if the selected set of vertices is a clique or anti-clique. For CLIQUECOVER the vertices are partitioned as was the case for BINPACKING. Each set in the partition is checked to see if it is a clique.

Team Building Problems (k-DM): Again, as for BINPACKING, a partition into teams is made and tested to see if each team contains exactly one member from each of the k groups of people.

Network Flow Problems (NETWORKFLOW): The decision variant is in P and, therefore, in NP.

Championship Problems (CHAMPIONSHIP): If there are m remaining games and r possible point distributions per game, then $m\lceil \log r \rceil$ bits suffice to describe any combination of outcomes. Once the outcomes of the games are given, it is easy to decide if the selected team is league champion.

Verification problems (SAT): Each $a \in \{0,1\}^n$ describes a truth assignment. Even for circuits it is easy to test if a given truth assignment satisfies the formula.

Number Theory Problems (PRIMES): it is easy to show that PRIMES $\in$ co-NP. Each potential divisor $j \in \{2, \ldots, n-1\}$ has a binary representation of length at most $\lceil \log n \rceil$. We can efficiently decide if n/j is an integer. The randomized primality test of Solovay and Strassen even shows that PRIMES $\in$ co-RP. In addition, it has been known for a long time that PRIMES $\in$ NP, although the proof of this fact is not as easy as the others we have presented here. More recently Agrawal, Kayal, and Saxena (2002) succeeded in showing that PRIMES $\in$ P (see also Dietzfelbinger (2004)).   □

The decision variants of the problems we have investigated (and of many others as well) belong to the class NP. The NP algorithms are very efficient but, due to their high error-probabilities, algorithmically worthless.

5.3 Alternative Characterizations of NP

For randomized algorithms with a runtime bounded by a polynomial $p(n)$, we want to separate the generation of random bits from the actual work of the algorithm. First, $p(n)$ random bits are generated and stored. Then A is "deterministically simulated" by using these stored random bits instead of generating random bits as the algorithm goes along. Aside from the time needed to compute $p(n)$, this gives rise to doubling of the worst-case runtime. That is,

> *When considering randomized algorithms, we can restrict our attention to algorithms that work in two phases:*
> - *Phase 1: determination of the input length n, computation of $p(n)$ (for a polynomial p), generation and storage of $p(n)$ random bits;*
> - *Phase 2: a deterministic computation that requires at most $p(n)$ steps and uses one random bit per step.*

In the imaginary world of nondeterministic algorithms, in the first phase sufficiently many bits are "guessed" (nondeterministically generated), and in the second phase they are tested to see if the guessed bits "verify" that the input can be accepted. One refers to this as the method of "guess and verify". These considerations do not lead to better algorithms, but they simplify the structural investigation of problems in NP, as we will show in two examples.

Theorem 5.3.1. *Every decision problem in NP can be solved by a deterministic algorithm with runtime bounded by $2^{q(n)}$ for some polynomial q.*

Proof. Let $p(n)$ be a polynomial that bounds the runtime of an NP algorithm A for a particular problem. The random bits generated in phase 1 of the algorithm form a random sequence from $\{0,1\}^{p(n)}$. It is easy to step through the $2^{p(n)}$ possible random bit sequences and to deterministically simulate the NP algorithm on each one in turn. The total computation time is bounded by $O\left(p(n)2^{p(n)}\right)$, which can be bounded by $2^{q(n)}$ for some polynomial $q(n) = O\left(p(n)\right)$. The deterministic algorithm accepts the input if and only if A accepts on at least one of the random sequences. By the definition of NP, the deterministic algorithm always makes the correct decision. $\square$

We can also interpret the two phases of an NP algorithm as follows: An input x of length n is extended by a 0-1 vector z of length $p(n)$. Then the deterministic algorithm A' of phase 2 works on the input (x, z). This leads to the following characterization of NP.

Theorem 5.3.2. *A decision problem L is in NP if and only if there is a decision problem $L' \in P$ such that L can be represented as*

$$L = \left\{ x \mid \exists z \in \{0, 1\}^{p(|x|)} : (x, z) \in L' \right\} .$$

Proof. If $L \in$ NP, then we can implement the discussion preceding the statement of the theorem. Assume we have a 2-phase algorithm A. The number of random bits on an input of length n is bounded by a polynomial $p(n)$, and the deterministic algorithm of phase 2 accepts a language $L' \in P$. An input x belongs to L if and only if there is a setting z of the random bits that causes the deterministic algorithm to accept (x, z) in the second phase. This is precisely the desired characterization.

If L can be characterized as in the statement of the theorem, then a randomized algorithm on input x can generate a random bit sequence z of length $p(|x|)$ and then check deterministically if $(x, z) \in L'$. If $x \in L$, then it will be accepted with positive probability, but if $x \notin L$, then it will never be accepted. □

The NP $\neq$ P-hypothesis can now be seen in a new light. Decision problems belong to NP if and only if they can be represented by a polynomially length-bounded existential quantifier $\left(\exists z \in \{0,1\}^{p(|x|)}\right)$ and a polynomially decidable predicate $\left((x, z) \in L'\right)$. The NP $\neq$ P-hypothesis is equivalent to the claim that the existential quantifier enlarges the set of represented problems. This characterization of NP is also known as the *logical* characterization of NP. Using DeMorgan's Laws we immediately obtain a logical characterization of co-NP as well, namely as the class of all languages L such that

$$L = \left\{ x \mid \forall z \in \{0,1\}^{p(|x|)} : \left((x, z) \in L'\right) \right\}$$

for some polynomial p and some language $L' \in P$. The conjecture that we cannot replace the existential quantifier in this characterization with a universal quantifier is equivalent to the statement that NP $\neq$ co-NP. The results from Section 5.2 can also be interpreted in this light. The decision variants of optimization problems are defined using existential quantifiers (e.g., is there a tour?) and polynomial predicates (is the cost bounded by D?). On the other hand, the set of prime numbers n is defined using a universal quantifier: For all k with $2 \le k < n$, k is not a divisor of n.

5.4 Cook's Theorem

Now we come to the seminal result that made the theory of NP-completeness for particular problems possible. We have seen through many examples that there are polynomial reductions between very different looking problems. Many decision variants of important optimization problems belong to NP, and the complexity class NP can be characterized not only in terms of algorithms, but also logically. But none of this brings us any closer to a proof that any particular problem is NP-complete, or even that there are any NP-complete problems. The hurdle lies in the definition of NP-completeness. To show that a problem is NP-complete, we need to reduce *every* problem in NP to our selected problem. That is, we must argue about problems about which we know nothing other than the fact that they belong to NP. Cook (1971) and independently Levin (1973) were able to clear this hurdle.

Here too we want to proceed algorithmically and keep the necessary resources as small as possible. Let L be a decision problem in NP for which there is an algorithm with runtime bounded by a polynomial $p(n)$. We have seen that the runtimes for most of the problems we are interested in (assuming a random access machine model) have been linear or at least quasi-linear. If we use Turing machines instead, the computation time is roughly squared, although for Turing machines with multiple tapes the slowdown can often be greatly reduced. Turing machines prove useful in this context because every step has only local effects. For every step t in a computation of a $q(n)$-bounded Turing machine, we can take an instantaneous snapshot of the Turing machine, which we will call the configuration at time t. It consists of the current state, the current contents of the tape cells, and the current location of the tape head. So inputs $x \in L$ can be characterized as follows: There are configurations $K_0, K_1, \ldots, K_{q(n)}$ such that K_0 is the initial configuration on input x, $K_{q(n)}$ is an accepting configuration (i.e., the current state is an accepting state $q \in Q^+$), and K_i, $1 \le i \le q(n)$, is a legal successor configuration of K_{i-1}. K_i is a legal successor configuration of K_{i-1} means that the Turing machine, for one of the two choices of the random bit used at step i of the computation, transforms configuration K_{i-1} into K_i.

Which of the problems has such properties that we hope will simplify our work of creating a transformation from the conditions just described into instances of that problem? Whether q is the current state at time t, or whether the tape head is at tape cell j at time t, etc., can be easily described using Boolean variables, and we are interested in whether certain dependencies between these variables are *satisfied*. So we have arrived at verification problems, and we select SAT as our target problem.

Although Turing machines work locally, for the ith configuration there are $2i + 1$ possible tape head positions. In order to simplify the arguments that follow, we will first simulate Turing machines with machines that work "even more locally".

Definition 5.4.1. *A Turing machine is* oblivious *if the position of the tape head until the time the machine halts depends only on the step t and not on the input x.*

Lemma 5.4.2. *Every (deterministic or randomized) Turing machine M can be simulated by a (deterministic or randomized, respectively) oblivious Turing machine M' in such a way that t computation steps of M are simulated by $O(t^2)$ computation steps of M'.*

Proof. The sequence of positions of the tape head of the Turing machine M' will be the following regardless of the Turing machine being simulated:

$$0, 1, 0, -1,$$
$$-1, 0, 1, 2, 1, 0, -1, -2,$$
$$-2, -1, 0, 1, 2, 3, 2, 1, 0, -1, -2, -3, \ldots,$$
$$-(j-1), \ldots, 0, \ldots, j, \ldots, 0, \ldots, -j, \ldots$$

The jth phase of the computation of M' will consist of $4j$ computation steps and will simulate the jth step of the Turing machine M. Thus t computation steps of M are simulated with

$$4 \cdot (1 + 2 + \cdots + t) = 2t(t+1) = O(t^2)$$

steps of M'.

How does the simulating Turing machine M' work? How does it count the positions? All of this is solved with a few simple tricks and by increasing the size of the tape alphabet and the internal memory (number of states). Prior to the tth step of M, cells $-(t-1)$ and $t-1$ should be marked to indicate the left and right ends of the portion of the tape being considered. This is not possible for $t = 1$, but for the first step the Turing machine can call upon its internal memory and "imagine" the two marks, both of which would mark cell 0 at the start of the computation. In addition, we must mark the tape position that machine M reads at step t. For step $t = 1$ this is again cell 0 and this information is again stored in the internal memory. The internal memory also keeps track of the state of machine M at each step, starting with the initial state of M for $t = 1$. The simulation is now easy to describe.

Starting from position $-(t-1)$, M' moves to the right looking for the cell that M reads at step t. This is easy to find with the help of its special marking. At this point, M' knows all the information that M has during its tth step. The state q is stored in the internal memory, and the symbol a that M reads from the tape, M' can also read from the tape (in the same cell that contains the tape head marker). If necessary, M' uses a random bit just like M. Now M' can store the new state q' in its memory and write the new tape symbol a' to the tape cell. Furthermore, M' knows if the tape head marker must be moved, and if so in which direction. For a move to the right, this is done in the next step. For a move to the left, M' remembers that this is still to be done. M' then searches for the right end marker and moves it to the right one cell. Then M' moves back to the left end marker and moves it one space to the left. If necessary, the tape head marker is moved to the left along the way. At this point, M' is ready to simulate the $(t+1)$st step of M. If M halts, then M' halts as well, making the same decision.   □

For our purposes, this simulation is fully adequate. If we use Turing machines with k tapes, we can use the same ideas to simulate them with oblivious one-tape Turing machines (see, for example, Wegener (1987)). Now we are prepared for Cook's Theorem.

Theorem 5.4.3 (Cook's Theorem). SAT *is* NP-*complete. Thus* NP = P *if and only if* SAT $\in$ P.

Proof. Since SAT is in NP, it is sufficient to show that every decision problem $L \in$ NP can be polynomially reduced to SAT. By Lemma 5.4.2, we can assume that the NP algorithm for L has a worst-case runtime of $p(n)$ and is implemented on an oblivious one-tape Turing machine. The reduction is a transformation with connected components. The components of the Turing machine M on input x with $|x| = n$ consist of the states, the random bits, and the contents of the tape. Here we use the fact that the tape-head position is independent of x. The components are represented by Boolean variables. To simplify notation we assume that the states are $q_0, \ldots, q_{k-1}$, that the tape alphabet consists of the symbols $a_1, \ldots, a_m$, and that a_m is the blank symbol.

- $Q(i, t)$, $0 \le i \le k - 1$, $0 \le t \le p(n)$: $Q(i, t) = 1$ represents that at step t, M is in state q_i. (The 0th step corresponds to the initialization.)
- $Z(t)$, $1 \le t \le p(n)$, represents the value of the tth random bit.
- $S(i, t)$, $1 \le i \le m$, $0 \le t \le p(n)$: $S(i, t) = 1$ represents that at step t, the symbol a_i is being read from the tape.

All together we use $(p(n) + 1) \cdot (|Q| + 1 + |\Gamma|) - 1 = O(p(n))$ Boolean variables.

The clauses will express the way M works in such a way that there will be values of the random bits $Z(1), \ldots, Z(p(n))$ for which M accepts input x if and only if the clauses are simultaneously satisfiable. Furthermore, we need to ensure that the variables represent things the way we are imagining. That is, we must satisfy the following conditions.

1. The variables for $t = 0$ correspond to the initial configuration of the computation.
2. The last configuration is accepting.
3. The variables represent configurations.
4. The tth configuration is the successor configuration of the $(t - 1)$st configuration according to the instructions of the Turing machine M.

We code these conditions as a conjunction of clauses. This can be done separately for each condition since conditions (1)–(4) are conjunctively joined.

(1) Since M starts in state q_0, it must be the case that $Q(0, 0) = 1$ and $Q(i, 0) = 0$ for all $i \ne 0$. For each j, let $t(j)$ be the first time that cell j is read. For each $0 \le j \le n-1$, $S(i, t(j))$ must have the value 1 if and only if $x_{j+1} = a_i$. (This is the only point at which the input x influences the transformation.) For all other j, $S(m, t(j))$ must have the value 1, since at the beginning of the computation the corresponding cells contain the blank symbol. Here we have not really made any clauses, rather we have replaced some of the Boolean variables with appropriate Boolean constants.

(2) For this we need a clause that is the disjunction of all $Q(i, p(n))$ for which q_i is an accepting state.

(3) At every time, the Turing machine is in exactly one state and reads exactly one symbol. Syntactically, this is the only condition placed on configurations. Formally, this means that for every $t \in \{0, \ldots, p(n)\}$, exactly one of

the variables $Q(i,t)$ and exactly one of the variables $S(i,t)$ has the value 1. So we have $2p(n)+2$ conditions, of which some have already been fulfilled by our actions under (1). Since the number of variables in each condition is $|Q|$ or $|\Gamma|$, and therefore $O(1)$, we can make our lives easy. Every Boolean function can be represented in conjunctive normal form, that is, as a conjunction of disjunctions (clauses). The number of clauses with r variables is bounded by 2^r, which in our case is $O(1)$, since the number of variables is $O(1)$. (In fact, for our function "exactly one input variable has the value 1", $O(r^2)$ clauses suffice.)

(4) Now we must code the semantics of the Turing machine M. The tth step of M depends on the state after the $(t-1)$st step (i.e., $Q(i,t-1)$, $0 \leq i \leq k-1$), on the random bit $Z(t)$, and on the symbol being read at time t (i.e., $S(i,t)$, $1 \leq i \leq m$). This is $|Q| + |\Gamma| + 1 = O(1)$ variables. The result of this step in the computation is expressed in the new state (i.e, the variables $Q(i,t)$ for $0 \leq i \leq k-1$) and in the symbol that is written to the tape cell (i.e., $S(i, N(t))$ for $1 \leq i \leq m$, where $N(t)$ is the next time after time t that M once again reads the cell that is read at time t). If $N(t) > p(n)$, then this information is irrelevant and need not be computed. In other words, the following $|Q| + |\Gamma| = O(1)$ equations must be satisfied for $0 \leq i \leq k-1$ and $1 \leq j \leq m$ to guarantee that M is being simulated:

$$Q(i,t) = f_i\left(Q(0,t-1),\ldots,Q(k-1,t-1),Z(t),S(1,t),\ldots S(m,t)\right)$$

and

$$S\left(j,N(t)\right) = g_j\left(Q(0,t-1),\ldots,Q(k-1,t-1),Z(t),S(1,t),\ldots,S(m,t)\right).$$

These $|Q| + |\Gamma|$ equations describe δ in our coding of states, symbols, and random bits. So these functions don't depend on t either. Every equation is true only for certain assignments of the variables that occur, and can therefore be expressed as a conjunction of $O(1)$ clauses. (An explicit description of the clauses can be found in Garey and Johnson (1979), but this is not needed for our purposes.)

All together we have $O(p(n))$ clauses of length $O(1)$, i.e., an instance of SAT with total length $O(p(n))$. The clauses can be computed in time $O(p(n))$. By first simulating all the movements of the Turing machine M for $p(n)$ steps, we can compute $t(j)$ and $N(t)$ for all t in time $O(p(n))$. Since the individual functions and equations each contain only $O(1)$ variables, they can be converted to conjunctive normal form in time $O(1)$.

If M accepts input x with random bits $z_1,\ldots,z_{p(n)}$, we can replace the variables in our SAT instance with the values that they represent in the computation of M and this will satisfy all the clauses. On the other hand, if there is an assignment for the variables that satisfies all of the clauses, then we obtain an accepting computation of M by setting the random bits according to the values of the variables $Z(t)$ in the satisfying assignment. Condition (1) ensures that M is correctly initialized. Condition (3) ensures that the variables represent a current state and a read tape symbol at every step in the computation. Condition (4) ensures inductively that the states and tape symbols follow the computation of M. Finally, condition (2) ensures that the computation accepts its input. □

Using this pioneering result it is significantly easier to prove the NP-completeness of additional decision problems. This is because of the transitivity of $\leq_p$. If $L \in$ NP and we can show that $K \leq_p L$ for some NP-complete problem K, then L is also NP-complete since for all $L' \in$ NP, $L' \leq_p K$, and from $K \leq_p L$ it follows that $L' \leq_p L$ for all $L' \in$ NP. Proofs of NP-completeness will tend to get easier and easier, since the number of known NP-complete problems is continually growing, and so we have an ever-growing selection of problems, and it is sufficient to polynomially reduce any one of them to a new problem to show that the new problem is NP-complete.

To prove the NP-completeness of a problem $A \in$ NP it is sufficient to reduce some NP-complete problem to A.

By the results from Chapter 4, we now know that the following problems are all NP-complete: SAT, 3-SAT, CLIQUE, INDEPENDENTSET, VERTEXCOVER, DHC, HC, and $\text{TSP}^{2,\Delta,\text{sym}}$. The optimization variants of these problems are all NP-equivalent.

6

NP-complete and NP-equivalent Problems

6.1 Fundamental Considerations

We now have the necessary tools at our disposal to prove the NP-completeness of decision problems, and we want to consider the ten groups of problems introduced in Section 2.2. In this chapter we are interested in the basic forms of the problems and in a few related inquiries. In Chapter 7 we will discuss special problem variants and investigate where the border between difficult (i.e., NP-complete) and easy (i.e., polynomial time computable) variants lies. By the results of Section 4.2, the NP-equivalence of evaluation and optimization variants follows from the NP-completeness of their related decision problems. Furthermore, we know from Section 5.2 that all the decision problems we will be considering are contained in NP. So to prove NP-completeness, it will be sufficient to polynomially reduce some NP-complete problem to the problem we are considering. On the one hand, we want to consider a large number of problems, and on the other hand, we don't want to discuss too many reductions in detail. Therefore, we will only discuss in detail those proofs that contain new ideas; for the others, we will limit ourselves to the significant ideas.

Three of the ten groups of problems have for the purposes of this chapter already been handled. Network flow problems are polynomially solvable. SAT and 3-SAT have been shown to be NP-complete, and from this is follows easily that further generalization such as SAT_{CIR} are also NP-complete. Finally, VERTEXCOVER has also been shown to be NP-complete.

6.2 Traveling Salesperson Problems

We have also treated traveling salesperson problems and have shown that the special variants HC, DHC, and $TSP^{2,\triangle,sym}$, and therefore all generalizations of these as well, are NP-complete. Now we want to consider three additional problems. We begin with the problem of determining whether a directed graph has a *Hamiltonian path* (directed Hamiltonian path, DHP). A Hamiltonian path is a path that visits each vertex of the graph exactly once. The corresponding problem for undirected graphs is called HP.

Theorem 6.2.1. DHP *and* HP *are* NP-*complete.*

Proof. The proof of Theorem 4.4.4 showed that 3-SAT $\leq_p$ DHC. The polynomial reduction given there provides a reduction 3-SAT $\leq_p$ DHP if we omit the two edges that reach $v_{1,1}$. Analogously to the proof that DHC $\leq_p$ HC (Theorem 4.3.1) we can show that DHP $\leq_p$ HP. $\square$

From the proof of Theorem 6.2.1 it even follows that it is NP-complete to determine if there is a Hamiltonian path from a selected vertex s to a selected vertex t. These results are not surprising, but we need them for the following result. In an undirected, connected graph, the edges of which have non-negative cost, a minimum spanning tree is a tree with minimum total costs of the edges that connects all the vertices in the graph. It is known that minimum spanning trees can be computed in time $O(n^2)$. Minimum spanning trees have the tendency to be "star-shaped"; in particular, there are often some vertices with high degree. If this is not desired in a particular application, one can add a bound k on the degree of the vertices and so obtain the problem of computing a *bounded-degree minimum spanning tree* (BMST).

Theorem 6.2.2. BMST *is* NP-*complete.*

Proof. Clearly, the decision variant of BMST is contained in NP. In the polynomial reduction HC $\leq_p$ TSP$^{2,\triangle,\text{sym}}$, we let $d_{i,j} = 1$ whenever $\{i,j\} \in E$ and $d_{i,j} = 2$ otherwise. We do the same thing for the reduction HP $\leq_p$ BMST, and add a degree bound of $k = 2$. A spanning tree with maximal degree 2 must be a Hamiltonian path. So a given graph has a Hamiltonian path if and only if the corresponding weighted graph has a spanning tree with maximal degree 2 and a cost of at most $n - 1$. $\square$

6.3 Knapsack Problems

It is always good to prove the NP-completeness of an especially restricted variant of a problem, since then the NP-completeness of all generalizations follows immediately (provided they are in NP). A very special knapsack problem is KNAPSACK*, where $u_i = w_i$ for all objects i. The decision variant – whether the weight limit W can be fully used – is equivalent to the question of whether there is a subset of the objects with total weight W. This is the question of whether there is an index set $I \subseteq \{1, \ldots, n\}$ so that the sum of all w_i, $i \in I$, is exactly W. In this form the problem is called SUBSETSUM. All of the problems we have considered so far have structures that express relationships between the objects being considered: Edges in graphs connect two vertices; in the championship problems, teams are connected by games; and in satisfiability problems variables may appear in more than one clause. This makes it possible to "code in" the structures of other problems. For SUBSETSUM we only have numbers and we need to express the structure of another problem using these numbers. The main idea of the reduction consists of reserving blocks of positions in the numbers. The structures of other problems are now coded in the same positions of different numbers. Since we form sums of numbers, we can construct connecting structures, but we must take care that the addition does not lead to "carries" from one block to another. This can be avoided through the use of "receiving blocks", more precisely blocks of positions in which all the numbers have zeros. In the following proof, we use decimal numbers and blocks of length 1. Receiving blocks are unnecessary since the sum of all digits in the same position will be bounded by 5 as a result of the construction, and so carries cannot occur.

Theorem 6.3.1. SUBSETSUM *is* NP-*complete.*

Proof. We describe a polynomial reduction from 3-SAT to SUBSETSUM. If the 3-SAT instance has m clauses $c_1, \ldots, c_m$ and uses n variables $x_1, \ldots, x_n$, we form $2n + 2m$ integers a_i and b_i for $1 \leq i \leq n$, and d_j and e_j for $1 \leq j \leq m$. Each of these integers will have $m + n$ decimal places. First we describe the last n decimal places, which will only contain zeros and ones. The numbers a_i and b_i have exactly one 1 in position i, and the numbers d_j and e_j have all zeros in these positions. The desired sum value S has a 1 in each of these positions (see Figure 6.3.1). So far it is clear that we are forced to choose for each i exactly one of a_i and b_i but that for the numbers d_j and e_j we still have free choice. The interpretation is now obvious: The choice of a_i represents $x_i = 1$ and the choice of b_i represents $x_i = 0$.

We code the clauses $c_1, \ldots, c_m$ in the front m decimal positions of the numbers a_i and b_i. One position is used for each clause. The clause c_j contains three literals and contributes a 1 to a_i if x_i occurs, a 1 to b_i if $\overline{x}_i$ occurs. If we select a satisfying assignment and decide between a_i and b_i accordingly, we will obtain in the position for c_j a sum of s_j, if clause c_j has s_j literals that are satisfied. So the clauses are simultaneously satisfiable if there is a choice of numbers a_i and b_i such that each of the first m positions of the sum is one of the values $\{1, 2, 3\}$ and each of the last n positions has the value 1. This is still not an instance of SUBSETSUM since there are many sum values that are equivalent to satisfiability of the clauses. We take care of this problem using slack elements, namely the numbers d_j and e_j. We will let $d_j = e_j$, and both numbers will have a 1 in position j and 0's everywhere else. Finally, we let S start with m 3's. Now if a choice of a's and b's leads to a value from among $\{1, 2, 3\}$ in position j, then we can select d_j and e_j, just d_j, or neither to force a 3 in that position. This is not possible if c_j is not satisfied. Then the sum of the a's and b's will have a 0 in position j, which can be increased at most to a value of 2 by adding d_j and e_j. Since we can construct all these numbers in time $O((n + m)^2)$, we have shown that 3-SAT $\leq_p$ SUBSETSUM. $\qquad \square$

	c_1	c_2	c_3	x_1	x_2	x_3	x_4
a_1	1	0	0	1	0	0	0
a_2	0	1	0	0	1	0	0
a_3	1	0	0	0	0	1	0
a_4	0	0	0	0	0	0	1
b_1	0	1	1	1	0	0	0
b_2	1	0	1	0	1	0	0
b_3	0	0	1	0	0	1	0
b_4	0	1	0	0	0	0	1
d_1	1	0	0	0	0	0	0
d_2	0	1	0	0	0	0	0
d_3	0	0	1	0	0	0	0
e_1	1	0	0	0	0	0	0
e_2	0	1	0	0	0	0	0
e_3	0	0	1	0	0	0	0
S	3	3	3	1	1	1	1

Fig. 6.3.1. An example of the reduction 3-SAT $\leq_p$ SUBSETSUM with $c_1 = x_1 + \overline{x}_2 + x_3$, $c_2 = \overline{x}_1 + x_2 + \overline{x}_4$, and $c_3 = \overline{x}_1 + \overline{x}_2 + \overline{x}_3$.

Corollary 6.3.2. KNAPSACK *and* PARTITION *are* NP-*complete.*

Proof. KNAPSACK is clearly a generalization of SUBSETSUM. PARTITION, on the other hand, is the special case of SUBSETSUM in which the required sum is exactly half the sum of the numbers s_i. The relation SUBSETSUM $\leq_p$ PARTITION is, nevertheless, easy to show. Let $(s_1, \ldots, s_n, S)$ be an instance of SUBSETSUM. We can assume that $0 \leq S \leq S^* := s_1 + \cdots + s_n$. We add to the set of numbers $\{s_1, \ldots, s_n\}$ the so-called *forcing components* $2S^* - S$ and $S^* + S$. Then the total of all the numbers is $4S^*$ and we must decide if there is a subset with sum $2S^*$. Since $(2S^* - S) + (S^* + S) = 3S^*$ to form such a subset sum we must select exactly one of $2S^* - S$ or $S^* + S$. There is a subset $I \subseteq \{1, \ldots, n\}$ such that the sum of all s_i for $i \in I$ is S if and only if there is a subset that together with $2S^* - S$ yields a sum of $2S^*$, in which case all the remaining numbers together with $S^* + S$ automatically also have the sum $2S^*$.   □

6.4 Partitioning and Scheduling Problems

Since the very specialized problem PARTITION is NP-complete, the NP-completeness of all generalizations that belong to NP follows immediately. Among these is the scheduling problem BINPACKING.

Corollary 6.4.1. BINPACKING *is* NP-*complete.*   □

We consider here one additional scheduling problem called SWI (sequencing with intervals) in order to present another reduction with a forcing component. A finite set of tasks A is given, and for each task $a \in A$ there is given a processing time $l(a)$, an earliest time the processing can begin $r(a)$ (release time), and a latest time for completion of the task $d(a)$ (deadline). The processing of a task may not be interrupted. The problem SWI consists in deciding whether the tasks can be performed by a processor in such a way that all the side-conditions are met. That is, the processing intervals of length $l(a)$ must be placed in an appropriate order.

Theorem 6.4.2. SWI *is* NP-*complete.*

Proof. Clearly SWI belongs to NP. We describe a polynomial reduction from PARTITION to SWI. Let $(s_1, \ldots, s_n)$ be an instance of PARTITION and define $S := s_1 + \cdots + s_n$. We generate $n+1$ tasks, $a_1, \ldots, a_{n+1}$. The tasks $a_1, \ldots, a_n$ represent the numbers $s_1, \ldots, s_n$. More precisely, $l(a_i) = s_i$, $r(a_i) = 0$, and $d(a_i) = S + 1$. The remaining task a_{n+1} is defined as a forcing component: $l(a_{n+1}) = 1$, $r(a_{n+1}) = S/2$, and $d(a_{n+1}) = S/2+1$. Since $d(a_{n+1}) - r(a_{n+1}) = l(a_{n+1})$, this task must be performed in the time interval $[S/2, S/2 + 1]$. The remaining tasks with a total processing time of S must be divided among the intervals $[0, S/2]$ and $[S/2+1, S+1]$. This is possible if and only if the numbers in the set $\{s_1, \ldots, s_n\}$ can be divided into two susbsets each with sum $S/2$. $\qquad\square$

6.5 Clique Problems

We already know that the problems CLIQUE and INDEPENDENTSET are NP-complete. In view of Chapter 10, we want to introduce a generalization of CLIQUE. Two graphs $G_1 = (V_1, E_1)$ and $G_2 = (V_2, E_2)$ are called *isomorphic* if they are identical up to the labeling of the vertices. Formally expressed, $|V_1|$ and $|V_2|$ must be equal, and there must be a bijection $f : V_1 \rightarrow V_2$ (a renaming of the vertices) such that $\{u, v\} \in E_1$ if and only if $\{f(u), f(v)\} \in E_2$. In Chapter 10 we will investigate the *graph isomorphism problem* (GRAPHISOMORPHISM), i.e., the problem of deciding whether two graphs are isomorphic. Here we consider the *subgraph isomorphism problem* (SI), where we must determine if there is a subgraph $G_1' = (V_1', E_1')$ of G_1 that is isomorphic to G_2. A subgraph G_1' of G_1 is determined by a selection of a set of vertices $V_1' \subseteq V_1$. The edge set E_1' then contains all edges from E_1 that go between vertices in V_1'. Clearly GRAPHISOMORPHISM $\leq_p$ SI (if $|V_1| = |V_2|$, then G_1 itself is the only subgraph that could be isomorphic to G_2), and CLIQUE $\leq_p$ SI (choose G_2 as a clique with k vertices).

Theorem 6.5.1. SI *is* NP-*complete.* $\qquad\square$

It remains to investigate the clique covering problem CLIQUECOVER. This problem will first be transformed into a more usual form. If $G = (V, E)$ has a clique covering $V_1, \ldots, V_k$, then the complement graph $\overline{G}$ has an anti-clique covering $V_1, \ldots, V_k$ and vice versa. By a *vertex coloring* of a graph $G' =$

(V', E') with k colors we mean a function $f : V \to \{1, \ldots, k\}$ (giving the coloring of the vertices) such that any pair of adjacent vertices have different colors $(f(v_1) \neq f(v_2)$ if (v_1, v_2) is an edge in the graph). The *graph coloring problem* (GC) consists in the computing of a vertex coloring using as few colors as possible. Clearly, vertices with the same color must form an anti-clique. So G can be covered with k cliques if and only if the complement graph $\overline{G}$ can be colored with k colors. So for the decision variants of these problems, CLIQUECOVER $\equiv_p$ GC.

Theorem 6.5.2. CLIQUECOVER *and* GC *are* NP-*complete.*

Proof. Based on the preceding discussion, it is sufficient to show that the NP-complete problem 3-SAT can be polynomially reduced to GC. Let an instance of 3-SAT be given that consists of clauses $c_1, \ldots, c_m$ over variables $x_1, \ldots, x_n$. We assume that every clause has exactly three literals. If necessary we can simply repeat literals. The number of allowed colors is set to 3. As a forcing component we form a triangle on vertices v_1, v_2, and v_3. These three vertices must receive different colors, and since the names of the colors don't matter, we will work under the assumptions that $f(v_1) = 1$, $f(v_2) = 2$, and $f(v_3) = 3$.

The literals $x_1, \overline{x}_1, \ldots, x_n, \overline{x}_n$ will be represented by $2n$ vertices that have the same names as the literals. The vertices x_i, $\overline{x}_i$, and v_3 are connected as a triangle. This forces the coloring $f(x_i) = 1$ and $f(\overline{x}_i) = 2$ with the interpretation that $x_i = 1$ or the coloring $f(x_i) = 2$ and $f(\overline{x}_i) = 1$ with the interpretation that $x_i = 0$. This makes the connection between variable assignments and vertex colorings. Now components representing the clauses must be constructed so that 3-colorings correspond to satisfying assignments. The component for the clause $c_j = z_{j,1} + z_{j,2} + z_{j,3}$ is shown in Figure 6.5.1. Note that the vertices $z_{j,1}$, $z_{j,2}$, and $z_{j,3}$ are vertices for the literals and that v_2 and v_3 belong to the forcing triangle.

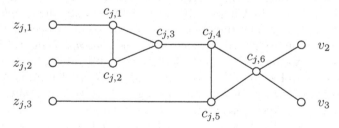

Fig. 6.5.1. The clause component in the polynomial reduction 3-SAT $\leq_p$ GC.

Since $f(v_2) = 2$ and $f(v_3) = 3$, it follows that $f(c_{j,6}) = 1$. Furthermore, $z_{j,1}, z_{j,2}$, and $z_{j,3}$ are not colored with 3. The following property, which can be easily verified by clever experimentation, shows that these components have constructed the desired connection between satisfying assignments and 3-colorings.

- Let $f(v_2) = 2$ and $f(v_3) = 3$. The c_j-component can be colored with three colors if and only if at least one of the vertices $z_{j,1}$, $z_{j,2}$, and $z_{j,3}$ is colored with 1.

The components for each clause c_j were made using different vertices $c_{j,l}$. All together we have $2n + 6m + 3$ vertices and $3n + 12m + 3$ edges that can be constructed in linear time.

If $a \in \{0,1\}^n$ is a satisfying assignment, we can color the vertices $v_1, v_2, v_3, x_i, \overline{x}_i, c_{j,6}, 1 \leq i \leq n, 1 \leq j \leq m$ as just described. Since c_j is satisfied, at least one of the vertices $z_{j,1}, z_{j,2}, z_{j,3}$ receives the color 1, and the clause component can be legally colored. On the other hand, for any legal coloring we can assume that $f(v_1) = 1$, $f(v_2) = 2$, and $f(v_3) = 3$. This forces $f(c_{j,6}) = 1$. As shown above, $f(z_{j,l}) = 1$ for at least one $l \in \{1, 2, 3\}$. Furthermore, the coloring corresponds to a variable assignment as described above. This assignment has the property that $z_{j,l}$ has the value 1 if $f(z_{j,l}) = 1$, so all the clauses are satisfied. □

In the proof of Theorem 6.5.2 we used a fixed value of 3 for the number of colors. We will use k-GC to denote the special case of GC in which the number of colors is fixed at k. So we have shown the following corollary.

Corollary 6.5.3. 3-GC *is* NP-*complete.* □

6.6 Team Building Problems

Now we present just a sketch of the proof that 3-DM is NP-complete.

Theorem 6.6.1. 3-DM *is* NP-*complete.*

Proof. It is sufficient to show that 3-SAT is polynomially reducible to 3-DM. We start again with m clauses $c_1, \ldots, c_m$ each with three literals over $x_1, \ldots, x_n$. We construct an instance of 3-DM with three groups of experts, each of which has $6m$ people. The first group is subdivided into n subgroups, one for each variable. If there are z_i clauses that contain either the literal x_i or the literal $\overline{x}_i$, then exactly $2z_i$ people belong to the subgroup for x_i: z_i people x_i^l $(1 \leq l \leq z_i)$ for the assignment $x_i = 1$, and z_i people $\overline{x}_i^l$ $(1 \leq l \leq z_i)$ for $x_i = 0$. A selection component for x_i is designed to force that the teams must be formed in such a way that all the people for $x_i = 0$ or all the people for $x_i = 1$ must remain unassigned to teams. To achieve this we assign z_i people from group 2 and z_i people from group 3 to potential teams in the manner described in Figure 6.6.1 for $z_i = 4$. In the figure, teams are indicated by triangles, the people in group 2 are $a_1, \ldots, a_4$, and the people in group three are $b_1, \ldots, b_4$.

Since $a_1, \ldots, a_4, b_1, \ldots, b_4$ do not appear in any other team, there are only two ways to place them all in teams. Either we choose T_1, T_3, T_5, and T_7

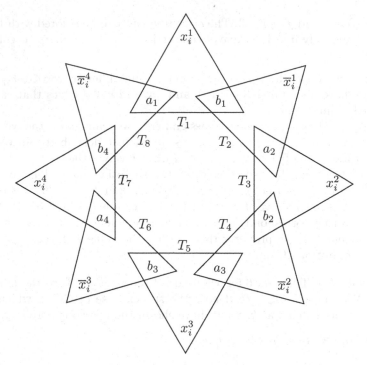

Fig. 6.6.1. A selection component from the reduction 3-SAT $\leq_p$ 3-DM.

with the interpretation that $x_i = 0$, or we choose T_2, T_4, T_6, and T_8 with the interpretation that $x_i = 1$. It is also clear from Figure 6.6.1 that this method would not work if we had only two groups of experts.

For the jth clause c_j, we have a person p_j^2 in group 2 and a person p_j^3 in group 3. These two people can only be in a team together, and need a third member from group 1, which is intended to represent the satisfaction of one of the literals occurring in c_j. If the literal x_i occurs in c_j, then there is a team (x_i^l, p_j^2, p_j^3). There are enough people for each literal so that each x_i^l (or $\overline{x}_i^l$) only occurs in one team. Finally, there are people q_j^2 and q_j^3 for $1 \leq j \leq 2m$, designed to form teams with the remaining people of group 1. These people are very flexible, and all triples (x_i^l, q_j^2, q_j^3) and $(\overline{x}_i^l, q_j^2, q_j^3)$ form potential teams.

Satisfying assignments lead to a formation of teams such that the selection components do not integrate the people representing the satisfied literals. So p_j^2 and p_j^3 find a third team member and then teams are formed with q_j^1 and q_j^2. On the other hand, any formation of teams on the selection components can be translated into a variable assignment. If all p_j^2 and p_j^3 belong to teams, then the variable assignment is satisfying. □

An important generalization of 3-DM is the *set cover problem*, SETCOVER, in which a set S, a number k and a sequence $A_1, \ldots, A_n$ of subsets of S are given and we must decide whether S is the union of k of the subsets A_i. An important application area is the minimization of depth-2 circuits. If we let S be the set of all people in an instance of 3-DM, and form a 3-element subset of S for each potential team, then we obtain a polynomial reduction 3-DM $\leq_p$ SETCOVER. That is,

Corollary 6.6.2. SETCOVER *is NP-complete.*   □

6.7 Championship Problems

We have already seen that the championship problem with the $(0,1,2)$-partition rule can be solved in polynomial time. With the introduction of the $(0,1,3)$-partition rule in the mid-1990's, the complexity theoretic investigation of this problem became interesting. The complexity of the championship problem changes dramatically with this new point rule.

Theorem 6.7.1. *The championship problem with the $(0,1,3)$-partition rule is NP-complete.*

Proof. Once again we will use 3-SAT as the starting point for our reduction. For the championship problem we will use another representation. We let the selected team win all its games and temporarily let all other games end in a tie. The other teams will be represented by vertices and labeled with a number $z \in \mathbb{Z}$ indicating that after these temporarily assigned outcomes the team has z more points than the selected team. The games that remain to be played are represented by edges between the opposing teams. The question is now whether the temporarily assigned outcomes can be modified in such a way that all vertices are labeled with non-positive values. At each edge, the outcome may be changed once. The effect is that one team receives two additional points, and the other team loses a point, since a 1:1 tie is converted into a 3:0 victory for one team.

Now let an instance of 3-SAT be given, i.e., clauses $c_1, \ldots, c_m$ over variables $x_1, \ldots, x_n$. We begin with the construction of variable components that are to reflect the assignment $x_i = 0$ or $x_i = 1$. Variables that do not occur will be ignored. For all other variables x_i, we form a binary tree in which the left subtree has as many leaves as there are occurrences of x_i in $c_1, \ldots, c_m$. Similarly the right subtree will have as many leaves as there are occurrences of $\overline{x}_i$. The root is labeled $+1$, the leaves are labeled -2, and the other vertices are labeled 0. Figure 6.7.1 shows an example.

Only the teams at the leaves will play additional games. In order to achieve a non-positive label, the root team must lose the game to one of its two children, and we will interpret a loss to the left child as $x_i = 0$ and a loss to the right child as $x_i = 1$. If the root loses to its right child, then the child

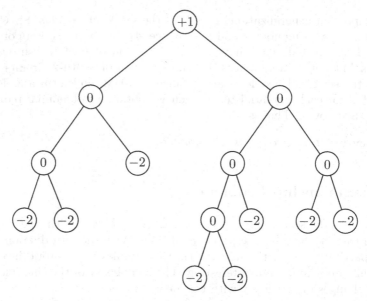

Fig. 6.7.1. A variable component from the reduction 3-SAT $\leq_p$ $(0,1,3)$ − CHAMPIONSHIP. In this example x_i occurs positively in three clauses and negatively in five clauses.

receives a value of $+2$, and must therefore lose to both of its children, ... This domino effect continues down to the leaves, which obtain the value 0. At this point, only the leaves in the left subtree (which represents $x_i = 1$) can still gain points. The construction of the clause components and the connections to the variable components are now obvious. The clause components consist of a single node (team) labeled $+1$. This team has three games to play, one for each of its literals. If the clause contains the literal x_i, then the team must play one of the leaves of the x_i component in the subtree representing $x_i = 1$. Of course, this is done in such a way that each leaf must play exactly one more game. This completes the construction of an instance of $(0,1,3)$-CHAMPIONSHIP. We have $O(m)$ teams and $O(m)$ games. The construction can be carried out in time $O(m)$.

From a satisfying assignment a for all of the clauses, we obtain the following modifications to the temporarily assigned game outcomes which result in the selected team becoming league champion. The roots of the variable components start the domino effect that corresponds to their assigned value. Then, for each clause component there is still one game against a team that represents a satisfied literal and can therefore receive two additional points. This game is lost by the team representing the clause. On the other hand, game outcomes that produce a championship for the selected team must use at least one of the two subtrees of each variable component in order to reduce the excess points at the root. We interpret this as the variable assignment.

The assignment must satisfy all the clauses since otherwise a clause compo-nent cannot reduce its excess points.   □

From this example we see that problems that do not belong to the typical repertoire of combinatoric optimization but come from decisions made by soccer functionaries can also be handled using the means of complexity theory.

Many very different-looking problems with direct or at least indi-rect connections to real applications prove to be NP*-complete or* NP*-equivalent. The proofs for* NP*-completeness use special features of the problems being considered but otherwise follow a common outline. One can therefore hope that proofs of* NP*-completeness for new problems can be obtained "almost routinely". Of the problems we have consid-ered so far, only the graph isomorphism problem* GRAPHISOMORPHISM *cannot be assigned one of the two categories "polynomially solvable" and "*NP*-equivalent".*

7

The Complexity Analysis of Problems

7.1 The Dividing Line Between Easy and Hard Versions of a Problem

We now return to the families of problems introduced in Section 2.2. We will use these examples to investigate just where the dividing line between easy and hard problems runs. To do this we will compare similar-looking problems such as the two covering problems VERTEXCOVER and EDGECOVER, and we will restrict the set of inputs of general problems like GC in various ways. Claims that particular problems are efficiently solvable will for the most part be omitted. Such proofs can be found in textbooks covering efficient algorithms. We will also omit some of the NP-completeness proofs.

All the variants of the traveling salesperson problem TSP that we have considered are NP-equivalent. The results of Section 6.2 have interesting implications for two other families of problems. While the problem of computing a minimum spanning tree can be done efficiently by means of Kruskal's algorithm, this problem becomes NP-equivalent if we place a bound on the degrees of the vertices in the desired spanning tree. Similarly, finding the shortest path from s to t can be done efficiently using Dijkstra's algorithm, but finding the longest cycle-free path from s to t is NP-equivalent. The hardness of the latter problems follows from the NP-completeness of the directed Hamiltonian path problem DHP.

SUBSETSUM and PARTITION are very specialized knapsack and partitioning problems that are hard. The hardness of these problems carries over to all more general variants of these problems. The class of scheduling problems has an especially rich structure. Various combinations of such parameters as the number of available processors, the speed of the processors, the suitability of the processors for specific tasks, the earliest start times for processing the tasks, the latest completion times, restrictions on the order in which tasks must be completed, or the option to interrupt tasks lead to an abundance of problems of differing complexity. Results about scheduling problems can be found in Lawler, Lenstra, Rinnooy Kan, and Shmoys (1993), and Pinedo (1995).

We have seen that the team building problem 2-DM is solvable in polynomial time, but that 3-DM (and therefore the problems k-DM for all $k \geq 3$) is NP-complete. With the help of an algorithm for 2-DM we can solve the edge covering problem EDGECOVER, but the vertex covering problem VERTEXCOVER is NP-complete.

Of the satisfiability problems, k-SAT is NP-complete if $k \geq 3$, and MAX-k-SAT is NP-complete for $k \geq 2$. For MAX-k-SAT we need to decide if at least l of the m clauses can be simultaneously satisfied, where l is a part of the input. So k-SAT is just the special case that $l = m$, from which it follows that MAX-k-SAT is NP-complete for $k \geq 3$. The proof that MAX-2-SAT is also NP-complete will not be given here, but this result has implications for the optimization of *pseudo-Boolean functions* $f : \{0,1\}^n \to \mathbb{R}$. Clauses can be "arithmetized" as follows: a disjunction of literals $z_1 + z_2 + \cdots + z_k$ is replaced by $1 - (1 - z_1)(1 - z_2) \cdots (1 - z_k)$ and $\bar{x}_i$ is replaced by $1 - x_i$. If we add the "values" of all the resulting clauses we get a *pseudo-Boolean polynomial* $f : \{0,1\}^n \to \mathbb{R}$ with the properties that $f(a)$ is the number of clauses satisfied by the assignment a and the degree of f is bounded by the maximum number of literals occurring in a single clause. From the NP-completeness of the decision variant of MAX-2-SAT it follows that the decision variant of the problem of maximizing a pseudo-Boolean polynomial of degree 2 is also NP-complete. Surprisingly, 2-SAT is solvable in polynomial time. To see this we transform an instance of 2-SAT into a directed graph on the vertices $x_1, \bar{x}_1, x_2, \bar{x}_2, \ldots x_n, \bar{x}_n$. Each clause $z_1 + z_2$ gives rise to a pair of edges $(\bar{z}_1, z_2)$ and $(\bar{z}_2, z_1)$, which represent the implications "$z_1 = 0 \implies z_2 = 1$" and "$z_2 = 0 \implies z_1 = 1$". All of the clauses can be simultaneously satisfied if and only if there is no variable x_i such that there are paths both from x_i to $\bar{x}_i$ and also from $\bar{x}_i$ to x_i in the resulting graph.

Vertex coloring problems have very special hard subproblems. 3-GC is NP-complete, and therefore k-GC is NP-complete for any $k \geq 3$. To show that 3-GC $\leq_p k$-GC, we add to the given graph $k - 3$ additional vertices which are connected to each other and to each vertex in the original graph. These new vertices will then require $k - 3$ colors, and none of these colors may be used for any of the original vertices. A greedy algorithm solves 2-GC in polynomial time. We take note of two further restrictions:

- k-d-GC is the restriction of k-GC to graphs with vertex degree at most d.
- k-GC$_\mathrm{pl}$ is the restriction of k-GC to planar graphs, i.e., to graphs that can be embedded in the plane without necessitating crossing edges.

The problem k-d-GC$_\mathrm{pl}$ results from applying both of the above restrictions at once. Now we get some problems that are trivial in the sense that in their decision variants all inputs are accepted. This is the case for k-d-GC when $k > d$, since regardless of how the at most d neighbors of a vertex have been colored, there will always be a color remaining for the vertex itself. Since the famous "Four Coloring Problem" has been solved, we know that every planar graph is 4-colorable. Therefore, k-GC_{pl} is trivial for $k \geq 4$ and, as we have previously seen, polynomial time decidable for $k \leq 2$. In contrast, the very special problem 3-4-GC_{pl} is NP-complete. This is the problem of deciding if a planar graph with maximal degree 4 is 3-colorable. This last claim follows by composing two polynomial reductions each using local replacement showing that 3-$GC \leq_p$ 3-$GC_{pl} \leq_p$ 3-4-GC_{pl}.

We begin with an instance G of 3-GC and an embedding of G in the plane with crossings. Figure 7.1.1 indicates how we replace an edge with three crossings. The subgraph P is the planar graph shown in Figure 7.1.2 with four outer vertices A, B, C, and D. A little experimenting easily shows the following:

- In every 3-coloring of P, A and C have the same color, and B and D have the same color.
- Every coloring f of A, B, C, and D with $f(A) = f(C)$ and $f(B) = f(D)$ can be extended to a 3-coloring of P.

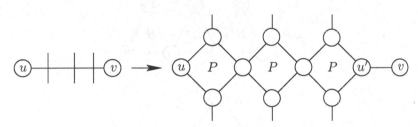

Fig. 7.1.1. Dealing with intersecting edges in 3-$GC \leq_p$ 3-GC_{pl}.

This construction guarantees that in Figure 7.1.1 the vertices u and u' receive the same color, so u and v must receive different colors. On the other hand, every coloring of the nonplanar graph can be translated into a coloring of the planar graph.

In the next step a vertex v with degree $d > 4$ is replaced with a planar graph H_d with d "outer" vertices with degree at most 2, and "inner" vertices with degree at most 4. In addition, this graph will be 3-colorable if and only if the outer vertices all have the same color. Then the d edges incident to v can be distributed among the d outer vertices of the graph representing v without changing the colorability properties. The construction is described in Figure 7.1.3 for $d = 6$. Since the vertices 1, 2, and 3 in H^* have degree 2, two copies of H^* can be fused at those vertices without increasing the degree of any vertex beyond 4.

Finally, we handle the championship problem with n teams. With the a-point rule, this problem is polynomial-time solvable. On the other hand, with the $(0, 1, 3)$-point rule, the problem becomes NP-complete. This result can be

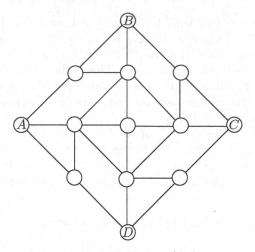

Fig. 7.1.2. The planar graph P.

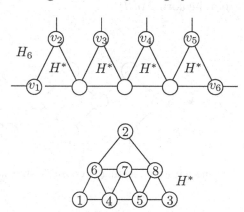

Fig. 7.1.3. The replacement of a vertex with degree 6 by a planar graph with maximal degree 4.

generalized to the $(0, 1, b)$-point rule for any $b \in \mathbb{Q}$ with $b > 1$ and $b \neq 2$. In this case, for example, the $(0, 1, 3/2)$-point rule can be better interpreted as the $(0, 2, 3)$-point rule, to which it is equivalent. Actual championship problems are more specific than the problems we have dealt with so far. Often leagues are scheduled in rounds in which each team plays exactly one game. $(0, 1, 3)$-CHAMPIONSHIP is still NP-complete for three remaining rounds, but polynomial-time solvable for two remaining rounds. It is not clear, however, if the given standings can actually be achieved in a league where each team plays each other twice (once at home and once away). In addition, the German Soccer League (Fußball Bundesliga), for example, uses a prescribed scheduling scheme that has strong "locality properties". Under these conditions, $(0, 1, 3)$-CHAMPIONSHIP is polynomial-time solvable for $O(\log^{1/2} n)$ remaining rounds.

Whether this problem is actually polynomial-time solvable for any number of remaining rounds is an open problem.

> For NP-*complete and* NP-*equivalent problems, it is worth considering whether one only needs an algorithm for a specialized problem variant, and if so to investigate the complexity of this specialized problem. We have used examples to show that the dividing line between easy and difficult problems can follow a surprising course.*

7.2 Pseudo-polynomial Algorithms and Strong NP-completeness

In Section 7.1 we did not handle an important possibility for restricting problems, namely to restrict the size of the numbers that occur in the instances. We consider here only natural numbers. Inputs with bit length n can contain numbers that are exponentially large with respect to n. On the other hand, most applications only require numbers of moderate size.

We are interested here in problems in which numbers that are not bounded by a polynomial in the input length are still meaningful. For the decision variant of the clique problem we ask about the existence of a clique of size k, where k is a parameter of the input. In principal, k can be any natural number. But the only meaningful values of k are in $\{2, \ldots, n\}$ since all graphs have cliques of size 1 and no graphs have cliques of size $k > n$. So CLIQUE is not of interest in this discussion. The same is true for all variants of the clique problem, for covering problems, team building problems, and verification problems. On the other hand, traveling salesperson problems, knapsack problems, partition problems, network flow problems, championship problems, and number theory problems of the sort for which the numbers that occur may meaningfully take on values that are not bounded by a polynomial in the length of the input, are in principle still meaningful. They are called large number problems.

For difficult problems (e.g., NP-equivalent problems) we pose the question: Are these problems still difficult if the numbers that occur are polynomially bounded in the length of the input? Number theory problems are a special case. An instance of PRIMES, for example, consists of exactly one number represented in binary. The value of this number is always exponential in the length of its binary representation. Thus it is not possible to polynomially restrict the size of the numbers that occur in instances of PRIMES. This situation is different for the other problems mentioned above. Because of the great importance of problems restricted to small numbers, large number problems that remain difficult when restricted in this way have received a special designation.

Definition 7.2.1. *A large number decision problem A is called* NP-complete *in the strong sense (or, more briefly,* strongly NP-complete*) if there is a polynomial $p(n)$ such that the problem is* NP-*complete when restricted to instances* *where all the numbers that occur are elements of* $\mathbb{N}$ *whose values are bounded by* $p(n)$, *where n is the length of the instance.*

Theorem 7.2.2. *The traveling salesperson problem* TSP *and the championship problem* CHAMPIONSHIP *with the* $(0, 1, a)$-*point rule are strongly* NP-*complete.*

Proof. We already know that TSP is NP-complete even when the distances are only allowed to take on values from the set $\{1, 2\}$. The largest number that occurs is then n, the name of the last city.

CHAMPIONSHIP is NP-complete with the $(0, 1, 3)$-point rule, and so the numbers in the instance are bounded by the number of teams, the number of games that remain to be played, and the current scores. In our reduction of 3-SAT to $(0, 1, 3)$-CHAMPIONSHIP in the proof of Theorem 6.7.1, no team plays more than three additional games, so the largest point difference that can be made up is 9 points. Thus $(0, 1, 3)$-CHAMPIONSHIP remains NP-complete when restricted to small numbers.   □

Under the assumption that NP $\neq$ P, the notion "strong NP-completeness" can complexity theoretically distinguish among NP-complete problems.

Theorem 7.2.3. *If* NP $\neq$ P, *then* KNAPSACK *is not strongly* NP-*complete.*

Proof. The claim will be proved by giving an algorithm for KNAPSACK that for polynomially bounded weight values runs in polynomial time. The algorithm uses the method of dynamic programming. Consider an instance of KNAPSACK with n objects and weight limit W. We will let KP(k, w) (for $1 \leq k \leq n$ and $0 \leq w \leq W$) denote the modified instance in which only the first k objects are considered and the weight limit is w. Let $U(k, w)$ be the largest utility that can be achieved for the instance KP(k, w), and let $D(k, w)$ be the decision for an optimal packing of the knapsack whether we pack object k $(D(k, w) = 1)$ or do not pack object k $(D(k, w) = 0)$. In addition, we give reasonable values for extreme values of the parameters: $U(k, w) = -\infty$, if $w < 0$; and $U(0, w) = U(k, 0) = D(k, 0) = 0$, if $w \geq 0$.

The algorithm now fills out a table row by row with the values $(U(k, g), D(k, g))$. If we are considering KP(k, w), we can pack object k, winning a utility of u_k, and reduce the weight limit for the remaining objects to $w - w_k$ (it is possible that $w - w_k < 0$). So we must consider the problem KP$(k - 1, w - w_k)$. If we decide not to pack object k, then we must consider KP$(k - 1, w)$. So

$$U(k, w) = \max\{U(k - 1, w),\ U(k - 1, w - w_k) + u_k\}.$$

Furthermore, we can set $D(k, w) = 1$ if $U(k - 1, w - w_k) + u_k \geq U(k - 1, w)$, and $D(k, g) = 0$ otherwise. The computation of $(U(k, w), D(k, w))$ can be done in time $O(1)$. The entire runtime amounts to $O(n \cdot W)$ and is polynomially bounded if W is polynomially bounded in n.   □

We call an algorithm for a large number problem *pseudo-polynomial* if for every polynomial $p(n)$ the algorithm runs in polynomial time on all inputs in which all numbers are natural numbers with size bounded by $p(n)$. Under the assumption that NP $\neq$ P, a pseudo-polynomial algorithm implies that a problem is not strongly NP-complete. From an algorithmic point of view, this can be expressed as follows:

If NP $\neq$ P, *then problems that are strongly* NP-*complete do not even have pseudo-polynomial algorithms.*

From this vantage point, it is worth taking another look at the proof of Theorem 6.3.1, i.e., at the proof that the special knapsack problem SUBSETSUM is NP-complete. For the reduction of 3-SAT to SUBSETSUM for instances of 3-SAT with inputs with m clauses and n variables we formed instances of SUBSETSUM with decimal length $n+m$. These are enormous numbers. A polynomial reduction that used only numbers with size bounded by some polynomial $p(n, m)$ would imply that NP = P since by Theorem 7.2.3, SUBSETSUM is polynomially solvable when restricted to small numbers.

BINPACKING is NP-complete even when restricted to two bins, but is pseudo-polynomially solvable using the pseudo-polynomial algorithm for SUBSETSUM. Somewhat more generally it can be shown that bin packing problems with a fixed number of bins are pseudo-polynomially solvable, and therefore not strongly NP-complete unless NP = P. Now we consider the other extreme case of bin packing. Suppose there are $n = 3k$ objects, k bins of size b, and that the sizes of the objects $a_1, \ldots, a_n$ are such that $b/4 < a_i < b/2$ and $a_1 + \cdots + a_n = k \cdot b$. This means that any two objects fit into a bin, but more than three never do. Now we must decide if the objects can be packed into k bins. If so, then each of the k bins contains exactly three objects, so this problem is called 3-PARTITION. In contrast to the bin packing problems with few bins and many objects per bin, this problem with many bins and at most three objects per bin is strongly NP-complete.

Theorem 7.2.4. 3-PARTITION *is strongly* NP-*complete.* $\square$

We will omit the technically involved proof (see Garey and Johnson (1979)), in which 3-DM is first reduced to 4-PARTITION with polynomially large numbers and then this problem is reduced to 3-PARTITION with polynomially large numbers. The problem 4-PARTITION is defined analogously to 3-PARTITION with $b/5 < a_i < b/3$ and $n = 4k$. Both polynomial reductions are interesting since in each case information is coded into numbers, as was the case in the proof that 3-SAT $\leq_p$ SUBSETSUM. The problem 3-PARTITION plays an important role as a starting point in proving that many other problems are strongly NP-complete. We will demonstrate this using BINPACKING and the scheduling problem SWI (sequencing with intervals) as examples.

Theorem 7.2.5. BINPACKING *and* SWI *are strongly* NP-*complete.*

Proof. The claim for BINPACKING is clear, since 3-PARTITION is a special case of BINPACKING. To prove the claim for SWI, we first describe a polynomial reduction from 3-PARTITION to SWI and then discuss the size of the numbers used in the reduction. An instance of 3-PARTITION consists of numbers $n = 3k$, b, and $a_1, \ldots, a_n$ such that $b/4 < a_i < b/2$ and $a_1 + \cdots + a_n = k \cdot b$. From this we construct an instance of SWI with n tasks $A_1, \ldots, A_n$ which represent the n objects of the instance of 3-PARTITION, and $k - 1$ forcing tasks $F_1, \ldots, F_{k-1}$. The tasks A_i may be started immediately $(r(A_i) = 0)$, their duration reflects the size of the corresponding objects $(l(A_i) = a_i)$, and they must be completed by time $d(A_i) = kb + k - 1$. The forcing tasks are defined by $r(F_i) = ib + i - 1$, $l(F_i) = 1$, and $d(F_i) = ib + i$. The time of their processing is forced, together they require $k - 1$ time, and they force the tasks $A_1, \ldots, A_n$ to be completed within k blocks of length b. So there is a packing of the n objects into the k bins if and only if the $n + k - 1$ tasks can be completed by one processor subject to the side conditions.

The largest number that appears in the instance for SWI is $kb + k - 1$. If the numbers in the input for 3-PARTITION are bounded by a polynomial $p(n)$, then $b \le p(n)$ and $kb + k - 1 \le k \cdot (p(n) + 1)$. So the strong NP-completeness of SWI follows from the strong NP-completeness of 3-PARTITION.   □

7.3 An Overview of the NP-completeness Proofs Considered

In the course of the last four chapters we have encountered many reductions, most of which have been polynomial reductions that have been used to prove the NP-completeness or even the strong NP-completeness of the decision variants of important problems. These results are summarized in Figure 7.3.1. Here we use NP$(p(n))$ to denote all decision problems that can be decided in nondeterministic time $O(p(n))$ by an oblivious Turing machine with one tape. Strongly NP-complete problems with large numbers are boxed. Polynomial reductions are represented by downward arrows. Next to the arrows we give the resources required by the reduction: first the computation time and then the size of the instance constructed by the reduction. For clarity we have omitted the $O(\cdot)$ in each case. So, for example, our reduction of 3-SAT to DHC applied to a Boolean formula with n variables in m clauses runs in time $O(n + m)$ and produces an instance of DHC with $O(n + m)$ vertices and $O(n + m)$ edges. For SAT, l refers to the length of the input. We have also used some additional abbreviations: CP for CHAMPIONSHIP, VC for VERTEXCOVER, SC for SETCOVER, and KP for KNAPSACK.

Figure 7.3.1 shows only a tiny piece of the much larger picture of known NP-completeness proofs. This diagram represents only those problems that have

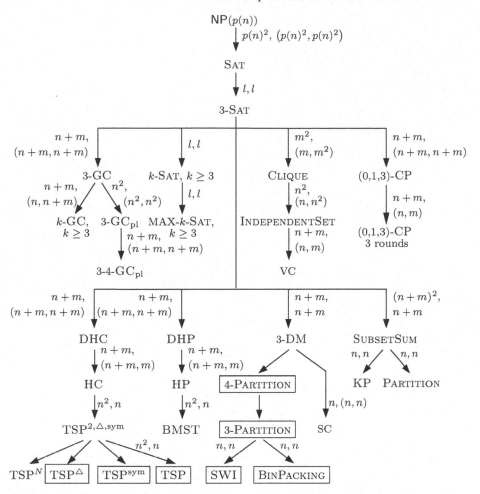

Fig. 7.3.1. An overview of NP-complete and strongly NP-complete problems.

been discussed here. The full picture of what is known about NP-completeness would be practically impossible to make: it would fill a large book by itself and we can safely assume that it would require updating nearly every day. Thus it was rather an understatement when we spoke in Chapter 1 of thousands of NP-complete problems.

> *The full picture of NP-complete and NP-equivalent problems is immense. The NP $\neq$ P-problem is a great intellectual challenge with far-reaching consequences.*

8

The Complexity of Approximation Problems – Classical Results

8.1 Complexity Classes

To this point we have understood optimization as a sharply defined criterion: Only the computation of a provably optimal solution counts as success, everything else is a failure. In cases where we can compute exact solutions to optimization problems, we should do so. But many optimization problems are NP-equivalent. For these problems, if we could efficiently compute solutions with values that are guaranteed to be at least close to the optimal value, this would be a good way out of the (conjectured) $NP \neq P$-dilemma. This is especially true for problems from real applications where the parameters are based on estimates, since exact optimization under these conditions is a fiction.

For a decision problem A we will use MAX-A or MIN-A to denote the related optimization problem. We are interested in optimization problems such that for each instance x there is a non-empty set $S(x)$ of *solutions* and each solution $s \in S(x)$ has a positive *value* $v(x, s)$ with respect to x. These conditions are met by the optimization problems we have encountered with the exception that sometimes solutions have a value of 0, for example an empty set of nodes for CLIQUE or VERTEXCOVER representing a graph with no edges. In the first case we can simply remove the empty set from the set of solutions $S(x)$, since there is always a trivial solution that is better, namely a clique of size 1. In the second case we can exclude graphs with no edges from consideration without significantly altering the problem. We insist that $v(x, s) > 0$ so that we can divide by $v(x, s)$.

Our goal is to compute good solutions $s \in S(x)$ and their values $v(x, s)$ in polynomial time. So we will require that for some polynomial p, the length of every solution $s \in S(x)$ and its value $v(x, s)$ be bounded by $p(|x|)$. For most problems the values of the solutions will be integers; one exception is the traveling salesperson problem MIN-TSP$^{d\text{-Euclid}}$. Finally, we must decide if we are interested in a solution with as large a value as possible (maximization problems) or in a solution with as small a value as possible (minimization problems). The goodness of a solution $s \in S(x)$ should measure "how close" the value of the solution $v(x, s)$ is to the value of an optimal solution $v_{opt}(x)$ for the instance x. This idea is well-motivated, but it also has the problem that the definition contains the unknown value $v_{opt}(x)$. If we could compute $v_{opt}(x)$ efficiently, then the underlying evaluation problem would be solvable in polynomial time. As we saw in Section 4.2, for most problems this implies that the optimization problem itself is solvable in polynomial time. So we will be forced to estimate $v_{opt}(x)$.

But first we want to formalize how we will measure the "closeness" of $v(x, s)$ to $v_{opt}(x)$. The most obvious idea is to consider the difference $v_{opt}(x) - v(x, s)$, or its absolute value. But in many cases this is inappropriate. A difference of 10 between a computed solution and an optimal solution for MIN-BINPACKING is awful if 18 bins suffice, but it is respectable when 1800 bins are needed. For MIN-TSP the problem is changed formally, but not substantially, when we express the distances in meters instead of kilometers. The same is true if we express the utility of objects in the knapsack problem using monetary units and switch from dollars to cents. In both cases the difference $v_{opt}(x) - v(x, s)$ would increase by a constant factor. That this difference should provide a good measure of the goodness of a solution is the exception rather than the rule. So instead we will use the usual measure of goodness, namely the ratio of $v_{opt}(x)$ to $v(x, s)$. The difficulties discussed above in our consideration of $v_{opt}(x) - v(x, s)$ do not arise. We follow the tradition of using the quotient $v_{opt}(x)/v(x, s)$ for maximization problems and the quotient $v(x, s)/v_{opt}(x)$ for minimization problems. This ensures that we obtain uniform values of goodness that always have a value of at least 1. But we have to accept that better solutions have a smaller goodness than worse solutions. This definition is always used for minimization problems. For maximization problems, the quotient $v(x, s)/v_{opt}(x)$ can also be found in the literature.

Definition 8.1.1. *For optimization problems the* approximation ratio $r(x, s)$ *for a solution s for instance x is defined by*

- $v_{opt}(x)/v(x, s)$ *for maximization problems, and*
- $v(x, s)/v_{opt}(x)$ *for minimization problems.*

For an optimization algorithm A we expect that for each instance x a solution $s_A(x)$ is computed, which will then have an approximation ratio of $r_A(x) := r(x, s_A(x))$. For $\varepsilon := \varepsilon_A(x) := r_A(x) - 1$, such a solution is called ε-*optimal*. For minimization problems the value of the computed solution is $100 \cdot \varepsilon$ % above the optimal value, and for maximization problem the optimal value is $100 \cdot \varepsilon$ % larger than the value of the computed solution, the value of which is $100 \cdot (\varepsilon/(1 + \varepsilon))$ % smaller than the optimal value. Just as we do not consider the computation time $t_A(x)$ of an algorithm for each input, instead of $r_A(x)$ we will investigate the *worst-case approximation ratio*

$$r_A(n) := \sup \{r_A(x) \colon |x| \leq n\} .$$

Sometimes the worst-case approximation ratio is not the best measure. For example, in Section 8.2 an efficient approximation algorithm A for BinPacking is presented for which

$$v(x, s_A(x)) \leq \frac{11}{9} \cdot v_{\text{opt}}(x) + 4 .$$

Thus

$$r_A(x) \leq \frac{11}{9} + \frac{4}{v_{\text{opt}}(x)} .$$

Since $v_{\text{opt}}(x) \geq 1$, it follows that $r_A(n) \leq 47/9$. Since we can efficiently recognize instances where all the objects fit into a single bin, we only need the estimate for the case that $v_{\text{opt}}(x) \geq 2$, which leads to $r_A(n) \leq 29/9$. For instances with large values of $v_{\text{opt}}(x)$, however, this approaches the much better approximation ratio of $11/9$. Therefore we use the notation r_A^∞ (*asymptotic worst-case approximation ratio*) to denote the smallest number b such that for every $\varepsilon > 0$ there is a value $v(\varepsilon)$ such that for all x with $v_{\text{opt}}(x) \geq v(\varepsilon)$ the relation $r_A(x) \leq b + \varepsilon$ holds. We will see that (under the assumption that NP $\neq$ P) there are problems for which the smallest asymptotic worst-case approximation ratio achievable in polynomial time is smaller than the smallest worst-case approximation ratio achievable in polynomial time.

An *approximation problem* is an optimization problem for which we do not necessarily demand the computation of an optimal solution but are satisfied to achieve a prescribed (perhaps asymptotic) approximation ratio in polynomial time. This raises the question of determining the complexity of approximation algorithms. We can also ask at what point (for what approximation ratio) the complexity switches from "NP-equivalent" to "polynomially solvable". When we considered optimization problems, we were able to restrict our attention to the treatment of their decision problem variants. Approximation problems have reasonable variants as evaluation problems: In the case of maximization problems, we can require that a bound b be computed so that the value of the optimal solution lies in the interval $[b, b \cdot (1 + \varepsilon)]$; for minimization problems the optimal value should be in the interval $[b/(1+\varepsilon), b]$. There is not, however, any meaningful decision variant for an approximation problem. For inputs x with $v(x, s) \leq b$ for all $s \in S(x)$, the question of whether the value of an optimal solution to a maximization problem lies in the interval $[b, b \cdot (1 + \varepsilon)]$ requires a statement about the value of an optimal solution.

Our definitions allow trivial solutions. For example, for Clique an algorithm can always output a single vertex as a clique of size 1. The result is an approximation ratio of at most n. If instead we consider all sets of vertices of size at most k, checking them in polynomial time to see which ones form a clique, and outputting the largest clique found, we are guaranteed an approximation ratio of n/k. Approximation ratios become interesting when they are not "trivially obtainable".

Definition 8.1.2. *Let $r\colon \mathbb{N} \to [1, \infty)$ with $r(n + 1) \geq r(n)$ be given.*

- *The complexity class APX($r(n)$) contains all approximation problems which can be solved by a polynomial-time algorithm A with a worst-case approximation ratio of $r_A(n) \leq r(n)$.*
- *We let APX denote the union of all APX(c) for $c \geq 1$.*
- *We let APX* denote the intersection of all APX(c) for $c > 1$.*

APX is the class of all approximation problems that can be solved in polynomial time with some constant maximal approximation ratio. The definition of APX* requires an APX(c) algorithm for each $c > 1$. This does not, however, imply the existence of an algorithm which given an $\varepsilon > 0$ computes an ε-optimal solution. Such an algorithm would have the advantage that its users could choose for themselves the approximation ratio they desired.

Definition 8.1.3. *A polynomial-time approximation scheme (abbreviated PTAS) for an approximation problem is an algorithm A that takes an input of the form (x, ε), where x is an instance of the approximation problem and $\varepsilon > 0$ is a rational number, and for a fixed ε produces in polynomial time (with respect to the length of x) a solution with worst-case approximation ratio at most $1 + \varepsilon$. The complexity class PTAS contains all optimization problems for which there is a polynomial-time approximation scheme.*

Even with a PTAS we have not satisfied all our wishes. Runtimes of $\Theta(n^{1/\varepsilon})$ or $\Theta(n \cdot 2^{1/\varepsilon})$ are allowed, since for a constant ε these are polynomially bounded. But for small values of ε, these runtimes are not tolerable, in contrast to runtimes of, for example, $\Theta(n/\varepsilon)$.

Definition 8.1.4. *A fully polynomial-time approximation scheme (abbreviated FPTAS) is a PTAS for which the runtime is polynomially bounded with respect to the length of x and the value of $1/\varepsilon$. The complexity class FPTAS contains all optimization problems for which there is a fully polynomial-time approximation scheme.*

If we restrict P to optimization problems, then

$$\mathsf{P} \subseteq \mathsf{FPTAS} \subseteq \mathsf{PTAS} \subseteq \mathsf{APX} \ .$$

For optimization problems which presumably do not belong to P, we are interested in determining whether they belong to FPTAS, PTAS, or at least to APX. In the case of APX, we are interested in finding as small a c as possible so that the problem belongs to APX(c). For still more difficult problems we are interested in slowly growing functions r so that the problems belong to APX($r(n)$). There is an obvious generalization of these classes from deterministic algorithms to randomized algorithms, but this will not be described in detail here.

Approximation algorithms that run in polynomial time for difficult op-
timization problems form a relevant alternative for applications. Com-
plexity classes are available to differentiate which approximation ratios
are achievable.

8.2 Approximation Algorithms

In order to get a feel for approximation algorithms a few examples of efficient
approximation algorithms are discussed here, although for many proofs we
will merely give pointers to textbooks on efficient algorithms. In addition, a
number of approximation results will be cited. We will start with approximation ratios that grow with the size of the instance and then continue with APX
algorithms, PTAS, and FPTAS.

We begin with two problems for which methods from Chapter 12 suffice
to show that they do not belong to APX if NP $\neq$ P. For MAX-CLIQUE an approximation ratio of $O(n/\log^2 n)$ can be obtained (Boppana and Halldórsson
(1992)). This is only a minor improvement over the trivial approximation ra-
tio of n or εn for arbitrary $\varepsilon > 0$. For the covering problem MIN-SETCOVER
it is also trivial to obtain an approximation ratio of εn. Here, however, it
was possible to achieve in polynomial time an approximation ratio of $O(\log n)$
(Johnson (1974)).

We will now present APX algorithms for a few problems. How good their
approximation ratios are will be discussed in Section 8.3 and in Chapter 12.
Our first example is MIN-VERTEXCOVER. We will use a simple "pebbling algorithm" in which we imagine placing pebbles on the vertices of the graph as
the algorithm proceeds. At the start of the algorithm, none of the vertices
are pebbled. In linear time we can traverse the list of edges and select an edge
if both of its vertices are still unpebbled. These two vertices are then pebbled.
The algorithm continues until there are no more edges that can be selected;
the output consists of the set of pebbled vertices. If the pebbled vertices did
not cover the edge $\{v, w\}$, then this edge could have been selected, so the pebbled vertices form a vertex cover of the edges. If k edges are selected, then the
vertex cover contains $2k$ vertices. The k edges have no vertices in common, so
at least k vertices are needed just to cover those edges. So we have obtained
an approximation ratio of 2.

The following interesting algorithm for MAX-3-SAT achieves an approximation ratio of 8/7 if all the clauses have exactly three *different* literals. For
each clause c_i there are 8 possible assignments for its three variables, and
seven of these satisfy the clause. Let X_i be the random variable that takes
on the value 1 if a random variable assignment satisfies the clause c_i and 0
otherwise. By Remark A.2.3, $E(X_i) = \text{Prob}(X_i = 1) = 7/8$; and by Theorem A.2.4 for m clauses if we let $X := X_1 + \cdots + X_m$, then we have the
equation $E(X) = (7/8) \cdot m$. So on average, $(7/8) \cdot m$ clauses are satisfied, but
never more than m. So a random variable assignment has an approximation

ratio of at most 8/7. Now we will *derandomize* this algorithm. For this we investigate the two possible values of the Boolean variable x_n, i.e., $x_n = 0$ or $x_n = 1$. It is simple to compute $E(X \mid x_n = b)$ for $b \in \{0, 1\}$ as a sum of all $a_i := E(X_i \mid x_n = b)$. Thus $a_i = 1$ if the clause is satisfied by $x_n = b$, $a_i = 7/8$ if the clause still has three unassigned variables, $a_i = 3/4$ if the clause still has two unassigned variables and the third literal has the value 0. In the course of this procedure there will be clauses with one unassigned variable and two literals with the value 0. Then the respective conditional expected value is $1/2$. Finally, the conditional expected value of X_i is 0 if all three literals have already been assigned "false". By Theorem A.2.9 we have

$$E(X) = \frac{1}{2} \cdot E(X \mid x_n = 0) + \frac{1}{2} \cdot E(X \mid x_n = 1) \, ,$$

and there is a value $b_n \in \{0, 1\}$ such that

$$E(X \mid x_n = b_n) \geq (7/8) \cdot m \, .$$

Since we have computed both conditional expected values, we can choose b_n suitably. Now we continue analogously for the two possible values of x_{n-1}. In the end we will have found $b_1, \ldots, b_n \in \{0, 1\}$ with $E(X \mid x_1 = b_1, \ldots, x_n = b_n) \geq (7/8) \cdot m$. This condition fixes the values of all the variables, and X is the number of clauses satisfied in this way. The runtime is $O(nm)$, since for each variable x_i we consider the clauses that result from setting $x_{i+1} = b_{i+1}, \ldots, x_n = b_n$.

For MIN-BINPACKING it is very simple to obtain an approximation ratio of 2. We pack each object in order into a bin, using a new bin only if it does not fit into any of the bins already used. If all the objects fit into one bin, we obtain the optimal solution. Otherwise, let b^* be the size of the contents of the least packed bin. If $b^* \leq b/2$, then by our strategy all the other bins are filled with contents at least $b - b^*$. So on average, the bins are always filled at least half-way, thus it is impossible to halve the number of bins used. A somewhat more complicated algorithm achieves in polynomial time an approximation ratio of $3/2$. Here we notice that the larger objects cause special problems. That leads to the following idea. First the objects are sorted by size, and the larger objects are packed first. Each object is packed into the bin with the smallest amount of free space that can still hold the object. The resulting strategy is referred to as "best-fit decreasing" (BFD). For this algorithm the relation

$$v(x, s_{\text{BFD}}(x)) \leq \frac{11}{9} v_{\text{opt}}(x) + 4$$

was proved (Johnson (1974)). As was already discussed in Section 8.1, this leads to an upper bound for the *asymptotic* worst-case approximation ratio of $11/9$. A polynomial algorithm of Karmarkar and Karp (1982) has an approximation ratio bounded by $1 + O((\log^2 v_{\text{opt}}(x))/v_{\text{opt}}(x))$, i.e., an asymptotic worst-case approximation ratio of 1. This kind of algorithm is also called an *asymptotic FPTAS*. In Section 8.3 and Chapter 12 we will discuss lower bounds for worst-case approximation ratios of polynomial-time algorithms.

Two results for traveling salesperson problems should be briefly mentioned. For MIN-TSP$^\triangle$ a worst-case approximation ratio of 3/2 can be guaranteed by a polynomial-time algorithm (see Hromkovič (1997)), and for MIN-TSP$^{d\text{-Euclid}}$ there is even a PTAS (Arora (1997)). For MIN-VERTEXCOVER and MAX-INDEPENDENTSET there is also a PTAS if we require that the graphs be planar (Korte and Schrader (1981)).

We will demonstrate the construction of a PTAS using as an example a simple scheduling problem for which even an FPTAS is known. The problem consists of scheduling n tasks on two processors in such a way that the maximal load of the processors is minimized. The processors are identical and require time a_i for the ith task. The basic idea is that the most important thing is to schedule the "large tasks" (those for which a_i is large) well, and that there cannot be all that many large tasks. Let $\varepsilon > 0$ be given and let $L := a_1 + \cdots + a_n$ be the total time required for the n tasks. A task will be considered large if it requires time at least εL. Then the number of large tasks is bounded by the constant $\lfloor 1/\varepsilon \rfloor$ and there are "only" at most $c := 2^{\lfloor 1/\varepsilon \rfloor}$ distributions of these large tasks between the two processors. For each of these c distributions the remaining tasks are scheduled "greedily", that is each task is assigned to the processor with the lightest load. From among the at most c solutions that result, the best one is chosen. The required computation time of $O(nc)$ is linear for a constant ε, but it is not a polynomial in n and $1/\varepsilon$. We now compare the maximal load in an optimal solution with the maximal load from the approximation algorithm. The optimal solution also distributes the large tasks between the two processors, and we consider the attempted solution of the approximation algorithm that begins by distributing the large tasks in exactly the same way. If all the smaller tasks can be handled by the processor with the lesser load after assigning the large tasks without increasing its load beyond the load of the other processor, then the approximation algorithm provides an optimal solution. Otherwise, the greedy algorithm ensures that the load of the two processors differs by at most εL. Thus the larger load is at most $\varepsilon L/2$ larger than the load of both processors if they are equally loaded. If the loads are equally distributed, the load for each processor is $L/2$. For an instance x, $v_{\text{opt}}(x) \geq L/2$ and $v(x, s) \leq L/2 + \varepsilon L/2 = (1 + \varepsilon)L/2$. Thus the solution is ε-optimal and we have designed a PTAS.

Finally, we want to discuss the ideas for an FPTAS for MAX-KNAPSACK (see also Hromkovič (1997)). In the proof of Theorem 7.2.3 we presented a pseudo-polynomial time algorithm for KNAPSACK using the method of dynamic programming. This algorithm was polynomially time-bounded in the case that the weights were polynomially bounded. In a similar fashion it is possible to design a pseudo-polynomial time algorithm that is polynomially time-bounded for polynomially bounded utility values and arbitrary weights. Now consider an arbitrary instance x of MAX-KNAPSACK. We can assume that $w_i \leq W$ for each object i. If we alter the utility values, we do not change the set of acceptable solutions, that is, the set of knapsack packings that do not violate the weight limit. The idea is to decrease the utility values by replacing a_i with $a_i' := \lfloor a_i \cdot 2^{-t} \rfloor$ for some integer $t > 0$. Figuratively speaking, we are striking the last t positions in the binary representation of a_i. If we choose t large enough, then the utility values will be polynomially bounded. We solve the instance x' with utility values a_i'. The solution s found in this way is optimal for the instance x'' with utility values $a_i'' := a_i' \cdot 2^t$ as well. As solution s^* for x we choose the better of solution s and the solution that simply chooses the object with the largest utility $a_{\max}$. If we choose t too large, then x and x'' are too dissimilar and the solution s^* might not be good. If we choose t too small, then the utility values are so large that the pseudo-polynomial-time algorithm doesn't run in polynomial time. But there is a suitable value for t so that the approximation ratio is bounded by $1 + \varepsilon$ and the runtime by $O(n^3/\varepsilon)$. The result is an FPTAS for MAX-KNAPSACK.

Here is a summary of the approximation ratios obtainable in polynomial time:

- $O(\frac{n}{\log^2 n})$ for MAX-CLIQUE,
- $O(\log n)$ for MIN-SETCOVER,
- 2 for MIN-VERTEXCOVER,
- 8/7 for MAX-3-SAT,
- 3/2 for MIN-BINPACKING,
- 3/2 for MIN-TSP$^\triangle$,
- PTAS for MIN-TSP$^{d\text{-Euclid}}$,
- PTAS for MIN-VERTEXCOVER$_{\text{planar}}$,
- PTAS for MAX-INDEPENDENTSET$_{\text{planar}}$,
- FPTAS for scheduling on two processors,
- FPTAS for MAX-KNAPSACK,
- asymptotic FPTAS for MIN-BINPACKING.

8.3 The Gap Technique

Now we investigate which approximation problems are difficult. Since the optimization problems we have considered are all NP-easy, this is also true for their respective approximation variants. If they are also NP-hard, then they are in fact NP-equivalent. A central technique for this kind of result is the so-called *gap technique*. The main principle of this technique is simple to explain. If we have an optimization problem such that for every input x and every solution $s \in S(x)$ the value of s is not in the interval (a, b) (i.e., either $v(x, s) \le a$ or $v(x, s) \ge b$), and it is NP-hard to determine which of $v_{\text{opt}}(x) \le a$ and $v_{\text{opt}}(x) \ge b$ holds, then it is NP-hard to obtain a worst-case approximation ratio that is smaller than b/a. For an instance x of a maximization problem with $v_{opt}(x) \leq a$, such an approximation algorithm could output only solutions s with $v(x, s) \leq a$. On the other hand, for an instance x with $v_{opt}(x) \geq b$, the algorithm would need to provide a solution with value $v(x, s)$ such that

$$v(x, s) \geq v_{opt}(x) \cdot \frac{a}{b} > b \cdot \frac{a}{b} = a .$$

But then the gap property implies that $v(x, s) \geq b$. Thus we would be able to distinguish instances x with $v_{opt}(x) \leq a$ from instances x with $v_{opt}(x) \geq b$. The consideration of minimization problems proceeds analogously. We will call problems of the type we have just described (a, b)-*gap problems*.

Remark 8.3.1. If an (a, b)-gap problem is NP-hard, then it is NP-hard to obtain a worst-case approximation ratio smaller than b/a for its optimization variant.

But how do we get (a, b)-gap problems? Gap problems can arise from polynomial reductions. If we reduce an NP-hard problem to a decision problem where we need to decide if an optimal solution to a maximization problem has value at least b, and if the rejected inputs all have values at most a, then we have an NP-hard (a, b)-gap problem. It would be great if in Cook's Theorem the constructed instances of SAT had a large gap, that is if either all the clauses were satisfiable or else at most some fraction $\alpha < 1$ of the clauses could be satisfied. Unfortunately, the proof of Cook's Theorem does not provide such a result. We can always satisfy all the clauses except one by setting the variables so that they simulate the computation of a Turing machine. Under such an assignment, the only clause that might not be satisfied is the clause coding that the final state is an accepting state.

Nevertheless there are very simple applications of the gap technique. In the polynomial reduction from HC to TSP (Theorem 4.3.1), edges were replaced with distances of 1, and missing edges were replaced by distances of 2. Round-trip tours that come from a Hamiltonian circuit in the graph, have a cost of n. Other tours have a cost of at least $n + 1$. This yields an NP-hard $(n, n+1)$-gap problem. In this case, it is easy to increase the size of the gap by replacing the distances of 2 with some polynomially long numbers, e.g., $n2^n$. Then tours that do not come from Hamiltonian circuits in the graph have cost at least $n2^n + n - 1$, so TSP is an NP-hard $(n, n2^n + n - 1)$-gap problem.

Theorem 8.3.2. *If* NP $\neq$ P, *then there is no polynomial-time algorithm for* MIN-TSP *with a worst-case approximation ratio of* 2^n. □

So the traveling salesperson problem is in its general form hard even with exponential approximation ratios, while the knapsack problem can be approximately solved with an FPTAS. This is an example of how analyzing approximation variants provides a finer complexity analysis than considering only pure optimization variants. But it is seldom as easy as it is in the case of TSP to prove the difficulty of very large approximation ratios.

For most of the optimization problems we consider we obtain at least weak inapproximability results. An optimization problem is called a *problem with small solution values* if the values of all solutions are positive integers and polynomially bounded in the length of the input. This is true of all scheduling problems, covering problems, clique problems, team building problems, and the optimization variants of verification problems. It is also true for large number problems like traveling salesperson problems, and knapsack problems, if we restrict the numbers that occur in the input to have values bounded by a polynomial in the length of the input. It is not immediately obvious how to think up a problem that even when restricted to small numbers in the inputs is not a problem with small solution values. Such a problem would arise, for example, if we defined the cost in a traveling salesperson problem to be the *product* of the distance values.

Theorem 8.3.3. *If* NP $\neq$ P, *then no* NP-*hard problem with small solution values has an FPTAS.*

Proof. Let $p(n)$ be a polynomial bound for the solution values. An FPTAS for $\varepsilon(n) := 1/p(n)$ is a polynomial-time approximation algorithm since the runtime is polynomially bounded in the length of the input n and $1/\varepsilon(n) = p(n)$. Since we are assuming that NP $\neq$ P and that the problem is NP-hard, this algorithm cannot compute an optimal solution for all inputs. Finally, the solution values lie in $\{1, \ldots, p(n)\}$, so every non-optimal solution shows that the worst-case approximation ratio is at least

$$p(n)/(p(n) - 1) = 1 + 1/(p(n) - 1) > 1 + \varepsilon(n) ,$$

which contradicts our assumption that there is an FPTAS.   □

This result has consequences especially for optimization problems whose decision variants are strongly NP-complete. We will call these optimization problems strongly NP-hard. If the restriction to the NP-hard variant with polynomial-size numbers is a problem with small solution values, then Theorem 8.3.3 can be applied.

We get large gaps for optimization problems whose decision variants are already NP-complete for small numbers.

Theorem 8.3.4. *If* NP $\neq$ P *and for some minimization problem with integer solution values it is* NP-*hard to decide whether* $v_{\text{opt}}(x) \leq k$, *then there is no polynomial-time algorithm with a worst-case approximation ratio smaller than* $1 + 1/k$. *The same is true for maximization problems and the decision whether* $v_{\text{opt}}(x) \geq k + 1$.

Proof. We prove the contrapositive. We will use the polynomial algorithm A with $r_A(n) < 1 + 1/k$ to solve the decision problem. An input x is accepted if and only if A outputs a solution s with $v(x, s) \leq k$. This decision is correct because if there is a solution s' with $v(x, s') \leq k$ but A outputs a solution s with $v(x, s) \geq k + 1$, then the worst-case approximation ratio is at least $(k + 1)/k = 1 + 1/k$, a contradiction.   □

Corollary 8.3.5. *If* NP $\neq$ P, *then* MIN-GC *has no polynomial-time algorithm with worst-case approximation ratio less than* 4/3, *and* MIN-BINPACKING *has no polynomial-time algorithm with worst-case approximation ratio less than* 3/2.

Proof. For GC the "$\leq$ 3-variant" (Corollary 6.5.3) is NP-complete, and for BINPACKING the "$\leq$ 2-variant" and even the special case of PARTITION are NP-complete.   □

Our results for MIN-BINPACKING show that the notions "in polynomial time achievable worst-case approximation ratio" and "in polynomial time achievable asymptotic worst-case approximation ratio" are different if NP $\neq$ P: The first parameter is 3/2 while the second is 1.

For MIN-GC there are much better results, but we want to use the classical techniques we have already introduced to show that if NP $\neq$ P, then there is no polynomial-time algorithm with *asymptotic* worst-case approximation ratio less than 4/3. For this we consider a graph $G = (V, E)$ with chromatic number $\chi(G)$.

We will construct in polynomial time a graph $G_k = (V_k, E_k)$ with $\chi(G_k) = k \cdot \chi(G)$. The $(3, 4)$-gap will then become a $(3k, 4k)$-gap, i.e., a gap with quotient 4/3 for arbitrarily large chromatic numbers. The construction first makes k disjoint copies of G and then adds an edge between two vertices if they are in different copies. In this way, each of the k copies must use a distinct set of colors, and since each copy requires $\chi(G)$ colors, $\chi(G_k) \geq k \cdot \chi(G)$. On the other hand, from an m-coloring of G we obtain a km-coloring of G_k using k "shades" of each of the m colors. Each of the copies of G receives its own "shade" but is otherwise colored according to the m-coloring of G. More formally, if vertex v in G is colored with color c, then the corresponding vertex in copy s of G in G_k is colored with color (c, s). So $\chi(G_k) \leq k \cdot \chi(G)$.

In summary, we have used the results from Section 8.2 and the straightforward application of the gap technique under the assumption that NP $\neq$ P to obtain the following results.

- MAX-KNAPSACK $\in$ FPTAS $-$ P,
- MIN-BINPACKING $\in$ APX $-$ PTAS,
- MIN-GC $\notin$ PTAS,
- MIN-TSP $\notin$ APX.

The PCP Theorem, which will be presented in Chapter 12, provides a method for applying the gap technique to many more problems.

8.4 Approximation-Preserving Reductions

Theorem 8.3.3 allows us to rule out the existence of an FPTAS for many problems under the assumption that NP $\neq$ P. Negative statements about containment in PTAS and APX are rarer. For this reason we are interested in reduction notions that would allow us carry over such conclusions from one problem to another. What properties do we anticipate for the reduction notions "$\leq_{\text{PTAS}}$" or "$\leq_{\text{APX}}$"? They should be reflexive and transitive, and $A \leq_{\text{PTAS}} B$ should ensure that $A \in$ PTAS if $B \in$ PTAS. Of course, the analogous statements should hold for $\leq_{\text{APX}}$. As for polynomial reductions, the subprogram for B will be called only once. Unlike for polynomial reductions, however, this call cannot come at the very end. The result of a call to the subprogram is a solution for an instance of problem B, which typically cannot be directly used as a solution for A. What we need is an efficient transformation that turns good approximation solutions for instances of problem B into "sufficiently good" approximation solutions for the given instance of problem A.

Definition 8.4.1. *A* PTAS reduction *of an optimization problem A to another optimization problem B (denoted $A \leq_{\text{PTAS}} B$) consists of a triple (f, g, α) of functions with the following properties:*

- *f maps instances x of problem A to instances $f(x)$ of problem B and can be computed in polynomial time;*
- *g maps triples (x, s, ε) where x is an instance of A, $s \in S_B(f(x))$ is a solution, and $\varepsilon \in \mathbb{Q}^+$, to solutions $g(x, s, \varepsilon) \in S_A(x)$, and g can be computed in polynomial time;*
- *$\alpha : \mathbb{Q}^+ \to \mathbb{Q}^+$ is a surjective polynomial-time computable function; and*
- *if $r_B(f(x), y) \leq 1 + \alpha(\varepsilon)$, then $r_A(x, g(x, y, \varepsilon)) \leq 1 + \varepsilon$.*

We will see in our subsequent investigation that this definition satisfies all our demands. Furthermore, these demands are "sparingly" met. So, for example, g need only be defined for instances of B that are produced by f from instances of A.

Lemma 8.4.2. *If $A \leq_{\text{PTAS}} B$ and $B \in$ PTAS, then $A \in$ PTAS.*

Proof. The input for a PTAS for A consists of an instance x of A and an $\varepsilon \in \mathbb{Q}^+$. In polynomial time we can compute $f(x)$ and $\alpha(\varepsilon)$, apply the PTAS for B on $(f(x), \alpha(\varepsilon))$, and obtain an $\alpha(\varepsilon)$-optimal solution $y \in S_B(f(x))$. Then we can compute in polynomial time $g(x, y, \varepsilon) \in S_A(x)$ and output the result as a solution for x. The last property of PTAS reductions ensures that $g(x, y, \varepsilon)$ is ε-optimal for x. □

Lemma 8.4.3. *If $A \leq_{\text{PTAS}} B$ and $B \in$ APX, then $A \in$ APX.*

Proof. Since $B \in$ APX, there is a polynomial-time approximation algorithm for B that computes δ-optimal solutions for some $\delta \in \mathbb{Q}^+$. Since the function α from the reduction $A \leq_{\text{PTAS}} B$ is surjective, there is an $\varepsilon \in \mathbb{Q}^+$ with $\alpha(\varepsilon) = \delta$. Now we can use the proof of Lemma 8.4.2 for this constant $\varepsilon > 0$ to obtain a polynomial-time approximation algorithm for A that guarantees ε-optimal solutions. □

This shows that we do not need a special reduction notion "$\leq_{\mathrm{APX}}$". For the sake of completeness we mention that $\leq_{\mathrm{PTAS}}$ is reflexive and transitive. The statement $A \leq_{\mathrm{PTAS}} A$ follows if we let $f(x) = x$, $g(x, y, \varepsilon) = y$, and $\alpha(\varepsilon) = \varepsilon$. If (f_1, g_1, α_1) is a PTAS reduction from A to B and (f_2, g_2, α_2) is a PTAS reduction from B to C, then there is a PTAS reduction (f, g, α) from A to C as illustrated in Figure 8.4.1, where $f = f_2 \circ f_1$, $\alpha = \alpha_2 \circ \alpha_1$, and $g(x, y, \varepsilon) = g_1(x, g_2(f_1(x), y, \alpha_1(\varepsilon)), \varepsilon)$.

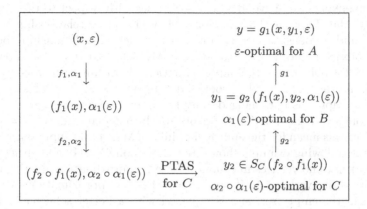

Fig. 8.4.1. The transitivity of PTAS reductions.

Some of the polynomial reductions that we have already designed turn out to be PTAS reductions for the corresponding optimization problems with the function g hidden in the proof of correctness.

Theorem 8.4.4.

1. MAX-3-SAT $\leq_{\mathrm{PTAS}}$ MAX-CLIQUE, *and*
2. MAX-CLIQUE $\equiv_{\mathrm{PTAS}}$ MAX-INDEPENDENTSET.

Proof. For the first statement we choose the transformation f from the proof of 3-SAT $\leq_{\mathrm{p}}$ CLIQUE (Theorem 4.4.3). In the proof of correctness, we implicitly showed how we can efficiently transform every clique of size k in problem $f(x)$ into a variable assignment of the original instance x that satisfies k clauses. We let this variable assignment be $g(x, y, \varepsilon)$ and let $\alpha(\varepsilon) = \varepsilon$.

The second statement follows analogously from the proof that CLIQUE $\equiv_{\mathrm{p}}$ INDEPENDENTSET (Theorem 4.3.4). In this case we can even set $g(x, y, \varepsilon) = y$ and $\alpha(\varepsilon) = \varepsilon$, since a set of vertices that is a clique in $G = (V, E)$ is an anti-clique in $\overline{G} = (V, \overline{E})$ and vice versa. $\square$

Finally, the "inflation technique" described at the end of Section 8.3 for the problem MIN-GC is an approximation-preserving reduction of that problem to itself such that the transformation produces graphs with larger chromatic numbers. But many of the polynomial reductions we have presented are not approximation preserving. For example, if we consider the reduction showing that SAT $\leq_p$ 3-SAT in the special case that the SAT-clauses each have length 4, then m clauses for MAX-4-SAT become $2m$ clauses for MAX-3-SAT, of which m clauses can be satisfied by giving all the new variables the value 1. So an approximation ratio of 2 for MAX-3-SAT has no direct consequences for the given instance of MAX-4-SAT.

The proof of Theorem 8.4.4 shows that the problems MAX-CLIQUE and MAX-INDEPENDENTSET have identical properties with respect to their approximability. But Theorem 4.3.4 not only showed a close relationship between CLIQUE and INDEPENDENTSET, but also a close relationship between INDEPENDENTSET and VERTEXCOVER. For MIN-VERTEXCOVER we know from Section 8.2 a polynomial-time approximation algorithm with worst-case approximation ratio of 2. In the proof that INDEPENDENTSET $\leq_p$ VERTEXCOVER, the input graph was not changed, only the bound k was changed, namely to $n - k$. From a vertex cover $V' \subseteq V$ we obtain the independent set $V'' = V - V'$. What does this mean for the approximability of MAX-INDEPENDENTSET? Nothing, as the following example shows. Let the graph $G = (V, E)$ consist of $n/2$ edges that have no vertices in common. The 2-approximation algorithm computes the entire vertex set $V' = V$, which has an approximation ratio of 2. V'' is then the empty set, and is replaced with a better solution consisting of a single vertex according to our comments in Section 8.1. The resulting approximation ratio of $n/2$, however, is very bad. In fact, we will see in Chapter 12 that MAX-CLIQUE and MAX-INDEPENDENTSET can only be very poorly approximated.

8.5 Complete Approximation Problems

The success of the theory of NP-completeness leads to the question of whether there is a class of optimization problems that can play the role of NP, and whether with respect to this class there is a class of $\leq_{PTAS}$-complete problems. The class NP can be defined as the class of problems for which given an instance x and a polynomially long proof attempt y we can decide in polynomial time whether y proves that x must be accepted by the given decision problem. For optimization problems, the solutions play the role of these proofs.

Definition 8.5.1. *An optimization problem A belongs to the complexity class* NPO *(non-deterministic polynomial-time optimization problems) if for an input (x, s) it is possible in polynomial time to check whether s is a solution for x and, if so, to compute $v(x, s)$. The class* NPO *restricted to maximization problems is denoted* Max-NPO, *and restricted to minimization problems,* Min-NPO.

It is tempting to extend the containments between complexity classes for approximation problems from Section 8.1 to

$$P \subseteq FPTAS \subseteq PTAS \subseteq APX \subseteq NPO .$$

But by our current definitions it is not true that APX $\subseteq$ NPO. From every decision problem, even non-computable problems, we obtain an APX-problem in the following way. For each instance x, let $S(x) = \{0,1\}$ with 1 corresponding to acceptance and 0 to rejection. Let the value of the correct decision be 2, and of the incorrect decision, 1. The corresponding maximization problem belongs to APX, since an output of 1 always has an approximation ratio of at most 2. But if the decision problem is not computable, then the function $v(x,1)$ is not computable either. Since NPO contains all of the practically relevant optimization problems, we will now restrict the classes P, FPTAS, PTAS, and APX to problems in NPO, but continue to use the same notation. Once we have restricted these classes in this manner, the containments listed above are true.

Definition 8.5.2. *An optimization problem A is* NPO-complete *if it belongs to* NPO *and all problems from* NPO *can be* $\leq_{PTAS}$-*reduced to A.* APX-complete, PTAS-complete, Max-NPO-*complete and* Min-NPO-*complete are defined analogously.*

We know from our study of NP-completeness that the main problem will be to find the first complete problem. After that, since the $\leq_{PTAS}$-reductions are transitive, it will suffice to reduce a known complete problem to another problem from the class being considered. Not until Chapter 12 will we be able to use the PCP Theorem to show that MAX-3-SAT is APX-complete. But there is a problem that we can show is NPO-complete using classical methods. As we already know, SAT-problems are good candidates for the "first" complete problem. An instance of the *maximum weight satisfiability* problem (MAX-W-SAT) consists of clauses and non-negative integer weights for the variables that appear in them. The solution set consists of all variable assignments. The value of a satisfying assignment is the maximum of 1 and the total weight of all the variables that are assigned 1. The value of other variable assignments is 1.

Lemma 8.5.3. MAX-W-SAT *is* Max-NPO-*complete.*

Proof. Clearly MAX-W-SAT belongs to Max-NPO. Now let $A \in$ Max-NPO. Our task is to design a $\leq_{PTAS}$-reduction of A to MAX-W-SAT. For A, we consider the following nondeterministic Turing machine. For each instance x of A, the machine nondeterministically generates a possible solution s. For this phase, any sequence of symbols of length at most $p(|x|)$ is allowed, where $p(n)$ is a polynomial bounding $|s|$ for all $s \in S(x)$ and all x with $|x| = n$. Now we check whether $s \in S(x)$. If so, we compute $v(x,s)$, write s and $v(x,s)$ to the tape and enter an accepting state. If not, we enter a rejecting state. The positions where s and $v(x,s)$ are written are the same for all inputs of the same length. Now we apply the transformation from the proof of Cook's Theorem to this Turing machine. Finally, we give the weights of the variables. For each j, the variable that codes whether the jth bit position of $v(x, s)$ contains a 1 receives the weight 2^j. All other variables receive weight 0. This describes the polynomial-time computable function f of the $\leq_{\text{PTAS}}$-reduction we are constructing.

Since for an instance x of A the solution set $S(x)$ is not empty, there is always at least one accepting computation, and therefore a satisfying assignment for the instance of MAX-W-SAT. The reverse transformation $g(x, y, \varepsilon)$ computes the variables that describe the solution s in the output of the Turing machine from knowledge of x and the satisfying assignment y. So we can compute s in polynomial time. Finally, we let $\alpha(\varepsilon) = \varepsilon$. If the solution y for the constructed instance of MAX-W-SAT codes the solution $s \in S(x)$ for the given instance x of A, then it also codes the value of $v(s, x)$, and by the definition of the variable weights, the weight of this assignment is $v(x, s)$. So if the solution for the MAX-W-SAT instance is ε-optimal, then the solution for the instance x of A obtained with the help of g is also ε-optimal.   □

Analogously we can define the problem MIN-W-SAT and show that it is Min-NPO-complete. In fact, MAX-W-SAT $\equiv_{\text{PTAS}}$ MIN-W-SAT. The proof is conceptually simple, but some technical hurdles must be overcome. We will not present this proof (see Ausiello, Crescenzi, Gambosi, Kann, Marchetti-Spaccamela, and Protasi (1999)), but draw the following conclusion from this result:

Theorem 8.5.4. MAX-W-SAT *and* MIN-W-SAT *are* NPO-*complete*.   □

9

The Complexity of Black Box Problems

9.1 Black Box Optimization

In practical applications *randomized search heuristics* such as randomized local search, simulated annealing, tabu search, and evolutionary and genetic algorithms have been used with great success. On the other hand, these algorithms never appear in textbooks on efficient algorithms as the best known algorithms for any problems. This is also justified, since for a given problem, a problem-specific algorithm will be better than general, randomized search heuristics. The advantage of search heuristics is that they can be used for many problems. Since they are not tailored to a particular problem, they ignore much of the information that supports the design of efficient algorithms. This distinction between problem-specific algorithms and randomized search heuristics is often unclear, since there are also hybrid variations, i.e., randomized search heuristics with problem-specific components. In that case, we are dealing with problem-specific algorithms, i.e., with normal randomized algorithms, which do not need any special treatment. Here we want to discuss scenarios in which the use of problem-specific algorithms is not possible.

In real applications, algorithmic problems arise as subproblems in a larger project. An algorithmic solution must be prepared in a short time, and experts in the design of efficient algorithms may not be available. In this situation "robust" algorithms, that is, algorithms that can be used to solve many problems, offer an alternative to craftfully designed, custom-fit software.

It can even happen that the function to be optimized is not available in closed form. When optimizing technical systems there are free parameters, the setting of which influences the system. The search space or solution space then consists of all allowed combinations of these parameters. Each setting of the parameters influences the system and its ability to complete its assigned task. So there is a function that assigns to each setting of the parameters a value of the resulting system. But for complicated systems, this function is not available in closed form; we can only derive these values by experimentally testing the system with a particular setting of the parameters. In practice, these experiments are often simulated with the help of computers, but the problems of choosing a suitable model and designing the simulation experiments will be ignored here.

Robust algorithms play an important role in applications, and so the question arises whether we can formulate these problems in such a way that they can be complexity theoretically investigated. In order to abstract away the technical system, we treat it as a *black box*. The black box provides, for a setting a of the parameters, the value $f(a)$. Since f is not available in closed form, we must use the black box to obtain values of f. In the classical scenario of optimization this corresponds to the computation of the value of a solution s for an instance x – i.e., $v(x, s)$ – except that in black box optimization x is unknown.

A *black box problem* is specified by a problem size n, the corresponding search space S_n, and the set F_n of possible problem inputs, which we identify with the corresponding functions $f : S_n \to \mathbb{R}$. The set F_n is not necessarily finite. Each of the optimization problems we have considered has a black box variant. For example, the traveling salesperson problem has a search space S_n consisting of all permutations of $\{1, \ldots, n\}$, and a function class F_n, that contains all functions $f_D : S_n \to \mathbb{R}$ such that f_D for a distance matrix D assigns to a permutation π the length of the corresponding tour. Or for the knapsack problem, the search space is $\{0, 1\}^n$ and the function class F_n consists of all $f_{u,w,W} : \{0, 1\}^n \to \mathbb{R}$, such that $f_{u,w,W}$ for a knapsack instance (u, w, W) assigns to each selection of objects the corresponding utility value if the weight limit is not exceeded and 0 otherwise. The difference between this and the scenario from before is that the algorithm has no access to D or (u, w, W). It is frequently the case that some properties of the target function are known. For $S_n = \{0, 1\}^n$ it may be that F_n consists of all pseudo-Boolean polynomials whose degree is at most d, for example. Another interesting class of functions is the class of *unimodal* functions, i.e., the class of functions that have a unique global optimum and for which each point that is not globally optimal has a Hamming neighbor with a better value.

A *randomized search heuristic* for a black box problem proceeds as follows:

- A probability distribution p_1 on S_n is selected, and $f(x_1)$ is computed (using the black box) for an $x_1 \in S_n$ selected at random according to p_1.
- For $t > 1$, using knowledge of $(x_1, f(x_1)), \ldots, (x_{t-1}, f(x_{t-1}))$ the algorithm does one of the following
  - ends the search, in which case the x_i with the best f-value is given as output, or
  - continues the search by selecting a new probability distribution p_t on S_n (dependent upon $(x_1, f(x_1)), \ldots, (x_{t-1}, f(x_{t-1}))$), in which case $f(x_t)$ is computed for an x_t chosen at random according to the new probability distribution p_t.

The randomized search heuristics mentioned above all fit into this scheme. Many of them do not actually store all of the available information

$(x_1, f(x_1)), \ldots, (x_{t-1}, f(x_{t-1}))$. Randomized local search and simulated annealing work with the current search point only; evolutionary and genetic algorithms work with a subset of search points called the *population*, the points of which are often referred to as individuals. In any case, the best result encountered is always stored in the background so that it can be given as the result of the algorithm, if no better solution is found.

The search is often interrupted before one knows whether an optimal solution has already been found. In order to evaluate a heuristic, we must then relate the expected runtime with the probability of success. Since stop rules represent only a small problem in practice, we will alter our search heuristics so that they never halt. We are interested in the *expected optimization time*, i.e., the expected time until an optimal solution is given to the black box. Since the evaluation of an x-value by the black box is considered difficult, we abstract away the time required to compute p_t and to select x_t and use the number of calls to the black box as our measure of time for these algorithms. This scenario is called *black box optimization*. The *black box complexity* of a black box problem is the minimal (over the possible randomized search heuristics) worst-case expected optimization time. This model makes it possible to have a complexity theory for randomized search heuristics and their specific application scenario.

One should ask about the reasonableness of this model. At the core of our examples is the fact that the function class F_n is known but not the actual target function f to be optimized. This makes problems more difficult. Heuristics can collect information about the target function since they learn function values for selected search points. Typical problem-specific algorithms are worthless for black box variants. On the other hand, we coarsen our measurement of runtime by counting only the number of calls to the black box. In this way, NP-hard problems can become polynomial-time solvable, as the example of maximizing pseudo-Boolean polynomials of degree 2 shows. The following deterministic search strategy needs only $\binom{n}{2} + n + 2 = O(n^2)$ black box calls. It obtains the f values for all inputs x with at most two 1's. Let e_0 be the input consisting entirely of 0's, e_i be the input with exactly one 1 in position i, and e_{ij} the input with two 1's in positions i and j with $i < j$. The unknown function can be represented as

$$f(x) = w_0 + \sum_{1 \leq i \leq n} w_i x_i + \sum_{1 \leq i < j \leq n} w_{ij} x_i x_j .$$

So we can compute the unknown parameters as follows:

- $w_0 = f(e_0)$,
- $w_i = f(e_i) - w_0$, and
- $w_{ij} = f(e_{ij}) - w_0 - w_i - w_j$.

Finally, given these parameters, f can be optimized with an exponential algorithm. In order to satisfy the demands of a black box algorithm, this optimal value x_{opt} is used as a last call to the black box.

We really don't want to allow algorithms like the one just described. One way out of this is to require that the runtime ignoring the black box calls also be bounded, say by a polynomial. But so far this has not simplified the proofs of lower bounds for the black box complexity of any particular problems. Such bounds will be proved in Section 9.3 without any complexity theoretic assumptions such as NP $\neq$ P or RP $\neq$ P. Another solution would be to limit the number of $(x, f(x))$ pairs that can be stored in a way that corresponds to the requirements of most randomized search heuristics actually used. Here, however, we are more interested in lower bounds and it is certainly the case that

A problem with exponential black box complexity cannot be efficiently solved by randomized search heuristics.

In Section 9.2 we present the minimax principle of Yao (1977) which provides us with a method for proving lower bounds for the black box complexity of specific problems. This method will be applied in Section 9.3 to selected problems.

9.2 Yao's Minimax Principle

The minimax principle of Yao (1977) still represents the only method available for proving lower bounds for *all* randomized search heuristics for selected classes of problems. For this method we must restrict F_n to finite classes of problems. Since S_n is finite, it is sufficient to restrict the image of the target function to a finite set such as $\{0, 1, \ldots, N\}$. It follows that there are only finitely many different "reasonable" deterministic search heuristics, where "reasonable" means that calls to the black box are never repeated. Randomized search heuristics can select the same search point more than once, but in that case the call to the black box is not repeated since the answer is already known from the first call. So there are only finitely many different calls and only finitely many different possible answers to each call, and therefore only finitely many deterministic search heuristics.

We are really dealing with only one active person, namely the person who is designing or selecting the randomized search heuristic, but it is useful to imagine a second person – an opponent – who chooses the target function $f \in F_n$ with the goal of maximizing the search time. We model our problem as a game between Alice, the designer of the randomized search heuristic A, and Bob, the devil's advocate or opponent who chooses $f \in F_n$. For a choice of A and f let $T(f, A)$ be the expected number of black box calls that are needed before a call is made to an optimal search point for f. Alice wants to minimize this cost. Since we have defined the black box complexity in relation to the most difficult function, it is Bob's goal to maximize the cost to Alice. From the perspective of game theory we are dealing with a *two-person zero-sum game*. The payoff matrix for this game has a column for every deterministic search heuristic A and a row for every function $f \in F_n$, and the matrix entries are given by $T(f, A)$. For a given choice of A and f, Alice pays Bob the amount $T(f, A)$. The choices of A and f happen independently of each other, and we allow both players to use randomized strategies.

A randomized choice of a deterministic algorithm leads to a randomized algorithm. The converse is true as well: If we bring together all the random decisions of a randomized algorithm into one random choice we obtain a probability distribution on the set of deterministic search heuristics. In this way we can identify the set of all randomized search heuristics with the set Q of all probability distributions on the set of deterministic search heuristics. For each choice of $q \in Q$ and the corresponding randomized search heuristic A_q, Alice's expected cost for f is denoted $T(f, A_q)$. Alice must fear the expected cost of $\max\{T(f, A_q) \mid f \in F_n\}$, which we will abbreviate as $\max_f T(f, A_q)$. This cost does not become larger if Bob is allowed to use a randomized strategy. Let P be the set of all probability distributions on F_n and f_p the random choice of $f \in F_n$ that corresponds to $p \in P$. Since $T(f_p, A_q)$ is the sum of all $p(f)T(f, A_q)$, we have

$$\max_f T(f, A_q) = \max_p T(f_p, A_q)$$

and Alice is searching for a q^* such that

$$\max_f T(f, A_{q^*}) = \min_q \max_f T(f, A_q) = \min_q \max_p T(f_p, A_q) \ .$$

From the perspective of Bob, the problem is represented as follows: If he chooses $p \in P$, then he is certain that Alice's expected cost will be at least $\min_q T(f_p, A_q)$. With the same arguments as before, this is the same as $\min_A T(f_p, A)$, and Bob is searching for a p^* such that

$$\min_A T(f_{p^*}, A) = \max_p \min_A T(f_p, A) = \max_p \min_q T(f_p, A_q) \ .$$

The Minimax Theorem that von Neumann proved already in the middle of the last century in his formulation of game theory (see Owen (1995)) says that two-person zero-sum games always have a solution. In our situation this means we have

$$\max_p \min_q T(f_p, A_q) = \min_q \max_p T(f_p, A_q) \ .$$

It follows by our observations that

$$v^* := \max_p \min_A T(f_p, A) = \min_q \max_f T(f, A_q).$$

The so-called *value of the game* v^* and optimal strategies can be computed efficiently by means of linear programming. Here efficiency is measured in terms of the size of the matrix $T(f, A)$, but is of no concern in our situation.

In all interesting cases, the set F_n and the set of deterministic search heuristics are so large that we are not even able to construct the matrix $T(f, A)$. We are only interested in the simpler part of the Minimax Theorem, namely

$$v_{\text{Bob}} := \max_p \min_A T(f_p, A) \leq \min_q \max_f T(f, A_q) =: v_{\text{Alice}} .$$

This inequality can be proven as follows. As we have seen, Alice can guarantee that her expected costs are not more than v_{Alice}. On the other hand, Bob can guarantee an expected value of at worst v_{Bob}. Since all the money is paid by Alice to Bob, and no money enters the game "from outside", $v_{\text{Bob}} > v_{\text{Alice}}$ would imply that Bob could guarantee an expected payment that is higher than the bound for the expected costs that Alice can guarantee in the worst case. This contradiction proves the inequality. The minimax principle of Yao consists of the simple deduction that for all $p \in P$ and all $q \in Q$,

$$\min_A T(f_p, A) \leq v_{\text{Bob}} \leq v_{\text{Alice}} \leq \max_f T(f, A_q) .$$

The achievement of Yao was to recognize that the choice of a randomized algorithm for the minimization of the worst-case expected optimization time for a function set (set of problem inputs) can be modeled as a two-person zero-sum game. In the following theorem we summarize the results we have obtained. After that we describe the consequences for proving lower bounds.

Theorem 9.2.1. *Let F_n be a finite set of functions on a finite search space S_n, and let $\mathcal{A}$ be a finite set of deterministic algorithms on the problem class F_n. For every probability distribution p on F_n and every probability distribution q on $\mathcal{A}$,*

$$\min_{A \in \mathcal{A}} T(f_p, A) \leq \max_{f \in F_n} T(f, A_q) . \qquad \square$$

The expected runtime of an optimal deterministic algorithm with respect to an arbitrary distribution on the problem instances is a lower bound for the expected runtime of an optimal randomized algorithm with respect to the most difficult problem instance. So we get lower bounds for randomized algorithms by proving lower bounds for deterministic algorithms. Furthermore, we have the freedom to make the situation for the deterministic algorithm as difficult as possible by our choice of a suitable distribution on the problem instances.

9.3 Lower Bounds for Black Box Complexity

In order to apply Yao's minimax principle, it is helpful to model deterministic search heuristics as *search trees*. The root symbolizes the first query to the black box. For each possible result of the query there is an edge leaving the root that leads to a node representing the second query made dependent upon that result. The situation is analogous at all further nodes. For every $f \in F_n$ there is a unique path starting at the root that describes how the search heuristic behaves on f. The number of nodes until the first node representing an f-optimal search point is equal to the runtime of the heuristic on f. For classes of functions where each function has a unique optimum, the search tree must have at least as many nodes as the function class has optima. Since we only have to make queries when we can't already we can't already compute the results, each internal node in the search tree has at least two descendants. Even for a uniform distribution of all optima, without further argument we don't obtain any better lower bound than $\log |S_n|$, i.e., a linear lower bound in the case that $S_n = \{0,1\}^n$. Such bounds are only seldom satisfying. An exception is the $\log(n!)$ lower bound for the general sorting problem, with which most readers are probably already familiar. Using the minimax principle of Yao, we obtain from this familiar bound for deterministic algorithms and a uniform distribution over all permutations, a lower bound for the worst-case expected runtime of any randomized algorithm. If we want to show lower bounds that are superlinear in $\log |S_n|$, we must prove that the search tree cannot be balanced.

We begin our discussion with two function classes that are often discussed in the world of evolutionary algorithms. With the help of black box complexity, the answers to the questions asked in the examples are relatively easy. The first function class symbolizes the search for a *needle in the haystack*. The function class consists of the functions N_a for each $a \in \{0,1\}^n$ where N_a is defined by $N_a(a) = 1$ and $N_a(b) = 0$ for $b \neq a$.

Theorem 9.3.1. *The black box complexity of the function class $\{N_a \mid a \in \{0,1\}^n\}$ is $2^{n-1} + \frac{1}{2}$.*

Proof. We obtain the upper bound by querying the points in the search space $\{0,1\}^n$ in random order. For each function N_a we find the optimum in the t-th query with probability 2^{-n} $(1 \leq t \leq 2^n)$. This gives the expected optimization time of

$$2^{-n}(1 + 2 + 3 + \cdots + 2^n) = 2^{n-1} + \frac{1}{2} .$$

We show the lower bound using Yao's minimax principle with the uniform distribution on $\{N_a \mid a \in \{0,1\}^n\}$. If a query returns the value 1, the algorithm can stop the search with success. So the interesting path in the search tree is the one that receives an answer of 0 to every previous query. On this path every $a \in \{0,1\}^n$ must appear as a query. At each level of the tree, only one new search point can be queried. So the expected search time is at least $2^{-n}(1 + 2 + 3 + \cdots + 2^n) = 2^{n-1} + \frac{1}{2}$. $\square$

The function class of all N_a clarifies the difference between the classical optimization scenario and the black box scenario. In the classical optimization scenario the function being optimized N_a (and therefore a) is known. The optimization is then a trivial task since the optimal solution is a. In the black box scenario, the common randomized search heuristics require an expected optimization time of $\Theta(2^n)$. This is inefficient in comparison to the classical optimization scenario, but by Theorem 9.3.1 it is asymptotically optimal in the black box scenario. In contrast to many claims to the contrary, the common randomized search algorithms on the class of all functions of the "needle in the haystack" variety are nearly optimal. They are slow because that problem is difficult in the black box scenario.

The black box scenario is very similar for functions that are *traps* for typical random search heuristics. For $a \in \{0,1\}^n$, the function T_a is defined by $T_a(a) = 2n$ and $T_a(b) = b_1 + \cdots + b_n$ for $b \in \{0,1\}^n$ and $b \neq a$.

Theorem 9.3.2. *The black box complexity of the function class* $\{T_a \mid a \in \{0,1\}^n\}$ *is* $2^{n-1} + \frac{1}{2}$.

Proof. The proof is analogous to the proof of Theorem 9.3.1. For the upper bound nothing must be changed. For the lower bound one must note that for each $b \in \{0,1\}^n$, the functions take on only two different values, namely $b_1 + \cdots + b_n$ and $2n$. The function value of $2n$ means that the query contains the optimal search point. $\qquad\square$

The functions T_a for $a \in \{0,1\}^n$ do in fact set traps for most of the common randomized search heuristics that have expected optimization time of $2^{\Theta(n \log n)}$. In contrast, the purely random search, where at each point in time the search point is selected according to the uniform distribution on the search space, is nearly optimal. This result is not surprising since common randomized search heuristics prefer to continue the search close to good search points. But for the functions T_a this is in general the wrong decision. On the other hand, the functions T_a are trivial in the classical optimization scenario.

Finally, we want to see a more complex application of Yao's minimax principle. It is often maintained that the common randomized search heuristics are fast on *all* unimodal functions. We can show that this is not true for many of these search heuristics by giving a cleverly chosen example. We want to show that in the black box scenario, *no* randomized search heuristic can be fast for all unimodal functions.

The class of unimodal pseudo-Boolean functions $f : \{0,1\}^n \to \mathbb{R}$ is not finite. But if we restrict the range of the functions to the integers z with $-n \leq z \leq 2^n$, then we have a finite class of functions. Now we need to find a probability distribution on these functions that supports a proof of a lower bound using Yao's minimax principle. One might suspect that the uniform distribution on this class of functions precludes an efficient optimization by deterministic search heuristics. But this distribution is difficult to work with, so we will use another distribution. We will consider paths $P = (p_0, \ldots, p_m)$ in $\{0,1\}^n$ consisting of a sequence of distinct points p_i such that the Hamming distance $H(p_i, p_{i+1})$ of two adjacent points is always 1 and p_0 is 1^n. For each such a path P there is a *path function* f_P defined by $f_P(p_i) = i$ and $f_P(a) = a_1 + \cdots + a_n - n$ for all a not on the path. The function f_P is unimodal since p_{i+1} is better than p_i for all i with $i < m$. For all other points a, any Hamming neighbor that contains one more 1 will be better. The idea behind the following construction is that "long random paths" make things difficult for the search heuristic. The search heuristic cannot simply follow the path step by step because the path is too long. On the other hand, even if we know the beginning portion of the path, it is difficult to generate a point "much farther down the path" with more than a very small probability. These ideas will now be formalized.

First we generate a random pseudo-path R on which points may be repeated. Let the length of the path be $l := l(n)$, where $l(n) = 2^{o(n)}$. Let $p_0 = 1^n$. We generate the successor p_{i+1} of p_i according to the uniform distribution of all Hamming neighbors of p_i. This means that we select a random bit to flip. From R we generate a path P by removing all the cycles from R in the following way. Again we start at 1^n. If we reach the point p_i along R and j is the largest index such that $p_j = p_i$, then we continue with p_{j+1}. We consider the probability distribution on the unimodal functions that assigns to the path function f_P the probability with which the random procedure just described generates the path P. Unimodal functions that are not path functions are assigned probability 0. Now we investigate deterministic search heuristics on random unimodal functions selected according to this distribution.

As preparation, we investigate the random pseudo-path R. With high probability, this path quickly moves far away from each point it reaches, and it is short enough that with high probability it will never again return to a point that it reached much earlier. In the next lemma we generalize and formalize this idea.

Lemma 9.3.3. *Let $p_0, p_1, \ldots, p_l$ be the random pseudo-path R, and let H be the Hamming distance function. Then for every $\beta > 0$ there is an $\alpha = \alpha(\beta) > 0$ such that for every $a \in \{0,1\}^n$ the event E_a that there is a $j \geq \beta n$ with $H(a, p_j) \leq \alpha n$ has probability $2^{-\Omega(n)}$.*

Proof. Let $E_{a,j}$ be the event that $H(a, p_j) \leq \alpha n$. Since $l = 2^{o(n)}$, there are $2^{o(n)}$ points p_j, and it suffices to bound the probability of the event $E_{a,j}$ by $2^{-\Omega(n)}$ for each $a \in \{0,1\}^n$ and $j \geq \beta n$. Now consider the random Hamming distance $H_t = H(a, p_t)$ for $0 \leq t \leq l$. If this distance is large, then for some time interval it will certainly remain "pretty large". If this distance is small, then the chances are good that it will grow quickly. Since we obtain p_{t+1} from p_t by flipping a randomly selected bit

$$\text{Prob}(H_{t+1} = H_t + 1) = 1 - H_t/n \, .$$

So if H_t is much smaller than $n/2$, then there is a strong tendency for the Hamming distance to a to increase.

Let $\gamma = \min\{\beta, 1/10\}$ and $\alpha = \alpha(\beta) = \gamma/5$. We consider the section $p_{j-\lfloor \gamma n \rfloor}, \ldots, p_j$ of R of length $\lfloor \gamma n \rfloor$, in order to give an upper bound on the probability of $E_{a,j}$. By the definition of α, the event $E_{a,j}$, (i.e., $H_j \leq \alpha n$) is equivalent to $H_j \leq (\gamma/5)n$.

If $H_{j-\lfloor\gamma n\rfloor} \geq 2\gamma n$, then H_j is certainly at least γn. So we can assume that $H_{j-\lceil\gamma n\rceil} < 2\gamma n$. Then during the entire section of R that we are considering, H_t is at most $3\gamma n \leq (3/10)n$. So we are dealing with $\lfloor\gamma n\rfloor$ steps at which H_t increases by 1 with probability at least $1 - 3\gamma \geq 7/10$ and otherwise decreases by 1. The Chernoff Inequality (Theorem A.2.11) guarantees that the probability that there are fewer than $(6/10)\gamma n$ steps among the $\lfloor\gamma n\rfloor$ steps we are considering that increase the Hamming distance is bounded by $2^{-\Omega(n)}$.

If we have $(6/10)\gamma n$ increasing steps, then we have an excess of at least $(6/10)\gamma n - (4/10)\gamma n = (\gamma/5)n$ increasing steps and the Hamming distance H_j is at least $(\gamma/5)n$. □

Lemma 9.3.3 has the following consequences. The pseudo-path R is constructed by a Markov process, that is, by a "memory-less" procedure. So $p_i, \ldots, p_l$ satisfy the assumptions of the lemma. For $a = p_i$ and $\beta = 1$, this implies that after more than n steps R reaches p_i again with probability at most $2^{-\Omega(n)}$. Since there are only $2^{o(n)}$ points p_i, the probability of a cycle of length at least n in R is bounded by $2^{-\Omega(n)}$. So with probability $1 - 2^{-\Omega(n)}$ the length of P is at least $l(n)/n$.

Theorem 9.3.4. *Every randomized search heuristic for the black box optimization of unimodal pseudo-Boolean functions has for each $\delta(n) = o(n)$ a worst-case expected optimization time of $2^{\Omega(\delta(n))}$. The minimal success probability of such a heuristic after $2^{O(\delta(n))}$ steps is $2^{-\Omega(n)}$.*

Proof. The proof uses Yao's minimax principle (Theorem 9.2.1). We choose $l(n)$ so that $l(n)/n^2 = 2^{\Omega(\delta(n))}$ and $l(n) = 2^{o(n)}$. By the preceding discussion, the probability that the length of P is less than $l(n)/n$ is exponentially small. We will use 0 as an estimate for the search time in these cases, and assume in what follows that P has length at least $l(n)/n$.

For the proof we describe a scenario that simplifies the work of the search heuristic and the analysis. The "knowledge" of the heuristic at any point in time will be described by

- the index i such that the initial segment $p_0, \ldots, p_i$ of P is known, but no further points of P are known; and
- a set N of points that are known not to belong to P.

At the beginning $i = 0$ and $N = \emptyset$. The randomized search heuristic generates a search point x and we define this step to be a successful step if $x = p_k$ with $k \geq i+n$. If it is not successful, i is replaced with $i+n$, and the search heuristic learns the next n points on the path. If x does not belong to the path, then x is added to N. To prove the theorem, it is sufficient to prove that for each of the first $\lfloor l(n)/n^2 \rfloor$ steps the probability of success is $2^{-\Omega(n)}$.

We consider first the initial situation with $i = 0$ and $N = \emptyset$. It follows directly from Lemma 9.3.3 with $\beta = 1$ that each search point x has a success probability of $2^{-\Omega(n)}$. In fact, the probability that P is still in the Hamming ball of radius $\alpha(1)$ around x after at least n steps is $2^{-\Omega(n)}$.

After m unsuccessful steps, $mn + 1$ points of the initial segment of P are known, and N contains at most m points. The analysis becomes more difficult because of the knowledge that these at most $mn + m + 1$ points will never again be reached by P. Let y be the last known search point that lies on P. The set M of path points $p_0, \ldots, p_{mn}$ and the points in N are partitioned into two sets M' and M'' such that M' contains the points that are far from y (more precisely: with Hamming distance at least $\alpha(1)n$ from y), and M'' contains the remaining points (the ones close to y). First we will work under the condition of event E that the points from M' do not occur again on the path. Since $\text{Prob}(E) = 1 - 2^{-\Omega(n)}$, the condition E can only have a small effect on the probability we are interested in. For a search point x, let x^* be the event that this point successfully ends the search. Then

$$\text{Prob}(x^* \mid E) = \text{Prob}(x^* \cap E) / \text{Prob}(E)$$

$$\leq \text{Prob}(x^*) / \text{Prob}(E) = \text{Prob}(x^*) \cdot (1 + 2^{-\Omega(n)}) \,.$$

So the success probability grows only by a factor close to 1, and so remains $2^{-\Omega(n)}$.

Finally, we must deal with the points in M''. Now we apply Lemma 9.3.3 for $\beta = 1/2$. After $n/2$ steps, with probability $1 - 2^{-\Omega(n)}$ P has Hamming distance at least $\alpha(1/2)n$ from y and from every other point in M. So we can apply the argument above on the remaining $n/2$ steps, but this time "far apart" will mean a distance of at least $\alpha(1/2)n$. This suffices to estimate the success probability as $2^{-\Omega(n)}$. □

Yao's minimax principle makes it possible to prove exponential lower bounds for randomized search heuristics that are used in black box scenarios.

Additional Complexity Classes and Relationships Between Complexity Classes

10.1 Fundamental Considerations

In Chapter 3 we introduced and investigated the fundamental complexity classes. The relationships between them were summarized in Theorem 3.5.3. Reductions serve to establish relationships between individual problems. If a problem is compared with a complexity class C, it can prove to be C-easy, C-hard, C-complete, or C-equivalent. In this way we learn something about the complexity of problems in relation to the complexity of other problems and in relation to complexity classes. The theory of NP-completeness has proven itself to be the best tool currently known for classifying as difficult many important problems under the hypothesis that NP $\neq$ P.

And so we have convinced ourselves that the investigation of complexity classes like NP that are defined in terms of algorithms that are not practically efficient can nevertheless be well-motivated.

In this chapter we return to these fundamental complexity classes and define new classes as well. We begin in Section 10.2 with the inner structure of NP and co-NP. In Section 10.4 we define and investigate the *polynomial hierarchy* of complexity classes that contain NP. To that end we define *oracle classes* in Section 10.3. While a Turing reduction may make use of an algorithm for a particular problem, we will now allow algorithms for any problem in an entire complexity class. We obtain new complexity theoretical hypotheses, some of which are stronger than the NP $\neq$ P-hypothesis but still well-supported. In later chapters we will draw consequences from these hypotheses that we do not (yet) know how to derive from NP $\neq$ P. In addition we obtain indications about which proof methods we *cannot* use to prove the NP $\neq$ P-conjecture.

Of course, all this begs the question, why all these considerations are related to NP and classes above NP, and why we don't continue with an investigation of algorithmically relevant classes like ZPP, RP, co-RP, and BPP. The main reason is that BPP $\neq$ P is not as well-supported a hypothesis as NP $\neq$ P. While we suspect that the NP-complete problems (and therefore a great number of well-studied problems) do not belong to P, there are hardly any such problems that we know belong to BPP but suspect do not belong to P. A proof that BPP = P would be a far-reaching and strong result, but it would not bring down the currently reigning view of the world of complexity classes – in contrast to a proof of NP = P. Among experts, the opinion is widely held that "P is close to BPP" but that P and NP are separated by the world of NP-complete problems. The notion "is close to" is, of course, not formalizable. We will further support these considerations in Section 10.5 where we investigate the relationship between NP and BPP.

10.2 Complexity Classes Within NP and co-NP

If NP = P, then since P = co-P it follows that co-NP = P and we only have the class of efficiently solvable problems. This is not only unexpected, it is also less interesting than the other case. From Section 5.1 we know that in P there are three equivalence classes with respect to the equivalence relation $\equiv_p$:

- all problems for which no input is accepted,
- all problems for which all inputs are accepted, and
- all other problems.

If NP $\neq$ P, then by definition the class NPC of all NP-complete problems forms a fourth equivalence class with respect to $\equiv_p$. Are there still more equivalence classes? This is equivalent to the question of whether or not the class NPI := NP $-$(P$\cup$NPC) is empty. Of course, we can't prove that any problem belongs to NPI, since then we would have proven that NP $\neq$ P. But perhaps there are problems that we suspect belong to NPI? Garey and Johnson (1979) list three problems which at that time were considered candidates for membership in NPI:

- the problem of linear programming (LP), i.e., the problem of determining whether a linear function on a space restricted by linear inequalities takes on a value at least as large as a given bound b;
- primality testing (PRIMES); and
- the graph isomorphism problem (GRAPHISOMORPHISM, or sometimes more briefly abbreviated as GI; see also Section 6.5).

It has been known for a long time already that LP $\in$ P (see, for example, Aspvall and Stone (1980)). PRIMES was known to belong to NP, co-NP, and even co-RP. Miller (1976) had already designed a polynomial-time primality test based on an unproven hypothesis from number theory. So PRIMES was also a candidate for membership in P. Finally, Agrawal, Kayal, and Saxena (2002) were able to prove that in fact PRIMES $\in$ P. Their arguments, however, have no consequences for the complexity of the factoring problem FACT. The proof that a number n is not prime is based on number theoretic arguments that have not (yet) been any help in computing a divisor of n. The conjecture that FACT is not polynomial-time solvable has not been shaken by the discovery of a polynomial-time primality test. In particular, cryptographic protocols like the RSA system and PGP that are based on the supposed difficulty of factoring, cannot be attacked with this primality test.

For GI there are no indications that GI $\in$ P. In Chapter 11 we will provide support for the conjecture that GI is not NP-complete. So for the moment, GI is the best-known decision problem that is conjectured to belong to NPI.

Since we want to concentrate on results about concrete algorithmic problems, the following existence result of Ladner (1975) will only be cited.

Theorem 10.2.1. *If* NP $\neq$ P, *then* NPI *is not empty and, in fact, contains problems that are incomparable with respect to* $\leq_p$. $\qquad\qquad\square$

So if NP $\neq$ P, then there are several $\equiv_p$-equivalence classes within NPI.

The power of the concept of polynomial reductions can be seen in the fact that almost all problems of interest have been proven to be either NP-equivalent or polynomial-time solvable. But if NP $\neq$ P, *then there is actually a rich structure of problems between* P *and* NPC.

We want to discuss the relationship between NP and co-NP. They are duals of each other since by definition co-co-NP = NP. This means that either NP = co-NP or neither class contains the other, since from NP $\subseteq$ co-NP it follows that co-NP $\subseteq$ co-co-NP = NP. In Section 5.3 we characterized NP using a polynomially bounded existential quantifier and polynomial-time predicates. Formally, $L \in$ NP if and only if there is a language $L' \in$ P and a polynomial p such that

$$L = \left\{ x \mid \exists z \in \{0,1\}^{p(|x|)} : (x,z) \in L' \right\} .$$

Languages in co-NP can be characterized in a dual manner. Formally, the existential quantifier is replaced by a universal quantifier. The NP $\neq$ P-hypothesis means that without the existential quantifier we cannot describe as many languages as with it. If we believe that in this sort of representation existential quantifiers cannot be replaced with universal quantifiers (and other languages $L' \in$ P), then this is equivalent to the NP $\neq$ co-NP-hypothesis. As was explained at the beginning of this section, a proof that NP $\neq$ co-NP implies that NP $\neq$ P. We have also seen that to prove that NP = co-NP, it suffices to show that NP $\subseteq$ co-NP. The following line of thought is intuitively obvious: If a hardest problem in NP, that is an NP-complete problem, belongs to co-NP, then all of NP belongs to co-NP. We will use this kind of reasoning often, so we formalize it here.

Theorem 10.2.2. *If* L *is* NP-*complete and* $L \in$ co-NP, *then* NP = co-NP.

Proof. As we have already discussed, it is sufficient to show that under the hypotheses of the theorem, if $L' \in$ NP, then $L' \in$ co-NP. But this is equivalent to $\overline{L} \in$ NP. We describe a polynomial-time bounded nondeterministic Turing

machine that accepts inputs $w \in \overline{L'}$ and rejects input $w \notin \overline{L'}$. Since L is NP-complete and $L' \in$ NP, $L' \leq_p L$. So there is a polynomial-time computable function f such that
$$w \in L' \Leftrightarrow f(w) \in L .$$
We apply this function f to the input w for $\overline{L'}$. It follows that

$$w \in \overline{L'} \Leftrightarrow f(w) \in \overline{L} .$$

Since $L \in$ co-NP, we can nondeterministically check whether $f(w) \in \overline{L}$ in polynomial time, and so we have a polynomial-time nondeterministic test for whether $w \in \overline{L'}$.   □

The NP $\neq$ co-NP-hypothesis implies that languages $L \in$ NP $\cap$ co-NP are neither NP-complete nor co-NP-complete. Before the proof that PRIMES $\in$ P, the fact that PRIMES $\in$ NP $\cap$ co-NP was the best indication that PRIMES was neither NP-complete nor co-NP-complete. For the graph isomorphism problem we know that GI $\in$ NP, but we do not know if GI $\in$ co-NP. So this kind of consideration provides no support for the conjecture that GI is not NP-complete.

Finally, the NP $\neq$ co-NP-hypothesis implies that NP-complete problems do not belong to co-NP. Therefore, it is not surprising that we have not been able to represent any of the known NP-complete problems with universal quantifiers and thus show them to belong to co-NP. In summary, we conjecture that the world within NP $\cup$ co-NP is as illustrated in Figure 10.2.1.

10.3 Oracle Classes

Already when we introduced Turing reductions $A \leq_T B$ in Section 4.1 we spoke of polynomial-time algorithms for A *with oracle* B. We will continue to use the notion of an oracle, although this term sounds somewhat mysterious and imprecise. In fact, we are simply talking about a subprogram for B, a call to which (usually called a *query*) is assigned a cost of 1. The term oracle is perhaps an unfortunate choice, but it is the usual designation for this sort of subprogram. Since we will only consider oracles for decision problems, we don't have to concern ourselves with how one should measure the cost of an oracle query when the response is longer than the question.

Definition 10.3.1. *The complexity class* P(L) *for a decision problem* L *contains all decision problems* L' *such that* $L' \leq_T L$, *that is, all problems* L' *that can be decided by polynomial-time algorithms with access to an oracle for* L. *The complexity class* P($\mathcal{C}$) *for a class* $\mathcal{C}$ *of decision problems is the union of all* P(L) *with* $L \in \mathcal{C}$.

If the complexity class $\mathcal{C}$ contains a $\leq_T$- or $\leq_p$-complete problem L^*, then P($\mathcal{C}$) = P(L^*), since each query to an oracle $L \in \mathcal{C}$ can be replaced by a polynomial-time algorithm that queries oracle L^*. In particular, P(NP) =

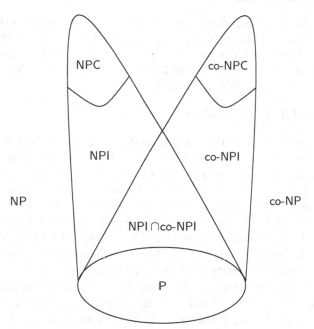

Fig. 10.2.1. The complexity world within NP ∪ co-NP under the assumption that NP ∩ co-NP ≠ P.

P(SAT). We suspect that P(NP) is a strict superclass of NP. Otherwise we would be able to replace all the queries to SAT in a polynomial-time algorithm with a single query at the very end, the answer to which we would not be allowed to change. In particular, co-NP ⊆ P(NP) since we can reverse the answer of the NP-oracle. These arguments even suggest that P(NP) is a strict superclass of NP ∪ co-NP. We can't prove any of this, however, since NP = P would imply that P(NP) = P(P) = P.

This operator cannot be iterated, since P(P(𝒞)) = P(𝒞): A polynomial-time computation in which we may make queries to a polynomial-time computation with oracle L is nothing more than a polynomial-time computation with oracle L.

In our earlier considerations, it was an important step to consider NP in addition to P. So now we want to consider NP(L) and NP(𝒞) in addition to P(L) and P(𝒞).

Definition 10.3.2. *For a decision problem L, the complexity class* NP(L) *contains all decision problem L' for which there is a nondeterministic polynomial-time algorithm with oracle L. For a class of decision problems 𝒞, the complexity class* NP(𝒞) *is the union of all* NP(L) *for L ∈ 𝒞.*

P(P) = P and NP(P) = NP, since the oracle queries can be replaced by (deterministic) polynomial-time algorithms. In order to become more familiar with these notions, we introduce a practically important problem that belongs to co-NP(NP) but is conjectured not to belong to either P(NP) or NP(NP). The language of all minimal circuits over all binary gates (MC) consists of all circuits with one output gate for which there is no circuit with fewer gates that computes the same Boolean function.

Theorem 10.3.3. MC ∈ co-NP(NP).

Proof. We will show that the complement $\overline{MC}$ is in NP(NP). Let C be a circuit, and let f be the function computed by C. In polynomial time we nondeterministically generate a circuit C' that has fewer gates than C. The function computed by C' we denote f'. From C and C' we form with one additional gate of type $\oplus$ (exclusive or) a new circuit C'' for which $f'' = f \oplus f'$. As oracle we select the NP-complete satisfiability problem for circuits, which we denote SAT$_{\text{CIR}}$. The oracle accepts C'' if and only if there is some a such that $f''(a) = 1$, that is, if and only if there is an a such that $f'(a) \neq f(a)$. In this case, the algorithm rejects C. If the oracle rejects C'', then $f' = f$, and C' is a smaller circuit that computes the same function that C computes. So the algorithm knows that C is not minimal and accepts C. Thus C is accepted on at least one computation path if and only if C is not minimal, as was desired. $\square$

As a final note, we point out that there is an alternative "exponential" notation for these classes that is also common in the literature. In this notation $P^{\mathcal{C}}$ and $NP^{\mathcal{C}}$ are used in place of $P(\mathcal{C})$ and $NP(\mathcal{C})$, for example.

10.4 The Polynomial Hierarchy

In Section 10.3 we prepared the tools to define a multitude of complexity classes. We will travel this path formally and look at a few properties of these complexity classes. Along the way, we will see that these complexity classes have clear, logical descriptions, from which we can construct complete problems. Their description supports the hypothesis that these complexity classes form a genuine hierarchy, that is, they form an increasing sequence of distinct complexity classes with respect to set inclusion.

Definition 10.4.1. *Let* $\Sigma_1 := NP$, $\Pi_1 := co\text{-}NP$, *and* $\Delta_1 := P$. *For* $k \geq 1$, *let*

- $\Sigma_{k+1} := NP(\Sigma_k)$,
- $\Pi_{k+1} := co\text{-}\Sigma_{k+1}$, *and*
- $\Delta_{k+1} := P(\Sigma_k)$.

The polynomial hierarchy (PH) *is the union of all* Σ_k *for* $k \geq 1$.

It is also consistent to let $\Sigma_0 = \Pi_0 = \Delta_0 = P$, and to extend the definition to all $k \geq 0$. As we saw in Section 10.3, $\Sigma_1 = NP$, $\Pi_1 = co\text{-}NP$ and $\Delta_1 = P$.

With the new notation, the statement if Theorem 10.3.3 can be expressed as $MC \in \Pi_2$. We list a few properties of the new complexity classes in order to get a picture of the relationships between them.

Lemma 10.4.2. *For the complexity classes within the polynomial hierarchy we have the following relationships:*

- $\Delta_k = \text{co-}\Delta_k = P(\Delta_k) \subseteq \Sigma_k \cap \Pi_k \subseteq \Sigma_k \cup \Pi_k \subseteq \Delta_{k+1} = P(\Pi_k)$.
- $\Sigma_{k+1} = NP(\Pi_k) = NP(\Delta_{k+1})$.
- $\Pi_{k+1} = \text{co-}NP(\Pi_k) = \text{co-}NP(\Delta_{k+1})$.
- $\Sigma_k \subseteq \Pi_k \Rightarrow \Sigma_k = \Pi_k$.

Proof. We have $\Delta_k = \text{co-}\Delta_k$, since by definition $\Delta_k = P(\Sigma_{k-1})$ and with Turing-reductions we can negate the answer at the end. Also, $P(\Delta_k) = P(P(\Sigma_{k-1})) = P(\Sigma_{k-1}) = \Delta_k$, since a polynomial algorithm that may query a polynomial-time algorithm with oracle $L \in \Sigma_{k-1}$ is nothing more than a polynomial-time algorithm that may make queries to the oracle $L \in \Sigma_{k-1} \subseteq \Delta_k$. Clearly $\Delta_k = P(\Sigma_{k-1}) \subseteq NP(\Sigma_{k-1}) = \Sigma_k$, and $\Delta_k = \text{co-}\Delta_k \subseteq \Pi_k$. The inclusion $P(\mathcal{C}) \subseteq NP(\mathcal{C})$ holds by definition for all complexity classes $\mathcal{C}$. Similarly, it follows from the definitions that $\Sigma_k \subseteq P(\Sigma_k) = \Delta_{k+1}$ and $\Pi_k = \text{co-}\Sigma_k \subseteq \text{co-}\Delta_{k+1} = \Delta_{k+1}$. Finally, $\Delta_{k+1} = P(\Sigma_k) = P(\Pi_k)$, since an oracle $L \in \Sigma_k$ is of the same use as an oracle $\overline{L} \in \text{co-}\Sigma_k = \Pi_k$. We can simply reverse the answers to the oracle queries.

By the same argument it follows that $\Sigma_{k+1} = NP(\Sigma_k) = NP(\Pi_k)$. From $\Sigma_k \subseteq \Delta_{k+1}$ it follows that $\Sigma_{k+1} = NP(\Sigma_k) \subseteq NP(\Delta_{k+1})$. For the reverse direction we must argue that an oracle $L \in \Delta_{k+1}$ can be replaced by an oracle $L' \in \Sigma_k$. Since $\Delta_{k+1} = P(\Sigma_k)$, an oracle $L \in \Delta_{k+1}$ can be replaced by a polynomial-time algorithm with oracle $L' \in \Sigma_k$. The result is a non-deterministic polynomial-time algorithm that queries a polynomial-time algorithm with oracle L'.

The third statement follows from the second by taking complements.

Finally, $\Sigma_k \subseteq \Pi_k$, implies that $\Pi_k = \text{co-}\Sigma_k \subseteq \text{co-}\Pi_k = \Sigma_k$ and thus that $\Sigma_k = \Pi_k$. □

Analogous to the representations in Chapter 3, we obtain the complexity landscape within the polynomial hierarchy depicted in Figure 10.4.1.

The conjecture that the classes of the polynomial hierarchy form a genuine hierarchy contains the conjecture that all the inclusions in Figure 10.4.1 are strict inclusions and that the classes Σ_k and Π_k are incomparable with respect to set inclusion. Thus we obtain the following complexity theoretical hypotheses:

- $\Sigma_k \neq \Sigma_{k+1}$,
- $\Pi_k \neq \Pi_{k+1}$,
- $\Sigma_k \neq \Pi_k$,
- $\Delta_k \neq \Sigma_k \cap \Pi_k \neq \Sigma_k \neq \Sigma_k \cup \Pi_k \neq \Delta_{k+1}$.

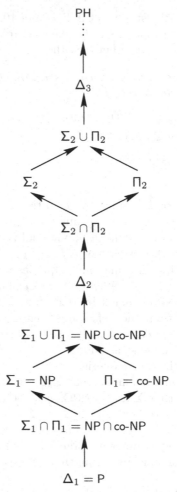

Fig. 10.4.1. The complexity landscape within the polynomial hierarchy. Arrows represent set inclusion.

Before investigating relationships between these hypotheses, we will derive a logical representation of the complexity classes Σ_k and Π_k. This will simplify later considerations.

Theorem 10.4.3. *A decision problem L belongs to the class Σ_k if and only if there is a polynomial p and a decision problem $L' \in P$ such that for $A = \{0,1\}^{p(|x|)}$,*

$$L = \{x \mid \exists y_1 \in A \, \forall y_2 \in A \, \exists y_3 \in A \ldots Q \, y_k \in A : (x, y_1, \ldots, y_k) \in L'\} .$$

The quantifier Q is chosen to be an existential or universal quantifier in such a way that the sequence of quantifiers is alternating.

Proof. We prove the theorem by induction on k. For $k = 1$ the statement was already proven in Theorem 5.3.2. Now suppose we have a representation of L of the type described for some $k \geq 2$. A nondeterministic algorithm can nondeterministically generate $y_1 \in A$. We allow the algorithm to access as oracle the decision problem

$$L^* := \{(x, y_1) \mid \exists y_2 \in A \, \forall y_3 \in A \ldots Q \, y_k \in A : (x, y_1, \ldots, y_k) \in \overline{L'}\} \, .$$

Recall that Q is the quantifier that makes the sequence of quantifiers alternate. Since $L \in \mathsf{P}$ implies that $\overline{L} \in \mathsf{P}$, by the inductive hypothesis $L^* \in \Sigma_{k-1}$. The nondeterministic algorithm queries the oracle L^* about (x, y_1) and reverses the answer. If $x \in L$, then there is some $y_1 \in A$ such that

$$\forall y_2 \in A \, \exists y_3 \in A \ldots Q \, y_k \in A : (x, y_1, \ldots, y_k) \in L'$$

is true. Therefore, $(x, y_1) \notin L^*$, and the nondeterministic algorithm accepts x. If $x \notin L$, then by DeMorgan's laws for all $y_1 \in A$,

$$\exists y_2 \in A \, \forall y_3 \in A \ldots Q \, y_k \in A : (x, y_1, \ldots, y_k) \notin L'$$

holds. So $(x, y_1) \in L^*$ for all $y_1 \in A$, and the nondeterministic algorithm does not accept x on any path. The runtime is polynomially bounded since y_1 has polynomial length.

Now suppose $L \in \Sigma_k$. Then L has a nondeterministic polynomial-time bounded algorithm A_L with oracle $L' \in \Sigma_{k-1}$. By the inductive hypothesis there is a decision problem $B \in \mathsf{P}$ such that

$$L' = \{z \mid \exists y_2 \in A \, \forall y_3 \in A \ldots Q \, y_k \in A : (z, y_2, \ldots, y_k) \in B\} \, .$$

There are two polynomials q and r such that the algorithm A_L on input x queries the oracle L' at most $q(|x|)$ times with queries of length at most $r(|x|)$. We can easily modify A_L and L' so that on every computation path for every input z of length $|x|$ exactly $q(|x|)$ queries are made, each of length $r(|x|)$. Then $x \in L$ if and only if there is an accepting computation path w with corresponding oracle queries $b_1, \ldots, b_{q(|x|)}$ and oracle answers $a_1, \ldots, a_{q(|x|)}$. We want to express this in a quantified expression of the desired form.

The quantified expression begins

$$\exists w, b_1, \ldots, b_{q(|x|)}, a_1, \ldots, a_{q(|x|)} \, .$$

Let C^* be the set of all $(x, w, b_1, \ldots, b_{q(|x|)}, a_1, \ldots, a_{q(|x|)})$, such that

- the ith query of A_L on input x along the computation path w is b_i if the previous queries are $b_1, \ldots, b_{i-1}$ and the answers received are $a_1, \ldots, a_{i-1}$; and
- x is accepted along this path.

Clearly $C^* \in \mathsf{P}$. It remains to check whether the answer a_i is the correct answer to query b_i. If $a_i = 1$, then we can check this answer via the formula

$$\exists y_2^i \in A \; \forall y_3^i \in A \ldots \; Q \, y_k^i \in A : (b_i, y_2^i, \ldots, y_k^i) \in B \; .$$

If $a_i = 0$, then we can check this answer via the formula

$$\forall y_2^i \in A \; \exists y_3^i \in A \ldots \; Q \, y_k^i \in A : (b_i, y_2^i, \ldots, y_k^i) \in \overline{B} \; .$$

Since a_i is not known in advance, we must combine both of these cases allowing the decision problem access to a_i:

$$\exists y_1^i \in A \; \forall y_2^i \in A \ldots \; Q \, y_k^i \in A : (b_i, a_i, y_1^i, \ldots, y_k^i) \in B^* \; ,$$

where B^* contains all vectors with $a_i = 1$ and $(b_i, y_1^i, \ldots, y_{k-1}^i) \in B$, and all vectors with $a_i = 0$ and $(b_i, y_2^i, \ldots, y_k^i) \in \overline{B}$. Here we see that the case $a_i = 0$ increases the number of quantifier alternations by 1. Now we can bring all these statements together. The first existential quantifier is over w and all b_i, a_i, y_1^i, $1 \le i \le q(|x|)$. The following universal quantifier is over all y_2^i, $1 \le i \le q(|x|)$. This continues until the kth quantifier. Finally, the decision problem B contains all $(x, w, b_1, a_1, y_1^1, \ldots, y_k^1, \ldots, b_{q(|x|)}, a_{q(|x|)}, y_1^{q(|x|)}, \ldots, y_k^{q(|x|)})$ with $(x, w, b_1, \ldots, b_{q(|x|)}, a_1, \ldots, a_{q(|x|)}) \in C^*$ and $(b_i, a_i, y_1^i, \ldots, y_k^i) \in B^*$, $1 \le i \le q(|x|)$. So $B' \in \mathsf{P}$. Now it is only a technical detail to make sure that behind each quantifier there is a Boolean variable vector of the same polynomial length $p'(|x|)$. □

Using DeMorgan's laws we obtain the following corollary.

Corollary 10.4.4. *A decision problem is in Π_k if and only if there is a polynomial p and a decision problem $L' \in \mathsf{P}$ such that if we let $A = \{0, 1\}^{p(|x|)}$, then*

$$L = \{x \mid \forall y_1 \in A \; \exists y_2 \in A \ldots \; Q \, y_k \in A : (x, y_1, \ldots, y_k) \in L'\} \; . \qquad □$$

Here is a summary of the results we have achieved:

> *The complexity classes Σ_k and Π_k contain problems that can be described with $k-1$ quantifier alternations, polynomially many variables, and a polynomial-time decidable predicate. They differ in the type of the first quantifier. The hypothesis that these classes are all different is the hypothesis that each new quantifier increases the descriptive power of such formulas and that it matters which type of quantifier is used first.*

This logical perspective simplifies the proof of the following results.

Theorem 10.4.5. *If $\Sigma_k = \Pi_k$, then $\mathsf{PH} = \Sigma_k$.*

This theorem clearly means that under the assumption that $\Sigma_k = \Pi_k$, the complexity landscape in Figure 10.4.1 "collapses" above $\Sigma_k \cap \Pi_k$, since all higher classes are equal to $\Sigma_k \cap \Pi_k$. So the complexity theoretical hypothesis $\Sigma_{k+1} \neq \Sigma_k$ is a stronger assumption than $\Sigma_k \neq \Sigma_{k-1}$, and the NP $\neq$ P-hypothesis is the weakest of all these assumptions. As was shown in Section 10.2, it follows from NP = P that NP = co-NP, i.e., that $\Sigma_1 = \Pi_1$ and PH = P.

Proof. We will show that $\Sigma_k = \Pi_k$ implies that $\Sigma_{k+1} = \Pi_{k+1} = \Sigma_k$. The argument can be completed using induction on k.

In the proof of Theorem 10.4.3 we proceeded very formally. Here we want to argue more intuitively. As an example, let's look at the case $k = 4$. From the perspective of Theorem 10.4.3, $\Sigma_4 = \Pi_4$, means that

$$\exists \forall \exists \forall \; P = \forall \exists \forall \exists \; P \; . \tag{10.1}$$

Behind the quantifiers we may only have polynomially many variables and P stands for decision problems from P, which may be different on the two sides of the equation. Now we consider Σ_5, that is, a problem of the form $\exists (\forall \exists \forall \exists \; P)$. The parentheses are not needed, but they are there to indicate that we want to apply Equation 10.1 to the bracketed expression to obtain an expression of the form $\exists \exists \forall \exists \forall \; P$. Two quantifiers of the same type can be brought together as a single quantifier. So every Σ_5-problem can be written in the form $\exists \forall \exists \forall \; P$ and so belongs to Σ_4. It follows that $\Sigma_5 = \Sigma_4 = \Pi_4$. $\Pi_5 = \Pi_4 = \Sigma_4$ follows analogously. $\qquad \square$

Corollary 10.4.6. *If* $\Sigma_k = \Sigma_{k+1}$, *then* PH $= \Sigma_k$.

Proof. $\Sigma_k \subseteq \Pi_{k+1}$. From $\Sigma_k = \Sigma_{k+1}$ it follows that $\Sigma_{k+1} \subseteq \Pi_{k+1}$ and by Lemma 10.4.2 $\Sigma_{k+1} = \Pi_{k+1}$ as well. Now Theorem 10.4.5 implies that PH $= \Sigma_{k+1}$. Together with the hypothesis of the corollary, it follows that PH $= \Sigma_k$. $\qquad \square$

The logical perspective of Theorem 10.4.3 leads to a canonical generalization of the well-known satisfiability problems like $\textsc{Sat}_{\text{CIR}}$ to *satisfiability problems of level k*. These problems deal with circuits C on k variable vectors $x_1, \ldots, x_k$ of length n so that for $A = \{0, 1\}^n$ we have

$$\exists x_1 \in A \; \forall x_2 \in A \ldots \; Q \, x_k \in A : C(x) = 1.$$

Here we let $C(x)$ denote the value of the circuit C when the input is $x = (x_1, \ldots, x_k)$. Since it is possible in polynomial time to verify the statement "$C(x) = 1$", it follows by Theorem 10.4.3 that $\textsc{Sat}_{\text{CIR}}^k \in \Sigma_k$. Just as SAT and $\textsc{Sat}_{\text{CIR}}$ are canonical candidates for NP $-$ P, $\textsc{Sat}_{\text{CIR}}^k$ is a canonical candidate for $\Sigma_k - \Sigma_{k-1}$. Of course, we have in MC a practically relevant problem that we suspect is in $\Pi_2 - \Pi_1$, but for very large values of k we can't expect to have practically relevant problems that we suspect are in $\Sigma_k - \Sigma_{k-1}$. How can we support the conjecture that there is a problem in $\Sigma_k - \Sigma_{k-1}$? Just as in the theory of NP-completeness it follows for Σ_k-complete problems L (see Definition 5.1.1) that either $\Sigma_k = \Sigma_{k-1}$ or $L \notin \Sigma_{k-1}$. Since we conjecture that $\Sigma_k \neq \Sigma_{k-1}$, we again have a strong indication that $L \notin \Sigma_{k-1}$.

With methods similar to those used in the proof of Cook's Theorem (Theorem 5.4.3), we obtain the following result.

Theorem 10.4.7. $\text{SAT}^k_{\text{CIR}}$ *is Σ_k-complete.*   □

Since the proof of Theorem 10.4.7 presents no new methods or ideas, we will omit it and conclude:

At every level Σ_k of the polynomial hierarchy there are complete problems. These complete problems are canonical candidates to separate the complexity classes Σ_{k-1} and Σ_k.

We have seen that PH = P follows from NP = P. This can serve as an additional argument for the NP $\neq$ P-hypothesis. We can extend the question of whether NP = P or NP $\neq$ P to oracle classes. We can ask whether NP(L) = P(L) or NP$(L) \neq$ P(L). If $L \in$ P, then this question is the same as the question of whether NP = P or NP $\neq$ P. One might even wager the conjecture that either for all languages L the relation NP(L) = P(L) holds or for all languages L the relation NP$(L) \neq$ P(L) holds. But this is false. There are languages A and B such that

$$\text{NP}(A) = \text{P}(A)$$

and

$$\text{NP}(B) \neq \text{P}(B) .$$

What does this result mean? We are not really interested in the oracles A and B, but we have here an indication about what sorts of proof methods *cannot* be used to prove NP $\neq$ P. Any attempted proof of NP $\neq$ P that uses techniques that would also imply NP$(A) \neq$ P(A) cannot succeed. There have already been several unsuccessful attempts to prove NP $\neq$ P where it was difficult to find the error in the proof. Nevertheless, one knew immediately that they could not be correct because NP$(A) \neq$ P(A) would have followed by the same techniques. Such restrictions on proof techniques limit the possible ways to prove the NP $\neq$ P-conjecture. A concentration of effort on fewer methods perhaps increases the chances of a solution of the NP $\neq$ P-question.

10.5 BPP, NP, and the Polynomial Hierarchy

The complexity classes BPP and NP play central roles in complexity theory: BPP is the class of problems efficiently solvable using randomized algorithms, and NP is the basis class for NP-completeness theory and contains many problems (in particular the NP-complete problems) that presumably are not efficiently solvable. What is the relationship between these two classes? It is

worthwhile to recall the differences between the underlying randomized algorithms of these two classes:

- NP algorithms: one-sided error, but large error-probability, e.g. $1 - 2^{-n}$.
- BPP algorithms: error-probability severely limited, e.g. by 2^{-n}, but two-
  sided error.

So it is at least possible that these classes are incomparable with respect to
the subset relation. On the other hand, our intuition is that BPP is "not much
bigger" than P, and so the inclusion BPP $\subseteq$ NP would add to our picture of
the complexity landscape without shaking the prevailing hypotheses such as
NP $\neq$ P. With respect to the polynomial hierarchy, the best known result is
that BPP $\subseteq \Sigma_2 \cap \Pi_2$. We will present the proof of this result in such a way
that we can draw further consequences from it.

Theorem 10.5.1. BPP $\subseteq \Sigma_2 \cap \Pi_2$.

Proof. Since by definition BPP = co-BPP, it is sufficient to show that BPP $\subseteq$
Σ_2. It then follows immediately that BPP = co-BPP $\subseteq$ co-$\Sigma_2 = \Pi_2$.

So let $L \in$ BPP be given. By Theorem 3.3.6 there is a randomized algorithm
for L with polynomial worst-case runtime and an error-probability bounded by
$2^{-(n+1)}$. Furthermore, we can assume that every computation path has length
$p(|x|)$ and that $p(n)$ is divisible by n. Since in the analysis that follows we will
need the inequality $p(n)/n \leq 2^n$, we will first deal with the at most finitely
many input lengths for which this is not the case. For these finitely many
inputs, a polynomial-time algorithm can simulate the randomized algorithm
on all computation paths and compute the correct result without losing the
property of being a polynomial-time algorithm.

For each input x of length n by our assumptions there are exactly $2^{p(n)}$
computation paths of the BPP algorithm. Because of the small error-rate, only
very few of these, namely at most $2^{p(n)-(n+1)}$ many, can give the wrong result.
For an input x we will let $A(x)$ be the set of computation paths $r \in \{0, 1\}^{p(n)}$
on which the BPP algorithm accepts, and $N(x)$ the set of remaining paths.
For all $x \in L$, $A(x)$ is much larger than $N(x)$. So for "significantly many"
$x \in L$, there must in fact be a common accepting computation path. On the
other hand, for $x \notin L$, the set $A(x)$ is very small. We want to take advantage
of this difference.

Let $k(n)$ be a size to be specified later. We will abbreviate $k(n)$ as k and
$p(n)$ as p in order to simplify the formulas. Let B be the language of all
triples (x, r, z) consisting of an input $x \in \{0, 1\}^n$ for the decision problem
L, k computation paths $r_1, \ldots, r_k \in \{0, 1\}^p$, and a so-called computation
path transformation $z \in \{0, 1\}^p$, for which $r_i \oplus z$ is in $A(x)$ for at least
one i. Here $\oplus$ stands for the component-wise exclusive or on vectors from
$\{0, 1\}^p$. The function $h_z(r) := r \oplus z$ is a bijective function onto the set $\{0, 1\}^p$
of computation paths. Since in deterministic polynomial time it is possible
to simulate a randomized algorithm with polynomially-bounded runtime on

polynomially many specified computation paths, $B \in P$ if k is polynomially bounded.

But what good is the problem B? We want to characterize L in the following way in order to use Theorem 10.4.3 to show that L is a member of Σ_2:

$$L = \{x \mid \exists r = (r_1, \ldots, r_k) \in \{0,1\}^{pk} \; \forall z \in \{0,1\}^p : (x, r, z) \in B\} . \quad (10.2)$$

What intuition do we have that such a characterization is possible? We have seen that many, but not necessarily all $x \in L$ have a common accepting path. By choosing sufficiently many computation paths $r_1, \ldots, r_k$, we can hope that for each $x \in L$ each transformation z transforms at least one of them into an accepting path. For $x \notin L$, the number of accepting paths is so small that this must fail to happen for at least one transformation z. This intuition can be confirmed for the choice $k := p/n$.

First let $x \in L$ and let $R(x)$ be the set of "bad" $r = (r_1, \ldots, r_k)$, i.e., the set of r for which there is a $z \in \{0,1\}^p$ such that for all i, $r_i \oplus z \in N(x)$. By showing that $|R(x)| < 2^{kp}$, we show the existence of a "good" r-vector such that for $x \in L$ the characterization above is correct. If $w_i = r_i \oplus z$, then $w_i \oplus z = r_i$. Thus $R(x)$ is the set of all $(w_1 \oplus z, \ldots, w_k \oplus z)$ such that $z \in \{0,1\}^p$ and $w_i \in N(x)$ for all i. So $|R(x)| \leq |N(x)|^k \cdot 2^p$. Since $x \in L$, by the small error-probability we have $|N(x)| \leq 2^{p-(n+1)}$. Because $k = p/n$ it follows that

$$|R(x)| \leq 2^{(p-(n+1)) \cdot k} \cdot 2^p = 2^{pk+p-nk-k} = 2^{pk-k} \leq \frac{1}{2} \cdot 2^{pk} .$$

This implies that at least half of the r-vectors are good.

Now suppose $x \notin L$. Since $|A(x)| \leq 2^{p-(n+1)}$, it follows that $|N(x)| \geq 2^p - 2^{p-(n+1)}$. Let $r = (r_1, \ldots, r_k) \in \{0,1\}^{pk}$ be given. We will show that there is a z such that $(x, r, z) \notin B$. For this to happen it must be that $r_i \oplus z \in N(x)$ for all i. We will let $Z_i(r)$ denote that set of all z such that $r_i \oplus z \in N(x)$. Because the $\oplus$-operator is bijective, $|Z_i(r)| = |N(x)| \geq 2^p - 2^{p-(n+1)}$. So there are at most $2^{p-(n+1)}$ z-vectors that are not contained in $Z_i(r)$. Thus there are at most $k \cdot 2^{p-(n+1)}$ z-vectors that are not contained in at least one $Z_j(r)$. Now consider values of n for which $k \leq 2^n$. Then $k \cdot 2^{p-(n+1)} \leq \frac{1}{2} \cdot 2^p$ and there is at least one z-vector that belongs to all $Z_i(r)$. For this z-vector $r_i \oplus z \in N(x)$ for all i, and thus $(x, r, z) \notin B$.

This verifies that L has the characterization given in Equation 10.2 and thus that $L \in \Sigma_2$. □

Our proof of Theorem 10.5.1 actually shows a slightly stronger result. We have just shown that $L \in \Sigma_2 = \text{NP(NP)}$. The NP-oracle used was "$\exists z \in \{0,1\}^p$ such that $(x, r, z) \notin B$". The nondeterministic algorithm generates $r = (r_1, \ldots, r_k)$ randomly. For $x \notin L$, the error-probability is 0. For $x \in L$, at most half of the r-vectors are bad and don't accept x, so the error-probability is bounded by $1/2$. So the outer algorithm is an RP algorithm. With an obvious definition, we have that L is actually contained in RP(NP).

Definition 10.5.2. *For a decision problem L the complexity class* RP(L) *contains all decision problems L' that can be decided by an* RP *algorithm with an oracle for L. For a class of decision problems $\mathcal{C}$ the complexity class* RP($\mathcal{C}$) *is the union of all* RP(L) *for $L \in \mathcal{C}$.*

ZPP(L), ZPP($\mathcal{C}$), BPP(L), BPP($\mathcal{C}$), PP(L), *and* PP($\mathcal{C}$) *are defined analogously.*

Using this definition we can formulate the preceding discussion as the following theorem.

Theorem 10.5.3. BPP $\subseteq$ RP(NP) $\cap$ co-RP(NP). $\qquad\qquad\qquad\qquad$ □

So at least we know that BPP contains no problems that are "far" from NP.

While BPP $\subseteq$ NP would be a new, far-reaching but not completely surprising result, a proof that NP $\subseteq$ BPP would completely destroy our picture of the complexity theory world. It is true that this would not immediately imply that NP = P, but all NP-complete problems would be solvable in polynomial time with small error-probability. That is, they would for all practical purposes be efficiently solvable. We will show the implication "NP $\subseteq$ BPP $\Rightarrow$ NP $\subseteq$ RP". Thus anyone who believes that NP $\subseteq$ BPP must also believe that NP $\subseteq$ RP and thus that NP = RP. These consequences could shake the belief in NP $\subseteq$ BPP, should it be held. If NP = RP, then we can push error-probabilities of $1 - 2^{-n}$ with one-sided error to error-probabilities of 2^{-n}, still with one-sided error. Unbelievable, but not provably impossible. On the way to our goal, we will prove that BPP(BPP) = BPP. We know that P(P) = P and conjecture that NP(NP) $\neq$ NP. This result shows that BPP as an oracle in a BPP algorithm is not helpful. It is also another indication that BPP is different from NP.

Theorem 10.5.4. BPP(BPP) = BPP.

Proof. Let $L \in$ BPP(BPP). Then there is an oracle $L' \in$ BPP such that $L \in$ BPP(L'). Let A denote the outer BPP algorithm. Let its worst-case runtime be bounded by the polynomial p_1 and its error-probability by $1/6$. (For the latter we use Theorem 3.3.6.) Let A' denote the BPP algorithm for L'. By Theorem 3.3.6 we can assume that the error-probability for A' is bounded by $1/(6 \cdot p_1(|x|))$. We replace the oracle queries with calls to the algorithm A'. The result is a new randomized algorithm that runs in polynomial time without any oracle. This algorithm can only make an error if the simulation of A' makes an error or the outer BPP algorithm makes an error despite a correct result from the simulation of A'. So the error-probability of our new algorithm is at most $p_1(|x|)/(6 \cdot p_1(|x|)) + 1/6 = 1/3$ and we have designed a BPP algorithm for L. $\qquad\qquad\qquad\qquad$ □

Remark 10.5.5. Since Theorem 3.3.6 also holds for all problems with unique solutions, we can generalize Theorem 10.5.4 with the same proof to the class of all BPP-problems with unique solutions. We will take advantage of this generalization later.

The following corollary hints that NP $\not\subseteq$ BPP.

Corollary 10.5.6. NP $\subseteq$ BPP $\Rightarrow$ PH $\subseteq$ BPP.

Proof. It suffices to show that for all k the inclusion $\Sigma_k \subseteq$ BPP follows from NP $\subseteq$ BPP. An obvious, but not quite correct, proof of the inductive step is the following:

$$\begin{aligned}
\Sigma_{k+1} &= \mathsf{NP}(\Sigma_k) \\
&\subseteq \mathsf{NP}(\mathsf{BPP}) \\
&\subseteq \mathsf{BPP}(\mathsf{BPP}) \\
&\subseteq \mathsf{BPP} ,
\end{aligned}$$

using the inductive hypothesis, the assumption that NP $\subseteq$ BPP, and Theorem 10.5.4, respectively for the three implications. The problem with this proof is that we have not shown that $\mathsf{NP}(\mathcal{C}) \subseteq \mathsf{BPP}(\mathcal{C})$ follows from NP $\subseteq$ BPP.

As it turns out $\mathsf{NP}(\mathsf{BPP}) \subseteq \mathsf{BPP}(\mathsf{NP})$ (without any additional assumptions) as we show in Lemma 10.5.7 below, and this suffices to complete our proof:

$$\begin{aligned}
\Sigma_{k+1} &= \mathsf{NP}(\Sigma_k) \\
&\subseteq \mathsf{NP}(\mathsf{BPP}) \\
&\subseteq \mathsf{BPP}(\mathsf{NP}) \\
&\subseteq \mathsf{BPP}(\mathsf{BPP}) \\
&= \mathsf{BPP} . \square
\end{aligned}$$

Lemma 10.5.7. $\mathsf{NP}(\mathsf{BPP}) \subseteq \mathsf{BPP}(\mathsf{NP})$.

Proof. Let $L \in \mathsf{NP}(\mathsf{BPP})$. We will let $n = |x|$ throughout this proof. This means that there is a language $B \in$ BPP and a polynomial p such that

$$x \in L \Leftrightarrow \exists y \in \{0,1\}^{p(n)} : (x,y) \in B .$$

Furthermore, by Theorem 3.3.6, there must be a BPP algorithm A_B for B with runtime bounded by a polynomial $q(n)$ and with error-probability bounded by $2^{-p(n)-2}$. Let C be the language consisting of all triples (x,y,r) such that $y \in \{0,1\}^{p(n)}$, $r \in \{0,1\}^{q(n)}$, and A_B accepts (x,y) along computation path r. Clearly $C \in$ P.

Now we give a BPP algorithm for L using an NP-oracle: on input x, randomly generate $r \in \{0,1\}^{q(n)}$ and accept if and only if there is a y such that $(x,y,r) \in C$. This algorithm can be carried out in polynomial time using an NP-oracle since $C \in$ P. It remains to show that the error-probability is appropriately bounded.

If $x \in L$, then there is a y_x such that $(x, y_x) \in B$, and hence

$$\begin{aligned}
\mathrm{Prob}(\text{our algorithm accepts } x) &= \mathrm{Prob}_r(\exists y : (x,y,r) \in C) \\
&\geq \mathrm{Prob}_r((x,y_x,r) \in C) \\
&\geq 1 - 2^{p(n)-2} .
\end{aligned}$$

And if $x \notin L$, then

$$\forall y \colon \mathrm{Prob}_r((x, y, r) \in C) \leq 2^{-p(n)-2} \, ,$$

so

$$\mathrm{Prob}_r(\exists y \colon (x, y, r) \in C) \leq 2^{p(n)} \cdot 2^{-p(n)-2} = 1/4 \, .$$

Thus our algorithm has two-sided error bounded by $1/4$, and $L \in \mathsf{BPP(NP)}$.

$\square$

Remark 10.5.8. Our proof of Lemma 10.5.7 can be generalized. (See, for example, Chapter 2 of Köbler, Schöning, and Torán (1993).) It is also worth noting that we are not using the full power of $\mathsf{BPP(NP)}$ in our proof, since only very limited access to the NP-oracle is required. This will lead to the definition of the $\mathsf{BP}(\cdot)$ operator in Section 11.3.

Now we come to the result announced above.

Theorem 10.5.9. $\mathsf{NP} \subseteq \mathsf{BPP} \Rightarrow \mathsf{NP} = \mathsf{RP}$.

Proof. By definition $\mathsf{RP} \subseteq \mathsf{NP}$, so we only need to show that $\mathsf{NP} \subseteq \mathsf{RP}$ follows from $\mathsf{NP} \subseteq \mathsf{BPP}$. For this it is sufficient to show that if $\mathsf{NP} \subseteq \mathsf{BPP}$, then $L \in \mathsf{RP}$ for some NP-complete problem L. All other problems in NP can be polynomially reduced to L.

We consider three variants of GC. Recall that GC is the problem of deciding for a graph $G = (V, E)$ and a number k whether the vertices of G can be assigned colors from a set of k colors in such a way that adjacent vertices always have different colors and that GC is NP-complete (Theorem 6.5.2). Colorings are arbitrary vectors $c = (c_1, \ldots, c_n) \in \{1, \ldots, n\}^n$, where c_i is the color of the ith vertex. Thus we can order colorings lexicographically. We will call a coloring legal if the two ends of each edge have different colors. LexGC is the problem of computing $f(G)$, the lexicographically least legal coloring that uses the fewest number of colors possible. This is not a decision problem, but it is a search problem with a unique solution. Finally, let MinGC be the problem of deciding for (G, c) with $c \in \{1, \ldots, n\}^n$ whether $c \geq f(G)$. In instances of this problem c is not required to be a legal coloring of G.

The statement $(G, c) \in \mathrm{MinGC}$ is equivalent to

$$\exists c' \in \{1, \ldots, n\}^n \ \forall c'' \in \{1, \ldots, n\}^n \colon \ (G, c, c', c'') \in B \, ,$$

where B contains the tuples (G, c, c', c'') such that

- c' is a legal coloring of G,
- $c' \leq c$, and
- at least one of the following conditions holds:
  - c'' is not a legal coloring of G,
  - $c'' \geq c'$,
  - c'' uses more colors than c'.

Clearly $B \in \mathsf{P}$, and by Theorem 10.4.3 this characterization of $(G, c) \in \mathrm{MINGC}$ shows that $\mathrm{MINGC} \in \Sigma_2$.

By Corollary 10.5.6, if $\mathsf{NP} \subseteq \mathsf{BPP}$, then $\mathsf{PH} \subseteq \mathsf{BPP}$. So in particular, $\mathrm{MINGC} \in \mathsf{BPP}$. Using binary search on $\{1, \ldots, n\}^n$, we can solve LEXGC with at most $\lceil \log n^n \rceil = \lceil n \log n \rceil$ queries to an oracle for MINGC, so $\mathrm{LEXGC} \in \mathsf{P(BPP)}$. By Remark 10.5.5, LEXGC can be solved in polynomial time by a randomized algorithm A with error-probability bounded by $1/3$. From this we can construct an RP algorithm A' for GC, proving the theorem.

The randomized algorithm A' receives as input a graph G and a number k. First A is simulated on input G. Let the result be c. A' accepts input (G, k) if and only if c is a legal coloring of G with at most k colors. The runtime of A' is polynomially bounded. If $(G, k) \notin \mathrm{GC}$, then there are no legal colorings of G with at most k colors, and the input (G, k) will be rejected with probability 1. If $(G, k) \in \mathrm{GC}$, then A' only fails to accept if A on input G made an error. So A' is an algorithm with one-sided error and an error-probability bounded by $1/3$.   □

The investigation of oracle classes has contributed to a better understanding of the relationships between classes we are interested in such as NP, BPP, *and* RP.

11

Interactive Proofs

11.1 Fundamental Considerations

In this chapter we define complexity classes in terms of interactive proofs. The motivation for these definitions is not immediately apparent, but the study of interactive proofs results in complexity classes with interesting properties and relationships to the complexity classes we already know. Much more important, however, are the results regarding the complexity of particular problems that can be obtained using this new perspective. In Section 11.3 we will present the arguments that we have already alluded to that lead us to believe that GRAPHISOMORPHISM is probably not NP-complete. In Section 11.4 we discuss interactive proofs that are convincing but do not reveal the core of the proof. Such proofs can be used in identification protocols. Finally, the PCP Theorem (see Chapter 12) and the theory of the complexity of approximation problems that arises from this theorem are based on the perspective introduced here, namely of solving problems via interactive proofs. Before we introduce the notion of interactive proof in Section 11.2 – a notion that goes back to Goldwasser, Micali, and Rackoff (1989) – we want to take a look at the notion of proof more generally.

Even in mathematics, the notion of a "formal proof" is fairly new. Strictly speaking, a formal proof requires a finite axiom system and a set of rules for drawing inferences from the axioms and already proven theorems. The advantage of this kind of proof is that it is easy to check the correctness of a proposed proof.

But the disadvantages of formal proofs outweigh their advantages. Formal proofs become unreadably long and obfuscate the important ideas of the proof. In the strict sense, this book contains no formal proofs. In practice, proofs are presented in such a way as to make them understandable. They are considered accepted when experts responsible for refereeing the results for a technical journal accept the proof. Often even these experts cannot understand the proof, and so they do not accept it, even though they cannot find an error. The referees then respond with questions for the authors in order to clarify the critical points in the proof. This interactive process continues until it becomes clear whether or not the proof can be accepted.

Thus the current reality is closer to the historical notion of proof. Socrates saw proofs as dialogues between students and teachers. The individuals involved in these dialogues have very different roles. The teacher knows a lot, and in particular knows the proof, while the student has more limited knowledge. We want to use such a role playing scenario in order to define complexity classes.

The role of the teacher will be played by a *prover*, Paul, and the role of the student will be played by a *verifier*, Victoria. Their tasks can be described as follows. For a decision problem L and an input x, Paul wants to prove that $x \in L$, and Victoria must check this proof. If $x \in L$, then there should be a proof that Victoria can efficiently check, but if $x \notin L$, then Victoria should be able to refute any proof attempt of Paul. The important difference between Paul and Victoria is that Paul has unlimited computation time but Victoria has only polynomial time to do her work.

In this model we can easily recognize the class NP. If $L \in$ NP, then by the logical characterization of NP there must be a language $L' \in$ P and a polynomial p such that

$$L = \{x \mid \exists y \in \{0,1\}^{p(|x|)} : (x,y) \in L'\} \, .$$

Given a proposed proof y from Paul, Victoria's polynomial verification algorithm consists of checking whether $(x,y) \in L'$. If $x \in L$, then there is a proof y that convinces Victoria. But if $x \notin L$, then every proof attempt y will be recognized as invalid.

If we consider classes like co-NP or Σ_k, the logical characterizations of which make use of a universal quantifier, the situation is a little different. For a characterization $\exists y_1 \forall y_2 \exists y_3 : (x, y_1, y_2, y_3) \in L'$ we can imagine a dialogue in which Paul begins with a proof attempt y_1 and in response to y_2 from Victoria finishes with the second part of the proof y_3. Now Victoria can check whether $(x, y_1, y_2, y_3) \in L'$. If $x \in L$, then this dialogue will work. But if $x \notin L$, then it could be the case that there is only *one* value y_2 for which Paul would be unable to find a value y_3 that leads Victoria to incorrectly accept x. Since Victoria only has polynomial time, perhaps she will be unable to compute this value y_2. Clearly a random choice for y_2 doesn't help in this case either. The situation is different, however, if there are sufficiently many such y_2 and we allow Victoria a small probability of making an error. After all, incorrect proofs are occasionally published even in refereed technical journals. So we will define interactive proofs in terms of randomized dialogues and small error-probabilities.

11.2 Interactive Proof Systems

Now that we have motivated the notion of interactive proofs and discussed possible realizations, we come to the formal definition.

Definition 11.2.1. *An* interactive proof system *consists of a communication protocol between two parties P (Paul, prover) and V (Victoria, verifier), each of which has a randomized algorithm. The communication protocol specifies who sends the first message. After a number of communication rounds that may depend on the input and on randomness, Victoria must decide whether or not to accept the input. The computation time for Victoria is bounded by a polynomial.*

We use $D_{P,V}(x)$ to denote the random variable that describes whether x is accepted by Victoria at the end of the protocol. $D_{P,V}(x)$ takes on the value 1 if x is accepted and 0 if x is rejected. The requirement that the algorithms P and V abide by the communication protocol C will be tacitly assumed throughout the following discussion.

Definition 11.2.2. *A decision problem L belongs to the complexity class* IP *if there is a communication protocol C and a randomized polynomial-time bounded algorithm V with the properties that*

- *There is a randomized algorithm P such that for all $x \in L$,*

$$\mathrm{Prob}(D_{P,V}(x) = 1) \geq 3/4 \, .$$

- *For all randomized algorithms P, if $x \notin L$, then*

$$\mathrm{Prob}(D_{P,V}(x) = 1) \leq 1/4 \, .$$

A problem $L \in$ IP belongs to IP(k) *if the communication protocol in the definition above allows at most k communication rounds, that is, at most k messages are exchanged.*

We can always arrange that Paul sends the last message, since it doesn't help Victoria any to send a message to which she receives no reply. The allowable error-probability of $1/4$ that appears in Definition 11.2.2 is to a certain extent arbitrary. Without increasing the number of communication rounds required, Paul and Victoria could carry out polynomially many simultaneous dialogues. At the end, Victoria could use the majority of these polynomially many individual "mini-decisions" as her decision for the expanded protocol. So by Theorem 3.3.6, the error-probability can be reduced from $1/2 - 1/p(n)$ to $2^{-q(n)}$, where p and q are polynomials. It is therefore sufficient to design interactive proof systems with an error-probability $1/2 - 1/p(n)$ to obtain interactive proof systems with error-probability $2^{-q(n)}$.

In Section 11.1 we informally discussed an interactive proof system for problems $L \in$ NP. There we only required one communication round in which

Paul sent y to Victoria. The decision of Victoria was to accept x if and only if $(x, y) \in L'$. Since this decision protocol is error-free, it follows that $NP \subseteq IP(1)$.

Since $IP(1)$ is already "quite large", we can suspect that IP is "really large". In fact, $IP = PSPACE$ (Shamir (1992)). Here $PSPACE$ denotes the class of all decision problems for which there are algorithms that require only polynomially bounded storage space (see Chapter 13). Since we will show in Chapter 13 that all the complexity classes of the polynomial hierarchy belong to $PSPACE$, IP is indeed a very large complexity class. We will concentrate our attention on interactive proof systems with a small number of communication rounds.

11.3 Regarding the Complexity of Graph Isomorphism Problems

To simplify notation, for the rest of this chapter we will use GI as an abbreviation for GRAPHISOMORPHISM. Recall that GI is the problem of determining whether two graphs $G_0 = (V_0, E_0)$ and $G_1 = (V_1, E_1)$ are isomorphic. They are isomorphic if they are identical up to the labeling of their vertices, that is, if G_1 is the result of applying a relabeling of the vertices to the graph G_0. The relabeling $\pi \colon V_0 \to V_1$ must be bijective and satisfy

$$\{u, v\} \in E_0 \Leftrightarrow \{\pi(u), \pi(v)\} \in E_1 .$$

It is simple to check whether $|V_0| = |V_1|$. Graphs with different numbers of vertices cannot be isomorphic, so we will assume in what follows that $V_0 = V_1 = \{1, \ldots, n\}$, and thus the set of bijections $\pi \colon \{1, \ldots, n\} \to \{1, \ldots, n\}$ is just the set S_n of permutations on $\{1, \ldots, n\}$.

Since $NP \subseteq IP(1)$, $GI \in IP(1)$. The proof consists of giving a suitable permutation π. Because of the asymmetry between Paul and Victoria and the difficulty of realizing universal quantifiers in an interactive proof system, most experts do not believe that $co\text{-}NP \subseteq IP(1)$ or even that $co\text{-}NP \subseteq IP(2)$. In particular, it is believed that the $co\text{-}NP$-complete problems do not belong to $IP(2)$. For this reason, the following result showing that $\overline{GI} \in IP(2)$ is an indication that GI is not NP-complete.

Theorem 11.3.1. $\overline{GI} \in IP(2)$.

Proof. The input consists of two graphs G_0 and G_1 with $V_0 = V_1 = \{1, \ldots, n\}$. Paul and Victoria use the following interactive proof system.

- Victoria randomly generates $i \in \{0, 1\}$ and $\pi \in S_n$. Then she computes $H = \pi(G_i)$, the graph that results from applying the permutation π to graph G_i, and sends the graph H to Paul.
- Paul computes $j \in \{0, 1\}$ and sends it to Victoria.
- Victoria accepts (G_0, G_1) if $i = j$. Accepting (G_0, G_1) means that Victoria believes the graphs G_0 and G_1 are *not* isomorphic.

Victoria can do her work in polynomial time. A permutation π can be represented as $(\pi(1), \ldots, \pi(n))$. When generating a random permutation, one must take care that each $\pi(i)$ is different from $\pi(1), \ldots, \pi(i-1)$. This can be done by generating the $\lceil \log(n - i + 1) \rceil$ bits of a random integer k which represents that for $\pi(i)$ we should choose the $(k+1)$st smallest as yet unused number. With probability less than $1/2$, $k > n - i + 1$ and so is too large. In this case we simply repeat the procedure up to n times. The probability that this method fails to produce a permuation is then less than $n/2^n$, which is so small that Victoria can just arbitrarily choose whether or not to accept the pair of graphs. By the robustness of the IP-classes with respect to small changes in the error-probability, this small amount of error won't make any difference. We have discussed the procedure for generating a random permutation in detail here, but in the future we will simply make statements like "generate a random $\pi \in S_n$" without further commentary.

If G_0 and G_1 are not isomorphic, then H is isomorphic to G_i but not to G_{1-i}. So Paul can determine i by applying all $\pi' \in S_n$ to G_0 and G_1, and comparing the results to H. He sets $j = i$ and sends this value to Victoria who will correctly accept (G_0, G_1). If Victoria decides to accept also in the (rare) case that she is unable to generate a random permutation, then this interactive proof system will have one-sided error.

If G_0 and G_1 are isomorphic, all three of the graphs that Paul has (G_0, G_1, and H) are isomorphic. In fact there will be exactly as many $\pi' \in S_n$ with $H = \pi'(G_0)$ as there are $\pi'' \in S_n$ with $H = \pi''(G_1)$. We want to take a closer look at this observation. Let $G^* = (V^*, E^*)$ with $V^* = \{1, 2, 3\}$ and $E^* = \{\{1, 2\}\}$. For π^* defined by $\pi^*(1) = 2$, $\pi^*(2) = 1$, $\pi^*(3) = 3$, we have $\pi^*(G^*) = G^*$. In general, the permutations π on G with $\pi(G) = G$ form the *automorphism group* of G, denoted $\operatorname{Aut}(G)$. These permutations form a group under composition of functions. Since the order (size) of a subgroup always divides the order of a group, $n!/|\operatorname{Aut}(G)|$ is an integer. We claim that there are exactly $|\operatorname{Aut}(H)|$ many $\pi' \in S_n$ with $H = \pi'(G_0)$. Since there is such a permutation π', the set of permutations $\pi^* \circ \pi'$ such that $\pi^* \in \operatorname{Aut}(H)$ form $|\operatorname{Aut}(H)|$ many permutations of the desired kind. Furthermore, there cannot be any more such permutations because if $\overline{\pi}(G_0) = H$ and $\pi'(G_0) = H$, then $\pi' \circ (\overline{\pi})^{-1}(H) = H$ and $\pi^* := \pi' \circ (\overline{\pi})^{-1} \in \operatorname{Aut}(H)$. So $(\pi^*)^{-1} \in \operatorname{Aut}(H)$ and $\overline{\pi} = (\pi^*)^{-1} \circ \pi'$ belongs to the set of permutations we already have.

By definition $\operatorname{Prob}(i = 0) = \operatorname{Prob}(i = 1) = 1/2$, and the only additional information for Paul is the random graph H. We have seen that H is (independent of the value of i) a random graph from the set of $n!/|\operatorname{Aut}(G_0)| = n!/|\operatorname{Aut}(G_1)|$ graphs that are isomorphic to G_0 and G_1. So $\operatorname{Prob}(i = 0 \mid H) = \operatorname{Prob}(i = 1 \mid H) = 1/2$ and Paul is in the situation of having to correctly provide the outcome of a fair coin toss. No matter how he decides, he will only succeed with probability $1/2$. So the entire interactive proof system has a one-sided error-probability just over $1/2$. For non-isomorphic graphs Victoria's decision is correct, and for isomorphic graphs, she makes an error with probability $\frac{1}{2} + \frac{n}{2^{n+1}}$. If we carry out the protocol twice and Victoria only accepts if both trials recommend acceptance, then her decision for non-isomorphic graphs remains correct and for isomorphic graphs the error-rate is approximately $1/4$. The number of communication rounds does not increase, since in each round the subprotocol can be carried out twice.   □

In the definition of interactive proof systems we combined nondeterminism and randomization with limited two-sided error, as we discussed in Section 11.1. The complexity class BP(NP) also combines nondeterminism and randomization (see Definition 10.5.2). In this case, a BPP algorithm may make repeated queries to an NP-oracle. In particular, the oracle answer may be negated and so BPP(NP) = co-BPP(NP). If instead we want to think of randomization as a "third quantifier" in addition to $\exists$ and $\forall$, then we want to rule out the negation of the oracle answer. This idea leads to the following definition of the operator BP($\cdot$) on a complexity class $\mathcal{C}$:

Definition 11.3.2. *A decision problem L belongs to BP($\mathcal{C}$) if there is a decision problem $L' \in \mathcal{C}$ with the following properties, where $r \in \{0,1\}^{p(|x|)}$ for some polynomial p and the probabilities are with respect to the choice of r:*

- *If $x \in L$, then $\mathrm{Prob}_r((x,r) \in L') \geq 3/4$.*

- *If $x \notin L$, then $\mathrm{Prob}_r((x,r) \in L') \leq 1/4$.*

It follows immediately from this definition that BP($\mathcal{C}$) $\subseteq$ BPP($\mathcal{C}$).

We can characterize BP(NP) as follows: There is a language $L' \in$ P and a polynomial p describing the lengths of r and y in dependence upon $|x|$ such that

- if $x \in L$, then $\mathrm{Prob}_r(\exists y \colon (x,r,y) \in L') \geq 3/4$;

- if $x \notin L$, then $\mathrm{Prob}_r(\exists y \colon (x,r,y) \in L') \leq 1/4$.

Note that our proof that NP(BPP) $\subseteq$ BPP(NP) (Lemma 10.5.7) actually showed that NP(BPP) $\subseteq$ BP(NP).

While for the class BP(NP) the entire computation time is polynomially bounded, for IP(2), Paul has unlimited time. The requirements regarding error-probability are the same for the two classes, so the following result is not surprising.

Theorem 11.3.3. BP(NP) $\subseteq$ IP(2).

Proof. Victoria and Paul use the characterization for a language $L \in$ BP(NP) given following Definition 11.3.2.

- Victoria randomly generates $r \in \{0,1\}^{p(|x|)}$ and sends r to Paul.
- Paul computes a $y \in \{0,1\}^{p(|x|)}$ and sends y to Victoria.
- Victoria accepts if $(x,r,y) \in L'$.

Since $L' \in$ P, Victoria can do her work in polynomial time. For all $y \in \{0,1\}^{p(|x|)}$ Paul can check the property $(x,r,y) \in L'$. If he finds a suitable y, he sends it to Victoria. If $x \in L$, this succeeds with probability at least $3/4$; but if $x \notin L$, then this succeeds with probability at most $1/4$. Thus $L \in$ IP(2).

$\square$

The interactive proof system used in the proof of Theorem 11.3.3 can also be described in the form of a fairy tale. King Arthur gives the wizard Merlin a task (x,r). Merlin is supposed to find y with $(x,r,y) \in L'$. This is a task that normal people cannot do in polynomial time, but Merlin is usually able to do it – even wizards must and can live with exponentially small error-probabilities. This view of BP(NP) has led to the names *Arthur-Merlin game* for this type of proof system and AM for the complexity class BP(NP).

By Theorem 11.3.3, a proof that $\overline{\mathrm{GI}} \in$ BP(NP) would be an even stronger indication that GI is not NP-complete. It is not known whether GI $\notin$ NPC follows from NP $\neq$ P. But from $\overline{\mathrm{GI}} \in$ BP(NP) and the assumption that $\Sigma_2 \neq \Pi_2$ (see Chapter 10) it follows that GI is not NP-complete. We will show this in Theorems 11.3.4 and 11.3.5.

Theorem 11.3.4. $\overline{\mathrm{GI}} \in$ BP(NP).

Proof. First we outline the basic ideas in the proof. Then we will go back and fill in the details. In order to show that $\overline{\mathrm{GI}} \in$ BP(NP), we are looking for a characterization of $\overline{\mathrm{GI}}$ that matches Definition 11.3.2. Let $x = (G_0, G_1)$. We can assume that G_0 and G_1 are defined on the vertex set $\{1, \ldots, n\}$. We will use $\equiv$ to represent graph isomorphism. So we need to come up with a y that contains enough information to distinguish between $G_0 \equiv G_1$ and $G_0 \not\equiv G_1$.

The basis for this distinction will be the sets

$$Y(G_i) := \{(H,\pi) \mid \pi \in \mathrm{Aut}(H) \text{ and } H \equiv G_i\},$$

and

$$Y := Y(G_0, G_1) := Y(G_0) \cup Y(G_1).$$

$|Y|$ can be used to determine whether $G_0 \equiv G_1$ or $G_0 \not\equiv G_1$. In the proof of Theorem 11.3.1 we saw that there are $n!/|\mathrm{Aut}(G_0)|$ many graphs H such that $H \equiv G_0$, so $|Y(G_i)| = n!$ for any graph G_i with n vertices. Furthermore, if $G_0 \equiv G_1$, then $Y(G_0) = Y(G_1)$, so $|Y| = |Y(G_0)| = n!$. But if $G_0 \not\equiv G_1$, then $Y(G_0) \cap Y(G_1) = \emptyset$, so $|Y| = |Y(G_0)| + |Y(G_1)| = 2n!$.

Of course, we don't see how to compute $|Y|$ efficiently. It suffices, however, to distinguish between the cases $|Y| = n!$ and $|Y| = 2n!$, which means that an approximate computation of $|Y|$ would be enough, and we may even allow a small error-probability. At the end of our proof we will see that the difference between $n!$ and $2n!$ is too small. So instead of Y we will use $Y' := Y \times Y \times Y \times Y \times Y$. Then $|Y'| = (n!)^5$, if $G_0 \equiv G_1$, and $|Y'| = 32 \cdot (n!)^5$, if $G_0 \not\equiv G_1$. The vector y from the characterization following Definition 11.3.2 will be made from strings y' and y''. The string y' must belong to Y', it is required that y' be a 0-1 string of fixed length, and we must be able to check whether $y' \in Y'$. The vector y'' will be another 0-1 string that will help us check whether $y' \in Y'$. A necessary condition for $(x, r, y) \in L'$ will therefore be that $y = (y', y'')$, where y' describes graphs $H_1, \ldots, H_5$ and permutations $\pi_1, \ldots, \pi_5$ and that y'' describes permutations $\alpha_1, \ldots, \alpha_5$ such that $\pi_i \in \mathrm{Aut}(H_i)$ and $H_i \equiv \alpha_i(G_0)$ or $H_i \equiv \alpha_i(G_1)$. These conditions can be checked in polynomial time.

Let the length of the description of y' be l. We will only consider such $y' \in \{0, 1\}^l$ that are contained in Y'. For reasons that will be clear shortly, we assume that $0^l \notin Y'$, which is certainly the case for obvious descriptions of graphs and permutations.

It's about time we describe how to obtain a randomized estimate for $|Y'|$. For this we will make use of a family of hash functions on the universe $U = \{0, 1\}^l$ with values in $\{0, 1\}^k$ for a value of k to be specified later. For a random choice of hash function from the family and for every $z \in \{0, 1\}^l$ with $z \neq 0^l$ we want to have the following property:

$$\mathrm{Prob}_h(h(z) = 0^k) = 2^{-k} .$$

We will be interested in the probability of the event "$\exists y' \in Y' : h(y') = 0^k$". It is obvious that this probability grows with $|Y'|$. Furthermore, for $z, z' \in \{0, 1\}^l$ such that $z \neq z'$, $z \neq 0^l$, and $z' \neq 0^l$, we want the events "$h(z) = 0^k$" and "$h(z') = 0^k$" to be independent. All probabilities are with respect to the random choice of a hash function.

Now we flesh out this proof idea. Our family of hash functions contains for each $k \times l$-matrix W over $\{0, 1\}$ the hash function $h_W(z) = W \cdot z$, where z is interpreted as a column vector and the computations are carried out in $\mathbb{Z}_2$, i.e., modulo 2. The random matrix W takes the place of the random vector r in the characterization following Definition 11.3.2. Finally, L' contains all $(x = (G_0, G_1), r = W, y = (y', y''))$ such that $y' \in Y'$, y'' contains the information described above for helping to check whether $y' \in Y'$, and $W \cdot y' = 0^k$. By the preceding discussion it is clear that $L' \in \mathrm{P}$, so it only remains to check the probability part of the characterization following Definition 11.3.2.

First we investigate the random hash function $h_W(z) = W \cdot z$. Here it will become clear why we must avoid the case that $z = 0^l$. We know for sure that $h_W(0^l) = 0^k$. Now let $z \neq 0^l$ and $z_j = 1$. The i-th bit of $h_W(z)$ is given by

$$w_{ij}z_j + \sum_{m \neq j} w_{im} \cdot z_m = w_{ij} + \sum_{m \neq j} w_{im} \cdot z_m$$

with sums taken mod 2. Since the values of $h_W(z)$ for $w_{ij} = 0$ and $w_{ij} = 1$ are different, the ith bit of $h_W(z)$ takes on the values 0 and 1 with probability $1/2$ each. Since the rows of W are chosen independently of each other, every value from $\{0, 1\}^k$ (including 0^k) has probability 2^{-k} of being equal to $h_W(z)$. Finally, if $z \neq z'$, $z \neq 0^l$, and $z' \neq 0^l$, then the random vectors $h_W(z)$ and $h_W(z')$ are independent. Suppose $z_j \neq z'_j$. Then $w_{ij}z_j = w_{ij}z'_j$ if and only if $w_{ij} = 0$, and therefore this event has probability $1/2$. Independent of the values of the sum of all $w_{im}z_m$ with $m \neq j$ and the sum of all $w_{im}z'_m$ with $m \neq j$, the ith bits of $h_W(z)$ and $h_W(z')$ agree with probability $1/2$. Once again the statement for vectors follows from the fact that the rows of W are chosen independently.

The next step is to investigate the random number S of all $y' \in Y'$ with $h_W(y') = 0^k$. The random variable S is the sum of the $|Y'|$ random variables $S(y')$, where $S(y') = 1$ if $h_W(y') = 0^k$ and otherwise $S(y') = 0$. By Remark A.2.3 it follows that $E(S(y')) = 2^{-k}$ and by Theorem A.2.4 it follows that $E(S) = |Y'| \cdot 2^{-k}$. Since $S(y')$ only takes on values 0 and 1, the variance is easy to compute straight from the definition: $V(S(y')) = 2^{-k} \cdot (1 - 2^{-k}) \leq 2^{-k}$. So by Theorem A.2.7, $V(S) \leq |Y'| \cdot 2^{-k} = E(S)$. Since $|Y'|$ is different in the two cases $G_0 \equiv G_1$ and $G_0 \not\equiv G_1$, it is good that $|Y'|$ shows up as a factor in the expected value of S. Furthermore, $V(S)$ is not very large.

The probability that we are interested in is

$$\text{Prob}(\exists y = (y', y'') : (x = (G_0, G_1), r = W, y = (y', y'')) \in L') .$$

If $y' \in Y'$, then there is also a corresponding y''. So we can represent the event more succinctly: we are interested in $\text{Prob}(\exists y' \in Y' : h_W(y') = 0^k)$, or using the notation used above, in $\text{Prob}(S \geq 1)$. This probability should be large if $E(S)$ is somewhat larger than 1, and small if $E(S)$ is somewhat smaller than 1. The choice of $k := \lceil \log(4 \cdot (n!)^5) \rceil$ achieves this.

If $G_0 \equiv G_1$, then

$$E(S) = (n!)^5 \cdot 2^{-\lceil \log(4 \cdot (n!)^5) \rceil} \leq 1/4 .$$

By the Markov Inequality (Theorem A.2.9) with $t = 1$,

$$\text{Prob}(S \geq 1) \leq E(S) \leq 1/4 ,$$

and we obtain for $(G_0, G_1) \notin \overline{GI}$ the desired small acceptance probability.

If $G_0 \not\equiv G_1$, then

$$E(S) = 32 \cdot (n!)^5 \cdot 2^{-\lceil \log(4 \cdot (n!)^5) \rceil}$$
$$\geq 32 \cdot (n!)^5 \cdot \frac{1}{2} \cdot 2^{-\log(4 \cdot (n!)^5)} = 4 .$$

Our goal is to show that $\text{Prob}(S \geq 1) \geq 3/4$, or equivalently that $\text{Prob}(S = 0) \leq 1/4$. In order to be able to apply the Chebychev Inequality (Corollary A.2.10), we use the fact that if $S = 0$, then $|S - E(S)| \geq E(S)$. We let $t := E(S)$ in the Chebychev Inequality. Then

$$\text{Prob}(S = 0) \leq \text{Prob}(|S - E(S)| \geq E(S))$$
$$\leq V(S)/E(S)^2 .$$

Earlier we showed that $V(S) \leq E(S)$ and $E(S) \geq 4$. From this it follows that

$$\text{Prob}(S = 0) \leq 1/E(S) \leq 1/4$$

and so $\mathrm{Prob}(S \geq 1) \geq 3/4$. For $(G_0, G_1) \in \overline{\mathrm{GI}}$ this is the large acceptance probability that was desired. All together we have characterized $\overline{\mathrm{GI}}$ in such a way that the statement $\overline{\mathrm{GI}} \in \mathrm{BP}(\mathrm{NP})$ has been proven according to Definition 11.3.2. $\square$

Theorem 11.3.5. *If* GI *is* NP-*complete, then* $\Sigma_2 = \Pi_2$.

Proof. For most parts of this proof we will find the operator notation of Chapter 10 convenient. In order to show that $\Sigma_2 = \Pi_2$, by Lemma 10.4.2 it is sufficient to show that $\Sigma_2 \subseteq \Pi_2$. So let $L \in \Sigma_2$ and thus representable as $\exists \cdot \forall \cdot \mathrm{P}$. If GI is NP-complete, then $\overline{\mathrm{GI}}$ is co-NP-complete and the $\forall$-operator can be replaced by an oracle for $\overline{\mathrm{GI}}$. By Theorem 11.3.4, $\overline{\mathrm{GI}} \in \mathrm{BP}(\mathrm{NP})$ and we can make use of the characterization of $\mathrm{BP}(\mathrm{NP})$ that was discussed following Definition 11.3.2. This means that there is a representation for L of the form $\exists \cdot \mathrm{BP} \cdot \exists \cdot \mathrm{P}$. Shortly we will show that from this it follows that there is a $\mathrm{BP} \cdot \exists \cdot \mathrm{P}$-representation. By Theorem 10.5.1 $\mathrm{BPP} \subseteq \Pi_2$ and $\mathrm{BP} \cdot \mathrm{P}$ can be replaced with $\forall \cdot \exists \cdot \mathrm{P}$. We can directly generalize the proof of Theorem 10.5.1 without any new ideas so that we can replace $\mathrm{BP} \cdot \exists \cdot \mathrm{P}$ with $\forall \cdot \exists \cdot \exists \cdot \mathrm{P}$ and so with $\forall \cdot \exists \cdot \mathrm{P}$. This representation proves that $L \in \Pi_2$ and $\Sigma_2 \subseteq \Pi_2$.

It remains to show the transformation from a $\exists (\mathrm{BP}) \exists \mathrm{P}$-representation into a $(\mathrm{BP}) \exists \mathrm{P}$-representation. If L has a $\exists (\mathrm{BP}) \exists \mathrm{P}$-representation, then there is a decision problem $L' \in \mathrm{P}$ such that

$$x \in L \Rightarrow \exists y \colon \mathrm{Prob}(\exists z \colon (x, y, z, r) \in L') \geq 3/4 \text{ , and}$$

$$x \notin L \Rightarrow \forall y \colon \mathrm{Prob}(\exists z \colon (x, y, z, r) \in L') \leq 1/4 \text{ ,}$$

where the probabilities above are with respect to the random vector r, and for $n = |x|$ the vectors y, z, and r have length $p(n)$. By repeating the procedure and taking a majority vote, we can reduce the error-probability to $2^{-p(n)}/4$. This makes z and r longer, but not x and y.

The statement "$\exists y \colon \mathrm{Prob}(\exists z \colon (x, y, z, r) \in L') \geq 1 - 2^{-p(n)}/4$" means that this y exists independent of the random vector r. From this it follows that

$$x \in L \Rightarrow \mathrm{Prob}(\exists (y, z) \colon (x, y, z, r) \in L') \geq 1 - 2^{-p(n)}/4 \geq 3/4.$$

In the second case $(x \notin L)$ we cannot argue in the same way. Assume for the sake of contradiction that there is an $x \notin L$ with

$$\mathrm{Prob}(\exists (y, z) \colon (x, y, z, r) \in L') > 1/4.$$

Then for more than a quarter of the r's there is a "good pair" (y, z). We write this as a table of the selected random vectors r with a respective good (y, z)-pair for each of these r's. Since there are only $2^{p(n)}$ vectors y, by the pigeonhole principle there is a y^* such that y^* occurs in the y-column for at least a fraction of $2^{-p(n)}$ of the r's in our table. This y^* is then a good choice for a fraction of more than $2^{-p(n)}/4$ of all r's. That is, for an $x \notin L$ we have

$$\exists y \,(\text{namely } y^*)\colon \text{Prob}(\exists z\colon (x,y,z,r) \in L') > 2^{-p(n)}/4 \,.$$

This contradicts the characterization of $x \notin L$ given above for the error-probability $2^{-p(n)}/4$. Thus the assumption must be false and we have

$$x \notin L \Rightarrow \text{Prob}(\exists (y,z)\colon (x,y,z,r) \in L') \le 1/4.$$

Thus we have obtained a $\mathsf{BP} \cdot \exists \cdot \mathsf{P}$-representation for L and the Theorem is proven.   □

In the example of the graph isomorphism problem we have seen that the consideration of the polynomial hierarchy, the characterization of its complexity classes, and the investigation of interactive proof systems have all contributed to the complexity theoretic classification of specific problems. The hypothesis that GI is not NP-complete is at least as well supported as the hypothesis that the polynomial hierarchy does not collapse to the second level.

11.4 Zero-Knowledge Proofs

The underlying idea of an interactive proof system is that Paul provides Victoria with enough information that she can check the proof with a small error-probability. So, for example, to convince Victoria that two publicly available graphs are isomorphic, Paul could send Victoria his secret π, the relabeling of the vertices that shows the two graphs are isomorphic. In any interactive proof system, Paul must send to Victoria some information related to the input. So in this sense, there are no interactive proof systems that reveal "zero knowledge". On the other hand, if Victoria could have computed the information sent by Paul herself in polynomial time and we consider polynomial time to be available, then it is as if Paul had revealed no information. But in such a case, Paul can't do any more than Victoria, so he has no secret information. Now let's go a step further and allow Victoria expected polynomial time. This means exponential time with correspondingly small exponential probability. If Paul does not want to reveal any knowledge (for example, he doesn't want to reveal any information about his password), then he has to assume that others are interested in this information. Among them are spies who may eavesdrop on the conversation and Victoria, who may deviate from the prescribed protocol if it helps her gain information from Paul. We will not, however, allow the spies to interfere with the conversation and send or modify messages. This all leads to the definition of *zero-knowledge proofs*.

Definition 11.4.1. *Let P and V be randomized algorithms of an interactive proof system for the decision problem L. This proof system has the* perfect zero-knowledge *property if for every polynomial-time randomized algorithm*

V' that can replace V (that is, V' must send the same type of messages), there is a randomized algorithm A with polynomially bounded worst-case expected runtime that for each $x \in L$ produces what is communicated between P and V' with the same probabilities.

For problems in P, Victoria can compute all the information herself, so perfect zero-knowledge proofs are only interesting for problems that lie outside of P. It is not immediately clear that there are any perfect zero-knowledge proofs for problems outside P, but for GI, which presumably does not belong to P, we have the following:

Theorem 11.4.2. *There is an interactive proof system for GI with the perfect zero-knowledge property.*

Proof. Let G_0 and G_1 be graphs so that Paul's secret is a permutation π^* with $G_1 = \pi^*(G_0)$. He would like to prove that G_0 and G_1 are isomorphic without giving away any information about π^* in the course of the conversation. The trick is to generate a random graph H that is isomorphic to G_0 and G_1 and later to give an isomorphism proving either that G_0 and H are isomorphic or that G_1 and H are isomorphic. To keep Paul from cheating in the case that G_0 and G_1 are not actually isomorphic, Victoria gets to decide later which of the two isomorphisms Paul must reveal. These considerations lead to the following interactive proof system:

- Paul randomly chooses $i \in \{0,1\}$ and $\pi \in S_n$, then he computes $H := \pi(G_i)$ and sends H to Victoria.
- Victoria randomly selects $j \in \{0,1\}$ and sends j to Paul.
- Paul computes $\pi' \in S_n$ and sends π' to Victoria.
- Victoria accepts if $H = \pi'(G_j)$.

Victoria can complete her work in polynomial time. If G_0 and G_1 are isomorphic, and $G_1 = \pi^*(G_0)$, then Paul can get Victoria to accept the input with certainty: If $i = j$, then Paul can choose $\pi' = \pi$; if $i = 1$ and $j = 0$, then $H = \pi(G_1)$ and $G_1 = \pi^*(G_0)$, so $H = \pi \circ \pi^*(G_0)$ and $\pi' = \pi \circ \pi^*$ will work; finally, if $i = 0$ and $j = 1$, then $H = \pi(G_0)$ and $G_0 = (\pi^*)^{-1}(G_1)$, so $H = \pi \circ (\pi^*)^{-1}(G_1)$, and $\pi' = \pi \circ (\pi^*)^{-1}$ will work. If the two graphs G_0 and G_1 are not isomorphic, Paul can still get Victoria to accept if $i = j$. But if $i \neq j$, then H and G_j are not isomorphic and there is no π' that will lead Victoria to accept. Since $\mathrm{Prob}(i \neq j) = 1/2$, the error-probability is $1/2$, and since the error is one-sided, we can reduce this to $1/4$ just as we did in Theorem 11.3.1.

In the conversation above, Victoria receives the triple (H, j, π') as information. In the case that G_0 and G_1 are isomorphic, H is a random graph that is isomorphic to G_0 and G_1, j is a random bit, and π' is a permutation such that $H = \pi'(G_j)$. Now let V' be an arbitrary polynomial-time randomized algorithm that computes the bit j. Then we can describe the algorithm A that simulates the communication as follows:

- Repeat until $i = j$:
  - randomly generate $i \in \{0,1\}$ and $\pi \in S_n$,
  - compute $H := \pi(G_i)$,
  - simulate V' for the situation in which Paul sent H and call the result j.
- A outputs the result (H, j, π), where these are the values from the last pass through the loop, i.e., the pass where $i = j$.

Each pass through the loop can be executed in polynomial time. Regardless of how V' computes the bit j, the bit i is the result of a fair coin toss and doesn't affect the computation of j, since the distribution of H is the same for $i = 0$ and $i = 1$. So i and j are the same with probability $1/2$. So by Theorem A.2.12, on average the loop must be executed 2 times, and the expected runtime is polynomially bounded for each input. Since $\pi \in S_n$ is chosen at random, if G_0 and G_1 are isomorphic, then H is a random graph isomorphic to G_0 and G_1. The pair (B, V') of algorithms computes a graph H chosen uniformly at random from the set of graphs that are isomorphic to G_0 and G_1, it computes a bit j according to V' and a permutation π' such that $H = \pi'(G_j)$. The algorithm A computes H according to the same probability distribution as (B, V'). Since A simulates V', it also computes j according to the same probability distribution as (B, V'). Finally, A outputs some π such that $H = \pi(G_i)$. Since $i = j$, this implies that $H = \pi(G_j)$. These considerations can be generalized to independent parallel runs of the protocol.   □

Paul's secret (password) in this example has the property that it is not completely secure. The graphs G_0 and G_1 are public knowledge, and the permutation π^* with $G_1 = \pi^*(G_0)$ is the secret or password. If someone could compute a permutation π with $G_1 = \pi(G_0)$, then he or she could pretend to be Paul and would withstand the identification protocol and get Victoria to accept. It would therefore be better to have an interactive proof system with the perfect zero-knowledge property not for GI but for some NP-complete or some even more difficult problem. We don't know how to do that. However, for NP-complete problems like HC, the problem of deciding if a graph has a Hamiltonian circuit, there are interactive proof systems with a weaker zero-knowledge property.

We assume the existence of a *one-way function*. A function $f : \{0,1\}^* \to \{0,1\}^*$ is a one-way function if it is one-to-one and computable in polynomial time, but it is not possible to compute information about the last bit of x from $f(x)$ in polynomial time. We will not give the formal definition here but will assume that knowing $f(x)$ is of no value if we are interested in the last bit of x. One-way functions permit an efficient *bit commitment*. For example, suppose Paul wants to leave a bit b as by a notary. The value remains secret, but in case of a disagreement it can be determined what value b has. For this, Paul generates a sufficiently long random bit sequence r and appends b to get x. Then he computes and makes public $f(x)$. In case of a disagreement, he must reveal x. Anyone can then apply f to x and compare the result to the publicly available value of $f(x)$. Paul can't be deceitful since f is one-to-one.

Here is an example of how bit commitment might work in practice. A sufficiently large prime number p is generated, and b is the parity of the bits in p. There are sufficiently many prime numbers that we needn't generate too many random numbers and test them for primality before we succeed in finding a prime. We have already indicated several times that PRIMES $\in$ P. Now a second smaller prime number $q < p$ is randomly generated and the product $n = pq$ is made public. In case of a disagreement, the unique prime divisors of n must be revealed, from which the parity of the bits of the larger divisor can easily be computed. In order for this bit commitment to be secure, we would have to assume that the factoring problem FACT cannot be solved in polynomial time, and that b cannot be efficiently computed from n in some other way.

Definition 11.4.3. *An interactive proof system has the zero-knowledge property under cryptographic assumptions if it has the perfect zero-knowledge property under the assumption that one-way functions exist.*

Theorem 11.4.4. *The Hamiltonian circuit problem* HC *has an interactive proof system with the zero-knowledge property under cryptographic assumptions.*

Proof. In our zero-knowledge protocol for graph isomorphism, Paul provided Victoria with a "scrambled" graph, and she could require Paul to "unscramble" the graph to show that it was isomorphic to one of the two input graphs of her choosing. This reveals Paul's deception at least half of the time if the two input graphs were not isomorphic. This time the rough idea is that Paul will provide an encoded version of a scrambled graph. Victoria can require Paul either to decode and unscramble the graph to show that it is isomorphic to the input graph, or she can require him to decode (but not unscramble) only a Hamiltonian circuit from the graph to show that such a circuit exists.

Let G be a graph for which Paul has secret knowledge of a Hamiltonian circuit H. Let the vertex set of G be $\{1, \ldots, n\}$ and let H be described by an edge list. The following interactive proof system is used:

- Paul selects a $\pi \in S_n$ at random and computes $\pi(G)$ and then puts the edge set of $\pi(G)$ in a random order. To describe π and the edge list $\pi(G)$, Paul sends Victoria a bit commitment for each bit.
- Victoria randomly chooses $i \in \{0, 1\}$ and sends i to Paul.
- If $i = 0$, then Paul decodes all of his bit commitments. If $i = 1$, then Paul only decodes the bit commitments for the bits describing the Hamiltonian circuit $\pi(H)$ in $\pi(G)$.
- If $i = 0$, then Victoria accepts if Paul really did commit to a permutation $\pi' \in S_n$ and the edge list of $\pi'(G)$. If $i = 1$, then Victoria accepts if the edges revealed by Paul form a Hamiltonian circuit on $\{1, \ldots, n\}$.

Victoria can do her work in polynomial time. If G has a Hamiltonian circuit, then Paul can follow the protocol and get Victoria to accept with certainty. If G does not have a Hamiltonian circuit, Paul can still commit to a pair $(\pi, \pi(G))$, but then he cannot fulfill the requirements if $i = 1$, since $\pi(G)$ has no Hamiltonian circuit. So at best, Paul can fulfill only one of the two requirements. Since he must decide what to do before he knows what i will be, he can only get Victoria to accept G with probability $1/2$. The error-probability can then be reduced to $1/4$ as we have seen before.

In the conversation just described, with probability $1/2$ Victoria receives a random permutation π and the description of $\pi(G)$, and with probability $1/2$ she receives a description of $\pi(H)$ for a Hamiltonian circuit H and some random permutation π. Under the assumption that one-way functions exist, the description of the bit commitments provides no usable information. The other information she can produce herself with probability $1/2$. A Hamiltonian circuit H can be described as a permutation π^* of the vertices $\{1, \ldots, n\}$. For a random π, $\pi \circ \pi^*$ is also a random permutation.   □

Our investigation of interactive proof systems with the zero-knowledge property shows that modern cryptographic procedures require complexity theory as a foundation.

The PCP Theorem and the Complexity of Approximation Problems

12.1 Randomized Verification of Proofs

In Chapter 11 interactive proof systems proved to be a useful tool. In this chapter we will investigate *probabilistically checkable proofs* (abbreviated PCP). With an appropriate restriction of resources we will obtain a new characterization of the complexity class NP. This characterization, the so-called PCP Theorem, is more than astounding, and a proof of its correctness is too complex to present here. In Section 12.2 we will prove a weaker result in order to gain a glimpse of the possibilities of probabilistically checkable proofs. The PCP Theorem is considered the most important result in complexity theory since Cook's Theorem. The theory of the complexity of approximation problems based on classical NP-completeness results which we presented in Chapter 8 doesn't get very far. The PCP Theorem provides new methods for investigating the complexity of approximation problems. In Section 12.3 we will look at two examples of inapproximability results – for MAX-3-SAT and CLIQUE – and in Section 12.4 we will prove the APX-completeness of MAX-3-SAT.

In Section 11.2 we showed that NP $\subseteq$ IP(1). The corresponding interactive proofs were only interactive in a restricted sense. Paul sends a proof that $x \in L$ to Victoria who then checks the proof deterministically and without error in polynomial time. If $x \in L$, then Paul can compute a proof that convinces Victoria. If $x \notin L$, then Victoria can expose any proof attempt as unconvincing. But the class NP is not taking advantage of the full power that IP(1) allows. Paul and Victoria are allowed to make use of randomness, and Victoria is allowed an error-rate of $1/4$. If Paul is only sending one message (the proof) and has unlimited computational power, then randomness is of no help to him: He can compute which proof attempt has the best properties and deterministically select this best attempt.

In order to characterize NP, we further restrict Victoria's resources. She may still use a randomized algorithm, but randomness will not be an arbitrarily available resource. The number of random bits allowed will be restricted.

Furthermore, Victoria will no longer be allowed two-sided error (as in interactive proofs) but must work with one-sided error. Specifically, co-RP-like errors will be allowed, that is, error-probabilities of up to $1/2$ for inputs that should *not* be accepted. So far, the familiar characterizations of problems in NP would still be allowed, without even making use of randomness. Now, however, we restrict Victoria's access to the proof. The proof is hidden, and Victoria – based on her knowledge of the input and her random bits – may compute a limited number of positions and ask that the bits of the proof in those positions be revealed. Victoria's access to the proof is *non-adaptive*: She must compute all the positions she wishes to read before reading any of them.

Definition 12.1.1. *For $r, q : \mathbb{N} \to \mathbb{N}$, an $(r(n), q(n))$-bounded probabilistic proof-checker is a polynomial time algorithm V. For an input x of length n and a proof P (a 0-1 vector), the algorithm V has access to x and a random vector $r \in \{0, 1\}^{O(r(n))}$. On the basis of this information, V computes up to $O(q(n))$ positions and receives as additional information the values of the bits of the proof P in those positions. Finally, the decision $V(x, r, P) \in \{0, 1\}$, whether x should be accepted or not, is computed.*

Since the verifier Victoria has only polynomially bounded computation time, she can read at most polynomially many random bits and proof bits. Therefore, we only consider polynomially bounded functions r (random bits) and q (query bits). We extend the definition to allow for r and q to be the constant function 0, and generalize our O-notation so that $O(0)$ is interpreted as 0. Using resource-bounded probabilistic proof checkers we can define complexity classes analogous to the classes defined using interactive proof systems.

Definition 12.1.2. *A decision problem L belongs to the complexity class $\mathsf{PCP}(r(n), q(n))$ (probabilistically checkable proofs with $O(r(n))$ random bits and $O(q(n))$ query bits), if there is an $(r(n), q(n))$-bounded probabilistic proof checker V with the following properties:*

- *If $x \in L$, then there is a proof $P(x)$ such that*

$$\mathrm{Prob}(V(x, r, P(x)) = 1) = 1 .$$

- *If $x \notin L$, then for all proofs P,*

$$\mathrm{Prob}(V(x, r, P) = 0) \geq 1/2 .$$

Once again the error threshold of $1/2$ is to a certain extent arbitrary. Since constant factors don't matter when counting the number of random bits or the number of query bits, we can perform constantly many independent proof attempts simultaneously. We accept an input only if this is the decision of *all* these proof attempts. In this way we can reduce the error-probability from any constant $\delta < 1$ to any constant $\varepsilon > 0$. We will let $\mathsf{PCP}(poly, q(n))$ denote the union of all $\mathsf{PCP}(n^k, q(n))$ for $k \in \mathbb{N}$; $\mathsf{PCP}(r(n), poly)$ is defined analogously.

Since we can consider the generation of the proof to be a nondeterministic process and since we allow co-RP-like errors, the following characterizations of P, NP, and co-RP come as no surprise.

Theorem 12.1.3.

- $P = PCP(0, 0)$,
- $NP = PCP(0, poly)$,
- $co-RP = PCP(poly, 0)$.

Proof. Consider a decision problem $L \in PCP(0, 0)$. Since $q(n) = 0$, Victoria cannot read any of the proof. This is equivalent to saying there is no proof. Furthermore, for all $x \notin L$ we must have $Prob(V(x, r, P) = 0) = 1$ (Since there are no random bits, all "probabilities" are either 0 or 1.) So $L \in P$.

$PCP(0, poly)$ allows arbitrarily long proofs, of which only polynomially many bits may be read. Since there are no random bits, for each x the same bit positions are always read, so the proof can be restricted to polynomial length, and the entire proof can then be read. Once again, since there are no random bits, no $x \notin L$ is accepted. So we obtain exactly the logical characterization of NP: For $x \in L$, there is at least one proof of polynomial length that convinces Victoria. For $x \notin L$ there is no proof that convinces her.

$PCP(poly, 0)$ can again be described with a scenario without any proofs, and we obtain exactly the characterization of co-RP. □

Equally straightforward is the proof of the following theorem regarding the nondeterministic simulation of an $(r(n), q(n))$-bounded probabilistic proof checker.

Theorem 12.1.4. *If $L \in PCP(r(n), q(n))$, then there is a nondeterministic Turing machine that decides L in time $2^{O(r(n) + \log n)}$.*

Proof. The nondeterministic Turing machine simulates the probabilistic proof checker for all $2^{O(r(n))}$ possible assignments of the random bit vector. For each assignment at most $p(n)$ bit positions are computed in polynomial time $p(n)$. For all of the at most $p(n) \cdot 2^{O(r(n))} = 2^{O(r(n) + \log n)}$ bit positions, the proof bits are nondeterministically generated. Then for the $2^{O(r(n))}$ assignments of the random bit vector, the computation of the proof checker is simulated. Finally the input is accepted if the proof checker accepts for all the assignments of the random bit vector. If $x \in L$, then there is a proof that causes the proof checker to accept with probability 1, that is, for all assignments of the random bit vector. If $x \notin L$, then for each proof the input is rejected for at least half of these assignments. So we obtain a nondeterministic algorithm for L. Since each computation of the proof checker takes at most $p(n) = 2^{O(\log n)}$ steps, the runtime of the nondeterministic Turing machine is bounded by $2^{O(r(n) + \log n)}$. □

As a corollary we obtain another characterization of NP.

Corollary 12.1.5. $NP = PCP(\log n, poly)$.

Proof. The inclusion $NP \subseteq PCP(\log n, poly)$ follows from Theorem 12.1.3, and the inclusion $NP \supseteq PCP(\log n, poly)$, from Theorem 12.1.4. □

12.2 The PCP Theorem

Corollary 12.1.5 contains the statement $NP \supseteq PCP(\log n, 1)$. One might suspect that $PCP(\log n, 1)$ is "much smaller" than NP. After all, what good are only constantly many bits of a proof? This intuition, however, turns out to be incorrect.

Theorem 12.2.1 (PCP Theorem). $NP = PCP(\log n, 1)$. □

The history of the PCP Theorem was described in great detail by Goldreich (1998). Feige, Goldwasser, Lovász, Safra, and Szegedy (1991) established the connection between resource-bounded probabilistically checkable proofs and inapproximability results. The PCP Theorem was proved in 1992 by Arora, Lund, Motwani, Sudan, and Szegedy (the journal version appeared in 1998). After that, the number of bit positions that needed to be read was reduced in a number of papers. It is sufficient to read only nine bits of the proof and then the error-probability is already bounded by 0.32. If the allowable error-probability is raised to 0.76, then we can get by with three bits of the proof. Variants of the PCP Theorem that allow for better inapproximability results have also been presented (for example, in Bellare, Goldreich, and Sudan (1998) and in Arora and Safra (1998)).

The proof of the PCP Theorem is too long and difficult to present here. It is a big challenge to find a proof of this theorem that is "digestible" for students. Those who don't shy away from some hard work can find a complete proof of the PCP Theorem that is clearly presented and well-written in the books by Ausiello, Crescenzi, Gambosi, Kann, Marchetti-Spaccamela, and Protasi (1999), and by Mayr, Prömel, and Steger (1998).

To show that $NP \subseteq PCP(\log n, 1)$, it suffices to show that some NP-complete problem like 3-SAT belongs to $PCP(\log n, 1)$. To see how reading only constantly many bits can help a probabilistic proof checker solve an NP-complete problem we want to give the proof of the following weaker theorem.

Theorem 12.2.2. $3\text{-SAT} \in PCP(n^3, 1)$.

Proof. Suppose we are given an instance of 3-SAT that consists of clauses $c_1, \ldots, c_m$ over the variables $x_1, \ldots, x_n$. A classical proof of the satisfiability of the clauses consists of giving an assignment $a \in \{0, 1\}^n$ that satisfies all the clauses. Each bit a_i is very "local" information; it only deals with the value of x_i. A probabilistically checkable proof of which only a few bits may be read should have the property that every bit contains a little information about each a_i. The information about a should be spread over the entire proof. Of course, we are thinking about the case when there is a satisfying assignment a. In this case we can think of the proof $P(a)$ corresponding to each satisfying assignment a as a coding of a. We must also discuss how we can recognize from $P(a')$ that a' is not a satisfying assignment. And later we must consider how to deal with proof attempts P' that are different from $P(a')$ for all $a' \in \{0,1\}^n$. Here we will only give an indication of the most important ideas. If P' is very different from all $P(a')$ then we will discover this with sufficiently high probability. Otherwise we want to "correct" P' into some $P'(a)$ and work with $P'(a)$ instead. So our code for each $a \in \{0,1\}^n$ must allow for efficient error correction (*error-correcting codes*).

The basis of our considerations is an *arithmetization* of the 3-SAT formula. The positive literals x_i will be replaced by $1 - x_i$, the negative literals $\overline{x}_i$ will be replaced by x_i, disjunctions will become products, and conjunctions will become sums. So, for example,

$$(x_1 + \overline{x}_2 + x_3) \wedge (\overline{x}_1 + \overline{x}_2 + x_4) \longrightarrow (1 - x_1) \cdot x_2 \cdot (1 - x_3) + x_1 \cdot x_2 \cdot (1 - x_4) \, .$$

It would have been more obvious to use a dual representation, but this way the degree of the resulting polynomial p is bounded by the number of literals per clause – in our case 3.

The polynomial p has the following properties. If a satisfies a clause, then the corresponding term is 0, while the term has value 1 for every non-satisfying assignment. So $p(a)$ is the number of unsatisfied clauses. We will see that it is advantageous to carry out all of our computations in $\mathbb{Z}_2$. Then $p(a)$ only indicates if the number of unsatisfied clauses is odd or even. If $p(a) = 1$, then we know with certainty that a does not satisfy all of the clauses, but if $p(a) = 0$, then we cannot be sure that a is a satisfying assignment. For some non-satisfying assignments the error-probability would then be 1. The idea now is to randomly ignore some of the clauses. If the number of unsatisfied clauses is even and we ignore some of the clauses, then the chances are good that the number of remaining clauses that are unsatisfied will be odd.

Formally, let p_i be the polynomial representing clause c_i. For a random bit vector $r \in \{0,1\}^m$, let p^r be the sum of all p_i with $r_i = 1$, that is, $p^r = r_1 p_1 + \cdots + r_m p_m$. For a satisfying assignment a, $p_i(a) = 0$ for all i, and thus $p^r(a) = 0$ for all r. For non-satisfying assignments a, $p^r(a)$ takes on the values 0 and 1 with probability $1/2$. We already used this property in the proof of Theorem 11.3.4 ($\overline{\text{GI}} \in \text{BP(NP)}$), but we repeat the argument. Since a is not a satisfying assignment, there is a j with $p_j(a) = 1$. Independent of the sum of all $r_i p_i(a)$ for $i \neq j$, this value becomes 0 or 1 with probability $1/2$ each when we add $r_j p_j(a) = r_j$. So checking whether $p^r(a) = 0$ has the desired properties. If a is a satisfying assignment, then $p^r(a) = 0$ for all r. If a is not a satisfying assignment, then the probability that $p^r(a) = 0$ is exactly $1/2$. Of course, in order to compute $p^r(a)$, Victoria must also know a.

Now we will reverse the situation for Victoria. As we have described things up until now, she knows p^r (the 3-SAT-formula) but not the input value a (a variable assignment) for $p^r(a)$. We will now compute three linear functions L_1^a, L_2^a, and L_3^a each depending on a. The function table of these functions will be the code for the proof a. Of course, Victoria doesn't know a, but she should be able to compute in polynomial time from p and r input vectors b^1, b^2, and b^3 such that from $L_1^a(b^1), L_2^a(b^2)$, and $L_3^a(b^3)$ she can compute the value of $p^r(a)$. She obtains the values $L_1^a(b^1), L_2^a(b^2)$, and $L_3^a(b^3)$ by reading certain portions of the proof, i.e., the code for a.

In order to learn more about the polynomial p^r, let's consider an arbitrary polynomial $q : \{0,1\}^n \to \{0,1\}$ with degree at most 3. If we expand q, it will consist of the following summands:

- $c_q \in \{0,1\}$, the constant term,
- terms of the form x_i for $i \in I_q^1$,
- terms of the form $x_i x_j$ for $(i,j) \in I_q^2$, and
- terms of the form $x_i x_j x_k$ for $(i,j,k) \in I_q^3$.

Since we are working in $\mathbb{Z}_2$, the coefficients are all either 0 (the term does not appear in the sum) or 1 (the term appears and the corresponding tuple belongs to the I_q-set of the appropriate degree). Now we define

- $L_1^a : \mathbb{Z}_2^n \to \mathbb{Z}_2$ by $L_1^a(y_1,\ldots,y_n) := \sum_{1 \le i \le n} a_i y_i$,

- $L_2^a : \mathbb{Z}_2^{n^2} \to \mathbb{Z}_2$ by $L_2^a(y_{1,1},\ldots,y_{n,n}) := \sum_{1 \le i,j \le n} a_i a_j y_{i,j}$, and

- $L_3^a : \mathbb{Z}_2^{n^3} \to \mathbb{Z}_2$ by $L_3^a(y_{1,1,1},\ldots,y_{n,n,n}) := \sum_{1 \le i,j,k \le n} a_i a_j a_k y_{i,j,k}$.

By definition L_1^a, L_2^a, and L_3^a are linear. They have function tables of length $2^n, 2^{n^2}$, and 2^{n^3}, so the code for a also has length $2^n + 2^{n^2} + 2^{n^3}$ and consists of the concatenation of the three function tables. For a given q, in polynomial time Victoria can compute c_q, I_q^1, I_q^2, and I_q^3. In addition she can compute the characteristic vectors c_q^1, c_q^2, and c_q^3 of I_q^1, I_q^2, and I_q^3. So, for example, bit (i,j) of c_q^2 is 1 if and only if $(i,j) \in I_q^2$, otherwise it is 0. Victoria reads the values $L_1^a(c_q^1)$, $L_2^a(c_q^2)$, and $L_3^a(c_q^3)$ in the codeword for a. Finally, she computes

$$c_q + L_1^a(c_q^1) + L_2^a(c_q^2) + L_3^a(c_q^3).$$

The claim is that in so doing, Victoria has computed $q(a)$. Clearly the constant term c_q is correct. Furthermore,

$$L_2^a(c_q^2) = \sum_{1 \le i,j \le n} a_i a_j (c_q^2)_{i,j} = \sum_{(i,j) \in I_q^2} a_i a_j .$$

$L_2^a(c_q^2)$ takes care of the terms of q that are of degree 2. The analogous statements hold for L_1^a and degree 1, and for L_3^a and degree 3. So we have found an encoding of $a \in \{0,1\}^n$ that is very long but can be used by Victoria to compute $p^r(a)$ in polynomial time using three selected positions.

Now we know what the proof should look like when there is a satisfying assignment: A satisfying assignment a is selected and the function tables for L_1^a, L_2^a, and L_3^a are used as the proof. We will check the proof by computing $p^r(a)$ for constantly many randomly chosen r and accept if they all have the value 0. For each of these tests it suffices to read three bit positions. The number of random bits is bounded by $O(n^3)$ since 3-SAT formulas without trivial clauses and without repeated clauses can have at most $2n + 4 \cdot \binom{n}{2} + 8 \cdot \binom{n}{3} = O(n^3)$ clauses and r describes a random choice of clauses. The error-probability for clause sets that are not satisfied is $1/2$ for each test, as we discussed above. At least that is the case for proofs of the type described. But in the case of unsatisfiable clause sets, we must react reasonably to all proofs. We will assume that these proofs have the "correct" length since we will never read any of the extra bits in a longer proof anyway, and shorter proofs simply offer additional chances to detect that they are undesirable.

So how are these proofs checked? We will use four modules:

- a linearity test,
- a function evaluator,
- a consistency test, and
- a proof verifier.

The linearity test serves to check whether a function table is describing a linear function. We will describe how this can be done with one-sided error reading only constantly many bits. But this test cannot work as desired if the proof merely includes the function table, since if the table contains only a single value that deviates from a linear function, then this will be detected with only a very small probability. We will therefore make a distinction between linear, almost linear, and other functions. These terms will be formalized later. We must be able to detect the "other functions", but we must accept that the "almost linear" functions may pass the linearity test. Linear functions will always pass the linearity test.

It will turn out that each almost linear function is "close" to exactly *one* linear function. So we will attempt to interpret the proof as if it contained this close linear function in place of the almost linear function it actually contains. The function evaluator's job is to compute for input values an estimate of the function value of this nearby linear function. If the function is linear, this estimate will always be correct. For almost linear functions the error-probability can be bounded by a constant $\alpha < 1$. Furthermore, by using repeated independent estimates and taking a majority decision, we can reduce the error-probability. The function evaluator will read only constantly many bits.

But there is another problem. It is not enough that the proof contain function tables of three linear functions. Since the functions L_1^a, L_2^a, and L_3^a all depend on a, they are related. The consistency test checks whether the three linear functions being considered (among them possibly the corrected versions of almost linear functions) are consistent, that is, if they come from the same input a. For consistent linear functions L_1^a, L_2^a, and L_3^a the test makes no errors. Inconsistent triples of linear or almost linear functions will be detected with constant error-probability $\beta < 1$. Once again, only constantly many bits will be read.

Finally, the proof verifier reads constantly many bits and tests as described above whether $p^r(a) = 0$ for random bit vectors r. If the proof contains L_1^a, L_2^a, and L_3^a, then the value of $p^r(a)$ is correctly computed. Otherwise the error-probability can be bounded by a constant $\gamma < 1$.

All together the proof (L_1^a, L_2^a, L_3^a) for a satisfying assignment a is always accepted. For unsatisfiable clause sets, a proof can be accepted if at least one of the following occurs:

- One of the three linearity tests fails to detect that one of the functions is not even almost linear.
- The consistency test fails to detect a triple of functions that are inconsistent. For this almost linear functions are corrected to linear functions.
- All the computed $p^r(a)$ have the value 0. Once again, almost linear functions are corrected to linear functions.
- One of the many function evaluations produces an incorrect value.

It is important to note that the function evaluator is used in the other modules. We will allow each linearity test an error-probability of $1/18$, i.e., a combined error-probability of $1/6$. The consistency test – under the assumption that the linearity tests make no errors – is allowed an error-probability of $1/6$. That leaves an error-probability of $1/6$ for the proof verifier – under the assumption that the other tests are all error-free. The proof verifier reads three bits. If we permit the function evaluator an error-probability of $1/10$, then for unsatisfiable clause sets a value of 0 is computed for $p^r(a)$ only if $p^r(a) = 0$ (probability $1/2$) or a function evaluation produces an incorrect value. So the overall error-probability of the proof verifier is bounded by $4/5$. Nine independent repetitions reduce this error-probability to less than $1/6$. Similar arguments allow us to compute the corresponding parameters for the other modules. So it suffices to show that every test has an error-probability bounded by some constant less than 1 and can be computed with the help of constantly many proof bits and $O(n^3)$ random bits in polynomial time. Then the PCP verifier can be made by assembling these modules.

We begin with the linearity test. Since we are working in the field $\mathbb{Z}_2$, $f : \mathbb{Z}_2^m \to \mathbb{Z}_2$ is linear if and only if $f(x + y) = f(x) + f(y)$ for all $x, y \in \mathbb{Z}_2^m$. We will say that a function f is δ-close to a function g if under the uniform distribution on $\mathbb{Z}_2^m$, $\text{Prob}_x(f(x) \neq g(x)) \leq \delta$. We will use the subscript on Prob to denote which element was chosen at random, always assuming a uniform distribution. The linearity test works as follows:

- Choose independent and random $x, y \in \mathbb{Z}_2^m$ and only consider f to be non-linear if $f(x + y) \neq f(x) + f(y)$.

This test has the following properties:

- If f is linear, it will pass the linearity test.
- If $\delta < 1/3$ and f is not δ-close to any linear function, then f passes the test with probability less than $1 - \delta/2$.

The first property is clear. The second property can be equivalently formulated as

- From $\mathrm{Prob}_{x,y}(f(x+y) \neq f(x) + f(y)) \leq \delta/2$ it follows that f is δ-close to some linear function g.

We will prove this claim by defining a linear function g and showing that f is δ-close to g. To define $g(a)$ we consider $f(a+b) - f(b)$ for all $b \in \mathbb{Z}_2^m$. For a linear function f this will always yield the value $f(a)$. So we let $g(a)$ be the value from $\{0, 1\}$ that occurs most frequently in the list of all $f(a+b) - f(b)$. In case of an equal number of 0's and 1's, we let $g(a) = 0$. It remains to show that

- g is δ-close to f, and
- g is linear.

The first property is proved by contradiction. Suppose that f and g are not δ-close. Then

$$\mathrm{Prob}_x(f(x) \neq g(x)) > \delta .$$

By the construction of g, for every $a \in \mathbb{Z}_2^m$

$$\mathrm{Prob}_y(g(a) = f(a+y) - f(y)) \geq 1/2 .$$

So it follows that

$$\mathrm{Prob}_{x,y}\left(f(x+y) - f(y) \neq f(x)\right)$$

$$\geq \mathrm{Prob}_{x,y}\left(f(x+y) - f(y) = g(x) \wedge g(x) \neq f(x)\right)$$

$$= \sum_{a \in \mathbb{Z}_2^m} 2^{-m} \cdot \mathrm{Prob}_y\left(f(a+y) - f(y) = g(a) \wedge g(a) \neq f(a)\right) .$$

For every a, either $g(a) = f(a)$ or $g(a) \neq f(a)$. In the first case the probability we are considering is 0, and in the second case the condition $g(a) \neq f(a)$ can be left out. So

$$\mathrm{Prob}_{x,y}\left(f(x+y) - f(y) \neq f(x)\right)$$

$$\geq 2^{-m} \cdot \sum_{\substack{a \in \mathbb{Z}_2^m \\ g(a) \neq f(a)}} \mathrm{Prob}_y\left(f(a+y) - f(y) = g(a)\right)$$

$$\geq 2^{-m} \cdot \sum_{\substack{a \in \mathbb{Z}_2^m \\ g(a) \neq f(a)}} \frac{1}{2} > \delta/2 ,$$

contradicting the assumption that $\mathrm{Prob}_{x,y}(f(x+y) \neq f(x) + f(y)) \leq \delta/2$. The last inequality follows since from $\mathrm{Prob}_x(f(x) \neq g(x)) > \delta$ it follows that more than $\delta \cdot 2^m$ of all $a \in \mathbb{Z}_2^m$ have the property that $g(a) \neq f(a)$.

For the proof of the linearity of g we investigate

$$p(a) := \mathrm{Prob}_x(g(a) = f(a+x) - f(x)) .$$

By the construction of g, $p(a) \geq 1/2$. We will show that, in fact, $p(a) \geq 1 - \delta$. Applying the assumption that

$$\mathrm{Prob}_{x,y}(f(x+y) \neq f(x) + f(y)) \leq \delta/2$$

to $x + a$ and y and also to x and $y + a$, and noting that for a random choice of $x \in \mathbb{Z}_2^m$, $x + a$ is also a random bit vector from $\mathbb{Z}_2^m$ yields

$$\mathrm{Prob}_{x,y}\left(f(x+a) + f(y) \neq f(x+a+y)\right) \leq \delta/2$$

and

$$\mathrm{Prob}_{x,y}\left(f(x) + f(y+a) \neq f(x+a+y)\right) \leq \delta/2 .$$

The probability of the union of these events is bounded above by δ, and the probability of the complement is bounded below by $1 - \delta$. By DeMorgan's laws, this is the intersection of the events $f(x+a) + f(y) = f(x+a+y)$ and $f(x) + f(y+a) = f(x+a+y)$, in particular a subset of the event $f(x+a) + f(y) = f(x) + f(y+a)$. Thus

$$\mathrm{Prob}_{x,y}\left(f(x+a) + f(y) = f(x) + f(y+a)\right) \geq 1 - \delta .$$

In order to take advantage of the independence of the selection of x and y, we write this equation as $f(x+a) - f(x) = f(y+a) - f(y)$. Then

$$1 - \delta \leq \mathrm{Prob}_{x,y}\left(f(x+a) - f(x) = f(y+a) - f(y)\right)$$

$$= \sum_{z \in \{0,1\}} \mathrm{Prob}_{x,y}\left(f(x+a) - f(x) = z \wedge f(y+a) - f(y) = z\right)$$

$$= \sum_{z \in \{0,1\}} \mathrm{Prob}_x\left(f(x+a) - f(x) = z\right) \cdot \mathrm{Prob}_y\left(f(y+a) - f(y) = z\right)$$

$$= \sum_{z \in \{0,1\}} \left(\mathrm{Prob}_x\left(f(x+a) - f(x) = z\right)\right)^2 .$$

If $z = g(a)$, then $\mathrm{Prob}_x(f(x+a) - f(x) = z) = p(a)$. Thus

$$\sum_{z \neq g(a)} \mathrm{Prob}_x\left(f(x+a) - f(x) = z\right) = 1 - p(a) ,$$

so

$$\sum_{z \neq g(a)} \left(\mathrm{Prob}_x\left(f(x+a) - f(x) = z\right)\right)^2 = (1 - p(a))^2 ,$$

and
$$1 - \delta \leq p(a)^2 + (1 - p(a))^2 \ .$$

Since, as we noted above, $p(a) \geq 1/2$, it follows that $1 - p(a) \leq p(a)$ and

$$p(a)^2 + (1 - p(a))^2 \leq p(a)^2 + p(a)(1 - p(a)) = p(a) \ ,$$

and thus $p(a) \geq 1 - \delta$, as was claimed.

We apply this result three times, using again the fact that not only x but also $x + a$ is a random bit vector from $\mathbb{Z}_2^m$. This gives

$$\mathrm{Prob}_x \left(g(a) = f(a + x) - f(x) \right) = p(a) \geq 1 - \delta,$$
$$\mathrm{Prob}_x \left(g(b) = f(b + a + x) - f(a + x) \right) = p(b) \geq 1 - \delta,$$
$$\mathrm{Prob}_x \left(g(a + b) = f(a + b + x) - f(x) \right) = p(a + b) \geq 1 - \delta.$$

Thus the intersection of the three events has probability at least $1 - 3\delta$. This also holds for any event implied by this intersection. In particular, adding the first two equations and subtracting the third, we get

$$\mathrm{Prob}_x \left(g(a) + g(b) = g(a + b) \right) \geq 1 - 3\delta \ .$$

Since by assumption $\delta < 1/3$,

$$\mathrm{Prob}_x (g(a) + g(b) = g(a + b)) > 0 \ .$$

But the equation $g(a) + g(b) = g(a + b)$ is true or false independent of the choice of x. A positive probability that can only take on a value of 0 or 1 must have the value 1. So $g(a) + g(b) = g(a + b)$ for all a and b and thus g is linear.

Now we turn to the function evaluator. The function evaluator receives as input the function table of a function $f : \mathbb{Z}_2^m \to \mathbb{Z}_2$ and an $a \in \mathbb{Z}_2^m$. For $\delta < 1/3$ it must have following properties:

- If f is linear, then the result is $f(a)$.
- If f is not linear, but δ-close to a linear function g, then the randomized function evaluator should output $g(a)$ with an error-probability bounded by 2δ.

The function evaluator works as follows:

- Chose an $x \in \mathbb{Z}_2^m$ at random and compute $f(x + a) - f(x)$.

The first property is clearly satisfied. The second property can be shown as follows. Since f and g are δ-close,

$$\mathrm{Prob}_x (f(x) = g(x)) \geq 1 - \delta$$

and

$$\mathrm{Prob}_x (f(x + a) = g(x + a)) \geq 1 - \delta \ .$$

Thus the probability that both events occur is at least $1 - 2\delta$. Both events together, however, imply that $f(x + a) - f(x) = g(x + a) - g(x)$, and by the linearity of g, this implies that $f(x + a) - f(x) = g(a)$. So the function evaluator has the desired properties.

For the consistency test, the function tables for f_1, f_2, and f_3 are available. The represented functions are either linear or δ-close to a linear function. For $\delta < 1/24$ the consistency test should have the following properties:

- If the function tables represent linear functions of the type L_1^a, L_2^a, and L_3^a for some $a \in \{0,1\}^n$, then the function tables pass the consistency test.
- If there is no $a \in \{0,1\}^n$ such that the functions f_1, f_2, and f_3 represented in the tables are δ-close to L_1^a, L_2^a, and L_3^a, then the consistency test detects this with an error-probability bounded by some constant less than 1.

The consistency test works as follows:

- Choose $x, x', x'' \in \mathbb{Z}_2^n$ and $y \in \mathbb{Z}_2^{n^2}$ independently at random.
- Define $x \circ x'$ by $(x \circ x')_{i,j} = x_i x_j'$ and $x'' \circ y$ by $(x'' \circ y)_{i,j,k} = x_i'' y_{j,k}$.
- Use the function evaluator to compute estimates b for $f_1(x)$, b' for $f_1(x')$, b'' for $f_1(x'')$, c for $f_2(x \circ x')$, c' for $f_2(y)$, and d for $f_3(x'' \circ y)$.
- The function tables pass the consistency test if $bb' = c$ and $b''c' = d$.

Linear functions L_1^a, L_2^a, and L_3^a always pass the consistency test. For them the function evaluator is error-free and

$$L_1^a(x) \cdot L_1^a(x') = \left(\sum_{1 \le i \le n} a_i x_i \right) \left(\sum_{1 \le j \le n} a_j x_j' \right) = \sum_{1 \le i,j \le n} a_i a_j x_i x_j' = L_2^a(x \circ x') .$$

Analogously it follows that $L_1^a(x'') \cdot L_2^a(y) = L_3^a(x'' \circ y)$. For the second property we use the fact that for $\delta < 1/24$ the error-probability of the function evaluator is bounded by $2\delta < 1/12$. This means that the error-probability of all six function evaluations together is bounded by $1/2$. Now assume that the function evaluations are without error. Let the linear function that is δ-close to f_1 have coefficients a_i and the linear function that is δ-close to f_2 have the coefficients $b_{i,j}$. Let $a_{i,j} := a_i a_j$. Now consider the matrices $A = (a_{i,j})$ and $B = (b_{i,j})$, and assume that the function evaluations are correct but the function tables are inconsistent. Then $A \ne B$. We represent the corresponding inputs x and x' as column vectors. The consistency test compares $x^\top A x'$ and $x^\top B x'$ and is based on the fact that for $A \ne B$ and random x and x' with probability at least $1/4$ the two values are different, and so the inconsistency is detected. If A and B differ in the jth column, then the probability that $x^\top A$ and $x^\top B$ differ in the jth position is $1/2$. This follows by the already frequently used argument regarding the value of the scalar products $x^\top y$ and $x^\top z$ for $y \ne z$ and random x. If $x^\top A$ and $x^\top B$ differ, then with probability $1/2$, $(x^\top A)x'$ and $(x^\top B)x'$ are also different.

If all the modules use the correct parameters, it follows that $3\text{-SAT} \in \text{PCP}(n^3, 1)$ and thus that $\text{NP} \subseteq \text{PCP}(n^3, 1)$. $\qquad \square$

In order to drastically reduce the number of random bits, we need to get by with much shorter proofs. One idea used is to replace the linear functions in our approach with polynomials of low degree. Then a so-called *composition lemma* is proved that produces from two verifiers with different properties an improved verifier. As we have already indicated, we won't go any deeper into the proof of the PCP Theorem. Our discussion should at least have made clear, however, that reading only constantly many bits of a proof can provide an amazing amount of information. But this only holds for proof attempts where false proofs are not always detected. The difficulty of reporting this result is shown in the following quotation from *The New York Times* on April 7, 1992:

> " In a discovery that overturns centuries of mathematical tradition, a group of graduate students and young researchers has discovered a way to check even the longest and most complicated proof by scrutinizing it in just a few spots ... "

12.3 The PCP Theorem and Inapproximability Results

The article just cited continues

> "... Using this new result, the researchers have already made a landmark discovery in computer science. They showed that it is impossible to compute even approximate solutions for a large group of practical problems that have long foiled researchers ...."

As examples, we want to show that this claim holds for MAX-3-SAT and MAX-CLIQUE.

The PCP Theorem makes it possible to make better use of the *gap technique* discussed in Section 8.3. Using the fact that 3-SAT $\in$ PCP$(\log n, 1)$, we will polynomially reduce 3-SAT to MAX-3-SAT in such a way the following properties are satisfied for a constant $\delta > 0$:

- If the given clause set is satisfiable, then the clause set produced by the reduction is also satisfiable.
- If the given clause set is not satisfiable, then at most a proportion of $1 - \delta$ of the clauses produced by the reduction are satisfiable.

We now choose an $\varepsilon > 0$ so that $1 + \varepsilon = 1/(1 - \delta)$. If MAX-3-SAT has a polynomial-time approximation algorithm with approximation ratio less than $1 + \varepsilon$, then it follows that NP = P. For in that case we can solve 3-SAT in the following way. First we use a reduction with the properties listed above, and then we apply the approximation algorithm MAX-3-SAT to the result and compute the proportion α of satisfied clauses. If $\alpha > 1 - \delta$, then the given clause set is satisfiable by the second property of the polynomial reduction. If $\alpha \leq 1 - \delta$, then by the first property of the reduction and the approximation ratio of the approximation algorithm, the clause set cannot be satisfiable. We will formalize this proof strategy in the theorem below.

Theorem 12.3.1. *There is a constant $\varepsilon > 0$ such that polynomial approximation algorithms for* MAX-3-SAT *with an approximation ratio less than $1 + \varepsilon$ only exist if* NP = P.

Proof. We will complete the application of the gap technique described above. By the PCP Theorem there are integer constants c and k such that there is a probabilistically checkable proof for 3-SAT that uses at most $c \cdot \log n$ random bits and reads at most k bits of the proof for instances of 3-SAT with n variables. We can assume that exactly $\lfloor c \cdot \log n \rfloor$ random bits are available and that always exactly k bits of the proof are read. There are then $N := 2^{\lfloor c \cdot \log n \rfloor} \le n^c$ assignments for the random bit vector. For each assignment of the random bits and each 3-SAT input there are exactly k bits of the proof that are read. So for each 3-SAT instance there can only be kN different bit positions that have a non-zero probability of being read. All other positions in the proof are irrelevant. So we can assume that the proof has length exactly kN. The set of possible proofs is then the set $\{0,1\}^{kN}$.

Let C be a set of clauses of length 3 on n variables. For this set C we consider N Boolean functions $f_r : \{0,1\}^{kN} \to \{0,1\}$ for $0 \le r \le N - 1$. The index r refers to the random bit vector, which will be interpreted as a binary number. For a fixed r and C, the k proof positions $j_r(1) < \cdots < j_r(k)$ that are read are also fixed. The value of $f_r(y)$ should take the value 1 if and only if the probabilistic proof checker accepts the proof y for clause set C with random bits r. Syntactically we describe all functions in dependence on all the bits $y = (y_1, \ldots, y_{kN})$ of the proof. But it is important that each function f_r essentially only depends on k of the y-variables. Now we can express the properties of the probabilistic proof checker as properties of the functions f_r.

- If the clause set is satisfiable, then there is a $y \in \{0,1\}^{kN}$ such that all $f_r(y) = 1$ for all $0 \le r \le N - 1$.
- If the clause set is not satisfiable, then for every $y \in \{0,1\}^{kN}$, $f_r(y) = 1$ for at most half of the r with $0 \le r \le N - 1$.

The polynomially many functions f_r only essentially depend on a constant number of variables. This makes it possible to compute the conjunctive normal forms for all of the functions f_r in polynomial time. For each function the conjunctive normal form has at most 2^k clauses of length k. Now we apply the polynomial reduction SAT $\le_p$ 3-SAT (Theorem 4.3.2) to replace the clauses of each function with clauses of length 3. This replaces each of the given clauses with $k^* = \max\{1, k - 2\}$ clauses. To see that the properties of the functions f_r described above carry over to the new clause sets we note that f_r has the value 0 if any one of its at most 2^k clauses has the value 0. After the described transformation we obtain for f_r at most $k^* \cdot 2^k$ clauses, and the value of f_r is 0 if any one of these clauses is unsatisfied. Thus

- If the original set of clauses is satisfiable, then the at most $k^* \cdot 2^k \cdot N$ newly formed clauses are simultaneously satisfiable.
- If the original set of clauses is not satisfiable, then for any assignment of the variables of the newly formed clauses, there are at least $N/2$ clauses (one each for half of the N f_r-functions) that are not satisfied.

For $\delta := (N/2)/(k^* \cdot 2^k \cdot N) = 1/(k^* \cdot 2^{k+1})$ at most a proportion of $1 - \delta$ of the clauses in the newly formed clause set are simultaneously satisfiable unless all the clauses are simultaneously satisfiable. By our preceding discussion we have proven the theorem for $\varepsilon := 1/(1 - \delta) - 1 > 0$.   □

The proof of Theorem 12.3.1 shows that we get better results if we can decrease the size of k but that the constant c only effects the degree of the polynomial that bounds the runtime. If $k = 2$, then we get a set of clauses each of length 2. For such a set of clauses we can determine in polynomial time if all the clauses are simultaneously satisfiable (see Section 7.1). Such a probabilistic proof checker for 3-SAT or some other NP-complete problem would imply that NP = P. Theorem 12.3.1 and the existence of a polynomial approximation algorithm with finite approximation ratio for MAX-3-SAT imply the following corollary.

Corollary 12.3.2. *If* NP $\neq$ P, *then* MAX -3- SAT $\in$ APX $-$ PTAS.   □

Now we turn our attention to MAX-CLIQUE. This problem stood at the center of the attempts to find "better PCP Theorems" (Arora and Safra (1998), Håstad (1999)). Here we are unable to prove the best known result but will be satisfied with the following theorem.

Theorem 12.3.3. *If* NP $\neq$ P, *then* MAX-CLIQUE $\notin$ APX.

Proof. Once again we use the gap technique. As in the proof of Theorem 12.3.1, we use a probabilistic proof checker for 3-SAT that uses $\lfloor c \cdot \log n \rfloor$ random bits and reads exactly k bits of the proof for a clause set on n variables. Once again let $N := 2^{\lfloor c \cdot \log n \rfloor} \le n^c$. For this probabilistic proof checker we construct the following graph in polynomial time. For each assignment of the random vector r we consider all 2^k assignments of the k bits of the proof that are read. Each assignment for which the proof is accepted is represented by a vertex in the graph, so the number of vertices is bounded above by $2^k \cdot N$. The vertices that belong to the same r form a group. Vertices from the same group are never connected by edges. Vertices from different groups are connected by an edge if and only if there are no contradictions in the assignment for the proof bits that both read.

If the given set of clauses is satisfiable, then there is a proof that is accepted for all assignments r. From each group we consider the vertices that represent this proof. By definition these vertices form a clique of size N.

If the given set of clauses is not satisfiable, then every proof is only accepted for half of the assignments r. If there is a clique of size $N' > N/2$, then by construction, the N' vertices must come from N' different groups. Furthermore, pairwise their read bits do not contradict each other. So there is a proof that is compatible with all of these partial assignments of proof bits. This proof will be accepted by N' (more than half) of the N assignments of r, in contradiction to the assumption that the given set of clauses is not satisfiable.

So if NP $\neq$ P, then there is no polynomial approximation algorithm for MAX-CLIQUE that achieves an approximation ratio of 2.

In contrast to the proof of Theorem 12.3.1, the constant k does not show up in the size of the resulting gap. The gap is 2 because the probabilistic proof checker has an error-probability bounded by $1/2$. But for each constant $d > 1$, there is a PCP$(\log n, 1)$-verifier for 3-SAT with an error-probability bounded by $1/d$. If we carry out the same proof but use this probabilistic proof checker instead, we obtain a gap of size d. This proves the theorem. $\square$

Our proof of Theorem 12.3.3 applied the PCP Theorem directly. In Theorem 8.4.4 we described a PTAS-reduction from MAX-3-SAT to MAX-CLIQUE with $\alpha(\varepsilon) = \varepsilon$. Using this we obtain for MAX-CLIQUE the same inapproximability result that we showed for MAX-3-SAT in Theorem 12.3.1. In contrast to MAX-3-SAT, MAX-CLIQUE has the property of *self-improvability*, which means that from a polynomial approximation algorithm with approximation ratio c we can construct an approximation algorithm with approximation ratio $c^{1/2}$. Since this increases the degree of the polynomial bounding the runtime, we can only repeat this constantly many times. The approximation ratio can then be reduced from c to $c^{1/2^k}$ for any constant k, and thus under $1 + \varepsilon$ for any $\varepsilon > 0$. This gives us a proof of Theorem 12.3.3 from Theorem 12.3.1 without applying the PCP Theorem directly.

For the proof of the property of self-improvability we consider for undirected graphs $G = (V, E)$ the *product graph* G^2 on $V \times V$. The product graph contains the edge $\{(v_i, v_j), (v_k, v_l)\}$, if

- $(i, j) \neq (k, l)$, and
- $\{v_i, v_k\} \in E$ or $i = k$, and
- $\{v_j, v_l\} \in E$ or $j = l$.

From a clique with vertices $\{v_1, \ldots, v_r\}$ in G we obtain a clique with vertices $\{(v_i, v_j) \mid 1 \leq i, j \leq r\}$ in G^2. Thus if cl(G) denotes the maximal clique size in G, then cl$(G^2) \geq$ cl$(G)^2$. On the other hand, suppose there is a clique of size m in G^2. Consider the vertex pairs (v_i, v_j) that form this clique. In the first or second component of these pairs there must be at least $\lceil m^{1/2} \rceil$ vertices. To show that cl$(G^2) \leq$ cl$(G)^2$ we will show that these $\lceil m^{1/2} \rceil$ vertices form a clique in G. If v_i and v_j both occur as first components in the vertex pairs of the clique in G^2, then there are v_k and v_l such that (v_i, v_k) and (v_j, v_l) also belong to the clique in G^2, and so are connected by an edge. But this implies by the definition of G^2 that $\{v_i, v_j\} \in E$. The arguments proceed analogously if v_i and v_j are second components of such vertex pairs. Thus cl$(G^2) =$ cl$(G)^2$.

To improve a polynomial c-approximation algorithm A for MAX-CLIQUE we compute for G the graph G^2 and apply A to G^2 to get a clique of size m, from which we compute a clique of size $\lceil m^{1/2} \rceil$ in G which we output. Then $\mathrm{cl}(G^2)/m \leq c$ and

$$\mathrm{cl}(G)/\lceil m^{1/2} \rceil \leq (\mathrm{cl}(G)^2/m)^{1/2} = (\mathrm{cl}(G^2)/m)^{1/2} \leq c^{1/2}.$$

This gives us a $c^{1/2}$ approximation algorithm with polynomially bounded runtime.

We won't derive any more inapproximability results. Kann and Crescenzi (2000) survey the best currently known results. For the optimization problems that we have dealt with most intensively we list the best known bounds in Table 12.3.1.

12.4 The PCP Theorem and APX-Completeness

In Section 8.5 we already showed that MAX-W-SAT and MIN-W-SAT are NPO-complete. Here we want to use the PCP Theorem to show that MAX-3-SAT is APX-complete. This result is the starting point for many further APX-completeness results, but we will not discuss these here. We have already seen that NP = P follows from MAX-3-SAT ∈ PTAS. In the first and deciding step of the proof, we show that MAX-3-SAT is Max-APX-complete, where Max-APX contains the maximization problems from APX. After that we show that every problem in Min-APX can be reduced to a maximization variant of itself with a $\leq_{\mathrm{PTAS}}$-reduction. Combining these gives the announced result.

We first want to discuss the idea of the proof of Max-APX-completeness. Consider a problem $A \in$ Max-APX that can be approximated in polynomial time with an approximation ratio of $r^* \geq 1$. The constant r^* could be very large. On the other hand, for small approximation ratios, MAX-3-SAT is a difficult problem. The approximate solution for A provides us with an interval $[a, r^* \cdot a]$ for the value of an optimal solution. We divide this interval into subintervals $I_i := [\tilde{r}^{i-1} \cdot a, \tilde{r}^i \cdot a]$, $i \geq 1$, for some $\tilde{r} > 1$. As long as $\tilde{r}$ is also a constant, we obtain constantly many subintervals. For each subinterval the quotient formed by the upper and lower ends is so small that the subproblem A_i consisting of all instances that have an optimal solution value in I_i is $\leq_{\mathrm{PTAS}}$-reducible to MAX-3-SAT. Of course, now we have the problem of building from solutions for the constructed instances of MAX-3-SAT, solutions of sufficiently good approximation ratio for the entire instance of A. These ideas will be carried out in the following Lemma.

Lemma 12.4.1. MAX-3-SAT *is* Max-APX-*complete.*

Proof. At the end of Section 12.3 we said that MAX-3-SAT is 1.249-approximable. But we can show that MAX-3-SAT ∈ APX directly by a simple argument. Each clause is satisfied by one of the following assignments: the

MAX-SAT	1.2987-approximable and APX-complete
MAX-k-SAT	$1/(1 - 2^{-k})$-approximable for $k \geq 3$, if all the clauses have k different literals, but not $(1/(1 - 2^{-k}) - \varepsilon)$-approximable
MAX-3-SAT	1.249-approximable, even if literals are allowed to appear more than once in a clause
MAX-2-SAT	1.0741-approximable, but not 1.0476-approximable; literals may appear in a clause more than once
MIN-VERTEXCOVER	2-approximable, but not 1.3606-approximable
MIN-GC	$O(n(\log \log n)^2/\log^3 n)$-approximable, but not $n^{1/7-\varepsilon}$-approximable; not even $n^{1-\varepsilon}$-approximable, if NP $\neq$ ZPP
MAX-CLIQUE	$O(n/\log^2 n)$-approximable, but not $n^{1/2-\varepsilon}$-approximable; not even $n^{1-\varepsilon}$-approximable, if NP $\neq$ ZPP
MIN-TSP	NPO-complete
MIN-TSP$^{\text{sym},\Delta}$	3/2-approximable and APX-complete
MAX-3-DM	$(3/2 + \varepsilon)$-approximable and APX-complete
MIN-BINPACKING	3/2-approximable, but not even $(3/2 - \varepsilon)$-approximable
	$(71/60 + 78/(71\text{opt}))$-approximable and also $(1 + (\log^2 \text{opt})/\text{opt})$-approximable where opt denotes the value of an optimal solution
MIN-SETCOVER	$(1 + \ln n)$-approximable, where n is the cardinality of the underlying set, but for some $c > 0$ not $(c \cdot \ln n)$-approximable, and not $((1-\varepsilon) \ln n)$-approximable, if polynomial-time nondeterministic algorithms can't be replaced by deterministic algorithms that run in time $O(n^{\log \log n})$

Table 12.3.1. Best known approximability and inapproximability results. The approximation ratios are with respect to polynomial-time algorithms, ε is always an arbitrary positive constant, and the negative results assume that NP $\neq$ P unless we mention otherwise.

assignment consisting entirely of 0's and the assignment consisting entirely of 1's. Whichever of these two assignments satisfies the most clauses has an approximation ratio bounded by 2.

Now let $A \in$ Max-APX and let r^* be a constant approximation ratio achievable by an algorithm G. We want to show that $A \leq_{\text{PTAS}} B = \text{MAX-3-SAT}$. In the definition of $\leq_{\text{PTAS}}$-reducibility (Definition 8.4.1), the demands on the approximation ratio of the approximate solution for A that comes from the approximate solution for B are given by

$$r_B(f(x), y) \leq 1 + \alpha(\varepsilon) \Rightarrow r_A(x, g(x, y, \varepsilon)) \leq 1 + \varepsilon .$$

For $\alpha \colon \mathbb{Q}^+ \to \mathbb{Q}^+$ we will use a linear function $\alpha(\varepsilon) = \varepsilon/\beta$ with $\beta > 0$. Then $1 + \alpha(\varepsilon)$ can take on every rational value $r > 1$, $\varepsilon = \alpha(\varepsilon) \cdot \beta$, and for $r = 1 + \alpha(\varepsilon)$, $1 + \varepsilon = 1 + \alpha(\varepsilon) \cdot \beta = 1 + (r - 1) \cdot \beta$. The demand on the approximation ratio of $g(x, y, \varepsilon)$ given above is equivalent to

$$r_B(f(x), y) \leq r \Rightarrow r_A(x, g(x, y, r)) \leq 1 + \beta \cdot (r - 1) .$$

The following choice of the parameter β turns out to be suitable:

$$\beta := 2(r^* \log r^* + r^* - 1) \cdot (1 + \varepsilon)/\varepsilon ,$$

where $\varepsilon > 0$ is now a constant for which Theorem 12.3.1 is satisfied. Furthermore, ε is chosen so that β is rational. The smaller the "difficult gap" for MAX-3-SAT, and the worse the given approximation ratio for A is, the larger β will be and the weaker the demands will be for the approximate solution for A that must be computed.

The case $r^* \leq 1 + \beta \cdot (r - 1)$ can be handled easily. The approximation algorithm G already provides a sufficiently good approximate solution. For all instances x of the problem A, let $f(x)$ be the same arbitrary instance of B. That is, we will define $g(x, y, r)$ independently of y. Let $g(x, y, r)$ be the solution $s(x)$ that algorithm G computes for instance x. Its approximation ratio is bounded by $r^* \leq 1 + \beta \cdot (r - 1)$ and so the demand on the approximation ratio $g(x, y, r)$ is met.

We can now assume that $b := 1 + \beta \cdot (r - 1) < r^*$. Unfortunately there is no way to avoid a few arithmetic estimations in this proof. First, let k be defined by $k := \lceil \log_b r^* \rceil$. From $b < r^*$ and the inequality $\log z \geq 1 - z^{-1}$ for $z \geq 1$ it follows that

$$k \leq \frac{\log r^*}{\log b} + 1 \leq \frac{\log r^*}{1 - 1/b} + 1$$

$$= \frac{b \cdot \log r^*}{b - 1} + \frac{b - 1}{b - 1} < \frac{r^* \log r^* + r^* - 1}{b - 1} = \frac{1}{b - 1} \cdot \frac{\beta \cdot \varepsilon}{2 \cdot (1 + \varepsilon)}$$

and

$$\frac{b-1}{\beta} < \frac{\varepsilon}{2k(1+\varepsilon)} .$$

From $b = 1 + \beta \cdot (r-1)$ it follows that

$$r = \frac{b-1}{\beta} + 1 < \frac{\varepsilon}{2k(1+\varepsilon)} + 1 .$$

We again let $s(x)$ denote the solution computed by algorithm G for instance x, we let $v_A(x, s)$ denote the value of this solution, and we let $v_{\mathrm{opt}}(x)$ denote the value of an optimal solution for x. Then

$$v_A(x, s) \leq v_{\mathrm{opt}}(x) \leq r^* \cdot v_A(x, s) \leq b^k \cdot v_A(x, s) ,$$

where the last inequality follows from the definition of k. Now we partition the interval of solution values into k intervals of geometrically growing sizes, that is, into the intervals $I_i = [b^i \cdot v_A(x, s), b^{i+1} \cdot v_A(x, s))$ for $0 \leq i \leq k - 1$.

First we deal with the intervals individually. For $0 \leq i \leq k - 1$ we consider the following nondeterministic polynomial-time algorithm G_i for instances of A:

- Nondeterministically generate a solution $s' \in S(x)$ (the definitions in Section 8.1 imply that this is possible in polynomial time).
- Accept the input if $v_A(x, s') \geq b^i \cdot v_A(x, s)$. In this case, leave s' and $v_A(x, s')$ on the work tape.

Now we can apply the methods of the proof of Cook's Theorem to express the language accepted by this algorithm as a 3-SAT formula γ_i. It is important to note that we can compute s' and its value $v_A(x, s')$ in polynomial time from a satisfying assignment for γ_i. This is because the satisfying assignment also codes the accepting configuration. We can design the algorithms A_i so that they all have the same runtime. This means that all of the formulas γ_i ($0 \leq i \leq k - 1$) will have the same number of clauses. Finally we define φ_i as the result of the transformation of γ_i as described in Theorem 12.3.1 and $f(x)$ as the conjunction φ of all φ_i for $0 \leq i \leq k - 1$. Using the construction from Theorem 12.3.1 we have also obtained that all the formulas φ_i have the same number m of clauses.

So we have a MAX-3-SAT instance with km clauses and therefore $v_{\mathrm{opt}}(\varphi) \leq km$. Now let a be an assignment of the variables in this formula. We assume that the approximation ratio of a is bounded by r. Then $v_{\mathrm{opt}}(\varphi) \leq r \cdot v_B(\varphi, a)$ and

$$v_{\mathrm{opt}}(\varphi) - v_B(\varphi, a) \leq (1 - 1/r) \cdot v_{\mathrm{opt}}(\varphi) \leq (1 - 1/r) \cdot km .$$

Now let r_i be the approximation ratio for the assignment a if we use a as a solution for the MAX-3-SAT instance φ_i. Since the formulas φ_j for $0 \leq j \leq k-1$ come from different algorithms, they are defined on disjoint sets of variables. Optimal assignments for the subproblems can be selected independently and form an optimal solution to the combined problem. So for all $i \in \{0, \ldots, k-1\}$,

$$
\begin{aligned}
v_{\mathrm{opt}}(\varphi) - v_B(\varphi, a) &= \sum_{0 \le j \le k-1} (v_{\mathrm{opt}}(\varphi_j) - v_B(\varphi_j, a)) \\
&\ge v_{\mathrm{opt}}(\varphi_i) - v_B(\varphi_i, a) \\
&= v_{\mathrm{opt}}(\varphi_i) \cdot (1 - 1/r_i) ,
\end{aligned}
$$

where the last equality follows from the definition of r_i. In the proof that MAX-3-SAT $\in$ APX we saw that it is always possible to satisfy half of the clauses, so $v_{\mathrm{opt}}(\varphi_i) \ge m/2$ and

$$
v_{\mathrm{opt}}(\varphi) - v_B(\varphi, a) \ge m \cdot (1 - 1/r_i)/2 .
$$

We combine the two bounds for $v_{\mathrm{opt}}(\varphi) - v_B(\varphi, a)$ and obtain

$$
m \cdot (1 - 1/r_i)/2 \le (1 - 1/r) \cdot km .
$$

With a simple transformation we get

$$
1 - 2k(1 - 1/r) \le 1/r_i .
$$

Now we go back and use our previously proven inequality

$$
r < \frac{\varepsilon}{2k(1+\varepsilon)} + 1 = \frac{\varepsilon + 2k(1+\varepsilon)}{2k(1+\varepsilon)}
$$

and obtain

$$
\begin{aligned}
1 - 2k(1 - 1/r) &> 1 - 2k \cdot \frac{\varepsilon}{\varepsilon + 2k(1+\varepsilon)} \\
&= 1 - \frac{\varepsilon}{1 + \varepsilon + \varepsilon/(2k)} \\
&= \frac{1 + \varepsilon/(2k)}{1 + \varepsilon + \varepsilon/(2k)} .
\end{aligned}
$$

Together it follows that

$$
r_i < \frac{1 + \varepsilon + \varepsilon/(2k)}{1 + \varepsilon/(2k)} = 1 + \frac{\varepsilon}{1 + \varepsilon/(2k)} < 1 + \varepsilon .
$$

This approximation ratio even guarantees that we get a satisfying assignment for φ_i when one exists. In our consideration of NP $\subseteq$ PCP$(n^3, 1)$, we saw that from the always accepted proof that a 3-SAT formula is satisfiable we can compute in polynomial time (with respect to the length of the proof) a satisfying assignment. This is also true for the proofs of the actual PCP Theorem, which only have polynomial length.

By construction there is a j such that $\varphi_0, \ldots, \varphi_j$ are satisfiable but $\varphi_{j+1}, \ldots, \varphi_{k-1}$ are not satisfiable. Then $v_{\text{opt}}(x) \in I_j$, so

$$b^j \cdot v_A(x, s) \leq v_{\text{opt}}(x) \leq b^{j+1} \cdot v_A(x, s) .$$

From the satisfying assignment of φ_j we can compute in polynomial time a solution s^* for the instance x of A that has a value that lies in the interval I_j. We define the result of this computation as $g(x, a, r)$. Since $v_{\text{opt}}(x)$ and $v_A(x, s^*)$ lie in I_j,

$$v_{\text{opt}}(x)/v_A(x, s^*) \leq b = 1 + \beta \cdot (r - 1) ,$$

and so $r_A(x, g(x, a, r)) \leq 1 + \beta \cdot (r - 1)$. This proves the lemma.   □

Now we only have to derive the announced relationship between minimization problems and maximization problems.

Lemma 12.4.2. *For every minimization problem $A \in$ APX there is a maximization problem $B \in$ APX such that $A \leq_{\text{PTAS}} B$.*

Proof. The basic idea is to set up a maximization problem based on the minimization problem by altering the evaluation function so that the direction of the goal is reversed. The obvious idea of replacing $v(x, s)$ with $-v(x, s)$ is not allowed because the values must be positive (see Section 8.1). The next obvious idea is to replace $v(x, s)$ with $b - v(x, s)$ for a large enough b. This is problematic since for instances x for which $v_{\text{opt}}(x)$ is much smaller than b, solutions for the given problem A that have a poor approximation ratio suddenly have a good approximation ratio after the transformation. Thus the value of b would have to depend on x.

Since $A \in$ APX, there is a polynomial-time approximation algorithm G for A with a worst-case approximation ratio bounded above by a constant $r^* \geq 1$. We can choose r^* to be an integer. Let $s^*(x)$ denote the solution computed by algorithm G for instance x. Our maximization problem B will have the same set of instances as A, and for each instance the same allowable solutions. The value of a solution for x is defined by

$$v_A(x, y) \leq v_A(x, s^*(x)) \Rightarrow v_B(x, y) := (r^* + 1) \cdot v_A(x, s^*(x)) - r^* \cdot v_A(x, y),$$

$$v_A(x, y) > v_A(x, s^*(x)) \Rightarrow v_B(x, y) := v_A(x, s^*(x)) .$$

This evaluation function v_B can be computed in polynomial time. We can use the approximation algorithm G as an approximation algorithm for the maximization problem B. By the definition of v_B, $v_B(x, s^*(x)) = v_A(x, s^*(x))$ and

$$v_A(x, s^*(x)) \leq v_{\text{opt},B}(x) \leq (r^* + 1) \cdot v_A(x, s^*(x)) .$$

From this it follows that $v_{\text{opt},B}(x)/v_B(x, s^*(x)) \leq r^* + 1$ and for the maximization problem B, G yields an approximation ratio bounded by $r^* + 1$, and so $B \in$ APX.

Now we need to design a $\leq_{\text{PTAS}}$-reduction from A to B. For this we define $f(x) = x$, so we consider the same instance for A and for B. The back transformation depends only on the instance x and the solution y but not on the approximation ratio r. As in the proof of Lemma 12.4.1, we measure the approximation ratio with r and not with ε. Then we define g by

$$v_A(x, y) \leq v_A(x, s^*(x)) \Rightarrow g(x, y, r) := y \;,$$

$$v_A(x, y) > v_A(x, s^*(x)) \Rightarrow g(x, y, r) := s^*(x) \;.$$

So g is polynomial-time computable. Finally, we let $\beta := r^* + 1$.

Now we need to check the following condition:

$$r_B(f(x), y) \leq r \Rightarrow r_A(x, g(x, y, r)) \leq 1 + \beta \cdot (r - 1) \;.$$

As in the definition of the evaluation function and the definition of g, we distinguish between two cases. The simpler case is the case that $v_A(x, y) > v_A(x, s^*(x))$. Then $s^*(x)$ is chosen as the result and $s^*(x)$ is better than y. Thus

$$r_A(x, g(x, y, r)) = r_A(x, s^*(x)) \leq r \leq r + (\beta - 1)(r - 1) = 1 + \beta \cdot (r - 1) \;,$$

where the last inequality follows because $\beta \geq 1$ and $r \geq 1$.

Now suppose $v_A(x, y) \leq v_A(x, s^*(x))$ so that $g(x, y, r) = y$. We have defined v_B just so that the condition we must show will be fulfilled. We have

$$r_A(x, g(x, y, r)) = r_A(x, y) = v_A(x, y)/v_{\text{opt}, A}(x)$$

and so it suffices to bound $v_A(x, y)$ from above by $(1 + \beta \cdot (r - 1)) \cdot v_{\text{opt}, A}(x)$. By the definition of $v_B(x, y)$,

$$v_A(x, y) = ((r^* + 1) \cdot v_A(x, s^*(x)) - v_B(x, y))/r^* \;.$$

By our assumption $r_B(f(x), y) = r_B(x, y) = v_{\text{opt}, B}(x)/v_B(x, y) \leq r$, and thus

$$v_B(x, y) \geq v_{\text{opt}, B}(x)/r \;.$$

A simple computation shows that $1/r \geq 2 - r$ if $r \geq 1$. Together we get

$$v_A(x, y) \leq ((r^* + 1) \cdot v_A(x, s^*(x)) - (2 - r)v_{\text{opt}, B}(x))/r^*$$
$$= ((r^* + 1) \cdot v_A(x, s^*(x)) - v_{\text{opt}, B}(x))/r^* + (r - 1) \cdot v_{\text{opt}, B}(x)/r^* \;.$$

First we give an estimate for the second summand. By the definition of v_B,

$$v_{\text{opt}, B}(x) \leq (r^* + 1) \cdot v_A(x, s^*(x)) \;.$$

Since $\beta = r^* + 1$ and $s^*(x)$ is r^*-optimal for A, it follows that

$$(r - 1) \cdot v_{\text{opt}, B}(x)/r^* \leq (r - 1) \cdot \beta \cdot v_A(x, s^*(x))/r^* \leq \beta \cdot (r - 1) \cdot v_{\text{opt}, A}(x) \;.$$

So the claim reduces to

$$((r^* + 1) \cdot v_A(x, s^*(x)) - v_{\text{opt},B}(x))/r^* \leq v_{\text{opt},A}(x) .$$

This inequality is even correct as an equality. Here we make use of the special choice of v_B which for a given instance x causes the same solution y^* to be optimal for both A and B. So $v_A(x, y^*) = v_{\text{opt},A}(x)$, $v_B(x, y^*) = v_{\text{opt},B}(x)$, and

$$v_B(x, y^*) = (r^* + 1) \cdot v_A(x, s^*(x)) - r^* \cdot v_A(x, y^*) .$$

From this it follows that

$$((r^* + 1) \cdot v_A(x, s^*(x)) - v_{\text{opt},B}(x))/r^* = v_{\text{opt},A}(x) .$$

Together we have

$$v_A(x, y) \leq (1 + \beta \cdot (r - 1)) \cdot v_{\text{opt},A}(x)$$

and the lemma is proved.   □

From Lemmas 12.4.1 and 12.4.2 we obtain our main result.

Theorem 12.4.3. Max-3-Sat *is* APX-*complete.*   □

This result is the starting point for using approximation-preserving reductions to obtain more APX-completeness results.

The PCP Theorem contains a new characterization of the complexity class NP. *The one-sided error and error-probability of* 1/2 *allowed in this characterization give rise to a large "gap" between the instances that are accepted and those that are rejected. This gap facilitates new applications of the gap technique for proving inapproximability results and completeness results for classes of approximation problems.*

13

Further Topics From Classical Complexity Theory

13.1 Overview

As was emphasized already in the introduction, the main focus of this text is on particular complexity theoretical results for important problems. So newer aspects like the complexity of approximation problems or interactive proofs have been placed in the foreground while structural aspects have been reduced to the bare essentials required for the desired results. But there are additional classical topics of complexity theory with results of fundamental importance. A few of these will be presented in this chapter.

The complexity classes we have investigated to this point have been based on the resource of computation time. An obvious thing to try is to develop an analogous theory for the resource of storage space. The resulting classes are defined in Section 13.2. It can be shown that all decision problems that are contained in the polynomial hierarchy can be decided using only polynomially bounded space and so are contained in the class PSPACE. This means that problems that are complete for PSPACE with respect to polynomial reductions do not belong to Σ_k unless $\Sigma_k = $ PSPACE. So these problems are also difficult with respect to the resource of time. PSPACE-complete problems will be introduced in Section 13.3.

The next natural question is whether there is a hierarchy of classes analogous to polynomial hierarchy – more precisely the *time* hierarchy – for space-based complexity classes. But the analogous hierarchy of classes does not exist because nondeterminism can be simulated deterministically in quadratic space (Section 13.4) and nondeterminism can simulate "co-nondeterminism" with the same space requirements (Section 13.5). Another place that one could use space bounds in place of time bounds would be to replace polynomial reductions – more precisely polynomial *time* reductions – with space-bounded reductions. Reductions that only require logarithmic space are a restriction on polynomial-time reductions and permit a view of the structure within P. The study of this structure leads to the discovery of problems in P that presumably cannot be solved by computers with many processors in polylogarithmic time. These issues will be discussed in Section 13.6. Finally, in Section 13.7 we introduce another variant of many problems. In Section 2.1 we distinguished between optimization problems, evaluation problems, and decision problems. In decision problems we ask whether or not there exists a solution with a certain property. A generalization of this is the counting problem, in which the number of such solutions must be computed.

13.2 Space-Bounded Complexity Classes

As we did for time-based complexity classes, we will use the Turing machine model to define space-bounded complexity classes. The space used by a nondeterministic computation on input x can be measured by counting the number of different tape cells that are visited during the computation. For nondeterministic computations we must consider all computation paths. Since for most problems it is necessary to read the entire input, sublinear space would not make much sense. But this is too coarse a measure of space. Instead, we consider Turing machines with two tapes. The input is located on an *input tape* on which the beginning and end are marked. The input tape is *read-only*, that is its contents can be read, but no new symbols can be written on the input tape. The second tape is the *work tape* and behaves like the tapes we are accustomed to, except that we will require this tape to be *one-way infinite*, that is we only allow addresses $i \geq 1$. The space used by a computation is measured solely in terms of the work tape, and is equal to the largest j such that work tape cell j is visited during the computation.

Definition 13.2.1. *The complexity class* DTAPE($s(n)$) *contains all decision problems that can be decided by a deterministic Turing machine using at most* $\lceil s(|x|) \rceil$ *space for each input x.* NTAPE ($s(n)$) *is defined analogously for nondeterministic Turing machines.* PSPACE *is the union of all* DTAPE(n^k) *for* $k \in \mathbb{N}$.

The notation is not entirely consistent since TAPE and SPACE refer to the same resource. But here as elsewhere we will go with the notation used most often. It is notable that the space bound $s(n)$ is taken very exactly. DTAPE(n) only allows n tape cells to be used on the work tape, whereas linear time allowed $O(n)$ computation steps. This can be explained by the following remark, in which we will show that for space bounds constant factors can be saved without any difficulty.

Remark 13.2.2. For every natural number k, DTAPE $(s(n))$ = DTAPE $(s(n)/k)$ and NTAPE $(s(n))$ = NTAPE $(s(n)/k)$.

Proof. If we replace the tape alphabet Γ with $\Gamma' := \Gamma^k \times \{1, \ldots, k\}$, then we can store k symbols from Γ on one tape cell and also mark which of them is "really" being read. The simulation using this idea is now obvious.   □

At this point we want to make a few comments about the class CSL for those who are familiar with the classes in the Chomsky hierarchy. Context sensitive languages are defined by context-sensitive grammars (for more information see, for example, Hopcroft, Motwani, and Ullman (2001)). Except for the generation of the empty string, context-sensitive languages are monotone, that is, the right side of each rule is not shorter than the left side. This allows the following nondeterministic algorithm that checks if $x \in L$ for a context-sensitive language L. On the work tape a region of length $|x|$ is marked. This is where a derivation starting with the start symbol will be nondeterministically generated. Derivations that do not stay within the space bounds indicated by the marked cells are terminated and x is rejected. Otherwise, the sequence generated is compared with the input x after every step. If they are found to be equal, x is accepted. This shows that $CSL \subseteq NTAPE(n)$. We will omit the proof of the other direction but state the result in the following theorem.

Theorem 13.2.3. $CSL = NTAPE(n)$.   □

This theorem shows that complexity classes based on space bounds can be used to characterize important classes of problems.

Connections between time and space bounds are interesting. The basic idea of the following consideration is simple. If a computation with restricted space uses too much time, then it must repeat a configuration (see Section 5.4). A configuration is an instantaneous snapshot of a Turing machine. The set of all possible configurations for an input of length n can be described by $Q \times \{1, \ldots, n\} \times \{1, \ldots, s(n)\} \times \Gamma^{s(n)}$, that is, by giving the current state $q \in Q$, the position $i \in \{1, \ldots, n\}$ on the input tape, the position $j \in \{1, \ldots, s(n)\}$ on the work tape, and the contents $y \in \Gamma^{s(n)}$ of the work tape. If there is an accepting computation path, then there is an accepting computation path that does not repeat any configurations and therefore has length at most $|Q| \cdot n \cdot s(n) \cdot |\Gamma|^{s(n)} = 2^{O(\log n + s(n))}$. Since we can count computation steps, we can terminate computation paths that have not halted after $|Q| \cdot n \cdot s(n) \cdot |\Gamma|^{s(n)}$ steps and reject the input along these paths. The only requirement is that $s(n)$ can be computed from n in time $2^{O(\log n + s(n))}$. This is true of all "reasonable" space bounds. So we make the following remark:

Remark 13.2.4. If $s(n)$ can be computed in space $s(n)$ and in time bounded by $2^{O(\log n + s(n))}$, then deterministic Turing machines using at most $s(n)$ space can be simulated by Turing machines that use space $s(n)$ and time $2^{O(\log n + s(n))}$. The same is true for nondeterministic Turing machines.

Between space and time there is at most an exponential blow-up if $s(n) \geq \log n$. Space bounds $s(n) = o(\log n)$ are a special case, since the position on the input tape can serve as auxiliary storage. This explains why some of the results that follow begin with the assumption that $s(n) \geq \log n$. From Remark 13.2.4 it follows immediately that $DTAPE(\log n) \subseteq P$.

Theorem 13.2.5. *If $s(n)$ can be computed in time $2^{O(\log n + s(n))}$, then nondeterministic Turing machines with space bound $s(n)$ can be simulated by deterministic Turing machines using time and space both bounded by $2^{O(\log n + s(n))}$.*

Proof. Let $L \in \mathsf{NTAPE}(s(n))$ and let M be the corresponding nondeterministic Turing machine. The configuration graph of M has a vertex for each of the $2^{O(\log n + s(n))}$ configurations. An edge goes from one configuration to another if the second is a possible successor configuration of the first for M. Using depth-first search we can check in linear time (with respect to the size $2^{O(\log n + s(n))}$) whether an accepting configuration is reachable from the initial configuration. □

In particular, $\mathsf{NTAPE}(\log n) \subseteq \mathsf{P}$.

We conclude this section with a comparison of the polynomial hierarchy and PSPACE.

Theorem 13.2.6. *For all $k \in \mathbb{N}$, $\Sigma_k \subseteq \mathsf{PSPACE}$, thus $\mathsf{PH} \subseteq \mathsf{PSPACE}$.*

Proof. We prove by induction on k that Σ_k and Π_k are subsets of PSPACE. $\Sigma_0 = \Pi_0 = \mathsf{P} \subseteq \mathsf{PSPACE}$, since it is not possible in polynomial time to use more than polynomial space. If $L \in \Sigma_k = \mathsf{NP}(\Pi_{k-1})$, then by the logical characterization of Σ_k there is a decision problem $L' \in \Pi_{k-1}$ and a polynomial p such that

$$L = \left\{ x \mid \exists y \in \{0,1\}^{p(|x|)} : (x, y) \in L' \right\}.$$

Now we try all values of y in lexicographical order. The storage of the current y requires only polynomial space $p(|x|)$, and by the inductive hypothesis, checking whether $(x, y) \in L'$ can be done in space that is polynomial in $|x| + p(|x|)$. So the space required for the entire algorithm is polynomially bounded in $|x|$. This proves that $\Sigma_k \subseteq \mathsf{PSPACE}$; $\Pi_k \subseteq \mathsf{PSPACE}$ follows analogously. □

In summary, for all $k \geq 1$,

$$\mathsf{DTAPE}(\log n) \subseteq \mathsf{NTAPE}(\log n) \subseteq \mathsf{P} \subseteq \mathsf{NP} \subseteq \Sigma_k \subseteq \mathsf{PSPACE} \subseteq \mathsf{NPSPACE}.$$

13.3 PSPACE-complete Problems

By Definition 5.1.1, a decision problem L is PSPACE-complete if it belongs to PSPACE and every decision problem $L' \in \mathsf{PSPACE}$ can by polynomially reduced to L, that is, $L' \leq_p L$. Just as NP-complete problems can be solvable in nondeterministic linear time, so PSPACE-complete problems don't necessarily require a lot of space. But since $\Sigma_k \subseteq \mathsf{PSPACE}$ (Theorem 13.2.6) and Σ_k is closed under polynomial reductions, a PSPACE-complete problem can only be in Σ_k if $\Sigma_k = \mathsf{PSPACE}$. So for PSPACE-complete problems it is "even less likely" than for NP-complete problems that they can be solved in polynomial time. Just as the generalization $\mathsf{SAT}^k_{\mathrm{CIR}}$ of SAT was the first problem that we showed to be Σ_k-complete, so it will be another obvious generalization of these problems that will be our first PSPACE-complete problem.

Definition 13.3.1. *A* quantified Boolean formula *consists of a Boolean expression $E(x)$ over $0, 1, x_1, \ldots, x_k$ and the Boolean operators $\wedge$ (AND), $+$ (OR), and $\neg$ (NOT), such that all the variables are quantified:*

$$(Q_1 x_1) \ldots (Q_k x_k) \colon E(x) \text{ with } Q_i \in \{\exists, \forall\}.$$

The decision problem QBF *is the decision problem of determining whether a quantified Boolean expression is true.*

In an instance of QBF the number of quantifier alternations is bounded only by the number of variables (minus 1). So QBF is a natural generalization of $\text{SAT}_{\text{CIR}}^k$.

Theorem 13.3.2. QBF *is* PSPACE-*complete.*

Proof. First we note that QBF $\in$ DTAPE$(n) \subseteq$ PSPACE, where n is the length of the input. Let k be the number of quantifiers (which equals the number of variables). It is easy to check whether a Boolean expression over constants is true in linear space. This is the claim when $k = 0$. In the general case we must consider both possible values of x_1 and for each evaluate a quantified Boolean expression with $k - 1$ quantifiers. To store the result of one of these evaluations while we compute the other requires only a constant amount of extra space, so by Remark 13.2.2, QBF $\in$ DTAPE$(n) \subseteq$ PSPACE.

Now we must show how to polynomially reduce an arbitrary problem $L \in$ PSPACE to QBF. By the results in Section 13.2 we can assume that L is decided by a Turing machine M in space $p(n)$ and time $2^{p(n)}$ for some polynomial p. As in the proof of Cook's Theorem (Theorem 5.4.3) we will represent the computation of M with a Boolean formula. We already know that we can express configurations using variables in space $p(n)$ and how to test a Boolean formula to see if the variables represent a possible configuration. We will use the abbreviated notation $\exists K$ and $\forall K$ for quantification over all the variables that represent configurations, and always assume that the test whether the variables describe a configuration is conjunctively added to the formulas described below. The formula $S(K, x)$ tests whether K is the initial configuration for input x, and $A(K)$ tests whether K is an accepting configuration. Finally, $T_j(K, K')$ tests for two configurations K and K' whether K' can be reached in 2^j steps from K.

Our first attempt to transform the input x for the decision problem L into a quantified Boolean formula $Q(x)$ is

$$Q(x) := \exists K_0 \exists K_a \colon (T_{p(n)}(K_0, K_a) \wedge S(K_0, x) \wedge A(K_a)).$$

It is clear that $x \in L$ if and only if $Q(x)$ is true, but $T_{p(n)}(K_0, K_a)$ is not yet in the proper syntactical form. Now we describe how to bring $T_j(K_1, K_2)$ into the proper form. For $j = 0$ we can reuse the construction from the proof of Cook's Theorem. By induction, the representation

$$T_j(K_1, K_2) = \exists K \colon (T_{j-1}(K_1, K) \wedge T_{j-1}(K, K_2))$$

is correct. Proceeding this way leads in the end to a syntactically correct but exponentially long representation, so this cannot be done in polynomial time.

The key idea of this proof is to have T_j get by with one call to T_{j-1} instead of two, as is needed in the formula above. We claim that $T_j(K_1, K_2)$ can be represented as

$$\exists K_3 \forall K_4 \forall K_5 \colon B(K_1, \ldots, K_5) + T_{j-1}(K_4, K_5) \tag{13.1}$$

with

$$B(K_1, \ldots, K_5) := \neg \Big[((K_4, K_5) = (K_1, K_3)) + ((K_4, K_5) = (K_3, K_2)) \Big] \, .$$

In case $T_j(K_1, K_2)$ is true, let K_3 be the configuration reached from configuration K_1 after 2^{j-1} steps. Then $B(K_1, \ldots, K_5)$ is clearly true for all pairs except for (K_1, K_3) and (K_3, K_2). But the entire expression is also true for these pairs since $T_{j-1}(K_1, K_3)$ and $T_{j-1}(K_3, K_2)$ are true. On the other hand, if K_3 witnesses that Formula (13.1) is true, then it follows that $T_{j-1}(K_1, K_3)$ and $T_{j-1}(K_3, K_2)$ and thus $T_j(K_1, K_2)$ are true. This formula can be applied to express $T_{p(n)}(K_0, K_a)$ in terms of a T_0-expression. For this we quantify over $3 \cdot p(n)$ configurations and there are $p(n)$ expressions of the form $B(K_1, \ldots, K_5)$ and then finally a T_0-expression. Since configurations can be described with polynomially many variables and can be checked for syntactic correctness with formulas of polynomial length, and since a test for the equality of two configurations only requires formulas of polynomial length, the entire formula $Q(x)$ has polynomial length. Its simple structure makes it possible to construct $Q(x)$ in polynomial time. This polynomial reduction of L to QBF proves the theorem.   □

There is a long list of **PSPACE**-complete problems (see, for example, Garey and Johnson (1979)). Interestingly many well-known games are **PSPACE**-complete, if they are generalized to arbitrary sizes. For the well-known board games go and checkers, there are obvious generalizations to boards of size $n \times n$. Such generalizations for games like chess, however, seem somewhat artificial. In any case, for these generalized games we have the following decision problem: given a legal placement of the game pieces and a player, does this player have a winning strategy? If it is Alice's turn to move, and her opponent is Bob, then this question can be expressed as

$$\exists \text{ move for Alice } \forall \text{ move for Bob } \exists \ldots \colon \text{ Alice wins.}$$

This representation has a certain similarity to quantified Boolean expressions. We will not present any proofs that particular generalized games lead to **PSPACE**-complete problems here. The fact that these problems are **PSPACE**-complete perhaps helps explain why for the usual sizes of boards it has not yet been possible to determine which player has a winning strategy.

Because of the *padding technique* used in the proof, we want to show that the *word problem for context-sensitive grammars* WCSL is PSPACE-complete. For WCSL an instance consists of a context-sensitive grammar G and a word w. The question is whether w can be generated by G.

Theorem 13.3.3. WCSL *is* PSPACE-*complete.*

Proof. Let (G, w) be an instance of WCSL. The remarks before Theorem 13.2.3 show that WCSL $\in$ NTAPE(n). In Section 13.4 we will show that NTAPE$(n) \subseteq$ DTAPE(n^2). Thus WCSL $\in$ PSPACE.

Now suppose $L \in$ PSPACE, and let M be a deterministic Turing machine that decides L in polynomial time using space bounded by $p(n) \geq n$. From L we construct a decision problem LONG(L). For some special symbol Z that has not yet been used, LONG(L) contains all strings $xZ^{p(|x|)-|x|}$ with $x \in L$. That is, to each word $x \in L$ we add $p(|x|) - |x|$ copies of the symbol Z. The length of this new word is then $p(|x|)$. We can choose p to be of such a simple form that checking whether the input has the right number of special symbols at the end can be done in $p(|x|)$ space. After that, all we need to do is decide whether $x \in L$. By assumption, this is possible using $p(|x|)$ space. Because of the artificial lengthening of the instances, it follows that LONG$(L) \in$ DTAPE(n). So by Theorem 13.2.3, LONG(L) is a context-sensitive language. The proof of Theorem 13.2.3 is constructive and shows how a context-sensitive grammar $G(L)$ for LONG(L) can be constructed from the corresponding linear space-bounded Turing machine M. Since the length of the description of M only depends on L and p and not on the input x, the time needed to compute $G(L)$ is a constant with respect to $|x|$. So from x we can compute $G(L)$ and the word $w = xZ^{p(|x|)-|x|}$ in polynomial time. By construction x belongs to L if and only if w can be generated by $G(L)$. $\square$

13.4 Nondeterminism and Determinism in the Context of Bounded Space

To simulate nondeterministic computations deterministically we simulate all of the exponentially many computation paths. This requires exponential computation time. But in terms of space use, we "only" need to keep track of which paths have already been simulated. That this doesn't require exponential space is not really very surprising.

Before we formulate this result, we want to point out a technical detail. Here and in Section 13.5, for a space bound $s(n)$ we want to be able to reserve a portion of the tape with $s(n)$ cells. This should be possible with $s(n)$ space available. Nevertheless, although this is possible for many important functions $s(n)$, it is not possible for all of them. So we will use the following definition to separate out the "good" space bounds.

Definition 13.4.1. *A function* $s : \mathbb{N} \to \mathbb{N}$ *is called* space constructible *if there is an* $s(n)$-*space-bounded deterministic Turing machine which for any input* x *computes the binary representation of* $s(|x|)$.

If we have $s(|x|)$ in binary representation, then we can mark a storage region of length $s(|x|)$ in space $s(|x|)$.

Theorem 13.4.2 (Savitch's Theorem). *If the function* $s(n) \geq \log n$ *is space constructible, then*

$$\mathsf{NTAPE}(s(n)) \subseteq \mathsf{DTAPE}(s(n)^2).$$

Proof. Let L be a decision problem in $\mathsf{NTAPE}(s(n))$, and let M be a nondeterministic Turing machine that decides L in space $s(n)$. We will build a Turing machine M' that decides L deterministically in space $O(s(n)^2)$. The theorem then follows by Remark 13.2.2.

On input x, the Turing machine M' first computes the binary representation of $s(|x|)$ and always describes configurations of M as configurations with $s(|x|)$ tape cells. This is possible because s is space constructible. By Remark 13.2.4 and the assumption that $s(n) \geq \log n$, we can assume that M runs in $s(n)$ space and $2^{c \cdot s(n)}$ time for some constant $c \in \mathbb{N}$. Later we will describe how we can deterministically check using $O((j+1)s(n))$ space whether M can get from configuration K_1 to configuration K_2 in 2^j steps. The claim follows by applying this to the initial configuration $K_0(x)$, the accepting configuration K_a, and $j = c \cdot s(n)$. For this we assume that there is only one accepting configuration. This is easily achieved by having the Turing machine erase the tape (formally by writing blank symbols in each cell) and moving the tape head to tape cell 1 before accepting.

For $j = 0$ the claim is simple, since we can generate from K_1 all possible successor configurations and compare them with K_2. For the inductive step we apply the predicate $T_j(K_1, K_2)$ from Section 13.3, which is true if K_2 can be reached in 2^j steps from K_1. Then

$$T_j(K_1, K_2) = \exists K_3 \colon (T_{j-1}(K_1, K_3) \wedge T_{j-1}(K_3, K_2)) .$$

We use extra space only to store j and to try out all K_3 in lexicographical order. So we need space for two configurations and for j. The configurations K_1 and K_2 are given. For each K_3 we use $O(j \cdot s(n))$ space to check whether $T_{j-1}(K_1, K_3)$ is true. In the negative case we generate the lexicographic successor of K_3 and work with it. In the positive case we use the same space to check whether $T_{j-1}(K_3, K_2)$ is true. If not, then we proceed as above; and if so, then $T_j(K_1, K_2)$ is true. If all K_3 are tested without success, then $T_j(K_1, K_2)$ is not true. Together for the test of T_j we require space for the test of T_{j-1} and extra space $O(s(n))$. So the total space required is $O((j+1) \cdot s(n))$ and the theorem is proved. □

Corollary 13.4.3. PSPACE = NPSPACE. □

Thus with respect to the resource of space, the analogous hierarchy to the polynomial hierarchy collapses to the lowest level, namely to PSPACE.

13.5 Nondeterminism and Complementation with Precise Space Bounds

The results from Section 13.4 can be interpreted to say that to simulate nondeterminism deterministically, a bit more space suffices, but we believe that for some tasks we need much more time. So it makes sense to investigate complexity classes for fixed space bounds $s(n)$. Starting with the complexity classes DTAPE($s(n)$), NTAPE($s(n)$), and co-NTAPE($s(n)$), and working analogously to the polynomial hierarchy we can define a sequence of space-bounded complexity classes. While we suspect that each class in the polynomial hierarchy is distinct, this is not that case for these space-bounded complexity classes even for a fixed space bound. We show that for "nice" functions with $s(n) \geq \log n$, NTAPE($s(n)$) = co-NTAPE($s(n)$), and so the "hierarchy" that we had imagined collapses to the first level. The question of whether in fact DTAPE($s(n)$) = NTAPE($s(n)$) has not yet been answered. For the special case that $s(n) = n$ this is the LBA problem (linear bounded automaton problem), namely the question of whether the word problem for context-sensitive grammars can be solved deterministically in linear space. In order to prove the theorem mentioned above, we need to "efficiently" simulate a nondeterministic algorithm co-nondeterministically. The efficiency required, however, is only in terms of space and not in terms of time.

Theorem 13.5.1 (Immerman und Szelepcsényi). *If the function $s(n)$ is space constructible and $s(n) \geq \log n$, then*

$$\text{NTAPE}(s(n)) = \text{co-NTAPE}(s(n)) .$$

Proof. It suffices to show that NTAPE($s(n)$) $\subseteq$ co-NTAPE($s(n)$) since then co-NTAPE($s(n)$) $\subseteq$ co-co-NTAPE($s(n)$) = NTAPE($s(n)$) follows immediately.

So let L be a language in NTAPE($s(n)$), and let M be a nondeterministic Turing machine that decides L in space $s(n)$. Because of the space-constructibility of $s(n) \geq \log n$ and Remark 13.2.4, we can assume that on every computation path M stops after at most $2^{c \cdot s(n)}$ computation steps for some constant $c \in \mathbb{N}$. If we could simulate every computation path deterministically in space $s(n)$, then we could improve Savitch's Theorem and solve the LBA problem.

Before we explain the proof idea we want to treat a few technical details. For an input x of length n, configurations of M will always be described for $s(n)$ space. Because $s(n)$ is space-constructible, we can mark off the corresponding regions on the tape. We will use counters that can take on values from $\{0, \ldots, 2^{c \cdot s(n)}\}$. Each counter can be stored in $c \cdot s(n) + 1$ tape cells.

So as long as we store no more than constantly many counters and configurations at one time, the required space will be bounded by $O(s(n))$ and by Remark 13.2.2, this is equivalent to space bounded by $s(n)$.

In order to prove that $L \in$ co-NTAPE$(s(n))$ we must reject inputs $x \in L$ on every computation path and we must accept inputs $x \notin L$ on at least one computation path. On some paths the nondeterministic algorithm M' for $\overline{L}$ will be certain that $x \in L$ and halt with the answer "$x \in L$". For $\overline{L}$, "$x \in L$" is equivalent to rejecting. On some paths M' will not be certain whether $x \in L$ or $x \notin L$. Since we must make the correct decision for all $x \in L$, algorithm M' will halt with the conclusion "$x \in L$" on these paths. This will guarantee a correct decision whenever $x \in L$. Furthermore, M' must guarantee for any $x \notin L$ there is at least one path on which one can be sure that $x \notin L$.

When can we be sure that $x \notin L$? Only if we know that none of the configurations that can be reached from the initial configuration $K_0(x)$ for x are accepting. Suppose we know the number of configurations $A(x)$ that can be reached from $K_0(x)$. Then we could proceed as follows. We step through the configurations of M in lexicographic order. To do this we only need to store the current configuration K. Then we check nondeterministically whether it is possible to get from $K_0(x)$ to K in $2^{c \cdot s(n)}$ steps. This requires space for a counter and two configurations that contain the amount of computation time already used, the configuration reached K', and a nondeterministically generated configuration K''. If K'' is not an immediate successor of K', then we halt with the output "$x \in L$". Now consider the case that the configuration K'' is an immediate successor of K'. If $K'' \neq K$, then we continue the process with $K' := K''$ and a new nondeterministically generated K''. If we find a reachable accepting configuration, then we stop with "$x \in L$". This process will stop after at most $2^{c \cdot s(n)}$ steps. We use another counter that starts with the value 1 for the initial configuration. For each other configuration K that we identify as reachable but not accepting, we increase the counter by one. If we have tried out all possible configurations K and haven't stopped, then we compare the configuration counter z with $A(x)$. In any case $z \leq A(x)$. If $z < A(x)$, then we have failed to classify at least one reachable configuration as reachable with our nondeterministic algorithm. So our attempt to identify all reachable configurations has failed and we halt and output "$x \in L$". On the other hand, if $z = A(x)$, we have identified all reachable configurations and determined that none of them are accepting. In this case we are certain that $x \notin L$ and we can output this result. For every reachable configuration there is a sequence of configurations of the length considered describing the corresponding computation. So for $x \notin L$ there is at least one computation path in the nondeterministic algorithm just described that leads to the result "$x \notin L$".

We have proved the theorem if we can show that $A(x)$ can be calculated nondeterministically. The nondeterministic computation of a number means that computation paths can be unsuccessfully terminated, that no path can provide an incorrect answer, and that at least one path must provide the correct answer.

The new idea in this proof is the nondeterministic computation of $A(x)$. The method used is called *inductive counting* because we inductively compute $A_t(x)$ (for $0 \leq t \leq 2^{c \cdot s(n)}$), the number of configurations that are reachable from $K_0(x)$ in at most t steps. Clearly $A_0(x) = 1$ since we have only the initial configuration. Now suppose we know $A_t(x)$ and need to compute $A_{t+1}(x)$. We consider all configurations K in lexicographic order and count those that are reachable in $t + 1$ steps. For each K and the correct value of $A_t(x)$, we check each configuration K' as described above to determine whether it can be reached in t steps. Configuration K is reachable in at most $t + 1$ steps if and only if it is one of the configurations reachable in at most t steps or an immediate successor of one of these configurations. All attempts that do not correctly identify all $A_t(x)$ configurations that are reachable in at most t steps are terminated unsuccessfully. In this way we never output an incorrect answer. But there must be a computation path along which each time all $A_t(x)$ configurations that can be reached in at most t steps are correctly identified. Along such paths it is correctly decided for each configuration K whether K can be reached in at most $t + 1$ steps. In this case $A_{t+1}(x)$ is correctly computed. Together we have the desired nondeterministic algorithm for computing $A(x)$ and so a nondeterministic algorithm for $\overline{L}$. The space constraints are not exceeded because we never need to store more than constantly many counters and configurations. □

13.6 Complexity Classes Within P

By Theorem 13.2.5 DTAPE($\log n$) $\subseteq$ NTAPE($\log n$) $\subseteq$ P. We are interested now in problems that are in P or in NTAPE($\log n$) but presumably not in DTAPE($\log n$). It is not immediately clear why we should be interested in such problems since practically speaking linear space is always available without any difficulty. The reason for our interest is the so-called *parallel computation hypothesis* which says that small space – in particular, logarithmic space – is closely related to polylogarithmic time on computers with polynomially many processors. This unexpected relationship will be considered in more detail in Chapter 14. Problems that are in P but presumably not in DTAPE($\log n$) are efficiently solvable but presumably do not "parallelize" well.

The investigation of the relationship between DTAPE($\log n$) and NTAPE($\log n$) leads to an analogue of the NP $\neq$ P-problem. This analogy becomes our guiding principle. We can't separate these classes, so we look for their most difficult problems. By the remarks at the beginning of Chapter 10, we can't do this in terms of polynomial – more precisely polynomial *time* – reductions. Within P it only makes sense to consider more restricted forms of reductions. When investigating P and NP we allowed polynomial algorithms. So for an investigation of the relationship between P and DTAPE($\log n$), also called LOGSPACE, the obvious thing to consider is algorithms that require only logarithmically bounded space. According to our current definitions, however, if we only allow logarithmic space, then our reductions can only compute outputs with lengths that are logarithmically bounded in the length of the input. This is not sufficient for building transformations from one problem to another. To get around this problem, we will give our Turing machines a write-only *output tape*, on which the output may be written from left to right. The space used on the output tape is not considered when calculating space bounds.

Definition 13.6.1. *A decision problem A is* log-space reducible *to a decision problem B, written $A \leq_{\log} B$, if there is a function f computable in logarithmic space that takes instances of A to instances of B in such a way that*

$$\forall x \colon x \in A \Leftrightarrow f(x) \in B \,.$$

Just as we have been using the abbreviation *polynomially reducible* for polynomial-time reducible, so now we will use the abbreviation *logarithmically reducible* for reducible in logarithmic space. This doesn't lead to confusion since we can't do meaningful computation in logarithmic time, and polynomial space contains all of PSPACE.

Definition 13.6.2. *Let C be a complexity class. A problem A is C-complete with respect to logarithmic reductions (log-space complete) if $A \in C$ and for every $B \in C$, $B \leq_{\log} A$.*

Since computations in logarithmic space can be simulated in polynomial time, $A \leq_{\log} B$ implies $A \leq_{\mathrm{p}} B$.

Logarithmic reductions have the properties that we expect of them:

- $\leq_{\log}$ is transitive.
- If $A \leq_{\log} B$ and $B \in \mathsf{DTAPE}(\log n)$, then $A \in \mathsf{DTAPE}(\log n)$.
- If $C \supseteq \mathsf{DTAPE}(\log n)$, L is C-complete with respect to logarithmic reductions, $L \in \mathsf{DTAPE}(\log n)$, then $C = \mathsf{DTAPE}(\log n)$.

We omit the proofs of these properties which follow the same scheme that we know from polynomial reductions. The only exception is that for an input x and the transformation function f, $f(x)$ cannot be computed and stored. So whenever the jth bit of $f(x)$ is needed, we compute it in logarithmic space, forgetting the first $j - 1$ bits. Since $f(x)$ has polynomial length, logarithmic space suffices to keep a counter that records the number of bits of $f(x)$ that have already been computed. To give these new notions some life, we introduce two important problems, one of which is P-complete and the other NTAPE($\log n$)-complete with respect to logarithmic reductions.

First we consider the *circuit value problem* CVP. An instance of the circuit value problem consists of a circuit C over the operators AND, OR, and NOT, and an input a for C. The circuit C has a designated output gate. We must compute the value $C(a)$ of this gate of C on input a. The practical significance of this problem is clear.

Theorem 13.6.3. CVP *is* P-*complete with respect to logarithmic reductions.*

Proof. CVP $\in$ P since we can evaluate the gates of C in topological order.

Now let $A \in$ P and let M be a deterministic Turing machine that decides A in polynomial time $p(n)$. Let x be an instance of length n for which we must check whether $x \in A$. At this point we will make use of a simple result that we will prove in Theorem 14.2.1, namely, that from a description of M we can compute in logarithmic space a circuit C_n such that for all inputs of length n, $x \in A$ if and only if $C_n(x) = 1$. So our reduction transforms x into (C_n, x) and $x \in A$ if and only if $(C_n, x) \in$ CVP. $\qquad\square$

This result is not surprising. If every circuit can be parallelized, that is, can be rewritten with small depth, then every polynomial-time solvable problem can be parallelized well.

One of the first algorithms that one learns is *depth-first search* (DFS) on directed and undirected graphs. Depth-first search can be used to solve the problem of *directed s-t-connectivity* (DSTCON) – the problem of determining whether there is a path from vertex s (source) to vertex t (terminal) in a directed graph G – in linear time.

Theorem 13.6.4. DSTCON *is* NTAPE$(\log n)$-*complete with respect to logarithmic reductions.*

Proof. First we show that DSTCON $\in$ NTAPE$(\log n)$. Starting with $z = 1$ and $v = s$ we can store a counter z and a vertex v. These are updated by replacing v by one of the vertices from its adjacency list and increasing the counter z by 1. If we ever have $v = t$, then the input is accepted. If the counter ever reaches $z = n$ without encountering t, then the input is rejected. Clearly this algorithm accepts precisely those graphs that have a path from s to t.

Now suppose $L \in$ NTAPE$(\log n)$ and M is a nondeterministic Turing machine that decides L in space $\log n$. We can assume that there is only one accepting configuration K_a. For every input x there is a configuration graph $G(x)$ with a vertex for each configuration of M. The graph has an edge from K to K' if M on input x can get from K to K' in one step. Our instance $f(x)$ of DSTCON will be the graph $G(x)$, the source vertex s corresponding to the initial configuration on input x and the terminal vertex $t = K_a$. By construction it is clear that $x \in L$ if and only if there is a path form s to t in $G(x)$. Furthermore, the function f can be generated in logarithmic space. The configurations have length $O(\log n)$, so they can be stored in logarithmic space. For each configuration the machine M induces an adjacency list of immediate successor configurations. $\qquad\square$

By the Theorem of Immerman and Szelepcsényi, DSTCON is also contained in co-NTAPE$(\log n)$. This is surprising since we have a hard time imagining the nondeterministic algorithm for $\overline{\text{DSTCON}}$. Only the proof of the theorem shows us how to obtain such an algorithm. On the other hand, it is reasonable to suspect that DSTCON $\notin$ DTAPE$(\log n)$ since otherwise DTAPE$(\log n) = $ NTAPE$(\log n)$.

13.7 The Complexity of Counting Problems

For many problems the optimization, evaluation, and decision variants are of practical importance. Often we can restrict our attention to the decision variant because the three variants are NP-equivalent (see Section 4.2). Now we add a further facet to these problems by considering a variant as *counting problem.*

If we want to check whether the specification S and the realization C of a circuit agree, then we can check whether $S \oplus C$ is satisfiable. The number of satisfying assignments for $S \oplus C$ gives the number of inputs on which C does not function as specified. We will let #SAT denote the problem of computing the number of satisfying assignments for a circuit. Many of the problems that we have considered have counting variants that can be defined in natural ways. Not all of them have practical significance like #SAT.

The counting variants of problems with NP-complete decision variants are clearly NP-hard. If we can compute the number of solutions, then we can decide if there are any. More interesting is the case of polynomially solvable problems for which the corresponding counting problem is difficult.

Recall the marriage problem. We can consider an instance as a bipartite graph G on two n-element sets of vertices U and V. An edge $\{u, v\}$ indicates that u and v can form a team (happy marriage). A *perfect matching* consists of n pairs so that each vertex is in exactly one pair. Many textbooks on efficient algorithms contain polynomial-time algorithms that solve this problem. For the problem of computing the number of perfect matchings (#PM), there is no known polynomial-time algorithm. How can we establish the difficulty of #PM in terms of complexity theory? We need a complexity class that for counting problems serves the role that NP served for decision problems.

Definition 13.7.1. *The complexity class #P (read: sharp P or number P) contains all counting problems #A for which there is a polynomial-time bounded nondeterministic Turing machine that for each instance x has exactly as many accepting paths as there are solutions for x.*

Remark 13.7.2. #SAT $\in$ #P and #PM $\in$ #P.

Proof. For #SAT we nondeterministically generate an input $a \in \{0,1\}^n$ for the circuit S (each a on exactly one path) and check whether a is a satisfying assignment for S.

Bipartite graphs G can be described by 0-1 matrices M where the rows represent the vertices in U and the columns the vertices in V. We let $M_{u,v} = 1$ if and only if $\{u, v\}$ is an edge in G. The number of perfect matchings in G is then equal to the *permanent* of M, defined by

$$\text{perm}(M) := \sum_{\pi \in S_n} M_{1,\pi(1)} \cdot M_{2,\pi(2)} \cdot \ldots \cdot M_{n,\pi(n)} \; .$$

Each permutation $\pi \in S_n$ corresponds to a possible perfect matching, and each product has the value 1 if this matching exists in G, and a value of 0 otherwise. #PM $\in$ #P. The witnessing nondeterministic Turing machine generates each permutation π on exactly one computation path and accepts if the value of the product corresponding to π is 1. This Turing machine accepts on the computation path for π if and only if π is a perfect matching.   □

Definition 13.7.3. *A counting problem #A is #P-complete if #$A \in$ #P and for every problem #$B \in$ #P, #$B \leq_T$ #A.*

Since the result of a counting problem is a number, it is not surprising that we use Turing reductions in this definition. Of course, if there is a function f that maps instances x of #B to instances $f(x)$ of #A in such a way that x and $f(x)$ have the same number of solutions, then #$B \leq_T$ #A. In the proof of Cook's Theorem there is a bijective correspondence between accepting computation paths of the given Turing machine and satisfying assignments of the SAT formula that is constructed. This proves the first part of the following theorem.

Theorem 13.7.4. *#SAT and #PM are #P-complete.*   □

We won't prove the claim for #PM (Valiant (1979)). It shows that the computation of the number of perfect matchings (i.e., of the permanent) is only possible in polynomial time if NP = P. Thus the theory of #P-completeness fulfills the expectations we had for it.

We end our considerations with the remark that we can decide in polynomial time whether the number of perfect matchings is even or odd. This problem is equivalent to the computation of $\text{perm}(M) \bmod 2$. Since in $\mathbb{Z}_2$ $-1 = 1$, the permanent and determinant are the same. It is well-known from linear algebra that the determinant of a matrix can be computed in polynomial time.

The Complexity of Non-uniform Problems

14.1 Fundamental Considerations

Although we have not made this explicit, our considerations to this point have been directed toward software solutions. If we want to design an efficient algorithm for an optimization problem like TSP or KNAPSACK, we are thinking of an algorithm that works for arbitrarily many cities or objects. When designing hardware, however, the situation is different. If a processor works with 64-bit numbers, then a divider for 64-bit numbers is supposed to compute the first 64 bits of the quotient.

The corresponding computational model is the *circuit*. Circuits for inputs of length n have Boolean variables $x_1, \ldots, x_n$ and Boolean constants 0 and 1 as inputs. They can be described as a sequence $G_1, \ldots, G_s$ of gates. Each gate G_i has two inputs $E_{i,1}$ and $E_{i,2}$ that must be among the previous gates $G_1, \ldots, G_{i-1}$ and the inputs. The gate G_i applies a binary operation op_i to its inputs. The functions that are computed by such circuits arise naturally. The input variables x_i and the Boolean constants 0 and 1 can be considered as functions as well. If the inputs to a gate G_i are realized by the functions $g_{i,1}$ and $g_{i,2}$, then gate G_i is realized by the function

$$g_i(a) := g_{i,1}(a) \,\mathrm{op}_i\, g_{i,2}(a) \,.$$

Circuits can be represented more visually as directed acyclic graphs. The inputs and gates form the vertices of the graph. Each gate has two in-coming edges representing its two inputs. In the general case, we must distinguish between the first and second input. If we restrict our attention to symmetric operators like AND, OR, and EXOR, then this is unnecessary. A circuit C realizes the function $f = (f_1, \ldots, f_m) \colon \{0,1\}^n \to \{0,1\}^m$ if each component function f_j is realized by an input or a gate. A circuit for addition on three bits is represented in Figure 14.1.1. The sum bit is computed in G_4 and the "carry bit" in G_5.

For the evaluation of the efficiency of circuits two different measures are available. The *circuit size* (or just size) of a circuit is equal to the number

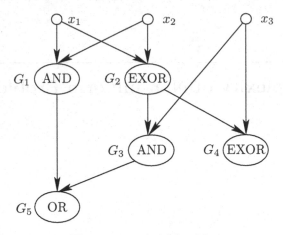

Fig. 14.1.1. A 3-bit adder.

of gates in the circuit and forms a measure of the hardware costs and the sequential computation time. We imagine that the gates are evaluated in the given order, and that the evaluation of each gate has cost 1. In reality, circuits are "parallel processors". In our example in Figure 14.1.1, gates G_1 and G_2 can be evaluated simultaneously, and once G_2 has been evaluated, G_3 and G_4 can be evaluated simultaneously. The depth of a gate is the length of the longest path from an input to that gate. All the gates with depth d can be evaluated simultaneously in the dth time step. The *circuit depth* (or just depth) of a circuit is the maximal depth of a gate in a given circuit. Our example adder has size 5 and depth 3.

Just as we have been concentrating our attention on decision problems, so here we will be primarily interested in Boolean functions $f : \{0,1\}^n \to \{0,1\}$ that have a single output. For the design of hardware, a particular input size may be important, but an asymptotic complexity theoretical analysis can only be based on a sequence $f = (f_n)$ of Boolean functions. A *circuit family* or sequence of circuits $C = (C_n)$ computes $f = (f_n)$ if each f_n is computed by C_n. This leads to the following relationship between decision problems on $\{0,1\}^*$ and sequences of Boolean functions $f = (f_n)$ with $f_n : \{0,1\}^n \to \{0,1\}$. For each decision problem there is a corresponding sequence of functions $f^A = (f_n^A)$ with

$$f_n^A(x) = 1 \Leftrightarrow x \in A \ .$$

On the other hand for any $f = (f_n)$ the decision problem A_f can be defined by

$$x \in A \Leftrightarrow f_{|x|}(x) = 1 \ .$$

On the basis of this relationship, in this chapter we will only consider inputs over the alphabet $\{0,1\}$.

For a sequence $f = (f_n)$ of Boolean functions we want to analyze the complexity measures of size and depth. So let $C_f(n)$ denote the minimal size of a circuit that computes f_n and let $D_f(n)$ be defined analogously for circuit depth. In Chapter 2 we claimed that the time complexity of a problem is a robust measure. Does this imply that the time complexity of A and the circuit size of f_A are related? Boolean functions can always be represented in disjunctive normal form. A naive analysis shows that their size and depth are bounded by $n \cdot 2^n$ and $n + \lceil \log n \rceil$, respectively. This is true even for sequences of functions (f_n^A) for which A is not computable. There are even noncomputable languages that for each length n contain either all inputs of that length or none of them. Then f_n^A is a constant function for each n and so has size 0.

Here the difference between software solutions (algorithms) and hardware solutions like circuit families becomes clear. With an algorithm for inputs of arbitrary length we also have an algorithm for any particular length n. On the other hand, we need the entire circuit family to process inputs of arbitrary length. An algorithm has a finite description, as does a circuit, but what about a circuit family? For a noncomputable decision problem A the sequence of DNF circuits just described is not even computable.

An algorithm is a *uniform* description of a solution procedure for all input lengths. When we are interested in such solutions we speak of a uniform problem. A circuit family $C = (C_n)$ only leads to a uniform description of a solution procedure if we have an algorithm that can compute C_n from n. It is possible for there to be very small circuits C_n for f_n that are very hard to compute and larger circuits C'_n for f_n that are much easier to compute. A circuit family $C = (C_n)$, where C_n has size $s(n)$, is called *uniform* if C_n can be computed from n in $O(\log s(n))$ space. In this chapter when we speak of uniform families of circuits we will be content to show that S_n can be computed in time that is polynomial in $s(n)$. It is always easy, but sometime tedious, to describe how to turn this into a computation in logarithmic space.

Every decision problem A on $\{0,1\}^*$ has a non-uniform variant consisting of the sequence $f^A = (f_n^A)$ of Boolean functions. The non-uniform complexity measures are circuit size and circuit depth where non-uniform families of circuits are allowed. A non-uniform divider can be useful. If we need a 64-bit divider, it only needs to be generated or computed once and then can be used in many (millions of) processors. So we are interested in the relationships between uniform and non-uniform complexity measures. In Section 14.2 we will simulate uniform Turing machines with uniform circuits in such a way that time is related to size and space to depth. Circuits can solve noncomputable problems, so they can't in general be simulated by Turing machines. We will introduce non-uniform Turing machines that can efficiently simulate circuits. Once again time will be related to size, and space to depth. Together it turns out that time for Turing machines and size for circuits are very closely related. The relationships between space and depth (and so parallel computation time) are also amazingly tight, but circuits do not provide a model of non-uniform computation that asymptotically exactly mirror the resource of storage space. Such a model will be introduced in Section 14.4.

For complexity classes that contain P, one can ask if all of their problems can be solved by circuits of polynomial size. In Section 14.5 we will show that this is the case for the complexity class BPP. If a similar result holds for NP as well, we obtain a new possibility for dealing with difficult problems. But this is only possible, as we will show in Section 14.7, if the polynomial hierarchy collapses to the second level. Before that we present a characterization of non-uniform complexity classes in Section 14.6.

> *Circuits form a fundamental hardware model. Only uniform circuits lead to an efficient algorithmic solution. New aspects of the complexity of problems are captured by the non-uniform complexity measures of circuit size and circuit depth. From a practical perspective, it is important to know if a problem is difficult because it requires large circuits or because it is not possible to compute small circuits efficiently.*

14.2 The Simulation of Turing Machines By Circuits

The goals of our considerations can be summarized as follows:

- Turing machines with small computation time can be simulated by uniform circuits with small size.
- Turing machines that use little space can be simulated by uniform circuits of small depth.

The first result compares the computation time of Turing machines with the time for the evaluation of a circuit. The second result implies that small space requirement makes possible an efficient computation via parallel processing and is a basis for the *parallel computation hypothesis* about the tight connection between storage space and parallel computation time.

What is the difficulty in simulating a Turing machine step by step with a circuit? Turing machines can incorporate branches (if-statements), and thus which tape cell is read at time t may depend on the input. It is true that configurations are only locally modified at each step, but where this modification occurs depends on the input. Oblivious Turing machines (see Definition 5.4.1) always read the same tape cell in the tth step regardless of the input. As we showed in Lemma 5.4.2, Turing machines can be simulated by oblivious Turing machines with only a quadratic slow-down. We mentioned there that one can actually get by with a logarithmic slow-down factor, i.e., that time $O(t(n) \log(t(n)))$ suffices for the simulation of any Turing machine by an oblivious Turing machine. So we will investigate how we can simulate oblivious Turing machines step by step with circuits.

The start configuration can be described by the input variables and Boolean constants at no cost. Assume we have described the first $t - 1$ computation steps and consider step t. Only the state and the symbol on the tape cell being read may change in this step. Since the state space Q and the tape alphabet Γ are finite, we only need constantly many bits of the description of the configuration to compute the new state and the new contents of the tape cell. More concretely, we are evaluating the Turing program $\delta : Q \times \Gamma \to Q \times \Gamma \times \{-1, 0, +1\}$, where the third component is constant for a given t since we are considering only oblivious Turing machines. Even the disjunctive normal form realization of a circuit for δ has only constant size with respect to the input length n. This constant will depend only on the complexity of δ. Together we obtain a circuit of size $O(t(n))$ to simulate $t(n)$ steps of a Turing machine. The circuit is uniform if the tape head position in step t can be efficiently computed, as is the case for the oblivious Turing machines mentioned above. In summary, we have the following result.

Theorem 14.2.1. *An oblivious $t(n)$ time-bounded Turing machine can be simulated by uniform circuits of size $O(t(n))$. A $t(n)$ time-bounded Turing machine can be simulated by uniform circuits of size $O(t(n) \log t(n))$.* $\qquad\Box$

The corresponding circuits also have depth $O(t(n) \log(t(n)))$. To get circuits with smaller depth we need a new idea.

Theorem 14.2.2. *An $s(n)$ space-bounded Turing machine can be simulated by uniform circuits of depth $O(s^*(n)^2)$, where $s^*(n) := \max\{s(n), \lceil \log n \rceil\}$.*

Proof. For space-bounded Turing machines we assume, as was described in Section 13.2, that the input is on a read-only input tape. The number of different configurations is bounded by $k(n) = 2^{O(\log n + s(n))} = 2^{O(s^*(n))}$. We consider the corresponding directed configuration graph that contains a vertex for each configuration. The edge set $E(x)$ depends on the input x. The edge (v, w) belongs to $E(x)$ if the Turing machine on input x can go from configuration v to configuration w in one step. Let the adjacency matrix of this graph be $A(x) = (a_{v,w}(x))$. It is important that $a_{v,w}(x)$ only depends on x_i in an essential way when the ith tape cell is being read in configuration v. So $a_{v,w}(x)$ is one of the functions 0, 1, x_i or $\overline{x}_i$. Thus each of the functions $a_{v,w}(x)$ can be computed by a circuit of depth 1. Now let $a_{v,w}^t(x) = 1$ if and only if on input x the configuration w can be reached from configuration v in t steps. For $t' \in \{1, \ldots, t-1\}$ we must go from configuration v to configuration u and then in $t - t'$ steps from configuration u to w. Thus

$$a_{v,w}^t(x) = \bigvee_u a_{v,u}^{t'}(x) \wedge a_{u,w}^{t-t'}(x) \, ,$$

where $\bigvee$ represents disjunction. The matrix A is the Boolean matrix product of $A^{t'}$ and $A^{t-t'}$. The depth needed to realize this matrix product is $1 + \lceil \log k(n) \rceil = O(s^*(n))$. Each of the conjunctions requires depth 1, and for each of the disjunctions a balanced binary tree can be used. Again from Section 13.2 we know that we reach an accepting configuration only if we can reach it in $k(n) \leq 2^{\lceil \log k(n) \rceil}$ steps. So we compute A^{2^i} for all $1 \leq i \leq \lceil \log k(n) \rceil$ with $\lceil \log k(n) \rceil = O(s^*(n))$ matrix multiplications. Finally we check if the input x

is accepted with a disjunction of all $a_{v_0,w}^{2^{\lceil \log k(n) \rceil}}(x)$ for the initial configuration v_0 and the accepting configurations w. The depth of this circuit is bounded by

$$1 + (1 + \lceil \log k(n) \rceil) \cdot \lceil \log k(n) \rceil + \lceil \log k(n) \rceil = O(s^*(n)^2) \,.$$

The corresponding circuits are uniform. The behavior of the Turing machine only plays a role in the computation of the $a_{v,w}(x)$.   □

It is not known how to simulate Turing machines with small time and small space bounds with circuits of small size *and* small depth simultaneously. Most likely there are no such simulations.

14.3 The Simulation of Circuits by Non-uniform Turing Machines

Circuit families $C = (C_n)$ form a non-uniform computation model because we are not concerned with how one comes up with circuit C_n for input length n. For a Turing machine to be able to simulate a circuit family it must also have free access to some information that depends on the length of the instance $n = |x|$ but not on the contents of the instance x. A *non-uniform Turing machine* is a Turing machine with two read-only input tapes. The first input tape contains the instance x, and the second input tape contains some helping information $h(|x|)$ that is identical for all inputs of length n. Because of the second input tape, the number of configurations of a non-uniform Turing machine that visits at most $s(n)$ tape cells is larger by a factor of $h(n)$ than the number for a normal Turing machine, namely $2^{\Theta(\log n + s(n) + \log h(n))}$. Frequently the second input tape is denoted as an oracle tape and the help as an oracle. The results of Section 14.2 can be generalized to the situation where we simulate non-uniform Turing machines with (non-uniform) circuits. The help $h(n)$ represents for C_n a constant portion of the input.

We will now show the following simulation results which go in the other direction from the results of Section 14.2:

- Small circuit families can be simulated by fast non-uniform Turing machines.
- Shallow circuit families can be simulated by non-uniform Turing machines with small space requirements.

The latter of these is the second support for the parallel computation hypothesis.

We will use the following notation for circuit families $C = (C_n)$:

- $s(n)$ for the size of C_n and $s^*(n)$ for $\max\{s(n), n\}$,
- $d(n)$ for the depth of C_n and $d^*(n)$ for $\max\{d(n), \lceil \log n \rceil\}$,
- f_n for the function computed by C_n,
- A_f for the decision problem corresponding to $f = (f_n)$.

Theorem 14.3.1. *The circuit family $C = (C_n)$ for a decision problem A_f can be simulated by a non-uniform Turing machine with two work tapes in time $O(s^*(n)^2)$ and space $O(s^*(n))$.*

Proof. For our help we let $h(n)$ be a description of the circuit C_n. This contains a list of all gates, which are represented as triples giving the operator, the first input, and the second input. For each input we note first the type (constant, input bit, or gate) and then its number. The length of this description is $O(s(n) \log s^*(n))$.

The Turing machine now processes the gates in their natural order. The first work tape is used to store the values of the previously evaluated gates. The second work tape will store a counter used to locate positions on the first work tape or the input tape. The help tape records where the input values for each gate is to be found. If the Turing machine knows the input values and the operator of a gate, then it can compute the output of this gate and append it to the list of previously known outputs. To evaluate the output of a gate, the Turing machine first retrieves the values of its inputs. For a constant this information is given directly on the help tape. Otherwise the index of the gate or input bit is copied from the help tape to the second tape. If the input is another gate, the head of the first work tape is brought to the left end of the tape. While we repeatedly subtract 1 from the counter stored on the second work tape until we reach the value 1, the tape head on the first tape is moved one position to the right each time. At the end of this procedure, the head on the first work tape is reading the information we are searching for. For an input bit we search analogously on the input tape. It is easy to see that for gate i or bit i, $O(i) = O(s^*(n))$ steps suffice. Since we must process $s(n)$ gates each with two inputs, the entire time is bounded by $O(s(n) \cdot s^*(n)) = O(s^*(n)^2)$. On the first work tape we never have more than $s(n)$ bits, and on the second work tape the number of bits is bounded by $s^*(n)$. $\square$

If we want to obtain a Turing machine with one work tape, we could use the simulation result mentioned in Section 2.3 and obtain a time bound of $O(s^*(n)^4)$. But in this case it is possible to give a direct description of a Turing machine with a time bound of $O(s^*(n)^2 \log s^*(n))$, but we will omit these details. If the given circuit family is uniform, then for an input of length n we can first compute C_n and then apply the simulation we have described.

Theorem 14.3.2. *The circuit family $C = (C_n)$ for a decision problem A_f can be simulated by a non-uniform Turing machine in space $O(d^*(n))$.*

Proof. We no longer have enough space to store the results of all the gates. But this is only necessary if the results of some gates are used more than once. This is not the case if the underlying graph of the circuit is a tree. It is possible to "unfold" circuits in such a way that they become trees. To do this we go through the graph of the circuit in topological order. As we encounter a vertex with r immediate successors we replace it and all of its predecessors with r copies. This increases the size but not the depth of the circuit. Circuits for which all gates have at most one successor are called *formulas*. In Figure 14.3.1 we show the result of unfolding the circuit from Figure 14.1.1.

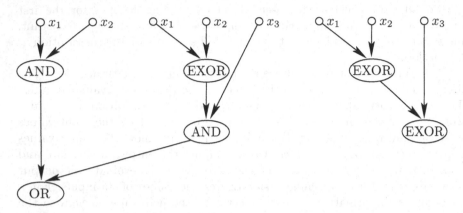

Fig. 14.3.1. The 3-bit adder as a formula.

As help for inputs of length n we use a formula F_n of depth $d(n)$ for f_n. Its description contains a list of all gates in the order of a post-order traversal. For a tree with one vertex this order consists of that vertex. Otherwise it consists of the results of a post-order traversal of the left subtree followed by that of the right subtree, followed by a description of the root. Gates will once again be described as triples of operation, left input, and right input. It is important that because we are using this order we will not need the numbers of the inputs that are gates. This will be seen in the proof of correctness. Formulas of depth $d(n)$ have at most $2^{d(n)} - 1$ gates, each of which can be described with $O(\log n)$ bits. So all together the length of the description is $O(2^{d(n)} \log n)$.

The Turing machine now processes the gates using post-order traversal. The work tape will be used to store the sequence of gate outputs that have not yet been used by their successor. Furthermore, as in the proof of Theorem 14.3.1 we use $O(\log n)$ space to locate values on the input tape. But how do we find values of the inputs to a gate? Because they are processed in the order of a post-order traversal, the left and right subtrees of a gate are processed immediately before that gate. The roots of these subtrees are the only gates whose values have not yet been used. So the values we need are at the right end of the list of gate outputs and the Turing machine works correctly.

Finally we show by induction on the depth d that there are never more than d outputs stored on the work tape. This implies that the space used is bounded by $O(\log n + d(n)) = O(d^*(n))$. The claim is clearly true when $d = 1$. Now consider a formula of depth $d > 1$. By the inductive hypothesis, $d - 1$

tape cells are sufficient to evaluate the left subformula. This result is stored in one cell, and along with the at most $d - 1$ tape cells needed to evaluate the right subformula, at most d tape cells are required. In the end only two tape cells are being used, and after evaluation of the root, only one tape cell is being used. □

If the given circuit family is uniform, then the information about a gate can be computed in space $O(\log 2^{d(n)}) = O(d(n))$. So in this case even a uniform Turing machine can get by with space $O(d^*(n))$.

There are close connections between circuit families and non-uniform Turing machines, and between Turing machines and uniform families of circuits. Circuit size is polynomially related to computation time, and circuit depth is polynomially related to space.

14.4 Branching Programs and Space Bounds

Now we want to introduce a non-uniform model of computation, the size of which characterizes the space used by non-uniform Turing machines asymptotically exactly. This model of computation has roots not only in complexity theory but also as a data structure for Boolean functions. For this reason there are two names commonly given to this model: *branching program* and *binary decision diagram* (abbreviated BDD).

A branching program works on n Boolean variables $x_1, \ldots, x_n$ and has only two types of elementary commands, which are represented as the vertices of a graph. A branching (or decision) vertex v is labeled with a variable x_i and has two out-going edges: one labeled 0, the other labeled 1. If v is reached in a computation, then the edge leaving v corresponding to the value of x_i is used to arrive at the next vertex. An output vertex w is labeled with a value $c \in \{0, 1\}$ and has no out-going edges. If w is reached, then the computation is complete and the value c is given as output. A branching program is a directed acyclic graph consisting of branching vertices (also called internal vertices) and output vertices (also called sinks).

Each vertex v in a branching program realizes a Boolean function f_v in the following way. To compute $f_v(a)$ we start at vertex v and carry out the commands at each vertex until we reach a sink. For branching programs there are two obvious complexity measures. The *length* of a branching program is the length of the longest computation path in the branching program and is a measure of the worst-case time required to evaluate the function. The *size* of a branching program is the number of vertices, and the branching program complexity $\mathrm{BP}(f)$ of a Boolean function f is defined as the minimal size of a branching program that computes f. This is the complexity measure that we will be interested in here. Figure 14.4.1 contains a branching program the input vertices of which realize the two output bits for the addition of three bits. To make the diagram more readable we have included two 1-sinks.

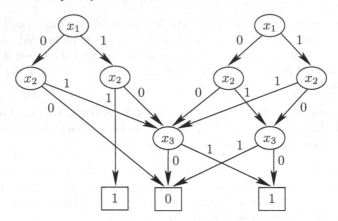

Fig. 14.4.1. A branching program for the addition of three bits.

So why is there a tight connection between the size of branching programs and the space required by non-uniform Turing machines? To evaluate f_v it is sufficient to remember the currently reached vertex. On the other hand, a branching program can directly simulate the configuration graph of a space-bounded Turing machine used in the proof of Theorem 14.2.2. We will formalize this in the theorem below, using $BP^*(f_n)$ to represent the larger of $BP(f_n)$ and n, and letting $s^*(n) = \max\{s(n), \lceil \log n \rceil\}$ just as before.

Theorem 14.4.1. *The decision problem A_f corresponding to $f = (f_n)$ can be solved by a non-uniform Turing machine in space $O(\log BP^*(f_n))$.*

Proof. For help on inputs of length n we use a description of a branching program G_n of minimal size for f_n. This description includes a list of the vertices, where each vertex is described by its type (inner vertex or sink), its number, and its internal information. For a sink the latter consists of the value that is output by the sink, and for an inner vertex it consists of a triple including the index of the variable to be processed, the index of the 0-successor, and the index of the 1-successor. Furthermore, we will always let the vertex representing f_n have index 1. In this way each of the $BP(f_n)$ vertices has a description of length $O(\log BP^*(f_n))$. We use the work tape to remember the current vertex, so at the beginning of the computation it contains the number 1. If a sink is reached, then we make the correct decision and stop the computation. Otherwise we search for the value of the variable to be processed on the input tape. After that the new current vertex is known, namely the x_i-successor. We look for its information on the help tape and update the current vertex index on the work tape.   □

Theorem 14.4.2. *An $s(n)$-space bounded Turing machine can be simulated by a branching program of size $2^{O(s^*(n))}$.*

Proof. We already know that the number of different configurations of the Turing machine on an input of length n is bounded by $2^{O(s^*(n))}$. The branching program G_n has a vertex for each of the configurations that is reachable from the start configuration. Accepting configurations are 1-sinks and rejecting configurations are 0-sinks. An inner vertex for configuration K is labeled with the variable x_i that is being read from the input tape in configuration K. The 0-child of this vertex is the configuration that is reached in one step from K if $x_i = 0$. The 1-child is defined analogously. Since we only consider Turing machines that halt on all inputs, the graph is acyclic and we have a branching program. The Boolean function describing the acceptance behavior of the Turing machine on inputs of length n is realized by the vertex labeled with the initial configuration.   □

What changes if the given Turing machine is non-uniform and the help has length $h(n)$? The number of configurations and therefore the size of the simulating branching program grows by a factor of $h(n) \leq 2^{\lceil \log h(n) \rceil}$. This has led to the convention of adding $\lceil \log h(n) \rceil$ to the space used by a non-uniform Turing machine. Or we could instead define $s^{**}(n) = \max\{s(n), \lceil \log n \rceil, \lceil \log h(n) \rceil\}$. The term $\lceil \log n \rceil$ has the same function for the input tape as the term $\lceil \log h(n) \rceil$ has for the help tape.

Corollary 14.4.3. *An $s(n)$-space bounded non-uniform Turing machine can be simulated by a branching program of size $2^{O(s^{**}(n))}$.*   □

These results can be summarized as follows for the "normal" case that $s(n) \geq \log n$, $\mathrm{BP}(f_n) \geq n$, and $h(n)$ is polynomially bounded:

Space and the logarithm of the branching program size have the same order of magnitude.

For a language $L \in \mathsf{NP}$, $L \in \mathsf{P}$, or $L \in \mathsf{NTAPE}(\log n)$, we can try to show that $L \notin \mathsf{DTAPE}(\log n)$ by proving a superpolynomial lower bound for the branching program size of the function $f^L = (f_n^L)$. This is the most common line of attack for such results. To this point, such lower bounds for branching program size grow more slowly than quadratically (see Chapter 16).

14.5 Polynomial Circuits for Problems in BPP

We have already discussed several times that BPP is "not much larger" than P. It is possible that BPP = P, but this is still an open question. Now we want to offer some support for the claim that problems in BPP are not much more difficult than problems in P. For a decision problem $A \in \mathsf{BPP}$ the Boolean functions $f^A = (f_n^A)$ can be computed by circuits of polynomial size. If these circuits were uniform, then it would follow that BPP = P. But so far, only non-uniform circuits for f_n^A have been found. The trick is that for a BPP algorithm we can choose the error-probability to be so low that by the pigeonhole principle there must be an assignment for the random bits for which the BPP algorithm makes no mistakes. We will choose this assignment of the random bits as help for a non-uniform Turing machine which can then be simulated by circuits as in Sections 14.2 and 14.3.

Theorem 14.5.1. *Decision problems $A \in$ BPP can be solved by polynomial-time deterministic non-uniform Turing machines. The Boolean functions $f^A = (f_n^A)$ have polynomially bounded circuit size.*

Proof. Since $A \in$ BPP, by Theorem 3.3.6 there is a randomized Turing machine M that decides A in polynomial time $p(n)$ with an error-probability bounded by $2^{-(n+1)}$. Now consider a $2^n \times 2^{p(n)}$-matrix such that the rows represent the inputs of length n and the columns represent the assignments of the random vector r. Since in $p(n)$ steps at most $p(n)$ random bits can be processed, we can restrict our attention to random vectors of length $p(n)$. Position (x, r) of the matrix contains a 1 if M on input x with random vector r is incorrect. Otherwise the matrix entry is 0. Since the probability of an error is bounded by $2^{-(n+1)}$, each row contains at most $2^{p(n)-(n+1)}$ 1's. The total number of 1's in the matrix is then bounded by $2^{p(n)-1}$ By the pigeonhole principle at least half of the columns must contain only 0's. We choose one of the corresponding random vectors r_n^* as help $h(n)$ for a non-uniform Turing machine M'. The Turing machine M' simulates M using $h(n) = r_n^*$ where M uses random bits. So M' is deterministic and makes no errors. Furthermore, the runtime of M' is bounded by $p(n)$. $\square$

For BPP algorithms with sufficiently small error-probability there is a golden computation path that works for all inputs of the same length. This computation path can be efficiently simulated – if it is known. The difficulty of *derandomizing* BPP algorithms is the difficulty of finding this golden computation path. Note that is not because there are so few of them: If the error-probability of the BPP algorithm is reduced to 2^{-2n}, then the fraction of golden computation paths among all computation paths is at least $1 - 2^{-n}$.

14.6 Complexity Classes for Computation with Help

Before we ask whether NP algorithms can be simulated by circuits of polynomial size, as BPP algorithms can be, we want to investigate more closely the complexity classes that arise from non-uniform Turing machines. In polynomial time only a polynomially long help can be read. So we will only allow polynomially long help. Furthermore, we will restrict ourselves to deterministic and nondeterministic polynomial-time computations. Generalizations of both of these aspects are obvious.

Definition 14.6.1. *The complexity class P/poly contains all decision problems that can be decided in polynomial time by non-uniform deterministic Turing machines with polynomially long help. NP/poly is defined analogously using nondeterministic Turing machines.*

The following characterization of P/poly follows from earlier results.

Corollary 14.6.2. P/poly *contains exactly those decision problems A for which $f^A = (f_n^A)$ has polynomially bounded circuit size.*

Proof. Theorem 14.3.1 says that the existence of polynomial-size circuits for $f^A = (f_n^A)$ implies that $A \in$ P/poly. Theorem 14.2.1 and the remarks at the beginning of Section 14.3 provide the other direction of the claim.   □

Now we can also present Theorem 14.5.1 in its customary brief form:

Corollary 14.6.3. BPP $\subseteq$ P/poly.   □

The NP $\overset{?}{=}$ P-question has a non-uniform analogue, namely the NP/poly $\overset{?}{=}$ P/poly-question. In order to get a better feeling for the class NP/poly we will present a characterization in terms of circuits for this class as well. Since NP expresses the use of an existential quantifier over a polynomially long bit vector, we must give our circuits the possibility of realizing existential quantifiers.

Definition 14.6.4. *A nondeterministic circuit C is a circuit for which the inputs are partitioned into input variables x and nondeterministic variables y. Each gate G in such a circuit computes the function $f_G : \{0,1\}^{|x|} \to \{0,1\}$ defined such that $f_G(a) = 1$ if and only if there is a $b \in \{0,1\}^{|y|}$ such that gate G computes the value 1 when the values of the x-variables are given by a and the values of the y-variables are given by b.*

Theorem 14.6.5. NP/poly *contains exactly those decision problems A for which the Boolean functions $f^A = (f_n^A)$ have nondeterministic circuits of polynomial size.*

Proof. First suppose that $A \in$ NP/poly. We can assume that we have a non-uniform nondeterministic Turing machine M for A that on inputs of length n takes exactly $p(n)$ steps for some polynomial p. The circuit C_n that simulates M on inputs of length n contains, in addition to the n input variables, constant inputs representing the help for M for inputs of length n, and nondeterministic input variables that describe the nondeterministic choices of M. With respect to this longer input, M works deterministically and can be simulated by a polynomial-size circuit. Considered as a nondeterministic circuit, with the appropriate partitioning of the inputs, this circuit computes the function f_n^A.

Now suppose we have nondeterministic circuits $C = (C_n)$ for $f^A = (f_n^A)$. The non-uniform Turing machine M receives as help for inputs of length n a description of the circuit C_n. M then randomly generates values for the nondeterministic inputs and simulates C_n on the extended input vector. Thus M decides A in polynomial time.   □

14.7 Are There Polynomial Circuits for all Problems in NP?

Since BPP $\subseteq$ P/poly, one can ask if it is also (or even) the case that NP $\subseteq$ P/poly. This would not lead directly to efficient algorithms for NP-equivalent problems, but we would at least have a better idea about what makes them difficult. Since polynomial reductions can be simulated by circuits of polynomial size, either all NP-complete problems are in P/poly, or P/poly contains no NP-complete problems. Since P $\subseteq$ P/poly, we can't hope to prove that NP $\not\subseteq$ P/poly. On the other hand, we believe that NP is so much farther from P than BPP is that NP can't be a subset of P/poly. We already know the way out of this situation. We will show that one of our well-founded complexity theoretic hypotheses is false if NP $\subseteq$ P/poly. In this case it is the hypothesis $\Sigma_2 \neq \Sigma_3$. Expressed differently, NP can only be a subset of P/poly if the polynomial hierarchy collapses to the second level, namely to Σ_2.

For the proof of this claim it suffices to show for some problem $A \in$ NP that

$$A \in \text{P/poly} \Rightarrow \Sigma_2 = \Sigma_3 \ .$$

The obvious choice for A is some NP-complete problem. The inputs of A have to be coded in binary, but this doesn't affect the complexity with respect to the usual descriptions of the problems we have considered. So what NP-complete problem should we choose? Based on our experience, the standard choice would be SAT or 3-SAT. This choice works here as well. But we will see in our proof that it is only important to choose an NP-complete problem with the following property:

Definition 14.7.1. *A decision problem is called* polynomially self-reducible *if it is Turing reducible to itself in such a way that all the queries made by the reduction are to instances of shorter length than the instance to be decided.*

Later we will see how this property gets used. First we show two examples of NP-complete problems that are polynomially self-reducible.

Lemma 14.7.2. SAT *and* CLIQUE *are polynomially self-reducible.*

Proof. For SAT we can decide instances with no variables directly in polynomial time. Otherwise we choose a variable x that occurs in our SAT instance φ, form instances $\varphi_0 = \varphi|_{x=0}$ and $\varphi_1 = \varphi|_{x=1}$, and query the subprogram for SAT on these two shorter instances. The formula φ is satisfiable if and only if at least one of φ_0 and φ_1 is satisfiable.

For CLIQUE we can decide instances with $n = 1$ or $k = 1$ directly in polynomial time. So let (G, k) be an instance of CLIQUE with $n, k \geq 2$. We select a vertex v from G with minimal degree. If the degree of this vertex is $n - 1$, then we have a complete graph and can again decide about the instance (G, k) directly. Otherwise we construct two graphs: G_1 is the result of removing v from G, and G_2 is the subgraph of G containing only those vertices connected to v by an edge. By our choice of v, both G_1 and G_2 have a shorter description than G. We query CLIQUE about (G_1, k) and $(G_2, k-1)$, and we accept only if at least one of these queries is accepted by CLIQUE. This decision is correct since G has a clique of size k if and only if there is a clique of size k that doesn't use vertex v or a clique of this size that contains v. But the second case is equivalent to the existence of a clique of size $k-1$ among the neighbors of v. $\qquad\square$

For a polynomially self-reducible problem A we will let M_A denote a polynomial-time Turing machine that decides A with queries to an A-subprogram for shorter instances of A. This same Turing machine can also be used with an oracle for a different decision problem B. In this case we will let $L(M_A, B)$ denote the language accepted by M_A with oracle B. Finally, for $C \subseteq \{0,1\}^*$ we let $C_{\leq n}$ denote the set of all $x \in C$ with $|x| \leq n$. Now we are ready to prove a technical lemma that allows us to draw consequences from the self-reducibility of A.

Lemma 14.7.3. *For a polynomially self-reducible decision problem A and a language $B \subseteq \{0,1\}^*$ if $L(M_A, B)_{\leq n} = B_{\leq n}$, then $A_{\leq n} = B_{\leq n}$.*

Proof. We prove the lemma by induction on n. For $n = 0$ the only allowed input is the empty string. Since there are no shorter strings, the subprogram for M_A cannot be called, and so $A_{\leq 0} = L(M_A, A)_{\leq 0} = L(M_A, B)_{\leq 0} = B_{\leq 0}$.

Now suppose that $L(M_A, B)_{\leq n+1} = B_{\leq n+1}$. Then $L(M_A, B)_{\leq n} = B_{\leq n}$, so by the inductive hypothesis $A_{\leq n} = B_{\leq n}$. We must show that $A_{\leq n+1} = B_{\leq n+1}$. For a string of length $n+1$ the Turing machine queries the subprogram only about strings y with $|y| \leq n$. So it doesn't matter if the subprogram is deciding A, $A_{\leq n}$, $B_{\leq n}$, or B since these are all the same on strings of length up to n. It follows that

$$A_{\leq n+1} = L(M_A, A)_{\leq n+1} = L(M_A, B)_{\leq n+1} = B_{\leq n+1},$$

with the last equality following from our assumption. This proves the lemma. $\qquad\square$

In what follows let A be a polynomially self-reducible NP-complete set like the ones we encountered in Lemma 14.7.2. Once again let M_A be a polynomial-time Turing machine that decides A with the help of queries to shorter instances of A. Our goal is to show that if $A \in$ P/poly, that is, if there exist polynomial-size circuits $C = (C_n)$ for $f^A = (f_n^A)$, then $\Sigma_2 = \Sigma_3$. It is important that instances of A be coded in binary. Circuits only work on inputs of a fixed length. For our purposes, it would be nice to have circuits that could process all instances of length up to m. So we will consider a circuit with input length $m + \lceil \log m \rceil$, such that the first $\lceil \log m \rceil$ input bits code a number $i \in \{1, \ldots, m\}$ and the original circuit C_i is then simulated on the next i input bits. It is easy to construct such a family of circuits $C^* = (C_m^*)$ from

the family $C = (C_n)$ in polynomial time and in such a way that the new circuits also have polynomial size. Now if a subprogram is called that simulates
circuit C_i for an arbitrary $i \leq m$, then we can replace this subprogram with a
program that simulates C_m^* instead. Within the subprogram we first compute
a suitable input for C_m^*. From this it follows that $L(M_A, C_m^*)_{\leq m} = A_{\leq m}$.
Said differently: For instances x of length i, $x \in L(M_A, C_m^*)$ if and only if
$C_i(x) = 1$. Based on this preliminary discussion we will now show how from
the assumption that there are polynomial-size circuits for the NP-complete
problem A, it follows that languages in Σ_3 are already contained in Σ_2.

Theorem 14.7.4. *If* NP $\subseteq$ P/poly, *then* $\Sigma_2 = \Sigma_3$.

Proof. Let A be a polynomially self-reducible NP-complete decision problem.
If NP $\subseteq$ P/poly, then there is a circuit family $C = (C_n)$ for A of polynomial
size that computes $f^A = (f_n^A)$. We will also make use of the polynomial-size
circuits C_m^* as described above.

Now let $L \in \Sigma_3$. By Theorem 10.4.3 there is an $\exists\forall\exists$-representation for L
with a polynomial-time predicate. We can turn this into an $\exists\forall$-representation
with an NP predicate. Since A is NP-complete, we can reduce the NP predicate
to A with a polynomial reduction f. Thus for some polynomial p we have

$$L = \{x: \exists y \, |y| \leq p(|x|) \, \forall z \, |z| \leq p(|x|): f(x, y, z) \in A\} \ .$$

The length of $f(x, y, z)$ is bounded by $q(|x|)$ for some polynomial q. We claim
that L can be characterized in the following way, where p' is a suitable polynomial.

$$
\begin{aligned}
L = \{x: \ &\exists(C, y) \text{ with } |C| \leq p'(|x|) \text{ and } |y| \leq p(|x|) \\
&\forall(w, z) \text{ with } |w| \leq q(|x|) \text{ and } |z| \leq p(|x|) \\
&C \text{ describes a circuit with size polynomial in } |x| \\
&\quad \text{for inputs of length at most } q(|x|), \\
&w \in L(M_A, C) \Leftrightarrow C_{|w|}(w) = 1, \text{ and} \\
&C \text{ computes the value 1 for } f(x, y, z)\} \ .
\end{aligned}
$$

In order for this to be a Σ_2 characterization, the three properties must be
checkable in polynomial time. For the first property this is clearly true for the
usual description of circuits. For the second property this follows since M_A is
polynomially time-bounded, we can replace subprogram calls with simulations
of C, and the evaluation of circuits can be done in polynomial time. Since f
can be computed in polynomial time, we can also check the third property in
polynomial time.

Finally, we show that this characterization of L is correct. First let $x \in L$.
For our circuit C we choose a circuit of polynomial size that checks for $(b, a) \in
\{0, 1\}^{\lceil \log q(|x|) \rceil} \times \{0, 1\}^{q(|x|)}$ whether the prefix of a of length $\text{bin}(b)$ belongs to
A. Here we are using $\text{bin}(b)$ to represent the number from $\{1, \ldots, q(|x|)\}$ that
is represented by b. We consider C as a circuit for inputs a with $|a| \leq q(|x|)$

that checks for membership in A. The correctness of the second condition follows from our preliminary discussion. By Lemma 14.7.3, C accepts exactly those instances that belong to A, and thus C accepts $f(x, y, z)$.

For the other direction we assume that x satisfies the logical characterization given above. By Lemma 14.7.3 the second condition implies that C accepts inputs $(b, a) \in \{0, 1\}^{\lceil \log q(|x|) \rceil + q(|x|)}$ if and only if the prefix of a specified by b belongs to A. From the third condition it follows that $f(x, y, z) \in A$. So $x \in L$ now follows from the previous characterization of L. This proves the theorem.   □

The results in Corollary 14.6.3 and Theorem 14.7.4 can be interpreted as saying that NP presumably contains problems that are more difficult (with respect to circuit size) than the problems in BPP. In particular, NP is probably not contained in BPP.

15

Communication Complexity

15.1 The Communication Game

The goal of complexity theory is to estimate the minimal resources needed to solve algorithmic problems. The lower bounds we have proven so far depend on complexity theoretic hypotheses or are with respect to specialized scenarios like the black box scenario. In this chapter and the next we will prove lower bounds for one resource without complexity theoretic assumptions but under the condition that some other resource is sufficiently restricted, i.e., so-called trade-off results. Among these will be results in Chapter 16 giving size lower bounds for bounded-depth circuits and or for bounded-length branching programs. Probably the earliest results of this type were about the area A and the parallel computation time T of VLSI circuits (see also Section 15.5). For certain functions $f = (f_n)$, Thompson (1979) showed that the product of area and the square of the runtime must grow asymptotically at least as fast as n^2, expressed formally: $AT^2 = \Omega(n^2)$. This means that area and runtime cannot both be small. Yao (1979) filtered out the core of the ideas used in the proof of these bounds and separated it from the specific applications. Out of this came the theory of communication complexity, which is based on the following *communication game*.

Alice and Bob cooperate to evaluate a function $f : A \times B \to C$ based on distributed information about the input. They need to compute $f(a, b)$ for $a \in A$ and $b \in B$. Alice knows a but not b, and Bob knows b but not a. How the input is distributed among Alice and Bob is part of the question. The goal is to come to a point where both Bob and Alice know that both of them know the value of $f(a, b)$. Communication complexity only deals with the case that A, B, and C are finite. In most of our examples we will be investigating Boolean functions with a single output, that is, the case where $A = \{0, 1\}^m$, $B = \{0, 1\}^n$, and $C = \{0, 1\}$.

The communication game places an emphasis on the information exchanged between Alice and Bob. The goal is to minimize the worst-case (with respect to the various inputs (a, b)) number of bits that Alice and Bob exchange. To make this precise we must explain the rules of the game. With knowledge of the function f but without knowledge of the particular input (a, b), Alice and Bob agree upon a *communication protocol P*.

Definition 15.1.1. *A communication protocol consists of a protocol tree T_P to evaluate f. The protocol tree is a binary tree in which each inner vertex has a 0-child and a 1-child. The leaves of the tree are labeled with values $c \in C$. Each inner vertex v is assigned to either Alice or Bob, and we will refer to them as A-vertices and B-vertices. For every vertex v there are sets $A_v \subseteq A$ and $B_v \subseteq B$ with the interpretation that only inputs $(a, b) \in A_v \times B_v$ can reach this vertex. Since the protocol will begin at the root of the tree for any instance (a, b), $A_v = A$ and $B_v = B$ for the root v. In addition, for each A-vertex v there is a decision function $g_v : A_v \to \{0, 1\}$, and for any internal vertex A-vertex v with children v_0 and v_1, $A_{v_i} = g_v^{-1}(i) \subseteq A_v$. The situation is analogous for the B-vertices.*

Alice and Bob compute $f(a, b)$ by traversing a path in the protocol tree in the following way. They begin at the root, which is thus reachable for all inputs. If at some point in the protocol, they are at an A-vertex v, then Alice computes $g_v(a)$, sends $g_v(a)$ to Bob, and they proceed to the $g_v(a)$-child of v. For the protocol to be suitable for the evaluation of f, it must be the case that the leaf eventually reached for the input (a, b) is correctly labeled with $f(a, b)$.

If Alice and Bob use protocol P, then they exchange exactly as many bits for input (a, b) as there are edges on the path from the root of T_P to the leaf $l(a, b)$. The depth $d_P(a, b)$ of the leaf $l(a, b)$ in T_P describes the amount of communication required for input (a, b). The *length* of the protocol P is defined to be the maximum of all $d_P(a, b)$ and is denoted $l(P)$. Finally, the communication complexity $C(f)$ of f is the minimal length of a protocol for evaluating f.

Since we are not concerned with the resources required to agree on a protocol, communication complexity is a non-uniform complexity measure. Furthermore, several aspects of the description and evaluation of the decision functions g_v at the inner vertices are abstracted. So a short protocol does not necessarily lead to an efficient general solution to the problem being considered. On the other hand, large lower bounds on communication complexity have the consequence that the problem is not efficiently solvable. We are therefore mostly interested in lower bounds and use upper bounds only to check how good the lower bounds are.

An example will help to clarify the definitions. Throughout this chapter we will use $\langle a \rangle$ to denote the integer represented by a binary string (or bit) a using the usual binary representation. For example $\langle 011 \rangle = 3$. The Boolean function $f(a_0, \ldots, a_3, b_0, \ldots, b_3, s_0, s_1)$ should have the value 1 if and only if $a_{\langle s \rangle} = b_{\langle s \rangle}$ for $\langle s \rangle = \langle s_0 \rangle + 2 \langle s_1 \rangle$. We first give an informal description of a protocol for evaluating f if Alice knows $a_0, \ldots, a_3$, and s_0 and Bob knows $b_0, \ldots, b_3$, and s_1:

- Alice sends s_0.
- Bob sends s_1.
- Bob computes $\langle s \rangle$ and sends $b_{\langle s \rangle}$.
- Alice computes $\langle s \rangle$ and sends 1 if and only if $a_{\langle s \rangle} = b_{\langle s \rangle}$.

The protocol tree for this example is illustrated in Figure 15.1.1, where the vertices are labeled to show who sends a bit and how it is computed. This protocol has length 4. The number of so-called *communication rounds* is 3 since along each path in the protocol tree the roles of sender and receiver are exchanged only twice.

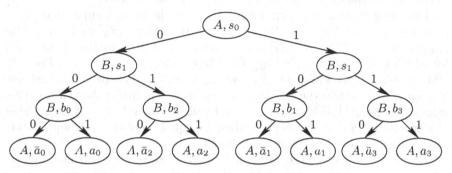

Fig. 15.1.1. A protocol tree. The last level has been omitted for the sake of clarity. The 1-edges lead to 1-leaves and the 0-edges lead to 0-leaves.

If instead Alice knows a_0, a_1, b_0, b_1, and s_0, and Bob knows a_2, a_3, b_2, b_3, and s_1, then the following protocol of length 3 can also be used:

- Alice sends s_0.
- Bob sends s_1.
- Alice and Bob compute $\langle s \rangle$. If $\langle s \rangle \leq 1$, then Alice can decide whether $a_{\langle s \rangle} = b_{\langle s \rangle}$ and send the result to Bob. Otherwise, Bob can decide if $a_{\langle s \rangle} = b_{\langle s \rangle}$ and send the result to Alice.

Before we discuss possible applications of the theory of communication complexity, we want to show by means of an example that it is not at all easy to design good protocols. Consider the following function $f_n : \{0,1\}^n \times \{0,1\}^n \rightarrow \{1, \ldots, n\}$. Alice interprets her input a as the characteristic vector of a set $S_A \subseteq \{1, \ldots, n\}$. That is, the set S_A contains i if and only if $a_i = 1$. Bob interprets b analogously as a set S_B. Together, Alice and Bob need to compute $f_n(a, b)$, the median of the multi-set $S_A \cup S_B$. If S_A and S_B together have s elements, then $f_n(a, b)$ is the element in position $\lceil s/2 \rceil$ of the sorted sequence of $S_A \cup S_B$. We will show that the communication complexity of f_n is $\Theta(\log n)$. In this case the lower bound $\lceil \log n \rceil$ is easy to show. Since it is possible that $S_A = \{i\}$ and $S_B = \emptyset$, each protocol tree must have a leaf labeled i. The lower bound now follows because binary trees with at least n leaves must have depth at least $\lceil \log n \rceil$.

It is also quite easy to design a protocol of length $O(\log^2 n)$. In this protocol Alice and Bob perform a binary search on $\{1, \ldots, n\}$ to locate the median M. The upper bound of $O(\log^2 n)$ will follow if we can find a protocol of length $O(\log n)$ with which Alice and Bob can decide whether $M \leq m$ for any $m \in \{0, \ldots, n\}$. For this, Alice sends the number of elements in S_A and the number of elements in $\{i \in S_A \mid i \leq m\}$. Now Bob can calculate the number of elements in $S_A \cup S_B$ (recall that we are considering all sets as multi-sets) and the number of elements in $\{i \in S_A \cup S_B \mid i \leq m\}$. This means he knows the answer to the question, which he can then send to Alice.

Designing a protocol with length $O(\log n)$ is more complicated. In a preparatory step, Alice and Bob exchange the values $|S_A|$ and $|S_B|$. This requires at most $2\lceil \log(n+1) \rceil$ bits. Now let k be the smallest power of 2 for which $k \geq |S_A|$ and $k \geq |S_B|$. Clearly $k < 2n$. Now Alice and Bob will add elements to the multi-sets S_A and S_B according to a prescribed scheme in such a way that in the end $|S_A| = |S_B| = k$ but the median of $S_A \cup S_B$ remains unchanged. Each number added will be either 1 or n. If the number of elements in $|S_A| + |S_B|$ is even, then an equal number of 1's and n's are used. Otherwise one more n is used than 1.

Alice and Bob know the value of k. Furthermore, they can maintain an interval of integers that are possible values for the median. Since we want the size of this interval I to be a power of 2, they begin with $I = \{1, \ldots, 2^{\lceil \log n \rceil}\}$. We will show the claim by giving a protocol of length 2 that will halve either k or $|I|$. After at most $\lceil \log n \rceil + \log k - 1 = O(\log n)$ of these steps, either $|I| = 1$ or $k = 1$. If $|I| = 1$, then Alice and Bob know the only element in I which is the median. If $k = 1$, then Alice and Bob exchange the only elements in S_A and S_B; the median is the smaller of the two.

Now we must describe the promised protocol of length 2. Alice computes the median a' of her current multi-set S_A, and Bob computes b' from S_B analogously. Let i be the smallest element in I. Alice considers the binary representation of $a' - i$, which has length $\lceil \log |I| \rceil$, and sends the most significant bit a^* to Bob. Bob does the analogous thing and sends b^* to Alice. If $a^* = b^*$, then for the overall median M it must be that the binary representation of $M - i$ begins with a^*. This suffices to halve the interval I: If $a^* = 0$, then I is replaced by its first half; otherwise I is replaced by its second half. Now consider the case that $a^* \neq b^*$. For reasons of symmetry it suffices to consider the case $a^* = 0$ and $b^* = 1$. Then Alice can remove the smaller half of the elements from S_A and Bob can remove the larger half of the elements from S_B. This cuts k in half but does not change the median. So the median problem has communication complexity $\Theta(\log n)$.

This example also shows that protocol trees are well-suited for structural considerations, but that it is better to describe specific protocols algorithmically.

In which areas can we find applications for the communication game? In networks or multiprocessor systems with distributed information, the communication complexity describes the least resources required to solve a problem. In this case we would need a communication game with many players. But often it is sufficient to consider the case where the players are divided into two groups, which are then represented by Alice and Bob. Since these examples are straightforward, we won't go into any more detail here.

In the example of VLSI circuits mentioned above, chips are rectangular regions with prescribed positions where the input bits are provided. Chips with area A can always be separated along a cut of length at most $A^{1/2} + 1$ so that approximately half of the inputs lie on each side of the cut. The two halves must "communicate" so that the chip can do its task. This idea will motivate our discussion in Section 15.5.

If we consider Turing machines with only one tape and divide the input in half, then enough information must flow across this dividing mark for the Turing machine to perform its task. In Section 15.5 we will use communication complexity to show that there are problems that require $\Omega(n^2)$ time on a one-tape Turing machine but only linear time on a two-tape Turing machine.

In Chapter 16 we will show that for functions with certain properties, circuits with severely limited depth and gates of unbounded fan-in must have many edges since each edge can contribute only a little to the communication that is needed. Branching programs with restrictions that we will describe later can be partitioned into layers in such a way that small branching programs lead to an efficient communication protocol for the represented function and a suitable partition of the input. So if the communication complexity of a function is large, the branching program must be large as well.

Before we get to these applications, we must show how we can prove lower bounds for communication complexity. In Section 15.2 we investigate the deterministic communication game described above. In Section 15.3 we investigate the case of one-sided but unbounded error, that is, non-deterministic protocols. And in Section 15.4 we investigate one- and two-sided errors that may only occur with small probability.

The communication game between Alice and Bob is an abstraction of many interesting problems. Questions are reduced to the core of the information exchanged between two modules involved in the solution. So in many models, lower bounds for communication complexity of specific functions have consequences for the complexity of the problem being considered.

15.2 Lower Bounds for Communication Complexity

The example of computing the median made it clear that we cannot argue naively to determine the communication complexity of a function. Even in our earlier example of a function f with ten input bits and two different partitions of the input, we only suspect that the given protocols of lengths 4 and 3 are optimal. The key to proofs of lower bounds lies in the investigation of protocol trees and the recognition that the set $I_v = A_v \times B_v \subseteq A \times B$ of all inputs that reach the vertex v has very special properties. The sets I_v for leaves v of a protocol tree, for example, form a partition of $A \times B$ since for each input the protocol defines a path ending at a leaf.

In a protocol tree for f with a leaf v marked with c it follows that f must be a constant function (with value c) on the set $A_v \times B_v$. So sets of the form $A' \times B'$ will play a special role and therefore should receive a special name. With this motivation we define the *communication matrix* of the function $f : A \times B \to C$. This matrix has $|A|$ rows representing the partial assignments $a \in A$, and $|B|$ columns representing the partial inputs $b \in B$. Position (a, b) of the matrix contains the value $f(a, b)$. So the communication matrix is just another form of the function table, one that reflects the partitioning of the input among Alice and Bob. Figures 15.2.1 and 15.2.2 show the communication matrices for $n = 3$ and the functions GT (greater than) and EQ (equality test). If $\langle a \rangle$ denotes the value of a interpreted as a number in binary, then $\mathrm{GT}_n(a, b) = 1$ if and only if $\langle a \rangle > \langle b \rangle$ and then $\mathrm{EQ}_n(a, b) = 1$ if and only if $\langle a \rangle = \langle b \rangle$.

	000	001	010	011	100	101	110	111
000	0	0	0	0	0	0	0	0
001	1	0	0	0	0	0	0	0
010	1	1	0	0	0	0	0	0
011	1	1	1	0	0	0	0	0
100	1	1	1	1	0	0	0	0
101	1	1	1	1	1	0	0	0
110	1	1	1	1	1	1	0	0
111	1	1	1	1	1	1	1	0

Fig. 15.2.1. The communication matrix of GT_3.

In Figure 15.2.1 the set $\{001, 010, 011\} \times \{011, 100, 101, 110, 111\}$ is indicated by the dashed outline. This set forms a submatrix or a *geometric rectangle*. On the other hand, in Figure 15.2.2 the indicated set is $\{000, 001, 100, 101\} \times \{010, 011, 110, 111\}$, which is geometrically a union of rectangles. We will refer to such sets as *combinatoric rectangles* since the row and column orderings in the communication matrix are arbitrary, and with a suitable reordering of the rows and columns any combinatoric rectangle be-

	000	001	010	011	100	101	110	111
000	1	0	0	0	0	0	0	0
001	0	1	0	0	0	0	0	0
010	0	0	1	0	0	0	0	0
011	0	0	0	1	0	0	0	0
100	0	0	0	0	1	0	0	0
101	0	0	0	0	0	1	0	0
110	0	0	0	0	0	0	1	0
111	0	0	0	0	0	0	0	1

Fig. 15.2.2. The communication matrix of EQ_3.

comes a geometric rectangle. Abbreviating, we will refer to $A' \times B'$ for any $A' \subseteq A$ and $B' \subseteq B$ simply as a *rectangle* of the communication matrix. Such a rectangle is called *monochromatic* if all $f(a,b)$ with $(a,b) \in A' \times B'$ have the same value. As we did for the graph coloring problem, we will identify colors and numbers. If we are interested in the function value c we will refer to c-rectangles.

We summarize this discussion as follows: A protocol of length l leads to a protocol tree with at most 2^l leaves. Therefore the input set can be partitioned into at most 2^l monochromatic rectangles. This can be reformulated into the following theorem making use of the fact that $C(f)$ is an integer.

Theorem 15.2.1. *Let $f : A \times B \to C$ be given. If every partition of $A \times B$ into monochromatic rectangles requires at least r rectangles, then the communication complexity of f cannot be smaller than $\lceil \log r \rceil$, that is, $C(f) \geq \lceil \log r \rceil$.*
□

Let's see how we can apply this theorem. We define the size of the rectangle $A' \times B'$ to be $|A'| \cdot |B'|$. If g_c is the size of the largest c-rectangle, then we will need at least $r_c := \lceil |f^{-1}(c)|/g_c \rceil$ c-rectangles. If the sum of all r_c with $c \in C$ is denoted r, then Theorem 15.2.1 provides a lower bound of $\lceil \log r \rceil$ for $C(f)$. This method is sufficient to produce a lower bound for EQ_n. We have $|EQ_n^{-1}(1)| = 2^n$, since for $a \in \{0,1\}^n$ exactly the pairs (a,a) are mapped to 1. On the other hand, no rectangle $A' \times B'$ with $|A'| \geq 2$ or $|B'| \geq 2$ can contain only pairs of the form (a,a). So $r_1 = 2^n$. Also $r_0 \geq 1$ and $r \geq 2^n + 1$, so $C(EQ_n) \geq \lceil \log(2^n + 1) \rceil = n + 1$. It is also easy to see that $C(EQ_n) \leq n+1$, since Alice can send her input of length n to Bob, and then he can compute the result and send it back to Alice.

Theorem 15.2.2. $C(EQ_n) = n + 1$.
□

For the function GT this argument is not sufficient. Figure 15.2.1 shows that a single 0-rectangle or 1-rectangle can cover one quarter of all the inputs. This gives a lower bound of 3. On the other hand, we really don't believe that GT is easier than EQ. By simply counting the inputs, we have been implicitly viewing all inputs as equal. But if a function has "easy subregions", then our counting argument breaks down. But we can generalize our method of "counting" using a probability distribution p on $A \times B$. We will define the p-size of $A' \times B'$ to be $p(A' \times B')$.

Theorem 15.2.3. *Let p be a probability distribution on $A \times B$. If for each monochromatic rectangle R, the condition $p(R) \leq \varepsilon$ is satisfied, then $C(f) \geq \lceil \log(1/\varepsilon) \rceil$.*

Proof. Since $p(A \times B) = 1$, every partition of $A \times B$ into monochromatic rectangles contains at least $\lceil 1/\varepsilon \rceil$ rectangles. The result now follows from Theorem 15.2.1.   □

Now we can apply this method to GT. Intuitively, $GT_n(a, b)$ is easy to compute if $\langle a \rangle$ and $\langle b \rangle$ are very different. Let $D = \{(a, b) \in \{0, 1\}^n \times \{0, 1\}^n : \langle a \rangle = \langle b \rangle$ or $\langle a \rangle = \langle b \rangle + 1\}$. We define a probability distribution p on $\{0, 1\}^n \times \{0, 1\}^n$ so that $p(a, b) = 1/(2 \cdot 2^n - 1)$ for all $(a, b) \in D$ and 0 otherwise. That is, p gives a uniform distribution on strings in D. In the communication matrix, these are the values on the main diagonal and just below the main diagonal. Any 0-rectangle R consists of exactly one diagonal entry, since if R contained both (a, a) and (b, b) with $a \neq b$, then it would also contain (a, b) and (b, a), but either $GT_n(a, b) = 1$ or $GT_n(b, a) = 1$. Thus for any 0-rectangle R, $p(R) \leq 1/(2 \cdot 2^n - 1)$. On the other hand, if a 1-rectangle R contained (a, b) and (a', b') with $\langle a \rangle = \langle b \rangle + 1$, $\langle a' \rangle = \langle b' \rangle + 1$, and $\langle a \rangle < \langle a' \rangle$, then R would also contain (a, b'). But $\langle a \rangle \leq \langle a' \rangle - 1 = \langle b' \rangle$, so $GT_n(a, b') = 0$. This shows that $p(R) \leq 1/(2 \cdot 2^n - 1)$ for all 1-rectangles R as well. By Theorem 15.2.3 we have

Theorem 15.2.4. $C(GT_n) = n + 1$.   □

If we look more closely at our proof of the lower bound for GT_n, we see that we considered the 0-rectangles and the 1-rectangles separately. We showed that each 0-rectangle can contain at most one input (a, b) with positive probability and that the same holds for 1-rectangles. When we can apply Theorem 15.2.3 in such a way, it is possible to give a simpler argument.

Definition 15.2.5. *For $f : A \times B \to C$ and $c \in C$ a subset $S \subseteq A \times B$ is called a c-fooling set if $f(a, b) = c$ for all $(a, b) \in S$ but if $(a, b) \in S$ and $(a', b') \in S$ with $(a, b) \neq (a', b')$, then at least one of $f(a, b')$ and $f(a', b)$ is different from c.*

The idea is that the inputs in S confuse Alice and Bob if they use a short protocol.

Theorem 15.2.6. *If there is a c-fooling set of size s_c for $f : A \times B \to C$ and $c \in C$, then*

$$C(f) \geq \left\lceil \log \sum_{c \in C} s_c \right\rceil .$$

Proof. It suffices to show that every partition of $A \times B$ into monochromatic rectangles requires at least s_c c-rectangles. Definition 15.2.5 guarantees that a c-rectangle cannot contain two elements from a c-fooling set. This proves the theorem. $\qquad\square$

For the function GT_n, the pairs (a, a) form a 0-fooling set of size 2^n and the pairs (a, b) with $\langle a \rangle = \langle b \rangle + 1$ form a 1-fooling set of size $2^n - 1$. Thus

$$C(\mathrm{GT}_n) \geq \lceil \log(2^n + 2^n - 1) \rceil = n + 1 .$$

We want to consider two additional functions that will play a role later. The function $\mathrm{DIS} = (\mathrm{DIS}_n)$ (disjointness test) interprets its inputs $a, b \in \{0, 1\}^n$ as characteristic vectors of sets $A, B \subseteq \{0, \ldots, n\}$ and tests whether $A \cap B = \emptyset$. In other words,

$$\mathrm{DIS}_n(a, b) = \neg(a_1 b_1 + \cdots + a_n b_n) ,$$

where $\neg$ stands for NOT and $+$ for OR. The function $\mathrm{IP} = (\mathrm{IP}_n)$ (inner product or scalar product) is defined by

$$\mathrm{IP}_n(a, b) = a_1 b_1 \oplus \cdots \oplus a_n b_n ,$$

where $\oplus$ stands for EXOR. That is, IP computes the scalar product over $\mathbb{Z}_2$. The function IP should not be confused with the complexity class IP that was introduced in Chapter 11.

Theorem 15.2.7. $C(\mathrm{DIS}_n) = n + 1$ *and* $n \leq C(\mathrm{IP}_n) \leq n + 1$.

Proof. As in the case of EQ_n, the upper bounds are obtained by having Alice send her entire input to Bob, who then calculates the result and sends it back to Alice.

For DIS_n the pairs $(a, \overline{a})$, where $\overline{a}$ denotes the bitwise complement of a, form a 1-fooling set of size 2^n. So we need at least 2^n 1-leaves and at least one 0-leaf. The lower bound follows.

For IP_n we go back to the counting method of Theorem 15.2.1. $|\mathrm{IP}_n^{-1}(0)| > 2^{2n}/2$, since for $a = 0^n$ the function IP_n takes on the value 0 for all (a, b), and for $a \neq 0^n$ this is the case for exactly half of the b's. We have made use of this last property in several contexts already. Now let a with $a_i = 1$ and $b_1, \ldots, b_{i-1}, b_{i+1}, \ldots, b_n$ be fixed. Then exactly one of the two values for b_i leads to an IP-value of 0. If we can show that every 0-rectangle R has at most 2^n inputs (a, b), then we will know that we need more than $2^n/2$ 0-rectangles to cover all the 0-inputs.

To estimate the size of a 0-rectangle R, we use the algebraic character of the scalar product. For a set $A \subseteq \{0,1\}^n$ let $\langle A \rangle$ be the subspace spanned by A in the $\mathbb{Z}_2$-vector space $\mathbb{Z}_2^n$. For each 0-rectangle $R = A \times B$, $\langle A \rangle \times \langle B \rangle$ is also a 0-rectangle. This follows from the following relationship, which is easy to verify:

$$\mathrm{IP}_n(a \oplus a', b \oplus b') = \mathrm{IP}_n(a,b) \oplus \mathrm{IP}_n(a,b') \oplus \mathrm{IP}_n(a',b) \oplus \mathrm{IP}_n(a',b') \,,$$

where $\oplus$ represents bitwise EXOR on the left side. So the largest 0-rectangle has the form $A \times B$ where A and B are orthogonal subspaces of $\mathbb{Z}_2^n$. The dimension of $\mathbb{Z}_2^n$ is n, and from the orthogonality of A and B it follows that $\dim(A) + \dim(B) \leq n$. Finally, the size of R is $|A| \cdot |B|$, and

$$|A| \cdot |B| = 2^{\dim(A)} \cdot 2^{\dim(B)} \leq 2^n \,. \qquad \square$$

The representation of the function f as a communication matrix M_f suggests applying methods from linear algebra to this matrix. This leads to the *rank lower bound method* for approximating the communication complexity of f.

Theorem 15.2.8. *Let* $\mathrm{rank}(f)$ *be the rank of the communication matrix* M_f *over* $\mathbb{R}$, *for an* f *with an image space* $\{0,1\}$. *Then*

$$\mathrm{C}(f) \geq \lceil \log \mathrm{rank}(f) \rceil \,.$$

Proof. We will show that every communication protocol for f requires a protocol tree T with at least $\mathrm{rank}(f)$ many 1-leaves. The theorem follows from this directly.

Let $A_v \times B_v$ be the set of inputs that reach the 1-leaf v in T. We form the matrix M_v that has a 1 in position (a,b) if and only if $(a,b) \in A_v \times B_v$. For each $a \in A_v$, M_v contains a row that is identical to the characteristic vector for B_v, and for each $a \notin A_v$, a row of 0's. So $\mathrm{rank}(M_v) = 1$ if $A_v \times B_v \neq \emptyset$, and $\mathrm{rank}(M_v) = 0$ otherwise. Furthermore, M_f is the sum of all M_v for the 1-leaves v. This follows because each input $(a,b) \in f^{-1}(1)$ leads to exactly one 1-entry in one of the matrices M_v. By the subadditivity of the rank function, letting $L(T)$ denote the set of 1-leaves in T, this leads to

$$\mathrm{rank}(M_f) \leq \sum_{v \in L(T)} \mathrm{rank}(M_v) \leq |L(T)| \,.$$

So the protocol tree for f has at least $\mathrm{rank}(M_f)$ many 1-leaves. $\qquad \square$

The communication matrix for EQ_n is the identity matrix and has full rank 2^n. From this it follows that there are at least 2^n 1-leaves. If we want to consider the number of 0-leaves as well, we can consider the negated function $\overline{\mathrm{EQ}}_n$. Let E_n be the $2^n \times 2^n$-matrix consisting solely of 1's. Then $\mathrm{rank}(E_n) = 1$. Since $M_f = E_n - M_{\overline{f}}$, it follows by the subadditivity of the rank function that

$\operatorname{rank}(M_f) \leq \operatorname{rank}(M_{\overline{f}}) + 1$. From this we get a lower bound of $2^n - 1$ for the number of 0-leaves and thus $C(\mathrm{EQ}_n) \geq n + 1$. The communication matrix for GT_n has rank $2^n - 1$ (see Figure 15.2.1), and the communication matrix of $\overline{\mathrm{GT}}_n$ has rank 2^n. So we can also derive $C(\mathrm{GT}_n) = n + 1$ using the rank method. For IP_n the communication matrix is only a little different from the much-studied Hadamard matrix H_n. For our purposes it is sufficient to define the Hadamard matrix with the help of the communication matrix for IP_n – namely, $H_n := E_n - 2 \cdot M_{\mathrm{IP}_n}$. Since H_n has full rank 2^n, we can close the gap in Theorem 15.2.7 and prove that $C(\mathrm{IP}_n) = n + 1$.

Nevertheless it can be tedious to go back to these methods for each new function. For this reason we are interested in a reduction concept that is tailored to the communication game.

Definition 15.2.9. *Let* $f : A \times B \to C$ *and* $g : A' \times B' \to C$ *be given. There is a* rectangular reduction *from* f *to* g, *denoted* $f \leq_{\mathrm{rect}} g$, *if there is a pair* (h_A, h_B) *of transformations* $h_A : A \to A'$ *and* $h_B : B \to B'$, *such that* $f(a, b) = g(h_A(a), h_B(b))$ *for all* $(a, b) \in A \times B$.

Since communication complexity abstracts away the costs of computation, we needn't place any requirements on the computational complexity of h_A and h_B.

Lemma 15.2.10. *If* $f \leq_{\mathrm{rect}} g$, *then* $C(f) \leq C(g)$.

Proof. Alice can compute $a' := h_A(a)$ herself, and Bob can compute $b' := h_B(b)$. Their communication protocol consists of using an optimal protocol for g on (a', b'). By the definition of $\leq_{\mathrm{rect}}$ this protocol is correct.   □

Up until now we have been satisfied to investigate communication complexity with given partitions of the inputs between Alice and Bob. In many applications (see Chapter 16) we need a stronger result: For every listing of the variables there must be a dividing point so that if we partition the variables so that Alice gets the variables before the dividing point and Bob the variables that come after, then the communication complexity of the function is large. This is not true for the functions EQ_n, GT_n, DIS_n, and IP_n that we have been considering. For the variable sequence $a_1, b_1, a_2, b_2, \ldots, a_n, b_n$ the communication complexity for every dividing point is bounded by 3. Using the so-called *mask technique* we obtain from each of these four functions a function that is difficult in the sense above. We define only the mask variant EQ_n^* of EQ_n since GT_n^*, DIS_n^*, and IP_n^* are defined analogously. The function EQ_n^* is defined on $4n$ variables $a_i, a_i', b_i, b_i', 1 \leq i \leq n$. The mask vector a' shortens the vector a to a^* by striking all a_i for which $a_i' = 0$. In the same way we get b^* from b using the mask vector b'. If a^* and b^* have different lengths, then $\mathrm{EQ}_n^*(a, a', b, b') := 0$. If a^* and b^* are of length m, then $\mathrm{EQ}_n^*(a, a', b, b') := \mathrm{EQ}_m(a^*, b^*)$.

Now consider an arbitrary sequence of $4n$ variables and place the dividing point at the position where we have first seen $\lceil n/2 \rceil$ a-variables or $\lceil n/2 \rceil$ b-variables. If we have seen $\lceil n/2 \rceil$ a-variables, then beyond the dividing point there must be at least $\lceil n/2 \rceil$ b-variables and vice versa. The following result shows that the mask variants of all the functions we have considered are difficult.

Theorem 15.2.11. *If Alice receives at least $\lceil n/2 \rceil$ a-variables and Bob at least $\lceil n/2 \rceil$ b-variables, then*

$$C(EQ_n^*) \geq C(EQ_{\lceil n/2 \rceil}) = \lceil n/2 \rceil + 1 \,.$$

Analogous results hold for GT_n^*, DIS_n^*, and IP_n^*.

Proof. Alice and Bob must handle all inputs (a, a', b, b'), in particular the case that a' selects exactly $\lceil n/2 \rceil$ of the a-variables given to Alice and b' selects exactly $\lceil n/2 \rceil$ b-variables given to Bob. Then what remains is the problem $EQ_{\lceil n/2 \rceil}$, in which Alice has all the a-variables and Bob has all the b-variables.
$\square$

Finally, we want to consider a structurally complicated function called the *middle bit of multiplication*, denoted $MUL = (MUL_n)$. The product of two n bit integers has a bit length of $2n$. The bit with place value 2^{n-1} (the bit in position $n-1$) is called the middle bit of multiplication. It is of particular interest that in many models of computation it is possible to reduce the computation of the other bits of multiplication to the problem of computing the middle bit. To make the representation easier, we will only consider the case that n is even.

Theorem 15.2.12. *If Alice and Bob each receive $n/2$ bits of the factor a and the bits of the other factor b are divided arbitrarily among them, then $C(MUL_n) \geq \lceil n/8 \rceil$.*

Proof. The idea of the proof is to find a subfunction of MUL_n for which we can use earlier results to give a lower bound of $\lceil n/8 \rceil$ for the communication complexity. We will replace many of the variables with constants in such a way that the resulting subfunction for the given partitioning of the variables between Alice and Bob has a high communication complexity.

We begin by choosing a distance $d \in \{1, \ldots, n-1\}$ such that the number m of pairs (a_i, a_{i+d}) with the following properties is as large as possible.

- Alice and Bob each have exactly one of the bits a_i and a_{i+d} in their inputs, and
- $0 \leq i \leq n/2 - 2$ and $n/2 \leq i + d \leq n - 1$.

We will motivate this choice by means of an example, which also helps to clarify the general case. For $n = 16$ and $d = 7$, suppose there are four pairs with the desired properties, namely (a_1, a_8), (a_3, a_{10}), (a_5, a_{12}), and (a_6, a_{13}), and that Alice knows a_1, a_6, a_{10}, and a_{12} and Bob knows a_3, a_5, a_8, and a_{13}. We want to reduce the computation of the middle bit to the computation of the carry bit for addition where the summands are divided between Alice and

Bob in such a way that for each bit position Alice knows the value in exactly one of the two summands (and Bob knows the other). If the second factor b has exactly two 1's – say in positions j and k – then the multiplication of $\langle a \rangle$ and $\langle b \rangle$ is just the addition of $\langle a \rangle \cdot 2^j$ and $\langle a \rangle \cdot 2^k$. Now we want to choose j and k so that

- the bit a_i from $\langle a \rangle \cdot 2^j$ and the bit a_{i+d} from $\langle a \rangle \cdot 2^k$ are in the same position; that is, we want $j - k = d$; and
- the pair $(i, i + d)$ with the largest i-value should end up in position $n - 2$.

So in our example we want $j = 8$ and $k = 1$ (see Figure 15.2.3).

		B	A		A		B		A	B		B		A									
a_{15}	a_{14}	a_{13}	a_{12}	a_{11}	a_{10}	a_9	a_8	a_7	a_6	a_5	a_4	a_3	a_2	a_1	a_0	0	0	0	0	0	0	0	0
0	0	0	0	0	0	0	a_{15}	a_{14}	a_{13}	a_{12}	a_{11}	a_{10}	a_9	a_8	a_7	a_6	a_5	a_4	a_3	a_2	a_1	a_0	0
								?															

(second summand labels: B A over a_{13} a_{12}, A over a_{10}, B over a_8, A B over a_6 a_5, B over a_3, A over a_1)

Fig. 15.2.3. The multiplication of $\langle a \rangle$ and $\langle b \rangle$ with two 1's in positions 1 and 8. The bits belonging to Alice and Bob are shown.

So that the middle bit of multiplication (its position is indicated by "?" in Figure 15.2.3) will be the same as the carry bit from the sum of the numbers formed from the selected pairs of numbers – in our example the numbers (a_6, a_5, a_3, a_1) and (a_{13}, a_{12}, a_{10}, a_8) – we proceed as follows. The pairs that lie between two selected pairs – in our example (a_4, a_{11}) and (a_2, a_9) – are set to $(0, 1)$. That way any carry from earlier positions will be passed on to the next position. All other bits that were not designated in Figure 15.2.3 are set to 0 so that they do not affect the sum. The result is represented in Figure 15.2.4.

0	0	a_{13}	a_{12}	1	a_{10}	1	a_8	0	a_6	a_5	0	a_3	0	a_1	0	0	0	0	0	0	0	0	0
0	0	0	0	0	0	0	0	0	a_{13}	a_{12}	1	a_{10}	1	a_8	0	a_6	a_5	0	a_3	0	a_1	0	0
									?														

Fig. 15.2.4. The summands after replacing some of the a-bits with constants.

The first j positions cannot generate carries, since there is at most one 1 in each of these positions. After this come a number of $(0,0)$ pairs which generate no carries, until we reach the first (a_i, a_{i+d}) pair. The pairs between the selected pairs pass along carries but generate no new carries. So the carry from the sum of the numbers formed from the a_i bits and the a_{i+d} bits reaches position $n - 1$. Since we have $(0,0)$ in that position, we obtain the problem of determining the carry bit of the sum of two m-bit binary numbers where Alice knows one of the bits in each of the m positions as a subproblem of computing the middle bit of multiplication. Since for addition the two bits in each position can be exchanged between the two summands without affecting the sum, we obtain the problem $\mathrm{CAR}_m(u, v)$ of computing the carry bit of the sum of an m-bit number u that Alice knows and an m-bit number v that Bob knows.

The theorem now follows from the following two claims.

1. $C(\mathrm{CAR}_m) = m + 1$.
2. It is possible to choose $m \geq \lceil n/8 \rceil - 1$.

To prove the first claim we consider the function GT_m, which by Theorem 15.2.4 has communication complexity $m + 1$. Since in general f and $\overline{f}$ have the same communication complexity, $C(\overline{\mathrm{GT}_m}) = m + 1$. Thus by Lemma 15.2.10 Claim 1 follows if we can show that $\overline{\mathrm{GT}_m} \leq_{\mathrm{rect}} \mathrm{CAR}_m$. To design the rectangular reduction we note that

$$\overline{\mathrm{GT}_m}(a, b) = 1 \Leftrightarrow \langle a \rangle \leq \langle b \rangle$$
$$\Leftrightarrow 2^m - \langle a \rangle + \langle b \rangle \geq 2^m$$
$$\Leftrightarrow \mathrm{CAR}_m(2^m - a, b) = 1 .$$

So the following transformations form a rectangular reduction $\overline{\mathrm{GT}_m} \leq_{\mathrm{rect}}$ CAR_m: Let $h_A(a) := a'$ with $\langle a' \rangle = 2^m - \langle a \rangle$ and $h_B(b) := b$.

The second claim follows with the help of the pigeonhole principle. Let k be the number of a_i with $0 \leq i \leq n/2 - 1$, that Alice knows. Then Alice knows $n/2 - k$ of the a_j, with $n/2 \leq j \leq n - 1$, and for Bob the situation is exactly reversed. Thus of the $n^2/4$ pairs (a_i, a_j) with $0 \leq i \leq n/2 - 1$ and $n/2 \leq j \leq n-1$, there are $k^2 + (n/2-k)^2$ pairs from which Alice knows exactly one bit. This number is minimized when $k = n/4$, and then it is $n^2/8$. Now by the pigeonhole principle at least $\lceil (n^2/8)/(n-1) \rceil \geq \lceil n/8 \rceil$ of these pairs (a_i, a_j) have the same index difference $d = j - i$. Since the case $i = n/2 - 1$ is forbidden, at least $\lceil n/8 \rceil - 1$ pairs can be chosen with the desired properties.
□

The communication matrix plays a central role in proofs of lower bounds for communication complexity. Protocol trees must have at least as many leaves as the number of monochromatic rectangles required to partition the communication matrix. In addition to the investigation of the maximal size of monochromatic rectangles with respect to an arbitrary probability distribution on the input set, fooling sets and the rank method can also be used to prove lower bounds for communication complexity.

15.3 Nondeterministic Communication Protocols

In Chapter 3 we introduced nondeterministic computation as randomized computation with one-sided error that need only be less than 1. We want to define nondeterministic communication protocols in the same way.

For randomized communication, the protocol specifies how many random bits Alice and Bob each have available. Alice's random vector r_A of length l_A is independent of Bob's random vector r_B of length l_B. Alice knows r_A, but not r_B, and Bob knows r_B, but not r_A. If the protocol calls for Alice to send a bit to Bob at vertex v, then which bit she sends may depend not only on the input a and the vertex v but also on r_A. The analogous statement is true for the bits Bob sends. So for any input (a, b) a random path is chosen in the *randomized protocol tree*. The error-probability for a protocol tree for f and the input (a, b) is the probability of reaching a leaf with a label that differs from $f(a, b)$.

If $r_A \in \{0, 1\}^{l_A}$ and $r_B \in \{0, 1\}^{l_B}$ are fixed, then we have a deterministic protocol that depends on (r_A, r_B). So a randomized protocol consists of the random choice of one of $2^{l_A + l_B}$ deterministic protocol trees. It helps to image a randomized balanced binary tree of depth $l_A + l_B$ followed by the deterministic protocol trees. Communication costs are caused by the deterministic protocol trees but not by the randomized tree that sits above them.

If we want to investigate one-sided error, we have to restrict our attention to decision problems, i.e., to functions $f : A \times B \to \{0, 1\}$. Nondeterminism is defined as one-sided error for inputs from $f^{-1}(1)$ with an error-probability that may be anything less than 1. In a protocol tree this means that for $(a, b) \in f^{-1}(0)$ all paths of positive probability end at 0-leaves, while for $(a, b) \in f^{-1}(1)$ there must be at least one path of positive probability that ends at a 1-leaf. If we consider all paths of positive probability and the labeling of the leaves that are reached we obtain the function value as a disjunction of these labels. Therefore we will speak of *OR-nondeterminism* in this case. Co-nondeterminism for f can be defined as nondeterminism for $\overline{f}$, or in terms of *AND-nondeterminism* since we obtain the result of the function by taking the conjunction of the labels of all leaves reached with positive probability. As a new kind of nondeterminism we introduce *EXOR-nondeterminism*. A randomized EXOR-protocol computes 1 exactly when an odd number of leaves with label 1 can be reached with positive probability. This type of nondeterminism has practical significance as a data structure for BDDs (see Wegener (2000)). Here we will investigate EXOR-nondeterminism as a representative of extended concepts of nondeterminism. Of further interest are mod_q classes (the number of paths to 1-leaves has a particular value mod$q$), and majority classes (the number of paths that reach the correct label is greater than $1/2$, which is the same as two-sided unbounded error).

Before we design nondeterministic protocols or prove lower bounds for nondeterministic communication complexity, we want to give a combinatorial characterization of this complexity measure. Recall that we proved lower bounds for deterministic communication complexity with the help of the minimal number $N(f)$ of monochromatic rectangles that can partition the communication matrix. We showed that $\lceil \log N(f) \rceil \leq C(f)$. For deterministic protocols it is necessary to work with partitions of the communication matrix since each input reaches exactly one leaf in the protocol tree. For nondeterministic protocols each input can reach many different leaves. But just as in Definition 15.1.1, the inputs that reach a leaf v with positive probability still form a rectangle. Now we define the combinatoric measures $C_{OR}(f)$, $C_{AND}(f)$, and $C_{EXOR}(f)$, with which we can characterize the nondeterministic communication complexity measures.

Definition 15.3.1. *For $f : A \times B \to \{0,1\}$, $N_{OR}(f)$ is the minimal number of 1-rectangles required to cover the 1-entries in the complexity matrix of f. $N_{AND}(f)$ is defined analogously using 0-rectangles and 0-entries in the communication matrix. Finally $N_{EXOR}(f)$ is the minimal number of rectangles needed so that (a,b) is covered an odd number of times if and only if $f(a,b) = 1$.*

The following result shows that these covering measures characterize nondeterministic communication complexity almost exactly.

Theorem 15.3.2. *The following relationships hold:*

- $\lceil \log N_{OR}(f) \rceil \leq C_{OR}(f) \leq \lceil \log(N_{OR}(f) + 1) \rceil + 1$,
- $\lceil \log N_{AND}(f) \rceil \leq C_{AND}(f) \leq \lceil \log(N_{AND}(f) + 1) \rceil + 1$,
- $\lceil \log N_{EXOR}(f) \rceil \leq C_{EXOR}(f) \leq \lceil \log(N_{EXOR}(f) + 1) \rceil + 1$.

Proof. The proof is analogous for all three claims. We will concentrate on the OR-case, i.e., the case for the usual nondeterminism. For the upper bound, Alice and Bob agree upon a minimal covering of the 1's in the communication matrix with 1-rectangles and on a numbering of the rectangles with numbers in $\{1, \ldots, N_{OR}(f)\}$. Alice investigates which of these rectangles intersect the rows for her input a. If there are no such rectangles, then she sends 0 to Bob as a binary number of length $\lceil \log(N_{OR}(f) + 1) \rceil$. In this case a 0-leaf is reached. Otherwise, Alice nondeterministically selects the number i of one of the 1-rectangles that intersect the a row and sends i to Bob. Bob can then decide if the input (a,b) is in the selected rectangle. He then sends this information to Alice. An accepting leaf is reached if and only if (a,b) is contained in the selected 1-rectangle.

For the lower bound we consider the protocol tree, in which at each vertex Alice or Bob decides, with the help of the information available to her or him, which bit to send. For a protocol tree of length $c = C_{OR}(f)$ this protocol tree has at most 2^c leaves and therefore at most 2^c 1-leaves. The inputs for which the vertex v is reached with positive probability again form a rectangle R_v. All inputs from R_v for a 1-leaf v are accepted. So the collection of all R_v for the 1-leaves v forms a cover of the 1's in the communication matrix with at most 2^c 1-rectangles. Thus $\log N_{OR}(f) \leq C_{OR}(f)$ and the claim follows since $C_{OR}(f)$ is an integer. □

This result led Kushilevitz and Nisan (1997) to define $C_{OR}(f)$ as $\log N_{OR}(f)$ and so as a purely combinatoric measure.

Which of our methods for the proof of lower bounds for deterministic communication complexity can also be used in the nondeterministic case? The methods in the deterministic case are

- estimation of the size of monochromatic rectangles, perhaps with respect to some probability distribution,
- the construction of large fooling sets as a special case of the method above, and
- the rank method.

If individual 1-rectangles can only cover an ε-portion of all 1's, then not only a partition but also a cover of the 1 entries requires at least $\lceil 1/\varepsilon \rceil$ many rectangles. So the first two methods restricted to 1's in the communication matrix lead to lower bounds for the length of OR-nondeterministic protocols. Of course the situation is analogous for the 0's in the communication matrix and AND-nondeterminism.

Theorem 15.3.3. *Let p be a probability distribution on $f^{-1}(1) \subseteq A \times B$. If for each 1-rectangle R the condition $p(R) \leq \varepsilon$ is satisfied, then $C_{OR}(f) \geq \lceil \log 1/\varepsilon \rceil$. If f has a 1-fooling set of size s, then $C_{OR}(f) \geq \lceil \log s \rceil$. Analogous results hold for 0-rectangles, 0-fooling sets, and $C_{AND}(f)$.* □

These methods don't provide any lower bounds for $C_{EXOR}(f)$ since the rectangles belonging to the leaves of an EXOR-protocol tree need not be monochromatic. On the other hand, the rank method does not help for OR- and AND-nondeterminism, as the example of EQ_n shows. In the proof of Theorem 15.2.8 the communication matrix was the sum of the matrices M_v which represented the 1-rectangles corresponding to 1-leaves. This was because each 1-input reaches exactly one 1-leaf. This condition is no longer fulfilled for nondeterministic protocols. But the situation is different for EXOR-nondeterminism – provided we add the matrices over $\mathbb{Z}_2$. It is precisely the 1-inputs that reach an odd number of 1-leaves and therefore lead to an entry of 1 in the $\mathbb{Z}_2$-sum of all the M_v. So the following theorem can be proved just like Theorem 15.2.8.

Theorem 15.3.4. *Let f be a Boolean function with image space $\{0,1\}$, and let $\mathrm{rank}_2(f)$ be the rank of the communication matrix M_f over $\mathbb{Z}_2$. Then*

$$C_{EXOR}(f) \geq \lceil \log \mathrm{rank}_2(f) \rceil \,.$$ □

The following matrix shows that $\mathrm{rank}_2(M)$ may be smaller than $\mathrm{rank}(M)$:

$$M = \begin{bmatrix} 1 & 1 & 0 \\ 1 & 0 & 1 \\ 0 & 1 & 1 \end{bmatrix} \,.$$

Theorem 15.3.5. *For nondeterministic communication complexity of the example functions* EQ_n, GT_n, DIS_n, IP_n, *and* MUL_n, *the following results hold:*

- $C_{\text{OR}}(\text{EQ}_n) \geq n$, $C_{\text{AND}}(\text{EQ}_n) \leq \lceil \log n \rceil + 2$, $C_{\text{EXOR}}(\text{EQ}_n) \geq n$.

- $C_{\text{OR}}(\text{GT}_n) \geq n$, $C_{\text{AND}}(\text{GT}_n) \geq n$, $C_{\text{EXOR}}(\text{GT}_n) \geq n$.

- $C_{\text{OR}}(\text{DIS}_n) \geq n$, $C_{\text{AND}}(\text{DIS}_n) \leq \lceil \log n \rceil + 2$, $C_{\text{EXOR}}(\text{DIS}_n) \geq n - \lfloor \log(n+1) \rfloor$.

- $C_{\text{OR}}(\text{IP}_n) \geq n - 1$, $C_{\text{AND}}(\text{IP}_n) \geq n$, $C_{\text{EXOR}}(\text{IP}_n) \leq \lceil \log n \rceil + 2$.

- *If and Alice and Bob each know* $n/2$ *bits of one of the factors, then* $C_{\text{OR}}(\text{MUL}_n) \geq \lceil n/8 \rceil - 1$, $C_{\text{AND}}(\text{MUL}_n) \geq \lceil n/8 \rceil - 1$, $C_{\text{EXOR}}(\text{MUL}_n) \geq \lceil n/8 \rceil - 1$.

Proof. We begin with the three upper bounds, which have similar proofs. In a nondeterministic protocol for $\overline{\text{EQ}}_n$ Alice can nondeterministically generate $i \in \{1, \dots, n\}$ and send i and a_i to Bob. Bob tests whether $a_i \neq b_i$, and sends the result to Alice. Alice accepts the input if $a_i \neq b_i$. Thus $C_{\text{AND}}(\text{EQ}_n) = C_{\text{OR}}(\overline{\text{EQ}}_n) \leq \lceil \log n \rceil + 2$. The same protocol with the test $a_i = b_i = 1$ shows that $C_{\text{AND}}(\text{DIS}_n) \leq \lceil \log n \rceil + 2$ and $C_{\text{EXOR}}(\text{IP}_n) \leq \lceil \log n \rceil + 2$. In the latter case there are exactly as many accepting computation paths as there are summands $a_i b_i$ with the value 1.

The lower bounds follow from Theorems 15.3.3 and 15.3.4 and from the results in Section 15.2 for the example functions. The function EQ_n has a 1-fooling set of size 2^n and the $\mathbb{Z}_2$-rank of the communication matrix is 2^n. The function GT_n has a 1-fooling set of size $2^n - 1$ and a 0-fooling set of size 2^n, and the $\mathbb{Z}_2$-rank of the communication matrix is $2^n - 1$. The function DIS_n has a 1-fooling set of size 2^n.

To estimate $C_{\text{EXOR}}(\text{DIS}_n)$ we describe a sufficiently large submatrix of the communication matrix that has full rank. For this we consider only inputs (a, b) for which a has exactly $\lfloor n/2 \rfloor$ 1's and b has exactly $\lceil n/2 \rceil$ 1's. We now select a convenient numbering of the rows and columns. If the input a belongs to the i-th row, then the bitwise complement $b := \overline{a}$ should belong to the i-th column. Using this numbering, the resulting submatrix is the identity matrix which only has 1's on the main diagonal. This is because two vectors with $\lfloor n/2 \rfloor$ or $\lceil n/2 \rceil$ 1's can only fail to have a 1 in the same position if one is the bitwise complement of the other. The identity matrix has full rank $\binom{n}{\lfloor n/2 \rfloor}$ over $\mathbb{Z}_2$. Since $\binom{n}{\lfloor n/2 \rfloor}$ is the largest of the $n + 1$ binomial coefficients $\binom{n}{k}$ for $k \in \{0, \dots, n\}$, $\binom{n}{\lfloor n/2 \rfloor} \geq 2^n/(n+1)$. So by the rank method it follows that $C_{\text{EXOR}}(\text{DIS}_n) \geq n - \lfloor \log(n+1) \rfloor$. The lower bound can be improved if we approximate the binomial coefficient using Stirling's formula.

In the proof of Theorem 15.2.7 we showed that $|\text{IP}_n^{-1}(0)| > 2^{2n}/2$ and that every 0-rectangle covers at most 2^n 0's. From this we obtain the lower bound for $C_{\text{AND}}(\text{IP}_n)$. The subfunction of IP_n, for which $a_n = b_n = 1$ is $\overline{\text{IP}}_{n-1}$. Since $C_{\text{OR}}(\overline{\text{IP}}_{n-1}) = C_{\text{AND}}(\text{IP}_{n-1}) \geq n - 1$, it follows that $C_{\text{OR}}(\text{IP}_n) \geq n - 1$.

Finally, we showed in the proof of Theorem 15.2.12 that $\mathrm{CAR}_{\lceil n/8 \rceil - 1}$ is a subfunction of MUL_n with the given partition of the variables. We reduced this problem to $\overline{\mathrm{GT}}_{\lceil n/8 \rceil - 1}$ via a rectangular reduction. Thus the lower bounds for MUL_n follow from the lower bounds for GT_n and the property that for any function f, $\mathrm{C}_{\mathrm{EXOR}}(\overline{f}) = \mathrm{C}_{\mathrm{EXOR}}(f)$. This last property is simple to show. The number of paths to 1-leaves is increased by 1 if at the root it is nondeterministically decided whether a 1-leaf is reached directly or the given protocol is used. $\square$

The communication complexity of any function $f : \{0,1\}^n \times \{0,1\}^n \to \{0,1\}$ is bounded above by $n + 1$. For many of the decision and optimization problems we have considered, a runtime of 2^n was the worst possible case, and exponentially better runtimes, that is polynomial time, were considered efficient. In analogy to this situation we will consider a function $f : \{0,1\}^n \times \{0,1\}^n \to \{0,1\}$ with polylogarithmic communication complexity as efficiently solvable by communication protocols. So we will let $\mathrm{P}_{\mathrm{com}}$, $\mathrm{NP}_{\mathrm{com}}$, co-$\mathrm{NP}_{\mathrm{com}}$, and $\mathrm{NP}_{\mathrm{com}}^{\mathrm{EXOR}}$ be the complexity classes of all functions $f = (f_n)$ with $f_n : \{0,1\}^n \times \{0,1\}^n \to \{0,1\}$ that have deterministic, OR-nondeterministic, AND-nondeterministic, or EXOR-nondeterministic communication complexity bounded by a polynomial in $\log n$.

Theorem 15.3.5 together with the fact that $\mathrm{C}_{\mathrm{OR}}(f) = \mathrm{C}_{\mathrm{AND}}(\overline{f})$ and the results from Section 15.2 says that the four complexity classes just defined are pairwise distinct. None of the three nondeterministic classes contains another. From this perspective we have answered many central questions with relatively simple methods. In conclusion, we will show that $\mathrm{P}_{\mathrm{com}} = \mathrm{NP}_{\mathrm{com}} \cap$ co-$\mathrm{NP}_{\mathrm{com}}$, formulating the result as an upper bound for deterministic communication complexity.

Theorem 15.3.6. $C(f) = O(\mathrm{C}_{\mathrm{OR}}(f) \cdot \mathrm{C}_{\mathrm{AND}}(f))$.

Proof. Alice and Bob agree on a cover of the 1-inputs of the communication matrix with $\mathrm{N}_{\mathrm{OR}}(f)$ 1-rectangles, and on a numbering of this cover. They also agree on a cover of the 0-inputs with $\mathrm{N}_{\mathrm{AND}}(f)$ 0-rectangles. These covers form the basis of their protocol which will make use of the following property of rectangles: If the rectangles R and R' both intersect row a and column b, then they both contain (a, b), and therefore their intersection is non-empty. This means that a 1-rectangle R and a 0-rectangle R' can share rows or columns, but not both. So for any 1-rectangle R and a set of 0-rectangles, either at least half of the set of 0-rectangles have no row in common with R or at least half of the set of 0-rectangles have no column in common with R.

The protocol consists of at most $\lceil \log \mathrm{N}_{\mathrm{AND}}(f) \rceil$ phases. In each phase only $\lceil \log \mathrm{N}_{\mathrm{OR}}(f) \rceil + O(1)$ bits are communicated. The bound then follows from Theorem 15.3.2. Alice and Bob maintain a candidate set K of all 0-rectangles from the chosen cover that could contain the particular input (a, b). At the beginning this set contains all $\mathrm{N}_{\mathrm{AND}}(f)$ rectangles in the cover of the 0's in the communication matrix. If $K = \emptyset$, then the communication ends with the result "$f(a,b) = 1$".

If $K \neq \emptyset$, then Alice checks whether there is a rectangle R in the 1-cover such that at most half of the 0-rectangles in K share a row with R. If there is such a rectangle, then Alice sends its index to Bob. Otherwise she informs Bob that there is no such rectangle. In the first case, both Alice and Bob can compute which 0-rectangles from K are still candidates, namely those that have a row in common with R. In this case the size of K has been reduced by at least half. In the second case Bob checks whether there is a rectangle R' belonging to the 1-cover that intersects column b and such that at most half of the 0-rectangles in K share a column with R'. He sends the corresponding message, and if his search was successful, the size of K has once again been cut in half.

Now we just need to describe what happens when neither Alice nor Bob find a suitable rectangle. In this case the communication ends with the result "$f(a,b) = 0$" because if $f(a,b) = 1$, then the rectangle R in the 1-cover that covers (a,b) must have the property that either at most half of the rectangles in K have a row in common with R or at most half of the rectangles in K have a column in common with R. Thus if $f(a,b) = 1$, then either Alice or Bob will find a suitable rectangle. □

Some functions have nondeterministic communication protocols that are exponentially shorter than the best deterministic ones. The class of such functions depends on the type of nondeterminism selected. Lower bounds for nondeterministic communication complexity can be derived from the lower bound methods for the deterministic case, but which methods can be carried over depends on the type of nondeterminism.

15.4 Randomized Communication Protocols

We now turn our attention to randomized communication protocols with small error- or failure-rates. As in Section 3.3 we will distinguish between the following situations:

- The protocol is error-free and we are interested in the worst-case (with respect to inputs) expected (with respect to the random bits) length of a protocol. The corresponding complexity measure is $R_0(f)$.
- The protocol is error-free, but it can fail, which we represent with the answer "?". For an allowed failure-rate of $\varepsilon < 1$ we have the complexity measure $R_{?,\varepsilon}(f)$.
- For functions $f : A \times B \to \{0,1\}$, one-sided error bounded by $\varepsilon < 1$ means that inputs from $f^{-1}(0)$ are processed without error while inputs from $f^{-1}(1)$ have an error-rate of at most ε. The corresponding complexity measure in this case is $R_{1,\varepsilon}(f)$.

- The complexity measure $R_{2,\varepsilon}(f)$ corresponds to protocols for which the error-probability is bounded by $\varepsilon < 1/2$ for all inputs. If $f : A \times B \to \{0,1\}$ this is two-sided error.

The question is how robust these complexity measures are against changes in the parameter ε. Communication protocols are algorithms and therefore the methods from Section 3.3 can be used. There we were considering polynomial time-bounded algorithms, and so polynomially many independent repetitions of the algorithm were unproblematic. Here, for a function $f : \{0,1\}^n \times \{0,1\}^n \to \{0,1\}$ the deterministic communication complexity is always bounded by $n + 1$. In many cases we can even determine the communication complexity asymptotically exactly. So if we only consider constant factors to be unproblematic, then we can only consider constantly many independent repetitions of a protocol to be unproblematic. The results and proofs in Section 3.3 and the comments just made lead directly to the following results.

Theorem 15.4.1. *For randomized communication complexity and $\varepsilon < 1$ the following relationships hold:*

- $R_0(f) \le 2 \cdot R_{?,1/2}(f)$.
- $R_{?,1/2}(f) \le 2 \cdot R_0(f)$.
- $R_{?,\varepsilon^k}(f) \le k \cdot R_{?,\varepsilon}(f)$.
- $R_{1,\varepsilon^k}(f) \le k \cdot R_{1,\varepsilon}(f)$.
- $R_{2,2^{-k}}(f) \le \lceil (2 \cdot \ln 2) \cdot k \cdot \varepsilon^{-2} \rceil \cdot R_{2,1/2-\varepsilon}(f)$ *for $0 < \varepsilon < 1/2$.* $\square$

We can also apply the proof that $\mathsf{ZPP} = \mathsf{RP} \cap \mathsf{co\text{-}RP}$ (Theorem 3.4.3) to communication complexity:

Theorem 15.4.2. *For $0 < \varepsilon < 1/2$ we have*

$$R_{?,\varepsilon}(f) \le R_{1,\varepsilon}(f) + R_{1,\varepsilon}(\overline{f}) .$$ $\square$

In order to learn how good randomized communication protocols can be, we will consider the example of the equality test EQ_n. The result $C_{AND}(EQ_n) \le \lceil \log n \rceil + 2$ from Theorem 15.3.5 can be interpreted in a new way. There we selected i at random and tested the property "$a_i \ne b_i$". If $a \ne b$, then with probability at least $1/n$ an index i is chosen for which $a_i \ne b_i$. So $R_{1,1-1/n}(\overline{EQ_n}) \le \lceil \log n \rceil + 2$. Independent repetitions do no allow us to achieve constant error-probabilities for short protocols. In order to have $(1 - 1/n)^k \le 1/2$, we would need $k = \Omega(n)$.

Now we will introduce one of the fundamental techniques for designing randomized communication protocols. For a deterministic decision of whether $a = b$, it is optimal for Alice to send Bob her entire input. If we allow errors, then it is sufficient for Alice to send Bob a *fingerprint* of a. Fingerprints of different individuals a and a' can only be the same with small probability. The term *fingerprint* can be a bit misleading. While a person's finger only has one fingerprint, we will assign to each $a \in \{0,1\}^n$ many different fingerprints in such a way that distinct inputs a and a' have only few fingerprints in common. So for a random choice of fingerprint, Bob can check the property "$a \neq b$" with small error-probability.

Theorem 15.4.3. $R_{1,1/n}(\overline{EQ}_n) = O(\log n)$.

Proof. Alice and Bob interpret their inputs as binary numbers $\langle a \rangle, \langle b \rangle \in \{0, \ldots, 2^n - 1\}$. Both of them compute the n^2 smallest prime numbers. From number theory we know that the size of these prime numbers is $O(n^2 \log n)$ and so each of these primes can be described with $O(\log n)$ bits. Alice randomly selects one of these prime numbers, and sends to Bob the type of fingerprint (p) and the fingerprint itself, namely $\langle a \rangle$ mod p. Bob checks whether $\langle a \rangle \equiv \langle b \rangle$ mod p, and sends the result of this test back to Alice. The input is rejected if $\langle a \rangle \equiv \langle b \rangle$ mod p. The length of this protocol is $\Theta(\log n)$ and inputs (a, b) with $a = b$ are always rejected. We need to approximate the probability that an input (a, b) is accepted if $a \neq b$. If there are k primes among the smallest n^2 primes for which $\langle a \rangle \equiv \langle b \rangle$ mod p, then this probability is k/n^2. We will show that there are fewer than n primes p such that $\langle a \rangle \equiv \langle b \rangle$ mod p, i.e., that $k < n$. For this we need a simple result from elementary number theory. If $\langle a \rangle \equiv \langle b \rangle$ mod m_1 and $\langle a \rangle \equiv \langle b \rangle$ mod m_2 for two relatively prime numbers m_1 and m_2, then $\langle a \rangle \equiv \langle b \rangle$ mod $m_1 m_2$ as well. The assumptions say that $\langle a \rangle - \langle b \rangle$ is an integer multiple of m_1 and an integer multiple of m_2. Since m_1 and m_2 are relatively prime, $\langle a \rangle - \langle b \rangle$ must then be an integer multiple of $m_1 m_2$. If $\langle a \rangle \equiv \langle b \rangle$ mod p for n prime numbers p, then this will also be true for their product. But since each of these primes is at least 2, their product must be greater than 2^n. But if $\langle a \rangle \equiv \langle b \rangle$ mod N for an integer N with $N \geq 2^n$, then $\langle a \rangle = \langle b \rangle$, so $a = b$. Thus the error-probability is bounded by $n/n^2 = 1/n$. $\square$

When we defined randomized communication protocols in Section 15.3 we emphasized that Alice knows r_A but not r_B and that Bob knows r_B but not r_A. What difference does it make if we have only one random vector of length $l_A + l_B$ which is known to both Alice and Bob? To distinguish between these two models, we will say that our original model uses *private coins*, and that the modified model uses *public coins*. We will use a superscripted "pub" in our notation to distinguish the public-coin complexity measures from their private-coin counterparts. Clearly Theorem 15.4.1 is still valid for protocols with public coins. Furthermore,

Remark 15.4.4. A protocol with private coins can be simulated by a protocol with public coins. So for example, $R_{2,\varepsilon}^{\mathrm{pub}}(f) \leq R_{2,\varepsilon}(f)$.

Proof. Let l_A and l_B be the lengths of the random vectors for Alice and Bob in a protocol with private coins. The protocol with public coins uses a random vector of length $l_A + l_B$. During the simulation, Alice uses the prefix of the random vector of length l_A, and Bob uses the suffix of length l_B. $\square$

Public coins sometimes lead to short and elegant protocols, as the following result shows.

Theorem 15.4.5. $R_{1,1/2}^{\text{pub}}(\overline{\text{EQ}}_n) \leq 2$.

Proof. Alice and Bob use a public random vector $r \in \{0,1\}^n$. Alice computes the $\mathbb{Z}_2$-sum of all $a_i r_i$ with $1 \leq i \leq n$ and sends the result $h_r(a)$ to Bob. The notation h_r should remind us of the hash function used in the proof of Theorem 11.3.4. Bob computes $h_r(b)$ and sends the result to Alice. They accept the input if $h_r(a) \neq h_r(b)$. The length of the protocol is 2. If $a = b$, then $h_r(a) = h_r(b)$ for all r and the protocol works without error. If $a \neq b$, then there is a position i with $a_i \neq b_i$. By symmetry it suffices to consider the case that $a_i = 0$ and $b_i = 1$. Let $h_r^*(a)$ be the $\mathbb{Z}_2$-sum of all $a_j r_j$ with $j \neq i$; $h_r^*(b)$ is defined analogously. Then $h_r(a) = h_r^*(a)$ and $h_r(b) = h_r^*(b) \oplus r_i$. So the probability that $h_r(a) = h_r(b)$ is exactly $1/2$ and so the error-rate is $1/2$. $\square$

Is it possible for $R_{1,\varepsilon}(f)$ and $R_{1,\varepsilon}^{\text{pub}}(f)$ or $R_{2,\varepsilon}(f)$ and $R_{2,\varepsilon}^{\text{pub}}(f)$ to differ even more strongly? It can be shown that $R_{1,1/4}(\overline{\text{EQ}}_n) \geq R_{2,1/4}(\overline{\text{EQ}}_n) = \Omega(\log n)$. On the other hand, by Theorems 15.4.5 and 15.4.1 it follows that $R_{1,1/4}^{\text{pub}}(\overline{\text{EQ}}_n) \leq 4$. Thus we already have an example where the difference between the two models is essentially as large as possible.

Theorem 15.4.6. *Let* $f: \{0,1\}^n \times \{0,1\}^n \to \{0,1\}$ *and* $\delta > 0$ *be given. Then*

- $R_{2,\varepsilon+\delta}(f) \leq R_{2,\varepsilon}^{\text{pub}}(f) + O(\log n + \log \delta^{-1})$, *and*
- $R_{1,\varepsilon+\delta}(f) \leq R_{1,\varepsilon}^{\text{pub}}(f) + O(\log n + \log \delta^{-1})$.

Proof. In this proof we use the fact that communication protocols are a non-uniform model. The protocols generated here are not in general efficiently computable. In this aspect and in the methodology we orient ourselves on the proof that $\text{BPP} \subseteq \text{P/poly}$ (Theorem 14.5.1, Corollary 14.6.3). In that case there was a *single* golden computation path. Here we will show that there are $t = O(n \cdot \delta^{-2})$ computation paths such that the random choice of one of these computation paths only lets the error-probability grow from ε to $\varepsilon + \delta$. From this the claims of the theorem follow easily. Alice and Bob agree on the good computation paths, and Alice generates with her private random bits a random $i \in \{1, \ldots, t\}$ and sends i to Bob using $O(\log t) = O(\log n + \log \delta^{-1})$ bits. Then Alice and Bob simulate the ith of the selected computation paths.

Suppose we have an optimal randomized communication protocol with a public random vector r of length l. The two cases, namely one-sided error and two-sided error, are handled with the same argument. Let $Z(a, b, r^*) = 1$ if the given protocol on input (a, b) with $r = r^*$ provides an incorrect result, and let $Z(a, b, r^*) = 0$ otherwise. We can imagine the Z-values as a matrix, the rows of which represent the inputs (a, b) and the columns the vectors r^*. By assumption, the proportion of 1's in each row is bounded by ε (for one-sided error the rows contain no 1's for $(a, b) \in f^{-1}(0)$. We want to show that there is a selection of t columns such that each row of the submatrix restricted to these columns has a proportion of at most $\varepsilon + \delta$ 1's (for one-sided error, of course, the shortened rows contain no 1's for $(a, b) \in f^{-1}(0)$). With these t random vectors – or, equivalently, with these t computation paths – we can complete the argument we began above. To be precise we must mention that columns may be chosen more than once.

We prove the existence of t such columns using the *probabilistic method* (see Alon and Spencer (1992)). This method proves the existence of an object with certain properties by designing a suitable random experiment and showing that the probability that the result of this experiment is an object with the desired properties is positive. The potential of this method was first recognized and employed by Erdős. In our case, we randomly and independently select t computation paths $r_1, \dots, r_t$. Let R be the random variable that takes on the values $r_1, \dots, r_t$ each with probability $1/t$. By definition

$$\mathrm{E}(Z(a, b, R)) = \sum_{1 \leq i \leq t} Z(a, b, r_i)/t \, .$$

But since $r_1, \dots, r_t$ are also randomly selected, we can use the Chernoff Inequality to prove that

$$\mathrm{Prob}\left(\sum_{1 \leq i \leq t} Z(a, b, r_i)/t \geq \varepsilon + \delta \right) \leq 2e^{-\delta^2 t} \, .$$

In Theorem A.2.11 we proved a form of the Chernoff Inequality in which $\mathrm{Prob}(X \leq (1 - \delta) \cdot \mathrm{E}(X))$ is bounded from above. Here we require a Chernoff Inequality for estimating $\mathrm{Prob}(X \geq (1+\delta) \cdot \mathrm{E}(X))$ (see Motwani and Raghavan (1995)). If $t = 2n\delta^{-2} + 1$, then $2\,e^{-\delta^2 t} < 2^{-2n}$. Since there are only 2^{2n} inputs (a, b), the probability that

$$\sum_{1 \leq i \leq t} Z(a, b, r_i)/t \geq \varepsilon + \delta$$

is smaller than 1 for any input (a, b). So the probability of a selection of $r_1, \dots, r_t$ such that the error-probability for each input is bounded by $\varepsilon + \delta$ is positive, and so t suitable vectors $r_1, \dots, r_t$ must exist. This completes the proof.   □

For a constant $\varepsilon < 1/2$ in the case of two-sided error (or $\varepsilon < 1$ in the case of one-sided error) we can choose a constant $\delta > 0$ such that $\varepsilon + \delta < 1/2$ ($\varepsilon + \delta < 1$ in the case of one-sided error). By Theorem 15.4.1 and Theorem 15.4.6 it follows that

$$\mathrm{R}_{2,\varepsilon}(f) = O(R_{2,\varepsilon}^{\mathrm{pub}}(f) + \log n)$$

and

$$\mathrm{R}_{1,\varepsilon}(f) = O(R_{1,\varepsilon}^{\mathrm{pub}}(f) + \log n) \, .$$

These results demonstrate a certain robustness of our model of randomized communication protocols with private coins. We have also already encountered a method for designing short randomized communication protocols. Lower bounds for one-sided error follow from lower bounds for nondeterministic communication protocols. But what is the situation for randomized communication protocols with two-sided error? As in Section 9.2 we will make use of the theory of two-person zero-sum games to characterize $R_{2,\varepsilon}^{\text{pub}}(f)$ using a measure for deterministic protocols and randomly selected inputs.

For $f : A \times B \to C$ we consider probability distributions p on $A \times B$ and investigate deterministic protocols such that the error-probability with respect to p is bounded by ε. We let $D_{p,\varepsilon}(f)$ denote the length of the shortest deterministic protocol that for a p-random choice of input yields an error-probability bounded by ε. The corresponding complexity measure is called (p, ε)-*distributional communication complexity*, but it is clearer to speak of this as the complexity of ε-approximations for f with respect to p.

Theorem 15.4.7. *For any function $f : A \times B \to C$ and each $\delta > 0$,*

- $R_{2,\varepsilon}^{\text{pub}}(f) \geq \max\{D_{p,\varepsilon}(f) \mid p \text{ a distribution on } A \times B\}$, *and*
- $R_{2,\varepsilon+\delta}^{\text{pub}}(f) \leq \max\{D_{p,\varepsilon}(f) \mid p \text{ a distribution on } A \times B\}$.

Proof. For the proof of the lower bound we assume there is a randomized communication protocol of length $R_{2,\varepsilon}^{\text{pub}}(f)$ with an error-probability of ε. The error-bound is valid for every input (a, b), and thus also for any input randomly selected according to the distribution p and $A \times B$. If the randomized protocol uses a random vector r of length l, then we are dealing with a random choice from among 2^l deterministic protocols. If all of these protocols had an error-probability greater than ε with respect to p, then the randomized protocol would also have an error-probability greater than ε, which would contradict the assumption. Therefore there must be a deterministic protocol with length $R_{2,\varepsilon}^{\text{pub}}(f)$ that has an error-probability bounded by ε with respect to p-random inputs.

For the proof of the other inequality we investigate the following two-person zero-sum game. For $d := \max_p\{D_{p,\varepsilon}(f)\}$, Alice can select a deterministic communication protocol P of length d and Bob gets to choose the input (a, b). The payoff matrix M has a 1 in position $((a, b), P)$ if the protocol P makes an error on input (a, b), otherwise this position contains a 0. Recall that Alice must pay this amount to Bob. By the definition of d, against each randomized strategy of Bob (that is, for each probability distribution p on $A \times B$), Alice has a deterministic strategy (that is, a deterministic communication protocol) for which her expected payout is bounded by ε. So the value of the game is bounded by ε. By the Minimax Theorem (see Owen (1995)) it follows that there is a randomized strategy for Alice (i.e., a probability distribution over the protocols of length at most d) that guarantees for each input (a, b) an error-probability of at most ε. For Alice and Bob to produce a common communication protocol from this, they must be able to make the corresponding random decision. This is possible using a common random vector, i.e., with public coins. To be precise, Alice and Bob would need an infinite sequence of random bits to correctly realize probabilities like, for example, $1/3$. But with finitely many random bits they can approximate any error-probability ε arbitrarily accurately. $\square$

We can omit the additive term δ for the error-probability if we allow the individual random bits to take on the value 1 with a probability that is not necessarily $1/2$ but is instead p_i for the ith random bit. We won't pursue this idea further here since we are primarily interested in the "$\geq$" part of Theorem 15.4.7. In order to prove lower bounds for $R_{2,\varepsilon}^{\mathrm{pub}}(f)$ we can choose a distribution p on $A \times B$ and prove a lower bound for $D_{p,\varepsilon}(f)$. This is one form of Yao's minimax principle.

Now, of course, we have the difficulty of proving lower bounds for $D_{p,\varepsilon}(f)$. Since we are once again dealing with deterministic protocols, we can hope to make use of our techniques involving sizes of rectangles with various properties. Since we may make errors on some of the inputs, the rectangles describing the inputs that lead to a leaf v may not be monochromatic. But if the error-probability is small, then these rectangles will either be small or *almost* monochromatic with respect to p. For $f : A \times B \to \{0,1\}$, a probability distribution p on $A \times B$, and a rectangle $R \subseteq A \times B$, let $R_0 := f^{-1}(0) \cap R$ and $R_1 := f^{-1}(1) \cap R$, and let the *discrepancy* of R with respect to f and p be defined by

$$\mathrm{Disc}_{p,f}(R) := |p(R_1) - p(R_0)| .$$

It follows that $\mathrm{Disc}_{p,f}(R) \leq p(R)$ and that small rectangles cannot have large discrepancy. Finally, let

$$\mathrm{Disc}_p(f) := \max\{\mathrm{Disc}_{p,f}(R) \mid R \subseteq A \times B \text{ and } R \text{ is a rectangle}\}$$

be the discrepancy of f with respect to p. The following result shows that a small discrepancy implies a large communication complexity with respect to the distribution, and thus a large communication complexity with respect to randomized protocols with two-sided error.

Theorem 15.4.8. *If f is a function $f : A \times B \to \{0,1\}$, p a probability distribution on $A \times B$, and $0 < \varepsilon \leq 1/2$, then*

$$D_{p,1/2-\varepsilon}(f) \geq \log(2\varepsilon) - \log(\mathrm{Disc}_p(f)) .$$

Proof. This result follows directly from the definitions and a simple calculation. We consider a deterministic protocol of length $d := D_{p,1/2-\varepsilon}(f)$ with an error-probability of at most $1/2 - \varepsilon$ with respect to p. The corresponding protocol tree has at most 2^d leaves $v \in L$ at which precisely the inputs in the rectangle $R_v \subseteq A \times B$ arrive. The rectangles R_v for $v \in L$ form a partition of $A \times B$. Let E^+ denote the set of all inputs on which the protocol works correctly, and let $E^- := (A \times B) - E^+$ be the set of all inputs on which the protocol makes an error. By our assumption, $p(E^-) \leq 1/2 - \varepsilon$ and so $p(E^+) \geq 1/2 + \varepsilon$. It follows that

$$
\begin{aligned}
2\varepsilon &\leq p(E^+) - p(E^-) \\
&= \sum_{v \in L} \left(p(E^+ \cap R_v) - p(E^- \cap R_v) \right) \\
&\leq \sum_{v \in L} |p(E^+ \cap R_v) - p(E^- \cap R_v)| \\
&= \sum_{v \in L} \mathrm{Disc}_{p,f}(R_v) \\
&\leq 2^d \, \mathrm{Disc}_p(f).
\end{aligned}
$$

Here we are only using the definitions of $\mathrm{Disc}_{p,f}(R)$ and $\mathrm{Disc}_p(f)$. We obtain the claim of the theorem by solving this inequality for $d := \mathrm{D}_{p,1/2-\varepsilon}(f)$. $\qquad\square$

It is not always easy to apply this method. As an example we will investigate IP_n.

Theorem 15.4.9. *If* $0 < \varepsilon \leq 1/2$, *then*

$$
\mathrm{R}^{\mathrm{pub}}_{2,1/2-\varepsilon}(\mathrm{IP}_n) \geq n/2 + \log \varepsilon \ .
$$

Proof. By Theorem 15.4.7 and Theorem 15.4.8 it suffices to prove for some distribution p on $\{0,1\}^n \times \{0,1\}^n$ an upper bound of $2^{-n/2}$ for the discrepancy of arbitrary rectangles $A \times B$. We will use the uniform distribution u on $\{0,1\}^n \times \{0,1\}^n$. In addition, we will replace the 1's in the communication matrix with -1's and the 0's with 1's. The result is the Hadamard matrix H_n introduced in Section 15.2. This has the advantage that we can now compute the discrepancy (now with respect to the colors 1 and -1) algebraically. By definition

$$
\begin{aligned}
\mathrm{Disc}_{u,\mathrm{IP}_n}(A \times B) &= \Big| \#\{(a,b) \in A \times B \mid H_n(a,b) = 1\} - \\
&\qquad \#\{(a,b) \in A \times B \mid H_n(a,b) = -1\} \Big| / 2^{2n} \\
&= \left| \sum_{(a,b) \in A \times B} H_n(a,b) \right| / 2^{2n}.
\end{aligned}
$$

Let $e_A \in \{0,1\}^{2^n}$ be the characteristic vector of $A \subseteq \{0,1\}^n$, and let e_B be the characteristic vector of $B \subseteq \{0,1\}^n$. Then $e_A^\top \cdot H_n \cdot e_B$ sums exactly those $H_n(a,b)$ with $(a,b) \in A \times B$. Thus

$$
\mathrm{Disc}_{u,\mathrm{IP}_n}(A \times B) = |e_A^\top \cdot H_n \cdot e_B| / 2^{2n}
$$

and it is sufficient to demonstrate an upper bound of $2^{3n/2}$ for $|e_A^\top \cdot H_n \cdot e_B|$. For this we can make use of the algebraic properties of H_n. For the $2^n \times 2^n$-identity matrix I_n it follows by simple computation that

$$H_n \cdot H_n^\top = 2^n \cdot I_n .$$

The matrix $H_n \cdot H_n^\top$ has in position (a, b) the entry

$$\sum_{c \in \{0,1\}^n} H_n(a, c) \cdot H_n(b, c) .$$

If $a = b$, then $H_n(a, c) = H_n(b, c) \in \{-1, +1\}$, $H_n(a, c) \cdot H_n(b, c) = 1$ and the sum is 2^n. As in the proof of Theorem 15.4.5, if $a \neq b$, then $\mathrm{IP}_n(a, c) = \mathrm{IP}_n(b, c)$ for exactly half of all $c \in \{0,1\}^n$. So half of all $H_n(a, c) \cdot H_n(b, c)$ have the value 1, and the other half have the value -1. Thus the sum of these values is 0. Since I_n has only one eigenvalue, namely 1, the only eigenvalue of $H_n \cdot H_n^\top = 2^n \cdot I_n$ is 2^n. From this it follows that the spectral norm $||H_n||_2$ of H_n has the value $2^{n/2}$. The norm of vectors is their Euclidean length. Thus $||e_A||_2 = |A|^{1/2} \leq 2^{n/2}$ and $||e_B||_2 \leq 2^{n/2}$. These norms measure how much vectors are lengthened when multiplied by the vector or matrix being investigated. Thus

$$|e_A^\top \cdot H_n \cdot e_B| \leq ||e_A||_2 \cdot ||H_n||_2 \cdot ||e_B||_2 \leq 2^{3n/2}$$

and $\mathrm{Disc}_{u, \mathrm{IP}_n}(A \times B) \leq 2^{-n/2}$ for arbitrary rectangles $A \times B$. $\qquad \square$

> *Randomized communication protocols, even with very small error-probabilities, can be exponentially shorter than deterministic communication protocols. It doesn't make much difference if the random bits are public or private. If with respect to some probability distribution on the inputs every rectangle of the communication matrix contains roughly half 0's and half 1's, then the randomized communication complexity of the corresponding function is large.*

15.5 Communication Complexity and VLSI Circuits

We will be satisfied with a naive understanding of VLSI circuits based on the simple model described below. The lower bounds we obtain for this simple model will certainly hold for any more realistically restricted model. We imagine a VLSI circuit as a rectangular grid of length l and width w. The grid has area $A := lw$ and consists of lw cells. Each cell can hold at most one bit of the input and is potentially connected only to the (at most four) cells with which it shares a cell wall. In each time unit at most one bit can be sent in one direction across each connection. For functions with one output y there is a cell that contains this result at the end of the computation. A VLSI circuit with eight inputs and one output is shown in Figure 15.5.1.

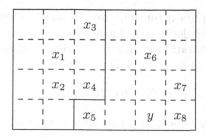

Fig. 15.5.1. A VLSI circuit of width 6 and length 4.

We can see from this diagram that it will always be possible to cut the circuit so that $\lfloor n/2 \rfloor$ inputs are on one side of the cut and $\lceil n/2 \rceil$ inputs are on the other side and such that the cut consists of at most $l + 1$ cell walls. By symmetry we can assume that $l \leq w$ and thus that $l \leq A^{1/2}$. In each time unit, at most $l + 1$ bits can be communicated across this cut. If we partition the input bits in such a way that Alice receives the bits on one side of the cut and Bob the bits on the other side, then we can establish a connection among the communication complexity of f with respect to this partition of the input bits, the area A, and the parallel computation time T of the VLSI circuit, namely

$$C(f) \leq (A^{1/2} + 1) \cdot T + 1 .$$

This is because in each of the T time steps at most $A^{1/2} + 1$ bits can be sent across the cut. This can be simulated by a deterministic communication protocol. The extra summand $+1$ is necessary, since in the VLSI circuit only one cell, i.e., only Alice or only Bob, must know the result. In a communication protocol this result must be communicated. Since the complexity of VLSI circuits is usually measured in terms of AT^2, our result can be expressed as $AT^2 = \Omega(C(f)^2)$.

As we see, we cannot partition the input arbitrarily. For the middle bit of multiplication (MUL), however, we have proven a linear lower bound for the communication complexity that is valid for any partition of the input bits that gives half of the bits of the first factor to each of Alice and Bob. If we modify our cut in the VLSI circuit so that it only takes into consideration the bits of the first factor, then we can still apply the observations above to obtain the following result:

Theorem 15.5.1. *For VLSI circuits that compute the middle bit of multiplication for two factors of length n, $AT^2 = \Omega(n^2)$.* □

15.6 Communication Complexity and the Computation Time of Turing Machines

Turing machines with k tapes and runtime $t(n)$ can be simulated by Turing machines with one tape and runtime $O(t(n)^2)$. Is this quadratic slowdown necessary? At least for linear runtimes we can answer these questions by giving a language that can be decided in linear time by a Turing machine with two tapes but requires quadratic time for any Turing machine with only one tape. For $f = (f_n)$ with $f_n : \{0,1\}^n \times \{0,1\}^n \to \{0,1\}$ let

$$L_f^* = \{acb : |a| = |c| = |b|, a, b \in \{0,1\}^*, c \in \{2\}^*, f_{|a|}(a,b) = 1\} .$$

Remark 15.6.1. The language L_{EQ}^* can be decided by a two-tape Turing machine in time $O(n)$.

Proof. In one pass over the input tape we can test whether the input has the form acb with $a, b \in \{0,1\}^*$ and $c \in \{2\}^*$, and simultaneously copy b to the second tape. By reading a and b at the same time, we can test whether they have the same length, and if so, we can compute $\mathrm{EQ}_n(a,b)$. Finally, we can check whether b and c have the same length. $\square$

More interesting than this simple observation is the proof of a lower bound for the runtime of Turing machines with only one tape.

Theorem 15.6.2. *If the language L_f^* for $f = (f_n)$ is decided by a one-tape Turing machine M in time $t(n)$, then*

$$\mathrm{R}_0^{\mathrm{pub}}(f_n) = O(t(3n)/n + 1) .$$

Proof. We want to design a randomized, error-free communication protocol for f_n that has a small expected length for every input. Alice knows $a \in \{0,1\}^n$, and Bob knows $b \in \{0,1\}^n$. In particular, each of them knows n and the way M works on the input $w = a2^n b$, where 2^n denotes a sequence of n 2's. With the help of the publicly known random vector, Alice and Bob select a random $i \in \{0, \ldots, n\}$. This is used to divide the tape of M between Alice and Bob. Alice receives the left portion, up to cell $n + i$, and Bob receives the rest. Since the head of M is reading a_1 at the beginning of the computation, Alice can simulate the first portion of the computation. When M crosses over the dividing line from left to right, Alice sends Bob the state of the Turing machine. This requires only $\lceil \log |Q| \rceil = O(1)$ bits. Now Bob can simulate the Turing machine until the dividing line is crossed from right to left and send Alice the state of the Turing machine at that point. This process continues until the machine halts. At that point, one of Alice and Bob knows the result and communicates it to the other. This protocol is error-free since M is error-free and correctly simulated.

Now let $z_i = z_i(a,b)$ be the number of computation steps at which the dividing line between tape cells $n + i$ and $n + i + 1$ is crossed. Since at each step at most one dividing line can be crossed and $|w| = 3n$ it follows that

$$z_0 + \cdots + z_n \leq t(3n)$$

and

$$(z_0 + \cdots + z_n)/(n+1) \leq t(3n)/n \ .$$

So on average, Alice and Bob send at most $t(3n)/n$ messages of length $O(1)$ and at the end one additional message of length 1. This proves the theorem.

$\square$

By Theorem 15.3.5 $C_{OR}(EQ_n) \geq n$, and thus $R_{1,2/3}(EQ_n) \geq n$. So by Theorem 15.4.6 $R_{1,1/2}^{pub}(EQ_n) = \Omega(n)$. By the variant of Theorem 15.4.1 for protocols with public coins, it follows that $R_0^{pub}(EQ_n) = \Omega(n)$. Finally, using Theorem 15.6.2 we obtain the desired result:

Theorem 15.6.3. *For one-tape Turing machines that decide L_{EQ}^* in time $t(n)$, $t(n) = \Omega(n^2)$.* $\square$

The results of the last two sections show that results about the communication complexity of specific problems can support the solution of problems from very different areas.

The Complexity of Boolean Functions

16.1 Fundamental Considerations

We have already emphasized several times that there is a close relationship between decision problems or languages $L \subseteq \{0,1\}^*$ and families of Boolean functions $f = (f_n)$ with one output. For each language L there is a family of functions $f^L = (f_n^L)$ such that $f_n^L \colon \{0,1\}^n \to \{0,1\}$ takes on the value 1 for input a if and only if $a \in L$. And for each $f = (f_n)$ with $f_n \colon \{0,1\}^n \to \{0,1\}$ there is a decision problem L_f that is the union of all $f_n^{-1}(1)$. When we consider families of Boolean functions, however, we focus our attention on the individual functions f_n; we are interested in non-uniform complexity measures like size and depth of circuits or the size and length of branching programs. In Chapter 14 we discussed the differences between uniform and non-uniform complexity measures and in Chapter 15 we investigated the non-uniform measure of communication complexity. Now we want to attempt to prove lower bounds for the complexity of Boolean functions with respect to the complexity measures just mentioned.

In principle this is an easy task. There are 2^{2^n} Boolean functions $f \colon \{0,1\}^n \to \{0,1\}$ and only $2^{O(s \log(s+n))}$ syntactically different circuits with s gates. This bound follows from the fact that each gate must realize one of finitely many operations and has as inputs two of the at most $s + n + 2$ possibilities. So for a suitable choice of $c > 0$, we cannot realize all of the Boolean functions with only $c \cdot 2^n / n$ gates. Now if we let f_n be the first function in a lexicographically ordered list of all function tables that has no circuit with $c \cdot 2^n / n$ or fewer gates, then we have a family $f = (f_n)$ of Boolean functions with high circuit complexity.

But this is not what we are after. We have been particularly interested in problems that are NP-easy, and especially in decision problems belonging to NP. In the same way, we want to concentrate now on families $f = (f_n)$ of Boolean functions for which the corresponding decision problem L_f is in NP. For restricted models, like depth-bounded circuits, we can show exponential lower bounds for functions $f = (f_n)$ for which the corresponding decision problems can be computed in polynomial or even in linear time. In order to rule out counting tricks and diagonalization arguments, we will restrict our attention to Boolean functions $f_n : \{0,1\}^n \to \{0,1\}$ that can be *explicitly defined*. In investigations that go beyond what we will cover here, there are various degrees of "explicitly defined", but for our purposes the requirement that $L_f \in \mathsf{NP}$ will suffice. The basic idea is to prove lower bounds for the complexity of explicitly defined Boolean functions with respect to non-uniform complexity measures that are as large as possible. For communication complexity we were able to prove linear lower bounds, which are the best possible. For circuits and branching programs we are still far from the best possible lower bounds. Therefore we pursue three related goals, namely

- the hunt for ever better bounds for explicitly defined Boolean functions and the various non-uniform complexity measures;
- the development of methods for proving lower bounds for various non-uniform complexity measures; and
- the estimation of the complexity of important Boolean functions.

The structure of this chapter follows the various non-uniform complexity measures. In Section 16.2 we investigate circuit size, and in Section 16.3, circuit depth. The special case of monotone circuits will be mentioned briefly. The results for general circuits are sobering. Much better results are possible if we remove the restrictions on the input degrees of the gates but drastically restrict the depth of the circuits. We will treat this model with generalized AND- and OR-gates in Section 16.4. We will also discuss some methods that work as well for generalized EXOR-gates. In Section 16.5 we will investigate an analogous model for so-called threshold circuits. These are important for two reasons. On the one hand we obtain a model for discrete neural nets without feedback, and on the other hand the limits of our techniques for proving lower bounds are especially clear to see in this model. In Section 16.6 we consider general and restricted branching programs. After developing methods for proving lower bounds and applying them to a few example functions in Sections 16.2–16.6, in Section 16.7 we introduce reduction concepts that allow us to extend these results from a few functions to many.

16.2 Circuit Size

Circuits are of clear importance as a canonical model of hardware. Recall that gates have two inputs and that any of the 16 Boolean functions can be applied to these inputs. The circuit size of f_n is the smallest number of gates that suffice to compute f_n. For a long time now, the record lower bound for explicitly defined Boolean functions has remained $3n - O(\log n)$. We should note that there is a trivial lower bound of $n - 1$ for all functions that depend *essentially* on all n inputs, where we say that a function f_n depends essentially on x_i if the two *subfunctions* $f_{n|x_i=0} : \{0,1\}^n \to \{0,1\}$ and $f_{n|x_i=1} : \{0,1\}^n \to$

$\{0, 1\}$ defined by $f_{n|x_i=b}(a) := f_n(a_1, \ldots, a_{i-1}, b, a_{i+1}, \ldots, a_{n-1})$ are different. In this case at least one gate must have each x_i as input. If f_n depends essentially on n variables, then the circuit consists of a directed acyclic graph with n inputs and one sink, corresponding to the output of the function. Since this graph is connected, it must contain at least $n - 1$ internal nodes, which correspond to the gates of the circuit. On the other hand, the few proofs of lower bounds of size $(2 + \varepsilon)n$ for $\varepsilon > 0$ are complicated. We will be satisfied to show a bound of $(2n - 3)$ using the method of *gate elimination* – the same method that forms the basis for all larger lower bounds.

The bound we will show is for a so-called *threshold function*. The threshold function $T^n_{\geq k}$ is defined on n inputs and returns a value of 1 if and only if at least k of the n inputs have the value 1. The negative threshold function $T^n_{\leq k}$ is the negation of $T^n_{\geq k+1}$.

Theorem 16.2.1. *The circuit size of $T^n_{\geq 2}$ is at least $2n - 3$.*

Proof. We will show the claim by induction on n. For $n = 2$, $T^n_{\geq 2}(x_1, x_2) = x_1 \wedge x_2$ and the claim is immediate, since $2n - 3 = 1$ and we can't possibly compute $T^n_{\geq 2}$ with no gates.

For the inductive step, the idea is to find a variable x_i such that replacing x_i with the constant 0 leads to a circuit with at least two fewer gates. The missing gates are said to have been *eliminated*. Since $T^n_{\geq 2|x_i=0}$ is equal to the function $T^{n-1}_{\geq 2}$ on the remaining variables, the remaining circuit must have at least $2(n - 1) - 3$ gates by the inductive hypothesis. If we have eliminated at least two gates, then the original circuit must have at least $2n - 3$, which demonstrates the claim.

So consider an optimal circuit for $T^n_{\geq 2}$ and its first gate G_1. This has two different variables as inputs, since otherwise there would be an equivalent circuit with fewer gates, contrary to the assumption of optimality. For the same reason, the operation of G_1 must be one of the ten Boolean operations that depend essentially on both inputs. As an exploration of cases shows, for inputs x_i and x_j these are the functions

$$(x_i^a \wedge x_j^b)^c \quad \text{and} \quad (x_i \oplus x_j)^c$$

for $a, b, c \in \{0, 1\}$. Here $x_i^1 = x_i$ and $x_i^0 = \overline{x}_i$. If we set $x_i = 0$, then the gates that have x_i as an input can be eliminated, since they can be combined with a preceding or following gate to form a single gate. Thus our goal is to show that one of the variables x_i and x_j is an input for at least one additional gate. Setting this variable to 0 will result in the desired elimination of at least two gates.

For the sake of contradiction assume that G_1 is the only gate that uses x_i and x_j as input. If G_1 is of the first type listed above, then the circuit for $x_j := \overline{b}$ is independent of x_i, although for $n \geq 3$ the function $T^n_{\geq 2|x_j=\overline{b}}$ depends essentially on all the rest of the variables. If G_1 is of the second type described above, then we get the same circuit for $x_i = x_j = 0$ as for

$x_i = x_j = 1$, contradicting the fact that these two subfunctions are different. This proves the theorem. □

Unfortunately, this method does not seem powerful enough to prove super-linear lower bounds. One potential hope is to consider functions $f_n : \{0,1\}^n \to \{0,1\}^n$, i.e., functions with n outputs. But so far, it has not been possible to prove superlinear lower bounds for any such function, even if we restrict the circuits to depth $O(\log n)$.

> *The investigation of the circuit size of explicitly defined Boolean functions shows clearly how insufficient our reservoir is for proving lower bounds for complexity with respect to practically important models of computation.*

Monotone circuits are circuits that use only AND- and OR-gates. Not all Boolean functions have monotone circuits; $\overline{x}_1$ for example has no such circuit. To describe the class of functions that can be computed by monotone circuits, we make use of a natural partial order ($\leq$) on $\{0,1\}^n$ defined by $(a_1, \ldots, a_n) \leq (b_1, \ldots, b_n)$ if and only if $a_i \leq b_i$ for all i. A Boolean function is called *monotone* if $f(a) \leq f(b)$ whenever $a \leq b$. It is not difficult to convince oneself that the monotone functions are exactly those functions that can be computed by monotone circuits. With a refinement of the technique of gate elimination, superlinear lower bounds have been proved for monotone circuits to compute monotone functions with n outputs. Here n^2 is the natural limit, since superquadratic bounds imply that at least one of the outputs has a su-perlinear lower bound. Methodologically it was an important step to be able to measure the progress of a computation at individual gates (Wegener (1982)). The breakthrough came when this progress was measured approximately in-stead of exactly. In this way in 1986 (journal version in 1990) Razborov was able to prove exponential lower bounds for the monotone circuit complexity of CLIQUE. His proof methods were then extended by Alon and Boppana (1987).

16.3 Circuit Depth

In Section 14.3 we defined formulas as circuits with underlying graphs that are trees, with the understanding that a variable may occur at many leaves of the formula tree. The *formula size* $L(f)$ of a Boolean function f is the minimal number of gates needed to compute f with a formula. Formula trees for f have at least $L(f)+1$ leaves, and so a circuit depth of at least $\lceil \log(L(f)+1) \rceil$. Since we can unfold circuits into formulas without increasing the depth (see Section 14.3), we have proven the following remark about the depth $D(f)$ of f.

Remark 16.3.1. For Boolean functions f,

$$D(f) \geq \lceil \log(L(f) + 1) \rceil.$$

The following converse is also true: $D(f) = O(\log L(f))$ (see, for example, Wegener (1987)). Thus the task of proving superlogarithmic bounds for the depth of functions is equivalent to the task of proving superpolynomial bounds for the formula size. But we are a long way from bounds of this size. The largest lower bound for formula size goes back to Nechiporuk (1966) and is $\Omega(n^2/\log n)$. This yields a circuit depth lower bound of $2\log n - \log\log n - O(1)$. This is only slightly better than the trivial lower bound of $\lceil \log n \rceil$ for functions that depend essentially on n variables.

This lower bound is based on the observation that small formulas are not able to compute functions that have an extremely large number of different subformulas. This method cannot be carried over to general circuits, however. It is known that there is an explicitly defined function with an asymptotically maximal number of different subfunctions and linear circuit size.

Theorem 16.3.2. *Let* $S_1, \ldots, S_k$ *be disjoint subsets of the variable set* $X = \{x_1, \ldots, x_n\}$, *such that* $f : \{0,1\}^n \rightarrow \{0,1\}$ *depends essentially on each variable* $x \in \cup_i S_i$, *and let* s_i *be the number of different functions on* S_i *that we obtain if we replace the variables in* $X - S_i$ *with constants in every possible way, then*

$$\mathrm{L}(f) \geq \Big(\sum_{1 \leq i \leq k} (2 + \log s_i) \Big)/4 - 1 \,.$$

Proof. We show the lower bound by showing a lower bound of $(2 + \log s_i)/4$ for the number of leaves t_i that belong to the variables in S_i.

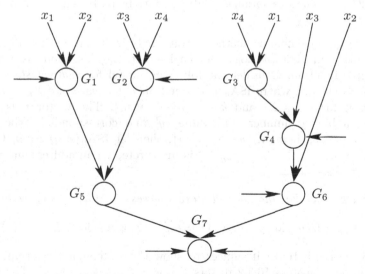

Fig. 16.3.1. A formula in which for $S_1 = \{x_1, x_2\}$ and $S_2 = \{x_3, x_4\}$ the vertices from W_1 are denoted with arrows from the left and the vertices from W_2 with arrows from the right.

Let W_i be the set of internal vertices (gates) in the formula tree that have S_i-leaves in both their left and right subtrees. For $w_i := |W_i|$, we have $w_i = t_i - 1$, since after removing all $(X - S_i)$-leaves and all vertices with fewer than two inputs, we are left with a binary tree with t_i leaves and w_i internal vertices. Now consider paths in the formula tree that start at S_i-leaves or at W_i-vertices, that end at W_i-vertices or at the root of the formula tree, and that contain no W_i-vertices as internal vertices. If we let p_i be the number of these paths, then $p_i \leq 2w_i + 1$, since only two of these paths arrive at each of these W_i-vertices plus one additional one at the root, if it is not a W_i-vertex. In Figure 16.3.1 (G_1, G_5, G_7) is such a path for $i = 1$. Let g be the function that is computed at the beginning of one of these paths after some assignment of all the variables not in S_i. Until we reach the last vertex along the path, we have a subformula that only has g and constants as inputs, and so computes one of g, $\bar{g}$, 0, or 1. So each of the p_i paths can only influence the output in one of four ways. Thus

$$s_i \leq 4^{p_i} \leq 4^{2w_i + 1} = 4^{2t_i - 1} = 2^{4t_i - 2} \,,$$

from which it follows that

$$\log s_i \leq 4t_i - 2 \quad \text{and} \quad t_i \geq (2 + \log s_i)/4 \,. \qquad \square$$

What is the largest this bound can be asymptotically? For s_i there are two upper bounds, namely

- $s_i \leq 2^{2^{|S_i|}}$, since the subfunctions are defined on $|S_i|$ variables, and
- $s_i \leq 2^{n - |S_i|}$, since we obtain the subfunctions by replacing $n - |S_i|$ variables with constants.

With the help of elementary methods from analysis, it can be shown that the Nechiporuk-bound is $O(n^2/\log n)$ for each function. This bound is achieved by a simple function. Consider the following model for *indirect storage access*: ISA $= (\text{ISA}_n)$, where ISA_n is defined on $n + k$ variables $x_0, \ldots, x_{n-1}$, $y_0, \ldots, y_{k-1}$ for $n = 2^m$ and $k := m - \lfloor \log m \rfloor$. The vector y is interpreted as a binary number with value $\langle y \rangle$ and corresponds to the $\langle y \rangle$th block of x of length m. If $\langle y \rangle \geq \lfloor n/m \rfloor$, then let $\text{ISA}_n(x, y) := 0$. Otherwise $x(y) := (x_{\langle y \rangle \cdot m}, \ldots, x_{\langle y \rangle \cdot m + m - 1})$ is interpreted as an address and we let $\text{ISA}_n(x, y) := x_{\langle x(y) \rangle}$.

Theorem 16.3.3. *For the indirect storage access function* (ISA) *we have*

$$\text{L}(\text{ISA}_n) = \Omega(n^2/\log n) \quad \text{and} \quad \text{D}(\text{ISA}_n) \geq 2 \log n - \log \log n - O(1) \,.$$

Proof. By Remark 16.3.1 it suffices to show the statement for formula size. We will apply Theorem 16.3.2 to sets S_i for $0 \leq i \leq \lfloor n/m \rfloor - 1$. The set S_i contains the variables $x_{i \cdot m}, \ldots, x_{i \cdot m + m - 1}$. In order to estimate the number of subfunctions on S_i, we consider the subfunctions that arise by setting the y-variables to constants in such a way that $\langle y \rangle = i$. This way the S_i-variables represent the direct address required to address a bit in the x-vector. More precisely, for any $\alpha \in \{0,1\}^{n-m}$, let f_α be the subfunction of ISA_n that results from setting y so that $\langle y \rangle = i$ and setting the x-variables in $X - S_i$ according to the bits of α. Since α forms a portion of the function table for f_α, the f_α's are distinct. Thus $s_i \geq 2^{n-m}$ and $\log s_i \geq n - m = \Omega(n)$. The claim now follows because the number of S_i sets that we are considering is $\lfloor n/m \rfloor = \Omega(n/\log n)$.

$\square$

There are no larger lower bounds known for the depth of circuits of explicitly defined Boolean functions, but there is a proof method that at least shows great potential. This method characterizes the depth of Boolean functions f using the communication complexity of a related relation R_f.

Definition 16.3.4. *For a Boolean function* $f : \{0,1\}^n \to \{0,1\}$ *there is a relation* $R_f \subseteq f^{-1}(1) \times f^{-1}(0) \times \{1, \ldots, n\}$ *that contains all* (a, b, i) *with* $a_i \neq b_i$. *In the communication game for* R_f, *Alice knows* $a \in f^{-1}(1)$, *Bob knows* $b \in f^{-1}(0)$, *and they must agree on an* $i \in \{1, \ldots, n\}$ *with* $a_i \neq b_i$.

The communication game always has a solution, since $a \in f^{-1}(1)$ and $b \in f^{-1}(0)$ must be different. Recall that $C(R_f)$ denotes the communication complexity of R_f. We now consider circuits with the usual inputs $x_1, \ldots, x_n, 0$, and 1, and the additional inputs $\overline{x}_1, \ldots, \overline{x}_n$. Furthermore, we will only allow AND- and OR- gates. The depth of f in this model will be denoted $D^*(f)$. It follows that

$$D(f) - 1 \leq D^*(f) \leq 2 D(f) .$$

The first of these inequalities follows because the negated inputs can reduce the depth of the circuit by at most 1. To see why the second inequality is true we temporarily consider negation to be without cost; that is, negation is allowed at any point in the circuit, but does not add to its depth. Using this modified definition of depth, we can construct a circuit that has the same depth and uses only NOT-, AND-, and EXOR-gates. Since $x \oplus y = \overline{x}y + x\overline{y}$, we can replace the EXOR-gates with circuits of depth 2. This gives a circuit with at most twice the depth using only AND-, OR-, and NOT-gates. Finally, using a "bottom-up" application of DeMorgan's Laws, we can force the negations up to the inputs without increasing the depth of the circuit. We will investigate D^* in order to obtain results about D.

Theorem 16.3.5. *If* f *is a non-constant Boolean function, then* $D^*(f) = C(R_f)$.

Proof. This surprising connection between depth and communication complexity will be illuminated by the proof. We begin with the "$\geq$" direction. Alice and Bob agree on a formula with optimal depth. They want to use their communication to find a path from the gate that computes f to an input x_i or $\overline{x}_i$ with $a_i \neq b_i$, which will then determine i with $(a, b, i) \in R_f$. The bound follows if for each gate along this path there is exactly one bit of communication.

Alice and Bob want to select their path in such a way that they only reach gates G that compute a function g with $g(a) = 1$ and $g(b) = 0$. This is initially true at the gate computing f since by assumption $f(a) = 1 \neq 0 = f(b)$. At gate G we let g_1 and g_2 denote the functions computed by its two inputs. There are two cases, depending on whether G is an AND-gate or an OR-gate. For an AND-gate, $g = g_1 g_2$, so $g_1(a) = 1$ and $g_2(a) = 1$. On the other hand, at least one of $g_1(b)$ and $g_2(b)$ must be 0. Bob can compute which of the two cases has occurred and communicate this to Alice with one bit. In this way Bob and Alice agree on an immediate predecessor G^*, such that $g^*(a) = 1$ and $g^*(b) = 0$. The case for OR-gates is dual to this. Now $g = g_1 + g_2$, $g_1(b) = 0$, $g_2(b) = 0$, and at least one of $g_1(a)$ and $g_2(a)$ is 1. This time Alice can determine the appropriate predecessor and communicate this to Bob. This discussion makes it clear that when they reach an input, it cannot be a constant. If the input is x_i, then $a_i = 1$ and $b_i = 0$; for $\overline{x}_i$, $a_i = 0$ and $b_i = 1$. In either case Alice and Bob have fulfilled their task.

The proof of the other direction is more complicated, although in a certain sense it is just a reversal of the proof just given. We start with an optimal protocol tree for R_f and transform it into a formula for f. Internal vertices at which Alice sends Bob a bit will become OR-gates and vertices at which Bob sends Alice a bit will become AND-gates. Leaves of the protocol tree with the answer $i \in \{1, \ldots, n\}$ are replaced by x_i or $\overline{x}_i$. The result is a formula with the same depth as the protocol tree, but we still need to decide which of the variables should be negated and to show that the resulting formula computes f.

Consider a leaf of the protocol tree with label i. From Section 15.2 we know that the set of inputs (a, b) that reach this leaf forms a rectangle $A \times B$. For all $(a, b) \in A \times B$, $a_i \neq b_i$. By the rectangle structure, either $a_i = 1$ and $b_i = 0$ for all $a \in A$ and $b \in B$, or $a_i = 0$ and $b_i = 1$ for all $a \in A$ and $b \in B$. Once again we see how useful it is to know that the inputs that reach a vertex in a protocol tree always form a rectangle. In the first case the leaf is labeled with x_i and in the second case with $\overline{x}_i$. This completes the description of the formula.

To show that this formula computes f, we will actually prove a stronger result. For each vertex v of the formula, let $A_v \times B_v$ be the rectangle of inputs (a, b) that reach v. We will show that if g_v is the function computed at v, then $g_v(a) = 1$ for $a \in A_v$, and $g_v(b) = 0$ for $b \in B_v$. The rectangle at the root r is $f^{-1}(1) \times f^{-1}(0)$, so this will prove that $g_r(a) = 1$ for $a \in f^{-1}(1)$ and $g_r(b) = 0$ for $b \in f^{-1}(0)$, so $g_r = f$.

The claim is proven by structural induction from the leaves of the formula to the root. At the leaves, the claim is true since we selected the literal at each leaf to make this work. Now consider an OR-vertex v and the rectangle $A_v \times B_v$. For the predecessors v_1 and v_2 we have $g_v = g_{v_1} + g_{v_2}$. Since Alice sent a bit to Bob at vertex v, A_{v_1} and A_{v_2} form a partition of A_v and $B_v =$

$B_{v_1} = B_{v_2}$. By the inductive hypothesis, for any $(a, b) \in A_{v_1} \times B_{v_1}$, $g_{v_1}(a) = 1$ and $g_{v_1}(b) = 0$. This implies that $g_v(a) = 1$. If $(a, b) \in A_{v_2} \times B_{v_2}$, then by the inductive hypothesis $g_{v_2}(a) = 1$ and $g_{v_2}(b) = 0$. From this it follows that $g_v(a) = 1$. For $(a, b) \in A_v \times B_v$, $a \in A_{v_1}$ or $a \in A_{v_2}$, and thus $g_v(a) = 1$. Furthermore, $b \in B_v = B_{v_1}$ and $b \in B_v = B_{v_2}$, so $g_v(b) = g_{v_1}(b) + g_{v_2}(b) = 0 + 0 = 0$. The argument for AND-vertices proceeds analogously, establishing the theorem.   □

> *The depth of f in circuits with AND-, OR-, and NOT-gates in which NOT-gates do not contribute to the depth is equal to the communication complexity of a certain relation R_f defined from f. Once again we see the broad applicability of the theory of communication complexity.*

The previous statement is valid even though the characterization from Theorem 16.3.5 has not yet led to any improved results about the depth of functions. Relations can have multiple correct answers, which makes the task of Alice and Bob easier but makes proofs of lower bounds more difficult.

Finally, we consider the case of monotone circuits. We will use D_m to denote the depth of monotone circuits. Of course, the "$\geq$" direction of Theorem 16.3.5 can be applied to the more restricted case of monotone circuits. Alice and Bob always reach a non-negated input x_i, and $a_i = 1$ and $b_i = 0$. In fact, they always realize the relation $M_f \subseteq f^{-1}(1) \times f^{-1}(0) \times \{1, \ldots, n\}$ that contains all (a, b, i) with $a_i = 1$ and $b_i = 0$. If we start with an optimal protocol tree for M_f and follow the proof of the "$\leq$" direction, then we obtain a monotone formula since at the leaves for every $(a, b) \in A \times B$, $a_i = 1$ and $b_i = 0$. So nothing must be changed in the proof that the formula computes f. Thus we have proven the following result.

Theorem 16.3.6. *If f is a non-constant monotone Boolean function, then* $D_m(f) = C(M_f)$.   □

This result has been used to obtain large lower bounds for the depth of monotone Boolean functions (see, for example, Kushilevitz and Nisan (1997)).

16.4 The Size of Depth-Bounded Circuits

As we discussed in Section 16.2, at the moment we cannot prove superlinear lower bounds for circuits of explicitly defined functions even if we restrict the circuits to be of depth $O(\log n)$. Depth restrictions of $o(\log n)$ are not meaningful, since then functions that depend essentially on n variables can no longer be computed. A more reasonable modification, is to allow gates to have more than two inputs. The number of inputs to a gate in a circuit is usually referred to as its *fan-in*. In the simplest model, we allow only AND- and OR-gates with unbounded fan-in and NOT-gates (which always have just one input). Since AND and OR are commutative and associative, the semantics of these large fan-in gates is clear. One could ask at this point whether it would be better to count edges or to continue to count vertices as our complexity measure. Since parallel edges between two vertices in this model can be replaced by a single edge, circuits with s gates can have at most $s \cdot (s + n)$ edges. And since we are interested in exponential lower bounds, we can continue to use the number of vertices as our measure of circuit size. If an OR-gate G has an OR-gate G' as one of its inputs, then G' can be replaced by its inputs. The analogous statement holds for AND-gates. Furthermore, the size is at most doubled if we push all the negations to the inputs using DeMorgan's Laws. Finally, by adding gates with one input we can arrange to have all edges running from level k' to $k' + 1$. This increases the number of gates by a factor of at most k if k is the depth of the circuit. The result of these measures is the following structure for circuits of depth k:

- inputs are $x_1, \ldots, x_n, \overline{x}_1, \ldots, \overline{x}_n, 0, 1$ and form level 0;
- the set of gates can be partitioned into k levels in such a way that all edges from gates in level k' go to gates in level $k' + 1$;
- all gates in a level are of the same type; and
- the gates on the odd-numbered levels are of a different type from those on the even-numbered levels.

OR-gates can be expressed as existential quantifiers (there is an input that has value 1) and AND-gates can be expressed as universal quantifiers. Circuits of depth k with an OR-gate at level k are therefore called Σ_k-circuits in analogy to the class Σ_k. Similarly, circuits with an AND-gate at level k are called Π_k-circuits. Σ_2-circuits are disjunctions of monomials, and circuits in this form are said to be in *disjunctive normal form* (DNF). This is confusing, since a normal form is supposed to be uniquely determined, and should therefore only refer to the disjunction of all minterms. Disjunctive form (DF) is a better designation, and we will sometimes use this less common term as well. Analogously, a Π_2-circuit corresponds to a conjunction of clauses, or a *conjunctive (normal) form* (abbreviated CNF or CF).

We have seen that we can restrict our attention to circuits where the gate type changes from level to level, i.e., alternates. The class of families $f = (f_n)$ of Boolean functions that have constant-depth polynomially-size circuits is for this reason denoted AC^0 (alternating class).

The *parity function* PAR $= (\mathrm{PAR}_n)$ is the EXOR of n variables. The parity function and its negation are the only functions for which every DF has the maximal number of 2^{n-1} monomials of length n and every CF has the maximal number of 2^{n-1} clauses of length n. Also, since setting some of the inputs to constants results in another parity function or its negation on the remaining variables, the parity function is a good candidate for proving lower bounds. In order to judge the quality of the lower bounds we achieve, we first prove an upper bound.

Theorem 16.4.1. *The parity function* PAR_n *can be computed by an alternating circuit of depth* $\lceil (\log n)/\log \log n \rceil + 1$ *and size* $O(n^2/\log n)$.

Proof. We begin with an EXOR-circuit for which the gates have a fan-in of $\lceil \log n \rceil$. In order to represent PAR_n, it is sufficient to build a balanced formula tree with $O(n/\log n)$ gates and depth $\lceil (\log n)/\log \log n \rceil$. Now we replace the EXOR-gates with both disjunctive and conjunctive forms. These each have size $2^{\lceil \log n \rceil - 1} + 1 \leq n + 1$. This increases the size of the circuit to $O(n^2/\log n)$ and the depth to $2 \cdot \lceil (\log n)/\log \log n \rceil$ levels that we imagine as $\lceil (\log n)/\log \log n \rceil$ layers of depth 2. The negations are again pushed to the inputs. The inputs of the gates G in the first level of a layer are gates from the second level of the preceding layer. Because we used both a DF form and a CF form, these functions are available at both an AND-gate and an OR-gate. We choose the gate of the same type as G, which means we can combine the second level of one layer with the first level of the next. In this way the depth is reduced to $\lceil (\log n)/\log \log n \rceil + 1$ without increasing the number of gates. $\square$

The following lower bound for PAR_n goes back to Håstad (1989). The statement that $\text{PAR}_n \notin \text{AC}^0$ had already been proved in some earlier papers with ever increasing lower bounds, but it was Håstad's *Switching Lemma* that revealed the core of such lower bounds.

Theorem 16.4.2. *Alternating circuits of depth k for* PAR_n *with $n \geq 2$ require at least* $2^{\lfloor n^{1/k}/10 \rfloor}$ *gates.* $\text{PAR} \notin \text{AC}^0$. *Achieving polynomial size requires at least depth* $(\log n)/(c + \log \log n)$ *for some constant c.*

Proof. The important part here is the lower bound. From this $\text{PAR} \notin \text{AC}^0$ and the statement regarding the depth of polynomial-size circuits follow by simple calculation.

We will prove the lower bound by induction on the depth k of the circuit. The trick in the inductive proof consists in looking more carefully at the functions computed at the gates in the second level of the circuit. Either all of these functions are represented as a DF or all as a CF. By symmetry, it suffices to consider only the first case. If we replace each DF with an equivalent CF, then the gates at levels 2 and 3 are all AND-gates and the two levels can be combined. Then we can apply the inductive hypothesis to the resulting circuit of depth $k - 1$.

Of course, the argument is not quite that simple. For the DF $x_1 x_2 + x_3 x_4 + \cdots + x_{n-1} x_n$, for example, every CF contains at least $2^{n/2}$ clauses, each of which has a length of at least $n/2$. Håstad applied the probabilistic method (see, for example, Alon and Spencer (1992)) to a random assignment of randomly selected variables. The number of variables that are fixed by this assignment should be chosen so that there are enough variables remaining and so that with positive probability all of the DFs can be replaced by *sufficiently small* CFs. An analysis of this procedure shows that it doesn't produce the desired result. So a new parameter s is introduced which measures the largest number of inputs to a gate in the first level. If s is small, as it is for a DF for $x_1x_2 + x_3x_4 + \cdots + x_{n-1}x_n$, then there is hope that long clauses can be replaced with the constant 1 with sufficiently high probability. These ideas are formalized in Håstad's *Switching Lemma*.

Lemma 16.4.3 (Håstad's Switching Lemma). *Let f be a DF over n variables with monomials of length at most s. Let $m > 0$ and let g be a random subfunction generated by the following random experiment. First $n - m$ variables are selected uniformly at random and then these variables are set to 0 or 1 independently with probability $1/2$. The probability that there is no CF for g with clauses of length at most t is smaller than $(5ms/n)^t$.* ☐

The technically challenging proof of the Switching Lemma will not be described here (see Razborov (1995)). We will use the Switching Lemma to prove the following claim:

- Let $S := 2^{\lfloor n^{1/k}/10 \rfloor}$, $\lfloor n^{1/k}/10 \rfloor \geq 1$, $n(i) := \lfloor n/(10 \log S)^{k-i+1} \rfloor$, and $i \in \{2, \ldots, k+1\}$. Then there is no alternating circuit for $\mathrm{PAR}_{n(i)}$ that has depth i, at most S gates on the levels $2, \ldots, i$, and at most $\log S$ inputs for each gate on level 1.

First we will show how the Theorem follows from this claim. If there were an alternating circuit for PAR_n with depth k and S gates, then we could replace this circuit with a circuit of depth $k + 1$ by computing $x_1, \overline{x}_1, \ldots, x_n, \overline{x}_n$ at level 1 with gates that each have one input. This circuit computes the function PAR_n in depth $k+1$, has at most S gates on the levels $2, \ldots, k+1$, and fan-in 1 at each gate at level 1 – a contradiction to the claim for $i = k + 1$.

The proof of the claim follows by induction on i. For $i = 2$, the number of variables is $n(2)$ and

$$
\begin{aligned}
n(2) &= \lfloor n/(10 \log S)^{k-1} \rfloor \\
&= \lfloor (10n \log S)/(10 \log S)^k \rfloor \\
&\geq 10 \log S > \log S.
\end{aligned}
$$

In order to compute $\mathrm{PAR}_{n(2)}$ in depth 2, we would need gates at level 1 with $n(2) > \log S$ inputs since all prime implicants and all prime clauses have this length. So the claim holds for $i = 2$.

For the inductive step we apply the Switching Lemma or its dual for CFs with $m(i) := \lfloor n(i)/(10 \log S) \rfloor$, $s := \log S$, and $t := \log S$. The probability that a DF or CF cannot be transformed in the desired way into a CF or DF is smaller than

$$
(5m(i)s/n(i))^t \leq (1/2)^{\log S} = 1/S .
$$

So the probability that at least one of the at most S DFs or CFs cannot be transformed in this way is smaller than 1. This implies that there is an assignment of $n(i) - m(i)$ of the $n(i)$ variables such that all DFs or CFs at the second level can be transformed in such a way that the second and third levels can be merged without increasing the number of gates but reducing the number of levels by 1. This results in an alternating circuit of depth $i - 1$ that computes either the parity function or its negation on $m(i) = n(i - 1)$ variables. For the equality $m(i) = n(i - 1)$ we are using the fact that for integers a, b, and j the equation $\lfloor a/b^j \rfloor = \lfloor \lfloor a/b^{j-1} \rfloor / b \rfloor$ holds. The number of the gates at levels $2, \ldots, i - 1$ remains bounded by S, and the gates at level 1 have at most $\log S$ inputs. This contradiction to the inductive hypothesis completes the proof of the theorem.   □

If we now allow EXOR-gates with arbitrarily many inputs, then we can compute more functions with polynomial size since parity only requires one gate. We can then replace OR-gates with AND- and NOT-gates, and since $\bar{x} = x \oplus 1$, NOT-gates can be replaced by EXOR-gates. If we have r parallel edges as inputs to an EXOR-gate, these can be replaced with $r \bmod 2$ edges. In this way we obtain an alternating circuit with AND- and EXOR-levels. If we think of EXOR as a $\mathbb{Z}_2$-sum, then we can extend this idea to $\mathbb{Z}_m$-sums. A MOD_m-gate outputs the value 1 if and only if the number of 1's among the inputs is an integer multiple of m. EXOR-gates are not the same as MOD_2-gates, but we can get a MOD_2 from an EXOR-gate by adding a constant 1 input. For MOD_m-gates, r inputs that realize the same function can be replaced by $r \bmod m$ edges, so again it makes sense to measure the size of such circuits by counting the number of gates. A MOD_m-gate counts modulo m, so the class of all families $f = (f_n)$ of Boolean functions that can be computed by alternating circuits with constant depth and polynomial size with AND- and MOD_m-gates is denoted $\mathsf{ACC}^0[m]$ (alternating counting class).

First we consider the case $m = 2$, which amounts to computation in the field $\mathbb{Z}_2$. This suggests the application of algebraic methods. Boolean functions can be interpreted as $\mathbb{Z}_2$-polynomials, and therefore have a *degree*, namely the degree of this polynomial. It is simple to compute functions with high degree. For example, we can compute the polynomial $x_1 x_2 \cdots x_n$, which has maximal degree n, with a single AND-gate. But this polynomial is similar to a polynomial of very low degree, namely the constant 0 with degree 0 – similar in the sense that these polynomials only differ on one input. We can measure the distance between two functions f and g by counting the number of inputs a such that $f(a) \neq g(a)$. Razborov (1987) used this idea to show that certain explicitly defined functions cannot belong to $\mathsf{ACC}^0[2]$. He showed that $\mathsf{ACC}^0[2]$ functions must be a small distance from a polynomial of low degree. To show that a function $f = (f_n)$ is not in $\mathsf{ACC}^0[2]$, it suffices to show that the distance between f and any polynomial of low degree is large. Of course this idea must be quantified and parameterized by the depth of the circuit. Razborov investigated the *majority function* – MAJ $= (\mathrm{MAJ}_n)$ which has the value 1 if and only if the input contains at least as many 1's as 0's – and proved the following result.

Theorem 16.4.4. *The majority function can be computed by alternating circuits using* AND- *and* MOD_2-*gates in* $O((\log n)/\log\log n)$ *depth and polynomial size, but any such circuit with depth* $o((\log n)/\log\log n)$ *must have superpolynomial size. In particular,* MAJ $\notin$ ACC^0[2].   □

Smolensky (1987) investigated the ACC^0[m]-classes more generally and proved the following result.

Theorem 16.4.5. *Let* p *and* q *be distinct prime numbers and let* k *be a constant with* $k \geq 1$. *Then* $MOD_p \notin$ ACC^0[q^k].

Only primes and power of primes allow an algebraic approach. For numbers like $m = 6$ that are the product of at least two distinct primes, it has not yet been possible to prove that explicitly defined functions cannot belong to ACC^0[m].

16.5 The Size of Depth-Bounded Threshold Circuits

Since PAR $\notin$ AC^0, in Section 16.4 we allowed EXOR-gates and more general MOD_m-gates. Analogously, the result that MAJ $\notin$ ACC^0[2] leads to the idea of allowing MAJ-gates. In order to capture negation, disjunction, and conjunction in a single type of gate and to make the availability of constant inputs unnecessary, we will allow all threshold functions $T^n_{\geq k}$ and all negated threshold functions $T^n_{\leq k}$ as gates. Recall that these gates check whether there are at least (or at most) k ones among the inputs to the gate. The resulting circuits are called *threshold circuits* and form an adequate model for discrete neural nets without feedback.

In threshold circuits it can make sense to have parallel edges. The carry bit (CAR) from the addition of two n bit numbers, for example, can be computed by a threshold gate with exponentially many edges. This is because $CAR_n(a, b)$ takes on the value 1 if and only if the following inequality is satisfied:

$$\sum_{0 \leq i \leq n-1} a_i 2^i + \sum_{0 \leq i \leq n-1} b_i 2^i \geq 2^n .$$

So we can choose the threshold value 2^n and use 2^i edges from each of a_i and b_i to the threshold gate. So we obtain two complexity measures for the size of threshold circuits, namely

- the number of edges (wires) and
- the number of gates.

If we are only interested in the number of gates, then we can imagine that the edges carry integer weights and that threshold gates check whether the weighted sum of the inputs reaches the threshold value. Since it has only been possible to prove exponential lower bounds for the size of threshold circuits with very small constant depth, we will use TC^{0,d} to represent the class of the families $f = (f_n)$ of Boolean functions that can be computed by threshold circuits with polynomially many unweighted edges in depth d. Surprisingly, the use of weighted edges only allows us to save at most one level (Goldmann and Karpinski (1993)).

The goal of this section is to show that IP $\notin$ TC^{0,2} (Hajnal, Maass, Pudlák, Szegedy, and Turán (1987)). This is the current limit of our ability to prove exponential lower bounds. It has not yet been possible to show that there are any explicitly defined functions that are not in TC^{0,3}. In order to get a feel for the model, we will begin with two positive results.

Theorem 16.5.1. PAR $\in$ TC^{0,2} *and* IP $\in$ TC^{0,3}.

Proof. The circuit for PAR$_n$ uses only $2 \cdot \lceil n/2 \rceil + 1$ gates. For the input $x = (x_1, \ldots, x_n)$ we put $T^n_{\geq k}(x)$ and $T^n_{\leq k}(x)$ at the first level for each odd $k \leq n$. If x contains an even number of 1's, then every pair $(T^n_{\geq k}(x), T^n_{\leq k}(x))$ contains exactly one 1, and so we obtain a 1 at exactly $\lceil n/2 \rceil$ of the gates on level 1. If x has an odd number m of 1's, then the pair $(T^n_{\geq m}(x), T^n_{\leq m}(x))$ produces two 1's, but all other pairs produce one 1 as before. In this case $\lceil n/2 \rceil + 1$ of the gates on level 1 produce a 1. So we can compute parity with a threshold gate on level 2 that has every gate on level 1 as input and a threshold value of $\lceil n/2 \rceil + 1$.

Since IP$_n(x)$ is the parity function applied to $(x_1 y_1, \ldots, x_n y_n)$, the preceding result implies that IP $\in$ TC^{0,3}. The values $x_1 y_1, \ldots, x_n y_n$ can be computed on level 1 using $T^2_{\geq 2}(x_i, y_i)$ for $1 \leq i \leq n$, and the parity function on these outputs can be computed using two additional levels.   □

We will show that IP $\notin$ TC^{0,2} by demonstrating that for any partitioning of the input bits of a function $f = (f_n)$ with small threshold circuits of depth 2 between Alice and Bob, there is a shorter randomized communication protocol with public coins and two-sided error than there can be for IP (see Theorem 15.4.9). In order to work out this connection to communication complexity, we consider slightly modified threshold circuits. Instead of negated threshold gates, we will allow a weight of -1 to be assigned to the edges. Since the constant 1 is also available to us, and since $T^n_{\leq k} = 1 - T^n_{\geq k+1}$, we can then replace negated threshold gates without increasing the number of edges by more than a factor of 2. For the output gate we want to transform a threshold value of k into a threshold value of 0 and at the same time ensure that the weighted sum of the inputs never has the value 0. To do this, we first double all in-coming edges and the threshold value from k to $2k$. Since the weighted sum will then always be even, the threshold value $2k$ is equivalent to the threshold value $2k - 1$. Now if we add $2k - 1$ inputs to the output gate each coming from the constant 1 with weight -1, and replace the threshold value with 0, we obtain a circuit with the same output value as before. Furthermore, the weighted sum of the inputs is always odd, and so never 0. Finally, we increase the number of inputs to the output gate to the next power of 2 by adding sufficiently many connections to the constant 0. Together this only increases the size of the circuit by a constant factor. In the following lemma we will call such circuits *modified threshold circuits*.

Lemma 16.5.2. *If $f : \{0,1\}^n \to \{0,1\}$ can be computed by a modified threshold circuit of depth 2 in which every gate has at most $M = 2^m$ inputs, then*

$$R_{2,\frac{1}{2}-\frac{1}{2M}}^{\text{pub}}(f) \le m + 2$$

for every partition of the inputs between Alice and Bob.

Proof. Alice and Bob use the given modified threshold circuit as the basis of their communication protocol. With their random bits they select a random input to the output gate. If we denote the inputs to this gate as $f_1, \ldots, f_M$, then $f(a) = 1$ if and only if $w_1 f_1(a) + \cdots + w_M f_M(a) \ge 0$ for the edge weights $w_i \in \{-1, 1\}$. Alice and Bob want to compute the value $f_i(a)$ for the randomly selected function f_i to determine a "tendency" for the weighted sum. The function f_i is a threshold function over at most M inputs and the inputs are variables. The weighted sum of the inputs takes on one of the $M + 1$ consecutive values $-j, \ldots, 0, \ldots, M - j$ where j is the number of negatively weighted inputs. Alice computes the portion of this sum that she can evaluate because she knows the input bits involved. She then sends this value to Bob using $m + 1$ bits. Now Bob can evaluate the threshold gate and send the result to Alice, after which they come to the following decision:

- If $f_i(a) = 0$, they use an additional (public) random bit and select the result at random, since a value of 0 does not indicate any tendency.
- If $f_i(a) = 1$, then their decision is 1 if $w_i = 1$, and 0 if $w_i = -1$. Here they are using the tendency indicated by $w_i f_i(a)$.

This protocol has length $m + 2$. Now we estimate the error-probability for the input a. Let k be the number of functions f_i with $f_i(a) = 1$ and $w_i = 1$, let l be the number of functions f_i with $f_i(a) = 1$ and $w_i = -1$, and let $M - k - l$ be the number of functions f_i with $f_i(a) = 0$. If $f(a) = 1$, then the weighted sum of all $w_i f_i(a)$ is positive and so $k \ge l + 1$. The probability of a false decision is given by

$$\frac{1}{M} \left(l + \frac{1}{2}(M - k - l) \right) = \frac{1}{2} + \frac{1}{2M}(l - k) \le \frac{1}{2} - \frac{1}{2M}.$$

For $f(a) = 0$, $l \ge k + 1$ and the result follows analogously.   □

Theorem 16.5.3. *For any constant $\alpha < 1/4$ and a sufficiently large n, threshold circuits of depth 2 for IP_n require at least $2^{\alpha n}$ edges. In particular, $\text{IP} \notin \text{TC}^{0,2}$.*

Proof. If $2^{\alpha n}$ edges suffice to compute the inner product with threshold circuits of depth 2, then for some constant c, $2^{\alpha n + c}$ edges suffice for modified threshold circuits, and by Lemma 16.5.2

$$R^{\text{pub}}_{2,1/2-1/2^{\alpha n+c+1}}(\text{IP}_n) \leq \alpha n + c + 2 \, ,$$

where Alice knows all the a-bits and Bob knows all the b-bits. By Theorem 15.4.9, for this partition of the input

$$R^{\text{pub}}_{2,1/2-1/2^{\alpha n+c+1}}(\text{IP}_n) \geq n/2 - \alpha n - c - 1 \, .$$

For $\alpha < 1/4$ and sufficiently large n, these bounds contradict each other, proving the theorem.   □

Among the current challenges in the area of circuit complexity are the following problems:

- *Show that explicitly defined Boolean functions cannot be computed by circuits with linear size and logarithmic depth.*
- *Show that the formula size for explicitly defined Boolean functions grows faster than $n^2/\log n$.*
- *Show that explicitly defined Boolean functions do not belong to* ACC⁰[6].
- *Show that explicitly defined Boolean functions do not belong to* TC⁰,³.

16.6 The Size of Branching Programs

Branching programs were motivated and defined in Section 14.4. The largest known lower bound for the branching program size of explicitly defined Boolean functions is based on the same ideas as the largest bound for formula size (see Section 16.3). As in Theorem 16.3.2, for $f : \{0,1\}^n \to \{0,1\}$, let $X = \{x_1, \ldots, x_n\}$ represent the set of input variables, let $S_1, \ldots, S_k$ be disjoint subsets of X, and let s_i be the number of different subfunctions of f on S_i that can be obtained by replacing all variables in $X - S_i$ with constants.

Theorem 16.6.1. *For disjoint sets $S_1, \ldots, S_k$ of variables on which f depends essentially,*

$$\text{BP}(f) = \Omega\Big(\sum_{1 \leq i \leq k, s_i \geq 3} (\log s_i)/\log \log s_i \Big) \, .$$

Proof. Let G be a branching program of minimal size for f and let t_i be the number of internal vertices of G that are marked with variables from S_i. It suffices to prove that for $s_i \geq 3$

$$t_i = \Omega((\log s_i)/\log \log s_i) \, .$$

Since f depends essentially on all variables in S_i, $t_i \geq |S_i|$. On the other hand, each of the s_i subfunctions of f on S_i can be realized by a branching program of size t_i+2 since if we replace all variables $X-S_i$ with constants, then the edges entering the vertices marked with these variables can be replaced with edges to the appropriate successor.

So we are interested in estimating the number of different functions that can be realized by a branching program with t_i internal vertices on $|S_i|$ variables. For the internal vertices there are $|S_i|^{t_i}$ different combinations of variable assignments. For the jth vertex there are for each out-going edge t_i+2-j possible successor vertices. So the number we are interested in is at most $|S_i|^{t_i}((t_i+1)!)^2$. This number is not allowed to be smaller than s_i. From the inequality $|S_i| \leq t_i$ we obtain

$$s_i \leq t_i^{t_i}((t_i+1)!)^2 = t_i^{O(t_i)} .$$

From this it follows that $t_i = \Omega((\log s_i)/\log\log s_i)$ for $s_i \geq 3$.   □

Theorem 16.6.2. $\mathrm{BP}(\mathrm{ISA}_n) = \Omega(n^2/\log^2 n)$.

Proof. We can make use of the analysis of ISA_n from the proof of Theorem 16.3.3. We obtain $\Omega(n/\log n)$ S_i-sets, for which $\log s_i = \Omega(n)$ and therefore $(\log s_i)/\log\log s_i = \Omega(n/\log n)$. The bound now follows from Theorem 16.6.1.   □

While there are not many methods for proving large lower bounds for the size of general branching programs for explicitly defined functions, the situation is better for length-bounded branching programs. We will investigate how a small branching program G for f leads to a communication protocol for f and a partition (a, b) of the variables between Alice and Bob. Alice and Bob agree on a numbering of the vertices in G and divide up the vertices between them. Variables for which Alice knows the value are called A-vertices, and the other internal vertices are B-vertices. By symmetry we can assume that the evaluation of f begins at an A-vertex. Alice follows the computation for the current input until she comes to a B-vertex or a sink. She then sends the number of this vertex to Bob. If this vertex was a sink, then both parties know $f(a, b)$ and have accomplished their task. Otherwise, Bob continues the computation until reaching an A-vertex or a sink, at which point he sends the number of this vertex to Alice. Alice and Bob continue in this fashion until the number of a sink is communicated. With respect to the partition of the input between Alice and Bob, we define the *layer depth* $\mathrm{ld}(G)$ as the maximal number of *messages* in the protocol just described. Analogously we could have broken the computation into A-sections and B-sections and defined $\mathrm{ld}(G)$ as the maximal number of such sections along a computation path. These considerations lead to the following result about the communication complexity $\mathrm{C}(f)$, where $|G|$ denotes the number of vertices in G.

Lemma 16.6.3. $\mathrm{C}(f) \leq \mathrm{ld}(G) \cdot \lceil \log |G| \rceil$.   □

From this lemma we obtain the following inequality:

$$|G| \geq 2^{C(f)/\operatorname{ld}(G)-1} .$$

In Chapter 15 we encountered functions f_n defined on n variables with $C(f_n) = \Theta(n)$. In the case of general branching programs, however, we cannot rule out the possibility that $\operatorname{ld}(G) = \Omega(n)$. The lower bound then becomes useless. For this reason we consider the following restricted variant of branching programs.

Definition 16.6.4. *Let* $X = \{x_1, \ldots, x_n\}$ *be the variable set under consideration. For* $s \in X^m$, *an* s-*oblivious branching program consists of* $m + 1$ *levels such that for* $1 \leq i \leq m$ *each vertex in level* i *is labeled with* s_i, *level* $m+1$ *contains sinks, and all edges run from level* i *to some level* j *with* $j > i$. *For a* k-*indexed BDD* (k-*IBDD*)*, s is a concatenation of* k *permutations of* X. *For a* k-*ordered BDD* (k-*OBDD*)*, s is a concatenation of* k *copies of one permutation of* X.

With oblivious branching programs we can hope that the variables can be divided between Alice and Bob in such a way that the layer depth remains small. The restricted branching programs that we just introduced, especially the 1-OBDDs (which we will abbreviate OBDDs) have practical importance as a data structure for Boolean functions. OBDDs with a fixed permutation of variables (also called a variable ordering) are the most common data structure for Boolean functions and support many operations on Boolean functions (see, for example, Wegener (2000)). This data structure is of limited practical value, however, if the functions being considered do not have small representations. This motivates the study of lower bounds for the size of these branching programs and selected functions. We will restrict our attention to the mask variant EQ_n^* of the equality test and to the computation of the middle bit of multiplication MUL_n. Recall that the communication complexity of EQ_n^* is at least m if Alice knows m of the a-variables and Bob knows m of the b-variables, or vice versa. The communication complexity of MUL_n is at least $\lceil m/8 \rceil$, if Alice and Bob each know m variables of one of the factors.

For the investigation of k-OBDDs, we give Alice an initial segment of the variables (with respect to the variable ordering), and give the rest to Bob. This bounds the layer depth by $2k$. For EQ_n^* the initial segment ends when for the first time $\lceil n/2 \rceil$ a-variables or $\lceil n/2 \rceil$ b-variables are in the segment. For MUL_n, we divide up the variables in such a way that Alice receives $\lceil n/2 \rceil$ and Bob $\lfloor n/2 \rfloor$ of the variables of the first factor. This leads to the following lower bounds.

Theorem 16.6.5. *The size of* k-*OBDDs that compute* EQ_n^* *or* MUL_n *is* $2^{\Omega(n/k)}$. $\qquad\qquad \square$

For k-IBDDs and s-oblivious branching programs we can only guarantee a small layer depth for small variable sets $A, B \subseteq X$. This leads to good lower bounds for the representation size of f if there is an assignment for the variables outside of $A \cup B$ such that the communication complexity of the resulting subfunction for the variable partition (A, B) is large. The functions EQ_n^* and MUL_n have this property.

For k-IBDDs, we start with two disjoint variable sets A and B, i.e., a partition of the variables between Alice and Bob. We consider the first variable ordering as a list and put a dividing line after we have seen for the first time either $\lceil |A|/2 \rceil$ A-variables or $\lceil |B|/2 \rceil$ B-variables at the beginning of the list. In the first case $\lceil |A|/2 \rceil$ A-variables before the dividing line and the at least $\lceil |B|/2 \rceil$ B-variables after the dividing line survive. The other case is analogous, and in either case only the surviving variables are considered from this point. This procedure always results in at least $\lceil |A|/2^k \rceil$ surviving A-variables and $\lceil |B|/2^k \rceil$ surviving B-variables. With respect to these variables the layer depth is at most $2k$. It can even happen that the layer depth is less, since A- or B-layers can be next to each other. For EQ_n^* we start by selecting the set of all a-variables for A and the set of all b-variables for B. For MUL_n we can divide up the variables of the first factor uniformly between A and B.

Theorem 16.6.6. *The size of k-IBDDs that represent* EQ_n^* *or* MUL_n *is at least* $2^{\Omega(n/(k \cdot 2^k))}$. $\qquad\qquad\qquad\qquad\qquad\qquad\qquad\qquad\qquad\qquad\qquad\qquad$ $\square$

Theorem 16.6.6 only leads to superpolynomial lower bounds for $k = o((\log n)/\log \log n)$. In the general case of k-oblivious branching programs, let $m = 4kn$ for EQ_n^* and let $m = 2kn$ for MUL_n. Then each variable occurs in s on average k times. Note that the variables can occur with different frequencies and do not necessarily occur exactly once in certain blocks. This situation requires subtler combinatoric methods to show that there are not small sets A and B for which the layer depth is small. For the functions EQ_n^* and MUL_n one can show a lower bound of $2^{\Omega(n/(k^3 \cdot 2^{4k}))}$ for the size of s-oblivious branching programs with $m = 4kn$ (EQ_n^*) or $m = 2kn$ (MUL_n).

The lower bound methods discussed here can also be applied to nondeterministic branching programs. Nondeterministic branching programs are allowed to have arbitrarily many 0- and 1-edges at each internal vertex. For each input a there are then $w(a)$ computation paths that lead to sinks. The output for OR-nondeterminism is 1 if and only if at least one of these paths ends at a 1-sink; for AND-nondeterminism all of the paths must end at a 1-sink, and for EXOR-nondeterminism there must be an even number of such paths. Lemma 16.6.3 can be generalized to all three kinds of nondeterminism. In the communication protocol, Alice and Bob can nondeterministically select a portion of the computation path within the appropriate layer. This results in the same lower bounds for MUL_n for all three types of nondeterminism. For EQ_n^* the result generalizes only for OR- and EXOR-nondeterminism. Lower bounds on nondeterministic communication complexity were given in Theorem 15.3.5.

Lower bounds for general, length-bounded, but not necessarily oblivious branching programs can only be proven with methods from outside the theory of communication complexity. The methods applied are more complicated and can be seen as a generalization of communication complexity (see, for example, Beame, Saks, Sun, and Vee (2003)). In particular, generalized rectangles play a central role in these investigations.

16.7 Reduction Notions

So far we have emphasized the development of methods for proving lower bounds and applied these methods only on a few example functions. With the help of suitable reduction concepts, we can extend these results to many more functions. In this section we will introduce these reduction concepts and give a few examples of how they are used. We will consider families $f = (f_n)$ of functions such that $f_n : \{0,1\}^{p(n)} \to \{0,1\}^{q(n)}$ for two polynomially bounded functions p and q. Since we again consider polynomial size to be efficiently computable, f_n may have $p(n)$ inputs. In most cases, $p(n)$ will grow linearly. By considering more than one output ($q(n) > 1$) we can treat functions like multiplication in their entirety. All of the reductions we are about to introduce will have the property that $f = (f_n)$ is reducible to $g = (g_n)$ if f_n can be efficiently represented using g_m-gates. Depending on the purpose at hand, we need to decide how to fairly measure the costs of using these g_m-gates.

To make the following definitions more understandable we first introduce the complexity class NC^1 (Nick's class, named after Nick Pippenger). NC^1 contains all families $f = (f_n)$ of Boolean functions that can be computed by circuits using arbitrary gates with fan-in 2 in logarithmic depth (and therefore in polynomial size).

Definition 16.7.1. *A family of functions $f = (f_n)$ is a* projection *of $g = (g_n)$ (denoted $f \leq_{\mathrm{proj}} g$) if for some polynomially bounded function r the bits of $f_n(x_1, \ldots, x_{p(n)})$ are realized at specified outputs of $g_{r(n)}(y_1, \ldots, y_{p'(r(n))})$, where for each $1 \leq i \leq p'(r(n))$, $y_i \in \{0, 1, x_1, \overline{x}_1, \ldots, x_{p(n)}, \overline{x}_{p(n)}\}$. If for each $j \in \{1, \ldots, p(n)\}$ there is at most one i with $y_i \in \{x_j, \overline{x}_j\}$, then the projection is a* read-once projection *(denoted $f \leq_{\mathrm{rop}} g$).*

Definition 16.7.2. *A family of functions $f = (f_n)$ is* AC^0-reducible *to $g = (g_n)$ (constant depth reducible, denoted $f \leq_{\mathrm{cd}} g$) if there are polynomial-size, constant-depth circuits for f_n that are allowed to use AND- and OR-gates with unbounded fan-in, NOT-gates, and g_m-gates. Each g_m-gate is considered to contribute m to the value of the size of such a circuit.*

Definition 16.7.3. *A family of functions $f = (f_n)$ is* NC^1-reducible *to $g = (g_n)$ (denoted $f \leq_1 g$) if there are polynomial-size circuits of logarithmic depth for f_n using gates with fan-in two and g_m-gates. Each g_m-gate is considered to contribute $\lceil \log m \rceil$ to the depth and m to the size of such a circuit.*

As always, we want our reductions to be transitive, and this can be easily shown for all four of these reductions. Furthermore, these reductions can be ordered as follows:

$$f \leq_{\text{rop}} g \Rightarrow f \leq_{\text{proj}} g \Rightarrow f \leq_{\text{cd}} g \Rightarrow f \leq_1 g \ .$$

Once again we omit the easy proofs.

How can we make use of these reducibilities? Projections make our life easy. In circuits or formulas for $g_{r(n)}$, the variables can simply be replaced according to the specifications of the projection. The result is a circuit or a formula for f_n. This shows that $C(f_n) \leq C(g_{r(n)})$, $L(f_n) \leq L(g_{r(n)})$, and $D(f_n) \leq D(g_{r(n)})$. A *monotone projection* is not allowed to use the negated variables $\overline{x}_1, \dots, \overline{x}_{p(n)}$. If we use only monotone projections, then the inequalities above hold for monotone circuits and formulas as well.

In a branching program for $g_{r(n)}$ we can replace the variables at the internal vertices according to the specifications of the projection. An $\overline{x}_j$-vertex becomes an x_j-vertex if we change the labeling on the out-going edges. An internal vertex with label 0 can be removed; all edges entering such a vertex can be routed directly to its 0-child. The same is true for the label 1. From oblivious branching programs we obtain oblivious branching programs, and the number of levels cannot increase. However, if we start with k-OBDDs or k-IBDDs, we are only guaranteed to end up with k-OBDDs or k-IBDDs if the projections are read-once. This is the reason for introducing $\leq_{\text{rop}}$-reductions.

In order to describe the application of the other two reducibilities, we introduce the complexity classes AC^k and NC^k. The class AC^k contains all families $f = (f_n)$ of Boolean functions that can be computed by polynomial-size alternating circuits of depth $O(\log^k n)$. With the interpretation $\log^0(n) = 1$ this is a canonical generalization of the class AC^0. The class NC^k contains all families $f = (f_n)$ of Boolean functions that can be computed by polynomial-size circuits of depth $O(\log^k n)$ using arbitrary gates of fan-in 2. The following properties can be easily proved:

- $g \in \text{AC}^k$ and $f \leq_{\text{cd}} g \Rightarrow f \in \text{AC}^k$;
- $g \in \text{NC}^k$ and $f \leq_1 g \Rightarrow f \in \text{NC}^k$.

So these reductions have the desired and expected properties. Now we will look at some specific reductions.

In Theorem 13.6.3 we showed that the circuit value problem CVP is P-complete. An instance of CVP consists of a circuit C and an input a of the appropriate length for C. The task is to evaluate C on input a. Since CVP $\in$ P, CVP $\in$ P/poly. If $f = (f_n) \in$ P/poly – and therefore computable by polynomial-size circuits $C = (C_n)$ – then $f \leq_{\text{rop}}$ CVP: For f_n we select the description of C_n, which consists of constants, and consider the evaluation of the circuit C_n on an input a for f_n. The result is $f_n(a)$, since C_n computes the function f_n. Thus we have shown the following result.

Theorem 16.7.4. CVP *is* $\leq_{\text{rop}}$*-complete for* P/poly.   □

We conclude with the consideration of several frequently used functions, namely the parity function PAR, the inner product function IP, the majority function MAJ, the multiplication function MUL (here considered to output all of the bits of the product), the sum of n n-bit numbers MADD (multiple addition), the squaring function SQU, the computation of the n most significant bits of the reciprocal of an n-bit number INV (inverse), and the computation of the n most significant bits of the quotient of two n-bit numbers DIV.

Theorem 16.7.5.

- PAR $\leq_{\mathrm{rop}}$ IP $\leq_{\mathrm{rop}}$ MUL $\leq_{\mathrm{rop}}$ SQU $\leq_{\mathrm{rop}}$ INV $\leq_{\mathrm{rop}}$ DIV,

- MAJ $\leq_{\mathrm{rop}}$ MUL,

- MADD $\leq_{\mathrm{rop}}$ MUL,

- SQU $\leq_{\mathrm{proj}}$ MUL, *and*

- MUL $\leq_{\mathrm{cd}}$ MADD.

Proof. PAR $\leq_{\mathrm{rop}}$ IP follows from the fact that $\mathrm{PAR}_n(x) = \mathrm{IP}_n(x, 1^n)$, where 1^n denotes the vector consisting of n 1's.

The proofs that IP $\leq_{\mathrm{rop}}$ MUL, MAJ $\leq_{\mathrm{rop}}$ MUL, and MADD $\leq_{\mathrm{rop}}$ MUL are all based on the same basic idea. When we multiply x and y, the sum of all $x_i y_{k-i}$ has the place value 2^k. This sum doesn't appear in its pure form in the product, since there may be carries from earlier positions and because carries from position k are combined with the sums for positions $k+1, k+2, \ldots$. However, if we separate the important positions in x and y by sufficiently many 0's, then we can avoid these "overlap effects". We know that the sum of all $x_i y_i$ for $1 \leq i \leq n$ has a bit length of $k = \lceil \log(n+1) \rceil$. Therefore, $\mathrm{MUL}_{n+(n-1)(k-1)}(x', y')$ with $x' = (x_{n-1}, 0^{k-1}, x_{n-2}, 0^{k-1}, \ldots, x_1, 0^{k-1}, x_0)$ and $y' = (y_0, 0^{k-1}, y_1, \ldots, 0^{k-1}, y_{n-1})$ takes on the value of $\mathrm{IP}_n(x, y)$.

x_2	0	x_1	0	x_0	*	y_0	0	y_1	0	y_2
		x_2y_0	0	x_1y_0	0	x_0y_0				
				x_2y_1	0	x_1y_1	0	x_0y_1		
						x_2y_2	0	x_1y_2	0	x_0y_2
						IP_3				

Fig. 16.7.1. An illustration of the projection IP $\leq_{\mathrm{proj}}$ MUL.

To prove that MAJ $\leq_{\mathrm{rop}}$ MUL we increase the number of inputs to MAJ by adding constant inputs until the number of inputs is the next larger number of the form $2^k - 1$. We do this in such a way that the majority value is not changed, namely by choosing an equal number of 0's and 1's if possible, else one more 1 than 0. Now if we multiply the new input x by y and separate the numbers with 0's as in the proof that IP $\leq_{\text{rop}}$ MUL, and set all the y_j to 1, then the resulting product is the binary representation of the sum of all x_i. Since we have $m = 2^k - 1$ bits, the most significant bit of the sum indicates the majority value. For the proof that MADD $\leq_{\text{rop}}$ MUL we need to get the binary representation of the sum of all x_i where this time each x_i is itself an n-bit number. This sum has a bit length of at most $n + \lceil \log n \rceil$, so it suffices to separate things with $\lceil \log n \rceil$ 0's.

For the proof of MUL $\leq_{\text{rop}}$ SQU we consider for factors x and y of bit length n the number $z = (x, 0^{n+1}, y)$ and claim that $\text{MUL}_n(x, y)$ is contained in $\text{SQU}_{3n+1}(z)$. This is because

$$\langle z \rangle^2 = (\langle x \rangle \cdot 2^{2n+1} + \langle y \rangle)^2 = \langle x \rangle^2 \cdot 2^{4n+2} + \langle x \rangle \cdot \langle y \rangle \cdot 2^{2n+2} + \langle y \rangle^2 \, .$$

Since $\langle y \rangle^2$ and $\langle x \rangle \cdot \langle y \rangle$ have a bit length of $2n$, there are no overlaps and $\text{SQU}_{3n+1}(z)$ contains $\langle x \rangle \cdot \langle y \rangle$.

The most difficult portion of this proof is showing that SQU $\leq_{\text{rop}}$ INV. The basic idea is to make use of the equality

$$1 + q + q^2 + q^3 + \cdots = 1/(1 - q)$$

for $0 \leq q < 1$. Here we see that the square of q is one of the summands of the reciprocal of $1 - q$. Ideally we would like to write $1 - q$ as a projection of q and again make sure that no undesired overlaps occur when we sum all the q_i's. Unfortunately this doesn't quite work, since it is not possible to express $1 - q$ as a projection of q.

We want to square the number $x = (x_{n-1}, \ldots, x_0)$. So we form the $(10n)$-bit number y with $\langle y \rangle := \langle x \rangle \cdot 2^{-t} + 2^{-T}$, $t := 4n$, and $T := 10n$. The extra summand 2^{-T} guarantees that we can write $1 - \langle y \rangle$ as a projection of $\langle x \rangle$. Furthermore, 2^{-T} is small enough that it doesn't produce any undesired overlaps. Figure 16.7.2 doesn't use the correct parameters, but is structurally correct and shows how we get $1 - \langle y \rangle$.

$1 =$	1	.	0	0	0	0	0	0	0	0	0
$\langle y \rangle =$	0	.	0	0	0	x_2	x_1	x_0	0	0	1
$1 - \langle y \rangle =$	0	.	1	1	1	$\overline{x}_2$	$\overline{x}_1$	$\overline{x}_1$	1	1	1

Fig. 16.7.2. The computation of $1 - \langle y \rangle$.

It remains to show that we can find $\langle x \rangle^2$ in the $10n$ most significant bits of $Q := 1/(1 - \langle y \rangle)$.

$$Q = 1 + \langle y \rangle + \langle y \rangle^2 + \langle y \rangle^3 + \cdots$$
$$= 1 + (\langle x \rangle \cdot 2^{-t} + 2^{-T}) + (\langle x \rangle \cdot 2^{-t} + 2^{-T})^2 + (\langle x \rangle \cdot 2^{-t} + 2^{-T})^3 + \cdots$$
$$= 1 + \langle x \rangle \cdot 2^{-t} + \langle x \rangle^2 \cdot 2^{-2t} + \text{ remainder}.$$

The remainder can be approximated for $n \geq 2$ by

$$2^{-10n} + 2^{-12n} + 2^{-20n} + 2 \cdot 2^{-9n} < 2^{-8n} \, .$$

So the $8n + 1$ most significant bits of $1/(1 - \langle y \rangle)$ represent the number $1 + \langle x \rangle \cdot 2^{-4n} + \langle x \rangle^2 \cdot 2^{-8n}$. Since $\langle x \rangle^2 \leq 2^{2n}$, once again we have no overlaps, and we find $\langle x \rangle^2$ in INV_{10n} applied to $1 - \langle y \rangle$.

Let y be an n-bit string such that $\langle y \rangle = 1$, then $\text{INV}_n(x) = \text{DIV}_n(y, x)$ and so $\text{INV} \leq_{\text{rop}} \text{DIV}$; and $\text{SQU}_n(x) = \text{MUL}_n(x, x)$ so $\text{SQU} \leq_{\text{proj}} \text{MUL}$. For the latter projection each x_i-bit is read twice.

The ordinary multiplication procedure taught in grade school requires computing the product $x_i y_j$ for all i and j with $0 \leq i, j \leq n - 1$. For this n^2 gates and depth 1 suffice. The "multiplication matrix" shown in Figure 16.7.1 can be interpreted as the addition of n numbers of bit length $2n - 1$. If we add $n - 1$ additional summands each with the value 0, then we can use a single MADD_{2n-1}-gate to compute $\text{MUL}_n(x, y)$. $\qquad\square$

To estimate the complexity of Boolean functions we begin by developing methods for proving lower bounds in the various models being considered. These methods are first applied to simple-looking functions and then extended to many other functions with the help of suitably defined reducibilities.

Final Comments

For discrete optimization problems the design of an algorithm in most cases is a trivial task. The search space – the set of possible solutions – is finite, and it is possible to go through the elements of the search space, evaluate them, and then select the optimal solution. But normally the size of the search space grows exponentially with the length of the problem description, so a brute force exploration of the search space for all lengths of interest is generally not practical. Thus the only algorithms that are really of interest are those that can get by with reasonable amounts of time and storage space. Users of algorithms might be satisfied with randomized algorithms that work with a small probability of error or failure, or with algorithms that only produce nearly optimal results. And often they only require algorithms for special cases of a more general problem.

Complexity theory is the discipline that tries to discover the border between problems that are efficiently solvable and those that are not. Complexity theory must react to new developments in the design of algorithms and deal with such things as problems with small numbers, approximation problems, black box problems (where only incomplete information about the input is available), and problems with fixed input length (as occur, for example, in the design of hardware).

There are many important problems for which no efficient algorithm is known, but for which we also have no proof that an efficient algorithm is impossible. In this rigorous sense, complexity theory has failed. But it has been largely successful in making statements regarding the relative difficulty of important problems. Such statements have the following form: "If A is efficiently solvable, then so is B", or equivalently, "If B is not efficiently solvable, then neither is A". Furthermore, it has been possible not only to compare pairs of problems in this way, but also to compare problems to entire classes of problems and to compare classes of problems with each other. The theory of NP-completeness is a milestone of scientific achievement, and new developments such as probabilistically checkable proofs have built an impressive structure on this foundation. If one is willing to accept well-founded hypotheses, then one obtains a fairly comprehensive view of where the borders for the design of efficient algorithms lie.

Complexity theory has not only reacted to algorithmic questions but has also had an independent development. The structural results obtained in this way can often be applied to gain an even clearer view of the complexity of specific problems.

If we are only interested in rigorous lower bounds on the resources required to solve problems – bounds that do not depend on any hypotheses – then the results are sobering. The situation is somewhat better in the black box scenario and in situations where we place bounds on some additional resource such as parallel computation time, or depth, or storage space. Trade-off results reveal the potential of the methods currently available for lower bounds on resource requirements.

In summary, complexity theory can be satisfied that it has found at least partial solutions to all new options for the design of algorithms. Complexity theory also has a future, since there are central problems that remain unsolved and since developments in the design of algorithms will continue to raise new and practically relevant questions.

A

Appendix

A.1 Orders of Magnitude and O-Notation

As was discussed in Chapter 2, the computation time of algorithms is measured in terms of parameters such as the length of the input. The most commonly used measure of computation time is the worst-case computation time with respect to the unit cost model. Computation times are then functions $t \colon \mathbb{N} \to \mathbb{N}$ that increase monotonically. But computation times can only rarely be computed exactly, and so they are bounded from above and below. In estimates like $\binom{n}{2} \leq n^2/2$ functions arise that are no longer integer-valued. For this reason we will work here with functions $f \colon \mathbb{N} \to \mathbb{R}^+$.

We want to compare computation times in such a way that "constant factors don't matter". Since its first use by Bachmann in 1892, O-notation (pronounced "big O") has established itself as the way to measure the growth rate, or order of magnitude, of functions $f \colon \mathbb{N} \to \mathbb{R}^+$, and therefore of computation times.

Our goal is to define the relations "$\leq$", "$\geq$", "$=$", "$<$", and "$>$" between functions, but first we will replace the strict definition $f \leq g$ (namely, $f \leq g$ if and only if $f(n) \leq g(n)$ for *all* $n \in \mathbb{N}$) with a weaker condition:

Definition A.1.1. $f = O(g)$ *has the interpretation that asymptotically f grows no faster than g, and is defined by the condition that $f(n)/g(n)$ is bounded above by a constant c.*

The notation $f = O(g)$ has the disadvantage of suggesting that $O(g) = f$, but this notation is not even defined. It is therefore useful to think of "$\leq$" when one sees O, so that it becomes clear that these relationships must be read from left to right and are not reversible. Or one can think of $O(g)$ as the set of all functions f such that $f = O(g)$. In this case, $f \in O(g)$ would be more suggestive notation. The notation $O(f) = O(g)$ is understood to mean that whenever $h = O(f)$, then $h = O(g)$. So we interpret

$$n^2 + \lceil n^{1/2} \rceil \leq n^2 + n = O(n^2) = O(n^3)$$

as follows: $n^2 + n = O(n^2)$, since $(n^2+n)/n^2 \le 2$. Furthermore, every function h with $h(n)/n^2 \le c$ also has the property that $h(n)/n^3 \le c$. With such a chain of "equations", we may omit the middle part and conclude that $n^2 + n = O(n^3)$. Now it is clear why the use of the equality symbol in O-notation has proved to be so advantageous. Otherwise, the previous relationship would have to be written as

$$n^2 + \lceil n^{1/2} \rceil \le n^2 + n \in O(n^2) \subseteq O(n^3) \,,$$

and the mixture of "$\le$", "$\in$", and "$\subseteq$" in one formula is confusing.

The following computation rules for O are useful:

- $c \cdot f = O(f)$ for $c \ge 0$,
- $c \cdot O(f) = O(f)$ for $c \ge 0$,
- $O(f_1) + \cdots + O(f_k) = O(f_1 + \cdots + f_k) = O(\max\{f_1, \ldots, f_k\})$ for any constant k, and
- $O(f) \cdot O(g) = O(f \cdot g)$.

The first two relationships are obvious; the third follows from

$$c_1 \cdot f_1(n) + \cdots + c_k \cdot f_k(n) \le (c_1 + \cdots + c_k) \cdot (f_1(n) + \cdots + f_k(n))$$
$$\le k \cdot (c_1 + \cdots + c_k) \cdot \max\{f_1(n), \ldots, f_k(n)\} \,,$$

and the fourth from

$$(c_1 \cdot f(n)) \cdot (c_2 \cdot g(n)) = (c_1 \cdot c_2) \cdot f(n) \cdot g(n) \,.$$

Once we have expressed "asymptotically $\le$" as O, the definitions of "asymptotically $\ge$", and "asymptotically $=$", follow in the obvious way:

- $f = \Omega(g)$ (read "f is big omega of g") has the interpretation that f grows asymptotically at least as fast as g, and is defined by $g = O(f)$.
- $f = \Theta(g)$ (read "f is big theta of g") has the interpretation that asymptotically f and g grow at the same rate and is defined by $f = O(g)$ and $g = O(f)$.

Finally, we come to the definitions of "asymptotically $<$" and "asymptotically $>$":

- $f = o(g)$ (read "f is little o of g") has the interpretation that asymptotically f grows more slowly than g and is defined by the condition that the sequence $f(n)/g(n)$ approaches 0.
- $f = \omega(g)$ (read "f is little omega of g") has the interpretation that asymptotically f grows more quickly than g and is defined by $g = o(f)$.

If we were to use the strict definition of $f \le g$, namely that $f(n) \le g(n)$ for all n, then many pairs of functions that are asymptotically comparable (like n^2 and $n + 10$, for example), would not be comparable. In this case,

$n+10 = O(n^2)$; in fact, $n+10 = o(n^2)$. Nevertheless, not all pairs of monotone functions are asymptotically comparable. Let

$$f(n) := \begin{cases} n! & n \text{ even} \\ (n-1)! & n \text{ odd} \end{cases}$$

and

$$g(n) := \begin{cases} (n-1)! & n \text{ even} \\ n! & n \text{ odd.} \end{cases}$$

Then f and g are monotone increasing, but $f(n)/g(n) = n$ for even n, and $g(n)/f(n) = n$ for odd n, so neither is bounded above by a constant. Thus neither $f = O(g)$ nor $g = O(f)$ are true. The runtimes of most algorithms, however, are asymptotically comparable.

Finally, we want to order the growth rates that typically occur as computation times. The growth rates $\log\log n$, $\log n$, n, 2^n, and 2^{2^n} serve as a basis. The difference between each successive pair is exponential since $2^{\log\log n} = \log n$ and $2^{\log n} = n$. We will use $\log^\varepsilon n$ as an abbreviation for $(\log n)^\varepsilon$. Then for all constants $k > 0$ and $\varepsilon > 0$,

$$(\log\log n)^k = o(\log^\varepsilon n),$$
$$\log^k n = o(n^\varepsilon),$$
$$n^k = o(2^{n^\varepsilon}),$$
$$2^{n^k} = o(2^{2^{n^\varepsilon}}).$$

As an example, we will show the second relation. We must show that $\lim_{n \to \infty} \frac{(\log^k n)}{n^\varepsilon} = 0$. It is a simple fact of analysis that for $\alpha > 0$, $\lim_{n \to \infty} a_n = 0$ if and only if $\lim_{n \to \infty} a_n^\alpha = 0$. Let $\alpha := 1/k$ and $\delta := \varepsilon/k$. Then we need to check if $\lim_{n \to \infty} (\log n)/n^\delta = 0$. The functions $\log n$ and n^δ can be extended in a canonical way to $\log x$ and x^δ, functions on $\mathbb{R}^+$. By l'Hospital's rule

$$\lim_{x \to \infty} \frac{\log x}{x^\delta} = \lim_{x \to \infty} \frac{\frac{d}{dx}\log x}{\frac{d}{dx}x^\delta} \tag{A.1}$$

$$= \lim_{x \to \infty} \frac{x^{-\delta}}{\delta \ln 2} \tag{A.2}$$

and this limit is clearly 0. The other relationships follow in a similar fashion. From these follow many more relationships, e.g., $n \log n = o(n^2)$, since $\log n = o(n)$. As an example, we obtain the following sequence of asymptotically ever faster growing orders of magnitude, where $0 < \varepsilon < 1$:

$\log \log n,$

$\log n,\ \log^2 n,\ \log^3 n,\ \ldots$

$n^\varepsilon,\ n,\ n \log n,\ n \log n \log \log n,\ n \log^2 n,\ n^{1+\varepsilon},\ n^2,\ n^3, \ldots$

$2^{n^\varepsilon},\ 2^{\varepsilon n},\ 2^n,$

$2^{2^n}.$

For a sum of constantly many orders of magnitude, one summand of which grows asymptotically faster than the others, the order of magnitude is that of this fastest growing summand. So, for example,

$$n^2 \log^2 n + 10 n^3 / \log n + 5n$$

has the order of magnitude of $n^3 / \log n$. For summands of the form $c \cdot n^\alpha$, i.e., for polynomials, the order of magnitude is precisely the order of magnitude of the term with the largest exponent.

Further simplifying, we obtain the following notions: A function $f : \mathbb{N} \to \mathbb{R}^+$ is called

- *logarithmic* if $f = O(\log n)$;
- *polylogarithmic* if $f = O(\log^k n)$ for some $k \in \mathbb{N}$, i.e., if asymptotically f grows no faster than a polynomial in $\log n$;
- *linear, quadratic,* or *cubic* if $f = O(n)$, $f = O(n^2)$, or $f = O(n^3)$;
- *quasi-linear* if $f = O(n \log^k n)$ for some $k \in \mathbb{N}$;
- *polynomially bounded* (or sometimes just *polynomial*) if $f = O(n^k)$ for some $k \in \mathbb{N}$;
- *superpolynomial* if $f = \Omega(n^k)$ for every $k \in \mathbb{N}$, i.e., if f grows faster than any polynomial;
- *subexponential* if $f = O(2^{n^\varepsilon})$ for every $\varepsilon > 0$;
- *exponential* if $f = \Omega(2^{n^\varepsilon})$ for some $\varepsilon > 0$; and
- *strictly exponential* if $f = \Omega(2^{\varepsilon n})$ for some $\varepsilon > 0$.

It is important to note in this context that superpolynomial, exponential, and strictly exponential denote lower bounds while the other terms refer to upper bounds. So, for example, n^2 is cubic (more precisely we could say that "n^2 grows asymptotically no faster than cubic"). If we want to express a lower bound, we can say that an algorithm requires at least cubic computation time. Functions like $n^{\log n}$ that are superpolynomial but subexponential are called *quasi-polynomial.*

If computation times depend on two or more parameters, we can still use O-notation. For example, $f(n, m) = O(nm^2 + n^2 \log m)$, if there is a constant c such that $f(n, m) / (nm^2 + n^2 \log m) \le c$ for all $n, m \in \mathbb{N}$.

For probabilities $p(n)$, it often matters how fast these converge to 0 or 1. In the second case, we can consider how fast $q(n) := 1 - p(n)$ converges to 0. By definition $p(n) = o(1)$ if and only if $p(n)$ converges to 0. This is true even for functions like $1/\log n$ and $1/(\log\log n)$ which become small "very slowly". We will call $p(n)$

- *polynomially small* if $p(n) = O(n^{-\varepsilon})$ for some $\varepsilon > 0$;
- *exponentially small* if $p(n) = O(2^{-n^{\varepsilon}})$ for some $\varepsilon > 0$; and
- *strictly exponentially small* if $p(n) = O(2^{-\varepsilon n})$ for some $\varepsilon > 0$.

The last of these can be expressed as $2^{-\Omega(n)}$, where $\Omega(n)$ expresses a lower bound but $2^{-\Omega(n)}$ expresses an upper bound.

A.2 Results from Probability Theory

Since we view randomization as a key concept, we will need a few results from probability theory. There are, of course, many textbooks that contain these results. But since we will consider here only the special cases that we actually need, we can choose a simpler and more intuitive introduction to probability theory.

For a random experiment we let S denote the *sample space*, that is, the set of all possible *outcomes* of the experiment. We can restrict ourselves to the cases where S is either finite ($S = \{s_1, \ldots, s_m\}$) or countably infinite ($S = \{s_1, s_2, \ldots\}$). In the first case the corresponding index set is $I = \{1, \ldots, m\}$, and in the second case $I = \mathbb{N}$. A *probability distribution* p assigns to each outcome s_i for $i \in I$ a probability $p_i \geq 0$. The sum of all the probabilities p_i for $i \in I$ must have the value 1.

An *event* A is a subset of the sample space S, i.e., a set of outcomes $\{s_i : i \in I_A\}$ for some $I_A \subseteq I$. The probability of an event A is denoted $\mathrm{Prob}(A)$ and is simply the sum of all p_i for $i \in I_A$. In particular, $\mathrm{Prob}(\emptyset) = 0$ and $\mathrm{Prob}(S) = 1$ for any probability distribution. Important statements concerning the probability of a union of events follow directly from this definition.

Remark A.2.1. A collection of events A_j for $j \in J$ is called *pairwise disjoint* if $A_j \cap A_{j'} = \emptyset$ whenever $j \neq j'$. For pairwise disjoint events A_j we have

$$\mathrm{Prob}\left(\bigcup_{j \in J} A_j\right) = \sum_{j \in J} \mathrm{Prob}(A_j) \,.$$

More generally, even if the events A_j are not pairwise disjoint we still have

$$\mathrm{Prob}\left(\bigcup_{j \in J} A_j\right) \leq \sum_{j \in J} \mathrm{Prob}(A_j) \,.$$

The following images can be helpful. We can imagine a square with sides of length 1. Each outcome s_i is represented as a subregion R_i of the square with area p_i such that the regions are disjoint for distinct outcomes. Area and probability are both measures. Events are now regions of the square, and the areas of these regions are equal to the sum of the areas of the outcomes they contain. It is clear that the areas of disjoint events add, and that in the general case, the sum of the areas forms an upper bound, since there may be some "overlap" that causes some outcomes to be "double counted". Our random experiment is now equivalent to the random selection of a point in the square. If this point belongs to R_i, then the outcome is s_i.

What changes if we know that event B has occurred? All outcomes $s_i \notin B$ are now impossible and so have probability 0, while the outcomes $s_i \in B$ remain possible. So we obtain a new probability distribution q. For $s_i \notin B$, $q(s_i) = 0$. This means that the sum of all q_i for $s_i \in B$ must have the value 1. The relative probabilities of the outcomes $s_i, s_j \in B$ should not change just because we know that B has occurred, so $q_i/q_j = p_i/p_j$. Therefore, for some constant λ

$$q_i = \lambda p_i ,$$

and

$$\sum_{i \in I_B} q_i = 1 .$$

From this it follows that

$$\lambda = \left(\sum_{i \in I_B} q_i \right) \Big/ \left(\sum_{i \in I_B} p_i \right) = 1/\operatorname{Prob}(B) .$$

So we define the *conditional probability* q by

$$q_i = \begin{cases} \dfrac{p_i}{\operatorname{Prob}(B)} & \text{if } s_i \in B \\ 0 & \text{otherwise.} \end{cases}$$

For an event A we obtain

$$q(A) = \sum_{i \in I_A} q_i = \sum_{i \in I_A \cap I_B} p_i/\operatorname{Prob}(B) = \frac{\operatorname{Prob}(A \cap B)}{\operatorname{Prob}(B)} .$$

For the conditional probability that A occurs under the assumption that B has occurred, the notation $\operatorname{Prob}(A \mid B)$ (read the probability of A given B) is used. So we have

$$\operatorname{Prob}(A \mid B) := \operatorname{Prob}(A \cap B)/\operatorname{Prob}(B) .$$

This definition only makes sense when $\operatorname{Prob}(B) > 0$, since condition B can only occur if $\operatorname{Prob}(B) > 0$. Often the equivalent equation

$$\operatorname{Prob}(A \cap B) = \operatorname{Prob}(A \mid B) \cdot \operatorname{Prob}(B)$$

is used. This equation can be used even if $\text{Prob}(B) = 0$. Although $\text{Prob}(A \mid B)$ is not formally defined in this case, we still interpret $\text{Prob}(A \mid B) \cdot \text{Prob}(B)$ as 0.

If $\text{Prob}(A \mid B) = \text{Prob}(A)$, then the probability of the event A does not depend on whether or not B has occurred. In this case the events A and B are said to be *independent* events. This condition is equivalent to $\text{Prob}(A \cap B) = \text{Prob}(A) \cdot \text{Prob}(B)$ and also to $\text{Prob}(B \mid A) = \text{Prob}(B)$ if $\text{Prob}(A) > 0$ and $\text{Prob}(B) > 0$. The equation $\text{Prob}(A \cap B) = \text{Prob}(A) \cdot \text{Prob}(B)$ shows that the term independence is in fact symmetric with respect to A and B. Events A_j for $j \in J$ are called *completely independent* if for all $J' \subseteq J$,

$$\text{Prob}\left(\bigcap_{j \in J'} A_j\right) = \prod_{j \in J'} \text{Prob}(A_j)$$

holds.

To this point we have derived conditional probability from the probability distribution p. Often we will go in the other direction. If we know the probability distribution of some statistic like income for every state, and we know the number of residents in each state (or even just the relative populations of the states), then we can determine the probability distribution for the entire country by taking the weighted sum of the regional probabilities. This idea can be carried over to probability and leads to the so-called *law of total probability*.

Theorem A.2.2. *Let B_j $(j \in J)$ be a partition of the sample space S. Then*

$$\text{Prob}(A) = \sum_{j \in J} \text{Prob}(A \mid B_j) \cdot \text{Prob}(B_j) .$$

Proof. The proof follows by simple computation.

$$\text{Prob}(A \mid B_j) \cdot \text{Prob}(B_j) = \text{Prob}(A \cap B_j)$$

and so by Remark A.2.1 we have

$$\sum_{j \in J} \text{Prob}(A \mid B_j) \cdot \text{Prob}(B_j) = \sum_{j \in J} \text{Prob}(A \cap B_j) = \text{Prob}\left(\bigcup_{j \in J} (A \cap B_j)\right)$$

$$= \text{Prob}\left(A \cap \bigcup_{j \in J} B_j\right) = \text{Prob}(A) . \qquad \square$$

Now we come to the central notion of a *random variable*. Formally, this is simply a function $X : S \to \mathbb{R}$. So one random variable on the sample space of all people could assign to each person his or her height; another random variable could assign each person his or her weight. But random variables are more than just functions, since every probability distribution p on the sample space S induces a probability distribution on the range of X as follows:

$$\text{Prob}(X = t) := \text{Prob}(\{s_i \mid X(s_i) = t\}) \, .$$

So the probability that X takes on the value t is simply the probability of the set of all outcomes that are mapped to t by X. While we usually can't "do calculations" on a sample space, we can with random variables. Before we introduce the parameters of random variables, we want to derive the definition of *independent random variables* from the notion of independent random events. Two random variables X and Y on the *probability space* (S, p) (i.e., a sample space S and a probability distribution p on that sample space) are called independent if the events $\{X \in A\} := \{s_i \mid X(s_i) \in A\}$ and $\{Y \in B\}$ are independent for all $A, B \subseteq \mathbb{R}$. A set of random variables $\{X_i \mid i \in I\}$ is called *completely independent* if the events $\{X_i \in A_i\}$ for $i \in I$ are completely independent for all events $A_i \subseteq \mathbb{R}$. The set of random variables $\{X_i \mid i \in I\}$ is *pairwise independent* if for any events $A_i, A_j \subseteq \mathbb{R}$ and any $i \neq j$, the events $\{X_i \in A_i\}$ and $\{X_j \in A_j\}$ are independent.

The most important parameter of a random variable is its *expected value* (or mean value) $E(X)$ defined by

$$E(X) := \sum_{t \in \text{im}(X)} t \cdot \text{Prob}(X = t) \, ,$$

where $\text{im}(X)$ denotes the image of the sample space under the function X. This definition presents no problems if $\text{im}(X)$ is finite (so, in particular, whenever S is finite). For countably infinite images the infinite series in the definition above is only defined if the series converges absolutely. This will not cause us any problems, however, since when we deal with computation times, the terms of the series will all be positive and we will also allow an expected value of ∞. Average-case runtime, as defined in Chapter 2, is an expected value where the input x with $|x| = n$ is chosen randomly. For the expected runtime of a randomized algorithm the input x is fixed and the expected value is taken with respect to the random bits that are used by the algorithm. Since we have defined conditional probability, we can also talk about *conditional expected value* $E(X \mid A)$ with respect to the conditional probability $\text{Prob}(X = t \mid A)$.

Expected value allows for easy computations.

Remark A.2.3. If X is a 0-1 random variable (i.e., $\text{im}(X)$ is the set $\{0, 1\}$), then

$$E(X) = \text{Prob}(X = 1) \, .$$

Proof. The claim follows directly from the definition:

$$E(X) = 0 \cdot \text{Prob}(X = 0) + 1 \cdot \text{Prob}(X = 1) = \text{Prob}(X = 1) \, . \qquad \square$$

This very simple observation is extremely helpful, since it allows us to switch back and forth between probability and expected value. Furthermore, expected value is linear. This can be explained simply. If we consider the balances in the accounts of a bank's customers as random variables (based on a random selection of a customer), and every balance is reduced by a factor of 1.95583 (to convert from German marks to euros), then the average balance will be reduced by this same factor. (Here we see a difference between theory and application, since in practice small differences occur due to the rounding of each balance to the nearest euro cent.) If two banks merge and the two accounts of each customer (perhaps with a balance of 0 for one or the other bank) are combined, then the mean balance after the merger will be the sum of the mean balances of the two banks separately. We will show that this holds in general for any random variables defined on the same probability space.

Theorem A.2.4. *Let X and Y be random variables on the same probability space. Then*

1. $E(a \cdot X) = a \cdot E(X)$ *for $a \in \mathbb{R}$, and*
2. $E(X + Y) = E(X) + E(Y)$.

Proof. Here we use a description of expected value that goes back to the individual outcomes of the sample space. Let (S, p) be the underlying probability space. Then

$$E(X) = \sum_{i \in I} X(s_i) \cdot p_i .$$

This equation follows from the definition of $E(X)$, since $\text{Prob}(X = t)$ is the sum of all p_i with $X(s_i) = t$. It follows that

$$E(a \cdot X) = \sum_{i \in I}(a \cdot X)(s_i) \cdot p_i = a \sum_{i \in I} X(s_i) \cdot p_i = a \cdot E(X)$$

and

$$E(X+Y) = \sum_{i \in I}(X+Y)(s_i) \cdot p_i = \sum_{i \in I} X(s_i) \cdot p_i + \sum_{i \in I} Y(s_i) \cdot p_i = E(X) + E(Y) .$$

$\square$

On the other hand, it is not in general the case that $E(X \cdot Y) = E(X) \cdot E(Y)$. This can be shown by means of a simple example. Let $S = \{s_1, s_2\}$, $p_1 = p_2 = 1/2$, $X(s_1) = 0$, $X(s_2) = 2$, and $Y = X$. Then $X \cdot Y(s_1) = 0$ and $X \cdot Y(s_2) = 4$. It follows that $E(X \cdot Y) = 2$, but $E(X) \cdot E(Y) = 1 \cdot 1 = 1$. The reason is that in our example X and Y are not independent.

Theorem A.2.5. *If X and Y are independent random variables on the same sample space, then*

$$E(X \cdot Y) = E(X) \cdot E(Y) .$$

Proof. As in the proof of Theorem A.2.4, we have

$$E(X \cdot Y) = \sum_{i \in I} X(s_i) \cdot Y(s_i) \cdot p_i .$$

We partition I into disjoint sets $I(t,u) := \{i \mid X(s_i) = t, Y(s_i) = u\}$. From this it follows that

$$E(X \cdot Y) = \sum_{t,u} \sum_{i \in I(t,u)} t \cdot u \cdot p_i = \sum_{t,u} t \cdot u \sum_{i \in I(t,u)} p_i$$

$$= \sum_{t,u} t \cdot u \cdot \mathrm{Prob}(X = t, Y = u).$$

Now we can take advantage of the independence of X and Y and obtain

$$E(X \cdot Y) = \sum_{t,u} t \cdot u \cdot \mathrm{Prob}(X = t) \cdot \mathrm{Prob}(Y = u)$$

$$= \left(\sum_{t} t \cdot \mathrm{Prob}(X = t) \right) \cdot \left(\sum_{u} u \cdot \mathrm{Prob}(Y = u) \right)$$

$$= E(X) \cdot E(Y).$$

$\square$

The claim of Theorem A.2.5 can be illustrated as follows. If we assume that weight and account balance are independent, then the mean balance is the same for every weight, and so the mean product of account balance and weight is the product of the mean account balance and the mean weight. This example also shows that data from everyday life typically only lead to "almost independent" random variables. But we can design experiments with coin tosses so that the results are "genuinely independent".

The expected value reduces the random variable to its weighted mean, and so expresses only a portion of the information contained in a random variable and its probability distribution. The mean annual income in two countries can be the same, for example, while the income disparity in one country may be small and in the other country much larger. So we are interested in the random variable $Y = |X - E(X)|$, which measures the distance of a random variable from its expected value. The kth central moment of X is $E(|X - E(X)|^k)$. The larger k is the more heavily larger deviations from the mean are weighted. Based on the discussion above, we might expected that the first central moment would be the most important, but it is computationally inconvenient because the function $|X|$ is not differentiable. As a standard measure of deviation from the expected value, the second central moment is usually used. It is called the *variance* of the random variable X and denoted by $V(X) := E((X - E(X))^2)$. Since $X^2 = |X|^2$, we can drop the absolute value. Directly from the definition we obtain the following results.

Theorem A.2.6. *Let X be a random variable such that $|E(X)| < \infty$, then*

$$V(X) = E(X^2) - E(X)^2$$

and for any $a \in \mathbb{R}$,

$$V(aX) = a^2 \cdot V(X).$$

Proof. The condition $|E(X)| < \infty$ guarantees that on the right side of the first claim we do not have the undefined quantity $\infty - \infty$. Then, since $E(X)$ is a constant factor, by linearity of expected value we have

$$V(X) = E((X - E(X))^2) = E(X^2 - 2 \cdot X \cdot E(X) + E(X)^2)$$
$$= E(X^2) - 2 \cdot E(X) \cdot E(X) + E(E(X)^2).$$

Finally, for each constant $a \in \mathbb{R}$, $E(a) = a$, since we are dealing with a "random" variable that always takes on the value a. So $E(E(X)^2) = E(X)^2$ and we obtain the first claim.

For the second claim we apply the first statement and use the equations $E((aX)^2) = a^2 \cdot E(X^2)$ and $E(aX)^2 = a^2 \cdot E(X)^2$. $\square$

Since $V(2 \cdot X) = 4 \cdot V(X)$ and not $2 \cdot V(X)$, it is not generally the case that $V(X + Y) = V(X) + V(Y)$. This is the case, however, if the random variables are independent.

Theorem A.2.7. *For pairwise independent random variables $X_1, \ldots, X_n$ we have*

$$V(X_1 + \cdots + X_n) = V(X_1) + \cdots + V(X_n).$$

Proof. The statement follows by simple computation. We have

$$V\left(\sum_{1 \le i \le n} X_i\right) = E\left(\left(\sum_{1 \le i \le n} X_i - E\left(\sum_{1 \le i \le n} X_i\right)\right)^2\right)$$

$$= E\left(\left(\sum_{1 \le i \le n} X_i - \sum_{1 \le i \le n} E(X_i)\right)^2\right)$$

$$= E\left(\sum_{1 \le i,j \le n} X_i \cdot X_j - 2 \sum_{1 \le i,j \le n} X_i \cdot E(X_j) + \sum_{1 \le i,j \le n} E(X_i) \cdot E(X_j)\right)$$

$$= \sum_{1 \le i,j \le n} \left(E(X_i \cdot X_j) - 2 \cdot E(X_i) \cdot E(X_j) + E(X_i) \cdot E(X_j)\right).$$

By Theorem A.2.5 it follows from the independence of X_i and X_j, that $E(X_i \cdot X_j) = E(X_i) \cdot E(X_j)$, and so the summands for all $i \ne j$ equal 0. For $i = j$ we obtain $E(X_i^2) - E(X_i)^2$ and thus $V(X_i)$. This proves the theorem. $\square$

The law of total probability can be extended to a statement about conditional expected value. Recall that $E(X \mid A)$ is the expected value of X with respect to the probability distribution $\text{Prob}(\cdot \mid A)$.

Theorem A.2.8. *Let $\{B_j \mid j \in J\}$ be a partition of the sample space S, and let X be a random variable. Then*

$$E(X) = \sum_{j \in J} E(X \mid B_j) \cdot \text{Prob}(B_j).$$

Proof. From the definitions we have

$$E(X) = \sum_{i \in I} X(s_i) \cdot p(s_i)$$

and

$$E(X \mid B_j) \cdot \text{Prob}(B_j) = \sum_{i \in I} X(s_i) \cdot \text{Prob}(s_i \mid B_j) \cdot \text{Prob}(B_j)$$

$$= \sum_{i \in I} X(s_i) \cdot \text{Prob}(\{s_i\} \cap B_j).$$

Since the sets B_j form a partition of the sample space, s_i is in exactly one of these sets, so

$$\sum_{j \in J} \text{Prob}(\{s_i\} \cap B_j) = p(s_i) .$$

So

$$\sum_{j \in J} E(X \mid B_j) \cdot \text{Prob}(B_j) = \sum_{j \in J} \sum_{i \in I} X(s_i) \cdot \text{Prob}(\{s_i\} \cap B_j)$$

$$= \sum_{i \in I} \left(X(s_i) \cdot \sum_{j \in J} \text{Prob}(\{s_i\} \cap B_j) \right)$$

$$= \sum_{i \in I} X(s_i) \cdot p(s_i)$$

$$= E(X) .$$

$\square$

This statement is not surprising. If we want to measure the mean weight of residents of a certain country, we can do this for each of several regions separately and then form a weighted sum, using the population proportions of the regions as weights.

Finally, we need a statement with which we can prove that the probability of "large" deviations from the expected value is "small". One very simple but extremely useful statement that makes this possible is the Markov Inequality. If we know that the mean annual income of a population is 40000 euros, then we can conclude from this that at most 4% of the population has an annual income that exceeds one million euros. For this to be the case we must make the assumption that there are no negative incomes. If more than 4% of the population earns at least one million euros, then these people alone contribute more than $0.04 \cdot 10^6 = 40000$ to the weighted mean. Since we have excluded the possibility of negative incomes, the mean income must be greater than 40000 euros. The *Markov Inequality* is a generalization of this result.

Theorem A.2.9 (Markov Inequality). *Let $X \geq 0$. Then for all $t > 0$,*

$$\text{Prob}(X \geq t) \leq E(X)/t .$$

Proof. We define a random variable Y on the same sample space that X is defined on as follows:

$$Y(s_i) := \begin{cases} t \text{ if } X(s_i) \geq t \\ 0 \text{ otherwise.} \end{cases}$$

By definition $Y(s_i) \leq X(s_i)$ for all i and therefore $Y \leq X$. By the definition of expected value this implies that $E(Y) \leq E(X)$. Similarly, it follows from the definitions of expected value and of Y that

$$E(Y) = 0 \cdot \text{Prob}(X < t) + t \cdot \text{Prob}(X \geq t)$$
$$= t \cdot \text{Prob}(X \geq t).$$

Putting these together we have

$$E(X) \geq E(Y) = t \cdot \text{Prob}(X \geq t) . \qquad \square$$

It is not so impressive that the Markov Inequality implies that at most 4% of the population can have an annual income in excess of one million euros. We suspect that the actual portion is much less. We obtain better estimates if we apply the Markov Inequality to specially chosen random variables. Using the random variable $|X - E(X)|^k$, for example, we obtain

$$\text{Prob}\left(|X - E(X)|^k \geq t^k\right) \leq E\left(|X - E(X)|^k\right) / t^k ,$$

or since $|X - E(X)|^k \geq t^k$ and $|X - E(X)| \geq t$ are equivalent,

$$\text{Prob}\left(|X - E(X)| \geq t\right) \leq E\left(|X - E(X)|^k\right) / t^k .$$

When computing $E\left(|X - E(X)|^k\right)$, as k increases, values of the random variables $|X - E(X)|$ that are smaller than 1 are weighted less heavily, and values that are greater than 1 are weighted more heavily. It is also worth noting that the denominator t^k changes with k. So it is very possible that we will achieve better results with larger values of k. For the case $k = 2$, the result is known as the *Chebychev Inequality*.

Corollary A.2.10 (Chebychev Inequality). *For all $t > 0$,*

$$\text{Prob}\left(|X - E(X)| \geq t\right) \leq V(X)/t^2 . \qquad \square$$

We now consider n independent coin tosses and want to investigate the random variable that counts the number of heads. Let $X_1, \ldots, X_n$ be random variables with $\text{Prob}(X_i = 0) = \text{Prob}(X_i = 1) = 1/2$. Then X_i measures the number of successes (tosses that result in heads) in the ith coin toss and $X := X_1 + \cdots + X_n$ measures the total number of successes. Note that $X_i^2 = X_i$. By Remark A.2.3, $E(X_i^2) = E(X_i) = 1/2$, and by Theorem A.2.6, $V(X_i) = 1/2 - (1/2)^2 = 1/4$. By Theorem A.2.4 and Theorem A.2.7, $E(X) = n/2$ and $V(X) = n/4$. Our goal is to show that for any constant $\varepsilon > 0$,

$\text{Prob}(X \geq (1 + \varepsilon) \cdot \text{E}(X))$ becomes very small as n increases. The Markov Inequality only provides the following estimate

$$\text{Prob}\,(X \geq (1 + \varepsilon) \cdot \text{E}(X)) \leq 1/(1 + \varepsilon)\,,$$

which is independent of n. With the Chebychev Inequality we obtain

$$\begin{aligned}
\text{Prob}\,(X \geq (1 + \varepsilon) \cdot \text{E}(X)) &= \text{Prob}\,(X - \text{E}(X) \geq \varepsilon \cdot \text{E}(X)) \\
&\leq \text{Prob}\,(|X - \text{E}(X)| \geq \varepsilon \cdot \text{E}(X)) \\
&\leq V(X)/\left(\varepsilon^2 \cdot \text{E}(X)^2\right) = \varepsilon^{-2} \cdot n^{-1}\,.
\end{aligned}$$

So the probability we are considering is polynomially small. The *Chernoff Inequality*, which we will derive shortly, will show that the probability is in fact strictly exponential small. The Chernoff Inequality also follows from the Markov Inequality. While for the Chebychev Inequality random variables were squared, or more generally the kth power Y^k was considered, for the Chernoff Inequality we will consider the random variable e^{-Y}. The stronger curvature of the exponential function as compared to polynomials makes a significantly better estimate possible, but only for certain random variables.

Theorem A.2.11 (Chernoff Inequality). *Suppose $0 < p < 1$ and $X = X_1 + \cdots + X_n$ for independent random variables $X_1, \ldots, X_n$ with $\text{Prob}(X_i = 1) = p$ and $\text{Prob}(X_i = 0) = 1 - p$. Then $\text{E}(X) = np$ and for all $\delta \in (0, 1)$ we have*

$$\text{Prob}\,(X \leq (1 - \delta) \cdot \text{E}(X)) \leq e^{-\,\text{E}(X)\delta^2/2}\,.$$

Proof. The statement about $\text{E}(X)$ follows from the linearity of expected value and $\text{E}(X_i) = p$ (Remark A.2.3).

A number $t > 0$ will be chosen later in the proof. Since the function $x \to e^{-tx}$ is strictly monotonically decreasing, $X \leq (1 - \delta) \cdot \text{E}(X)$ is equivalent to $e^{-tX} \geq e^{-t(1-\delta)\,\text{E}(X)}$. So by the Markov Inequality we have

$$\begin{aligned}
\text{Prob}\,(X \leq (1 - \delta) \cdot \text{E}(X)) &= \text{Prob}\left(e^{-tX} \geq e^{-t(1-\delta)\,\text{E}(X)}\right) \\
&\leq \text{E}\left(e^{-tX}\right)/e^{-t(1-\delta)\,\text{E}(X)}.
\end{aligned}$$

Now we compute $\text{E}(e^{-tX})$. Since $X_1, \ldots, X_n$ are independent, this is the random variables $e^{-tX_1}, \ldots, e^{-tX_n}$ are also independent. Thus

$$\begin{aligned}
\text{E}\left(e^{-tX}\right) &= \text{E}\left(e^{-t(X_1 + \cdots + X_n)}\right) \\
&= \text{E}\left(\textstyle\prod_{1 \leq i \leq n} e^{-tX_i}\right) \\
&= \textstyle\prod_{1 \leq i \leq n}\left(\text{E}(e^{-tX_i})\right).
\end{aligned}$$

And since X_i only takes on the values 0 and 1, it follows that

$$\begin{aligned}
\text{E}\left(e^{-tX_i}\right) &= 1 \cdot (1 - p) + e^{-t} \cdot p \\
&= 1 + p\left(e^{-t} - 1\right).
\end{aligned}$$

It follows that
$$E\left(e^{-tX}\right) = \left(1 + p(e^{-t} - 1)\right)^n.$$

By a simple result from calculus, $1 + x < e^x$ for all $x < 0$, and since $t > 0$, $p\left(e^{-t} - 1\right) < 0$ and

$$E\left(e^{-tX}\right) < e^{p(e^{-t}-1)n} = e^{(e^{-t}-1)\cdot E(X)}.$$

In the last step we took advantage of the fact that $E(X) = np$. Now we let $t := -\ln(1 - \delta)$. Then $t > 0$ and $e^{-t} - 1 = -\delta$. Thus

$$E\left(e^{-tX}\right) < e^{-\delta\cdot E(X)}.$$

Finally, we substitute this result into our first estimate and obtain

$$\text{Prob}\left(X \le (1 - \delta)\, E(X)\right) < e^{-\delta\cdot E(X)}\big/e^{(\ln(1-\delta))(1-\delta)\, E(X)}$$
$$= e^{(-(1-\delta)\ln(1-\delta)-\delta)\, E(X)}.$$

From the Taylor series for $x \ln x$ it follows that

$$(1 - \delta) \ln(1 - \delta) > -\delta + \delta^2/2.$$

Inserting this leads to the Chernoff Inequality. $\qquad\square$

We return now to our example, where $p = 1/2$. Then $X \ge (1 + \varepsilon)\cdot E(X)$ has the same probability as $X \le (1 - \varepsilon)\cdot E(X)$, since X is symmetrically distributed about $E(X)$. For a coin toss, we are simply reversing the roles of the two sides of the coin. Thus

$$\text{Prob}\left(X \ge (1 + \varepsilon)\cdot E(X)\right) \le e^{-\varepsilon^2 n/4}$$

is in fact strictly exponential small.

Frequently we encounter the following problem when investigating randomized algorithms. Such an algorithm may proceed in phases. Each phase has a probability of p of succeeding, in which case we stop the algorithm. Otherwise a new phase is begun that is completely independent of the preceding phases. Let X be a random variable that takes on the value t if the first success occurs in the tth phase. Since the phases are completely independent,

$$\text{Prob}(X = t) = q^{t-1}p,$$

where $q := 1 - p$. That is, outcome $X = t$ is equivalent to the failure of the first $t - 1$ phases followed by success in the tth phase. This probability distribution is known as the *geometric distribution*. We are interested in the expected value of this distribution.

Theorem A.2.12. *Let X be geometrically distributed with parameter p. Then* $E(X) = 1/p$.

Proof. By definition

$$E(X) = \sum_{1 \le k < \infty} k \cdot q^{k-1} \cdot p$$

$$= p \cdot (\ q^0$$

$$+ q^1 + q^1$$

$$+ q^2 + q^2 + q^2$$

$$+ q^3 + q^3 + q^3 + q^3$$

$$+ \cdots \qquad\qquad).$$

The first column has the value $1/(1-q) = 1/p$. Analogously, the value of the ith column (factor out q^{i-1}) is q^{i-1}/p. So

$$E(X) = p \cdot \tfrac{1}{p} \cdot \sum_{1 \le i < \infty} q^{i-1} = \tfrac{1}{p} \ . \qquad\qquad \square$$

References

1. Agrawal, M., Kayal, N. and Saxena, N. (2002). PRIMES is in P. Tech. Report Dept. of Computer Science and Engineering. Indian Inst. of Technology Kanpur.
2. Ahuja, R.K., Magnanti, T.L. and Orlin, J.B. (1993). *Network Flows. Theory, Algorithms and Applications*. Prentice–Hall.
3. Alon, N. and Boppana, R.B. (1987). The monotone circuit complexity of Boolean functions. Combinatorica 7, 1–22.
4. Alon, N. and Spencer, J. (1992). *The Probabilistic Method*. Wiley.
5. Arora, S. (1997). Nearly linear time approximation schemes for Euclidean TSP and other geometric problems. Proc. of 38th IEEE Symp. on Foundations of Computer Science, 554–563.
6. Arora, S., Lund, C., Motwani, R., Sudan, M. and Szegedy, M. (1998). Proof verification and the hardness of approximation problems. Journal of the ACM 45, 501–555.
7. Arora, S. and Safra, S. (1998). Probabilistic checking of proofs: A new charaterization of NP. Journal of the ACM 45, 70–122.
8. Aspvall, B. and Stone, R.E. (1980). Khachiyan's linear programming algorithm. Journal of Algorithms 1, 1–13.
9. Ausiello, G., Crescenzi, P., Gambosi, G., Kann, V., Marchetti-Spaccamela, A. and Protasi, M. (1999). *Complexity and Approximation*. Springer.
10. Balcázar, J.L., Díaz, J. and Gabarró, J. (1988). *Structural Complexity*. Springer.
11. Beame, P., Saks, M., Sun, X. and Vee, E. (2003). Time-space trade-off lower bounds for randomized computation of decision problems. Journal of the ACM 50, 154–195.
12. Bellare, M., Goldreich, O. and Sudan, M. (1998). Free bits, PCP and non-approximability – towards tight results. SIAM Journal on Computing 27, 804–915.
13. Bernholt, T., Gülich, A., Hofmeister, T., Schmitt, N. and Wegener, I. (2002). Komplexitätstheorie, effiziente Algorithmen und die Bundesliga. Informatik–Spektrum 25, 488–502.

14. Boppana, R. and Halldórsson, M.M. (1992). Approximating maximum independent sets by excluding subgraphs. BIT 32, 180–196.

15. Clote, P. and Kranakis, E. (2002). *Boolean Functions and Computation Models.* Springer.

16. Cook, S.A. (1971). The complexity of theorem proving procedures. Proc. 3rd ACM Symp. on Theory of Computing, 151–158.

17. Dietzfelbinger, M. (2004). *Primality Testing in Polynomial Time.* LNCS 3000. Springer.

18. Feige, U., Goldwasser, S., Lovász, L., Safra, S. and Szegedy, M. (1991). Approximating clique is almost NP-complete. Proc. of 32nd IEEE Symp. on Foundations of Computer Science, 2–12.

19. Garey, M.R. and Johnson, D.B. (1979). *Computers and Intractability. A Guide to the Theory of NP-Completeness.* W.H. Freeman.

20. Goldmann, M. and Karpinski, M. (1993). Simulating threshold circuits by majority circuits. Proc. of the 25th ACM Symp. on Theory of Computing, 551–560.

21. Goldreich, O. (1998). *Modern Cryptography, Probabilistic Proofs and Pseudorandomness.* Algorithms and Combinatorics, Vol.17. Springer.

22. Goldwasser, S., Micali, S. and Rackoff, C. (1989). The knowledge complexity of interactive proof-systems. SIAM Journal on Computing 18, 186–208.

23. Håstad, J. (1989). Almost optimal lower bounds for small depth circuits. In: Micali, S. (ed.) *Randomness and Computation.* Advances in Computing Research 5, 143–170. JAI Press.

24. Håstad, J. (1999). Clique is hard to approximate within $n^{1-\varepsilon}$. Acta Mathematica 182, 105–142.

25. Håstad, J. (2001). Some optimal inapproximability results. Journal of the ACM 48, 798–859.

26. Hajnal, A., Maass, W., Pudlák, P., Szegedy, M. and Turán, G. (1987). Threshold circuits of bounded depth. Proc. of 28th IEEE Symp. on Foundations of Computer Science, 99–110.

27. Hemaspaandra, L. and Ogihara, M. (2002). *The Complexity Theory Companion.* Springer.

28. Homer, S. (2001). *Computability and Complexity Theory.* Springer.

29. Hopcroft, J.E., Motwani, R. and Ullman, J.D. (2001). *Introduction to Automata Theory, Languages and Computation.* Addison-Wesley Longman.

30. Hopcroft, J.E. and Ullman, J.D. (1979). *Introduction to Automata Theory, Languages and Computation.* Addison-Wesley.

31. Hromkovič, J. (1997). *Communication Complexity and Parallel Computing.* Springer.

32. Johnson, D.S. (1974). Approximation algorithms for combinatorial problems. Journal of Computer and System Sciences 9, 256–278.

33. Kann, V. and Crescenzi, P. (2000). A list of NP-complete optimization problems. www.nada.kth.se/~viggo/index-en.html

34. Karmarkar, N. and Karp, R.M. (1982). An efficient approximation scheme for the one-dimensional bin packing problem. Proc. of 23rd IEEE Symp. on Foundations of Computer Science, 312–320.

35. Karp, R.M. (1972). Reducibility among combinatorial problems. In: Miller, R.E. and Thatcher, J.W. (eds.). *Complexity of Computer Computations*, 85–103. Plenum Press.

36. Korte, B. and Schrader, R. (1981). On the existence of fast approximation schemes. In: *Nonlinear Programming*. Academic Press.

37. Kushilevitz, E. and Nisan, N. (1997). *Communication Complexity*. Cambridge University Press.

38. Ladner, R.E. (1975). On the structure of polynomial time reducibility. Journal of the ACM 22, 155–171.

39. Lawler, E.L., Lenstra, J.K., Rinnooy Kan, A.H.G. and Shmoys, D.B. (1985). *The Traveling Salesman Problem. A Guided Tour of Combinatorial Optimization*. Wiley.

40. Lawler, E.L., Lenstra, J.K., Rinnooy Kan, A.H.G. and Shmoys, D.B. (1993). Sequencing and Scheduling: Algorithms and Complexity. In: Graves, S.C., Rinnooy Kan, A.H.G. and Zipkin, P.H. (eds.). *Handbook in Operations Research and Management Science*, Vol. 4, *Logistics of Production and Inventory*, 445–522. North–Holland.

41. Levin, L.A. (1973). Universal sorting problems. Problems of Information Transmission 9, 265–266.

42. Martello, S. and Toth, P. (1990). *Knapsack Problems*. Wiley.

43. Mayr, E., Prömel, H.J. and Steger, A. (1998) (eds.). *Lectures on Proof Verification and Approximation Algorithms*. LNCS 1367. Springer.

44. Miller, G.L. (1976) Riemann's hypothesis and tests for primality. Journal of Computer and System Sciences 13, 300–317.

45. Miltersen, P.B. (2001). Derandomizing complexity classes. In Pardalos, P.M., Rajasekaran, S., Reif, J. and Rolim, J. (eds.). *Handbook of Randomization*. Kluwer.

46. Motwani, R. and Raghavan, P. (1995). *Randomized Algorithms*. Cambridge University Press.

47. Nechiporuk, É.I. (1966) A Boolean function. Soviet Mathematics Doklady 7, 999–1000.

48. Nielsen, M.A. and Chuang, I.L. (2000). *Quantum Computation and Quantum Information*. Cambridge University Press.

49. Owen, G. (1995). *Game Theory*. Academic Press.

50. Papadimitriou, C.M. (1994). *Computational Complexity*. Addison–Wesley.

51. Pinedo, M. (1995). *Scheduling: Theory, Algorithms and Systems*. Prentice–Hall.

52. Razborov, A.A. (1987). Lower bounds on the size of bounded depth networks over a complete basis with logical addition. Math. Notes of the Academy of Sciences of the USSR 41, 333–338.

53. Razborov, A.A. (1990). Lower bounds for monotone complexity of Boolean functions. American Mathematical Society Translations 147, 75–84.
54. Razborov, A.A. (1995). Bounded arithmetics and lower bounds in Boolean complexity. In: Clote, P. and Remmel, J. (eds.). *Feasible Mathematics II.* Birkhäuser.
55. Schönhage, A., Grotefeld, A.F.W. and Vetter, E. (1999). *Fast Algorithms: A Multitape Turing Machine Implementation.* Spektrum Akademischer Verlag.
56. Shamir, A. (1992). IP=PSPACE. Journal of the ACM 39, 869–877.
57. Shasha, D. and Lazere, C. (1998). *Out of Their Minds. The Lives and Discoveries of 15 Great Computer Scientists.* Copernicus (Springer).
58. Singh, S. (1998). *Fermat's Last Theorem.* Fourth Estate.
59. Sipser, M. (1997). *Introduction to the Theory of Computation.* PWS Publishing Company.
60. Smolensky, R. (1987). Algebraic methods in the theory of lower bounds for Boolean circuit complexity. Proc. of 19th ACM Symp. on Theory of Computing, 77–82.
61. Solovay, R. and Strassen, V. (1977). A fast Monte-Carlo test for primality. SIAM Journal on Computing 6, 84–85.
62. Stinson, D.R. (1995). *Cryptography. Theory and Practice.* CRC Press.
63. Stockmeyer, L.J. (1977). The polynomial time hierarchy. Theoretical Computer Science 3, 1–22.
64. Strassen, V. (1986). The work of Leslie G. Valiant. Proc. of the Int. Congress of Mathematics, Berkeley, Ca.
65. Thompson, C.D. (1979). Area-time complexity for VLSI. Proc. of 11th ACM Symp. on Theory of Computing, 81–88.
66. Valiant, L.G. (1979). The complexity of computing the permanent. Theoretical Computer Science 8, 189–201.
67. van Leeuwen, J. (1990) (ed.). *Handbook of Theoretical Computer Science.* Elsevier, MIT Press.
68. Wagner, K. and Wechsung, G. (1986). *Computational Complexity.* VEB Deutscher Verlag der Wissenschaften.
69. Wegener, I. (1982). Boolean functions whose monotone complexity is of size $n^2/\log n$. Theoretical Computer Science 21, 213–224.
70. Wegener, I. (1987). *The Complexity of Boolean Functions.* Wiley. Freely available via http://ls2-www.cs.uni-dortmund.de/~wegener.
71. Wegener, I. (2000). *Branching Programs and Binary Decision Diagrams – Theory and Applications.* SIAM Monographs on Discrete Mathematics and Applications.
72. Wegener, I. (2002). Teaching nondeterminism as a special case of randomization. Informatica Didactica 4 (electronic journal).
73. Yao, A.C. (1977). Probabilistic computations: Towards a unified measure of complexity. Proc. of 18th Symp. on Foundations of Computer Science, 222–227.

74. Yao, A.C. (1979). Some complexity questions related to distributed computing. Proc. of 11th ACM Symp. on Theory of Computing, 209–213.
75. Yao, A.C. (2001). Lecture upon receiving the Turing Award. July 8, 2001, Chersonissos, Crete.

Index

#P   198
#P-complete   199
#SAT   198, *see also* SAT
δ-close   168
$\leq_1$ *see* NC^1-reduction
$\leq_{cd}$ *see* AC^0-reduction
$\leq_{proj}$ *see* projection
$\leq_{rop}$ *see* read-once projection
$\leq_{log}$ *see* logarithmic reduction
$\oplus$ *see* parity
$\leq_T$ *see* Turing reduction
$\equiv_T$ *see* Turing equivalent
$\leq_p$ *see* polynomial reduction
$\leq_{PTAS}$ *see* PTAS reduction
$\leq_{rect}$ *see* rectangular reduction
ε-optimal   100
3-DM   83
3-PARTITION   95
3-SAT   51, *see also* SAT
4-PARTITION   95

AC^0 260
AC^0-reduction   271
ACC$^0[m]$ 263
AC^k 272
Agrawal   68, 128
Ahuja   16, 49
algorithm   18
  deterministic   39, 69
  nondeterministic   39
  pseudo-polynomial time   105
  randomized   8, 27, 39, 44, 69, 102
algorithmic complexity   23, 24
Alice   190, 219, 257

Alon   242, 254, 261
alternating counting class   263
AM   151
AND-gate   252
AND-nondeterminism   233
anti-clique   53, *see also* independent
  set
approximation problem   101
approximation ratio   100
APX*   102
arithmetization   165
Arora   105, 164, 175
Arthur-Merlin game   151
Aspvall   128
asymptotic FPTAS   105
asymptotic worst-case approximation
  ratio   101
Ausiello   10, 114, 164
Aut(G) *see* automorphism group
automorphism group   149
average-case runtime   23, 28

Bachmann   279
Balcázar   10
baseball   17
basketball   17
BDD   *see* binary decision diagram
Bellare   164
Bernholt   17
best-fit decreasing   104
BFD   *see* best-fit decreasing
big O notation   162, 279
bin packing problem   15, 47, 48, 52, 80,
  178

binary decision diagram   9, 209
binary decision tree   10
bit commitment   157
black box   8, 116
black box complexity   117
black box optimization   117
black box problem   116
BMST   *see* bounded-degree minimum spanning tree
Bob   190, 219, 257
Bollig   VI, VII
Boolean
   formula   9, 10
   function   9, 10
Boppana   103, 254
bounded error   36
bounded-degree minimum spanning tree   78
bounded-error probabilistic polynomial time   33, *see* BPP
bouquet   18
BinPacking   *see* bin packing problem
BPP   29, 33, 40
branching program   9, 10, 209, 251, 267
Bundesliga   17, 92

$\mathcal{C}$ 35
$\mathcal{C}$-complete   65, 196
$\mathcal{C}$-easy   65
$\mathcal{C}$-equivalent   65
$\mathcal{C}$-hard   65
CAR   *see* carry bit
carry bit   264
CC   *see* clique cover problem
central moment   288
championship problem   16, 53, 54, 68, 85, 91, 94
Chebychev Inequality   291
checkers   190
Chernoff Inequality   33, 242, 292
chess   190
chip   17
Chomsky hierarchy   187
chromatic number   109
Chuang   21
Church-Turing Thesis   20, 22, 25, 26, 45
circuit   9, 10, 201, 251
   nondeterministic   213

circuit depth   202, 252, 254
circuit size   252, 260
circuit value problem   196, 272
clause   17
Clique   *see* clique problem
clique   15
clique cover problem   16, 47, 68
clique problem   16, 47, 48, 52, 56, 68, 81, 103, 111, 175, 178, 214, 254
Clote   10
co-$\mathcal{C}$ 35
coin toss   31
combinatoric rectangle   224
communication complexity   9, 10, 219, 220
communication game   219
communication matrix   224
communication protocol   220
communication rounds   221
complement   29
complete   *see* $\mathcal{C}$-complete
   PSPACE   188
completely independent   285, 286
completeness
   NP   7, 10, 77
complexity class   26
composition lemma   173
computable   43, 203
computation
   parallel   20
   quantum   20
computation path   39
computation time   *see* runtime
conditional probability   284
configuration of a Turing machine   71, 187
conjunction   17
conjunctive (normal) form   17, 74, 260
co-NP   40
consistency test   167, 172
constant depth reduction   *see* AC^0-reduction
context-sensitive language   187
Cook   71, 72, 107, 113
Cook's Theorem   72, 189, 199
counting problem   198
covering problem   15
CP   *see* championship problem
Crescenzi   10, 114, 164

cryptographic assumptions   158
cryptography   18, 30
CSL   187
cubic   282
CVP   *see* circuit value problem

Díaz   10
decision problem   29
depth-first search   197
derandomization   66, 104, 212
determinant   199
DFS   *see* depth-first search
DHC   14, *see also* Hamiltonian circuit
   problem
DHC^{SYM} *see* HC
DHP   *see* directed Hamiltonian path
   problem
Dietzfelbinger   68
Dijkstra   20
directed Hamiltonian path problem   78
directed *s-t*-connectivity   197
discrepancy   244
disjointness test   227
disjunction   17
disjunctive (normal) form   17, 260
distributional communication complexity   243
division function   273
DNA-computer   20
Droste   VI, VII
DTAPE($s(n)$)   186
dynamic programming   94

easy
   NP-   106
edge cover problem   15, 68
EDGECOVER   *see* edge cover problem
EP   28, 30
EQ*   229
EQ$_n^*$ 269
equality test (EQ)   224
Erdős   242
error-correcting code   165
error-probability   29
essentially dependent   252
evaluation problem   13
event   283
exor   *see* parity
EXOR-gate   252

EXOR-nondeterminism   233
expected optimization time   117
expected polynomial time   *see* EP
expected value   286
explicitly defined   252
exponential   282
exponentially small   283

FACT   *see* factoring
factoring   18, 128
failure-probability   28
fan-in   259
Feige   164
Fermat's Last Theorem   4
fingerprinting technique   239
flow   16, *see also* network flow problem
fooling set   226
forcing component   80, 82
formula   208
   quantified Boolean   189
formula size   254
FPTAS   *see* fully polynomial-time
   approximation scheme
Frens   VII
fully polynomial-time approximation
   scheme   102
function evaluator   167, 171

Gülich   17
Gabarró   10
gadget   51
Gambosi   10, 114, 164
game   190
gap technique   106, 173–175
Garey   10, 56, 74, 95, 128, 190
gate   201
gate elimination   253, 254
GC   *see* graph colorability problem
geometric distribution   293
geometric rectangle   224
GRAPHISOMORPHISM   *see* graph
   isomorphism problem
Giel   VI
go   190
golden computation path   212, 241
Goldmann   265
Goldreich   27, 164
Goldsmith   VII
Goldwasser   145, 164

grammar 41
  context free 41
graph coloring problem 82, 109, 143,
  178
graph isomorphism problem 81, 128
greater than (GT) 224
Gronemeier VII
Grotefeld 3, 22
growth rate 279, 281
guess 39
guess and verify 69

Håstad 175
Hadamard matrix 229, 245
Hajnal 265
Halldórsson 103
Hamiltonian circuit problem 49,
  56, 107, 158, see also traveling
  salesperson problem
Hamiltonian path 78
Hamiltonian path problem 78
Hamming distance 122
handball 17
hard see also C-hard
  NP- 106
hardware 201
hash function 152, 241
Håstad 261
HC 14, see also Hamitonian circuit
  problem
help 206
hockey 17
Hofmeister VI, 17
Homer 10
Hopcroft 3, 10, 19, 22, 187
HP see Hamiltonian path problem
Hromkovič 10, 105

I don't know 28
IBDD see indexed BDD
Immerman 9, 193, 197
inapproximability 108
independent events 27, 285
independent random variables 286
independent set 16
independent set problem 16, 47, 52,
  68, 81, 111
indexed BDD 269
indirect storage access 256, 268

inductive counting 195
inner product 227, 265, 273
input tape 186
interactive proof system 147
inverse function 273
investment advisers 37
IP 147
IP see inner product
IS see independent set problem
ISA see indirect storage access
isomorphism
  graph 81

Jägersküpper VII
Jansen VII
Johnson 10, 56, 74, 95, 103, 104, 128,
  190

k-dimensional matching 83
k-dimensional matching problem 16,
  178, 198
k-DM see k-dimensional matching
  problem
Köbler 143
Kann 10, 114, 164
Karmarkar 104
Karp 46, 104
Karpinski 265
Kayal 68, 128
Kirchhoff rule 16
knapsack problem 15, 47, 68, 78, 80,
  94, 105, 116
KNAPSACK see knapsack problem
Kranakis 10
Kushilevitz 10, 235, 259

l'Hospital 281
Ladner 129
language 29
large number problems 93
Las Vegas algorithm 28
law of total probability 285
Lawler 14, 15, 90
layer depth 268
LBA problem 193
ld see layer depth
length of a branching program 209
Lenstra 14, 15, 90
Levin 71
linear 282

linear bounded automaton   193
linear programming   128
linearity test'   167, 168
literal   17
local replacement   51, 56
log-space complete   196
log-space reduction   196
logarithmic   282
logarithmic cost model   20
logarithmic reduction   196
LOGSPACE   196
Long(L)   191
Lovász   164
lower bound   3, 21, 24, 25, 223
Lund   164

Maass   265
MADD   *see* multiple addition function
Magnanti   16, 49
MAJ   *see* majority function
majority function   263, 273
majority vote   33
Marchetti-Spaccamela   10, 114, 164
Markov Inequality   31, 290
Markov process   124
marriage problem   16, 53, 198
Martello   15
mask technique   229
MAX-2-SAT   178
MAX-3-SAT   161, 173, 177, 178, 184
MAX-k-SAT   161, 178
maximization problem   99
maximum weight satisfiability   113
Max-NPO   112
MAX-SAT   47
Mayr   10, 164
Micali   145
middle bit of multiplication   230, 247
Miller   128
Miltersen   66
minimal circuits   132
minimax principle   118, 244
Minimax Theorem   119
minimization problem   99
minimum spanning tree   78
Min-NPO   112
minterm   260
modified threshold circuit   266
MOD$_m$-gate   263

monochromatic   225
monomial   17
monotone Boolean function   254
monotone circuits   254
monotone projection   272
Monte Carlo algorithm   28
Motwani   6, 10, 19, 22, 164, 187, 242
multiple addition function   273
multiplication function   273
multiprocessor systems   10

NC^1-reduction   271
NC^k 272
Nechiporuk   255
needle in the haystack   121
network flow problem   16, 49, 53
neural nets   252
NETWORKFLOW   *see* network flow
    problem
Nielsen   21
Nisan   10, 235, 259
non-adaptive   162
non-uniform   220
nondeterminism   39
nondeterministic Turing machine   39
NP   39
NP-complete   96
    strongly   93, 94, 96
NPO   112
NTAPE($(s(n))$)   186
number theory   18, 128

O *see* big O notation
OBDD   *see* ordered BDD
oblivious   71, 204
Ogihara   10
one-sided error   29, 34, 61
one-way function   157
opponent   118
OR-gate   252
OR-nondeterminism   233
oracle   45, 130
oracle class   127
order of magnitude   279
Orlin   16, 49
outcome of a random experiment   283
output tape   196
Owen   243

P   26, 40

padding technique   191
pairwise disjoint   283
pairwise independent   286
Papadimitriou   10
parallel computation   10
parallel computation hypothesis   195, 204, 206
parity   17
parity function   260, 265, 273
PARTITION   52, 80, 81, *see* partition problem
partition problem   15
path
    computation   *see* computation path
path function   122
Paul   146
PCP Theorem   8, 10, 164
$PCP(r(n), q(n))$ 162
pebbling algorithm   103
perfect matching   198
permanent   198, 199
perpetual motion machines   2
PH   *see* polynomial hierarchy
pigeonhole principle   211
Π_k-circuit   260
Pinedo   15, 90
planar graph   90
polylogarithmic   282
polynomial hierarchy   8, 127, 132
polynomial reduction   60, 61
polynomial-time approximation scheme   102
polynomial-time many-one reduction   *see* polynomial reduction
polynomial-time reduction   *see* polynomial reduction
polynomially bounded   282
polynomially equivalent   60, 64
polynomially self-reducible   *see* self-reducible
polynomially small   283
population   117
PP   33, 40
Prömel   10, 164
primality testing   18, 30, 33, 68, 93, 128, 158
PRIMES   *see* primality testing
private coins   240
probabilistic method   242, 261

probabilistic proof-checker   162
probabilistically checkable proofs   161
probability   23
probability amplification   31
probability space   286
problem
    algorithmic   6
    approximation   10, 17
    decision   21, 35, 46
    evaluation   35, 46
    maximization   182
    minimization   182
    optimization   33, 35, 46
    search   13, 21, 33
product graph   176
projection   271
proof verifier   167
Protasi   10, 114, 164
protocol length   220
protocol tree   220
    randomized   233
prover   146
pseudo-polynomial   95
PSPACE   186
PTAS   *see* polynomial-time approximation scheme
PTAS reduction   110
public coins   240
Pudlák   265

QBF   *see* quantified Boolean formula
quadratic   282
quality of a solution   33
quasi-linear   282
quasi-polynomial   282
query   130
QuickSort   27, 28

Rackoff   145
Raghavan   6, 242
random bit   27
random polynomial time   *see* RP
random polynomial time with one-sided error   *see* RP
random variable   285
randomization   7, 39
randomized protocol tree   233
randomized search heuristic   115, 116
rank lower bound method   228

Razborov   254, 262, 263
read-once projection   271
read-only   186, 205, 206
reciprocal function   273
rectangle   225
rectangular reduction   229
recursive   *see* computable
reduction   7
register machine   19, 21, 22
restriction   52, 56
Rinnooy Kan   14, 15, 90
RP   29, 32, 40
RP*   32, *see also* NP

s-oblivious branching program   269
s-t-connectivity   197
Safra   164, 175
sample space   283
SAT   17, 51, 68, 72, 79, 103, 111, *see also*
     satisfiability problem
SAT$_{CIR}$ 17, 137, *see also* SAT
satisfiability   *see* SAT
satisfiability problem   17, 137, 164, 173,
     178, 198, 214
satisfiability problem of level k 137
satisfiable   17
SAT$_{CIR}^{k}$ 137, 188
Sauerhoff   VI
Savitch   9
Savitch's Theorem   192
Saxena   68, 128
scalar product   *see* inner product
Schönhage   3, 22
Schöning   143
Schaefer   VII
scheduling problem   15
Schmitt   17
search tree   120
self-improvability   176
self-reducible   214–216
sequencing with intervals   80, 95
set cover problem   85, 103, 178
SETCOVER   *see* set cover problem
#P   198
#P-complete   199
Shmoys   14, 15, 90
SI   *see* subgraph isomorphism problem
Σ_k-circuits   260
similar

algorithmically   43, 45, 61
    complexity theoretically   43
simple   *see* C-simple
Singh   4
Sipser   10, 56
size of a branching program   209
Smolensky   264
soccer   17, 55, 92
Socrates   8
software   201
Solovay   30, 68
solution
    to an approximation problem   99
sorting   20
space constructible   192
space-bounded complexity   186
specification   17
Spencer   242, 261
SQU   *see* squaring function
squaring function   273
s-t-DHP   78
Steger   10, 164
Stinson   18
Stirling's formula   236
Stone   128
Storch   VII
Strassen   5, 30, 68
strictly exponential   282
strictly exponentially small   283
strongly NP-complete   108
strongly NP-hard   108
structural complexity   8, 10, 185
subexponential   282
subfunctions   252
subgraph isomorphism problem   81
subset sum problem   78, 79, 95
SUBSETSUM   *see* subset sum problem
Sudan   164
superpolynomial   282
surveillance problem   15
SWI   *see* sequencing with intervals
Switching Lemma   261
Szegedy   164, 265
Szelepcsényi   9, 193, 197

$T_{\geq k}^{n}$ 253
$T_{\leq k}^{n}$ 253
team building   16
threshold circuit   264

threshold function 253
threshold gate 264
time *see* runtime
top-down programming 45
Torán 143
total probability
  law of 285
Toth 15
tournament 27
trap 122
traveling salesperson problem 14, 48,
    49, 67, 94, 99, 105, 107, 116, 178
TSP 14, *see also* traveling salesperson
    problem
TSP$^\Delta$ 14, *see also* traveling salesper-
    son problem
TSP$^{d\text{-Euclid}}$ 14, *see also* traveling
    salesperson problem
TSP^N 14, *see also* traveling salesper-
    son problem
TSP$^\Delta$ 105
Turing equivalent 45, 49, 63
Turing machine 21, 45, 71, 113, 186
  non-uniform 203, 206
  oblivious 96, 204
  one-tape 223
  randomized 27, 39
  two-tape 223
Turing reduction 45, 61
Turán 265
two-person zero-sum game 118
two-sided error 29

Ullman 3, 10, 19, 22, 187
unbounded-error probabilistic polyno-
    mial time 33, *see* PP
unfold 207
uniform 203
uniform cost model 20
unimodal function 116
unit cost model 22, 279
upper bound 3, 21, 24, 25

utility 15

Valiant 199
value
  of a game 119
  of a solution 99
van Leeuwen 10
van Melkebeek VII
verification problem 17
verifier 146
vertex coloring 81
vertex cover problem 15, 47, 52, 68,
    103, 105, 112, 178
Vetter 3, 22
Victoria 146
VLSI circuits 219, 223, 246
volleyball 17
von Neumann 119
VERTEXCOVER *see* vertex cover
    problem

Wagner 10
Wechsung 10
Wegener 6, 10, 17, 72, 254, 255
Witt VI
word problem 191
work tape 186
worst-case approximation ratio 100
worst-case expected runtime 27, 28
worst-case runtime 23, 26

Yao 4, 118, 244

zero-error *see* ZPP
zero-knowledge proofs 155
zero-knowledge property
  perfect 155
  under cryptographic assumptions
    158
zero-sum game 243
ZPP 28–30, 32, 40
ZPP* 32